SPORTS CULTURE & PERSONALITY

DON CALHOUN

Leisure Press

West Point, N.Y. • Berkeley, CA

For Lisa, With Love

A publication of Leisure Press.
P.O. Box 3, West Point, N.Y. 10996

Library of Congress Catalog Card No. 80-84355
ISBN 0-918438-68-3

Cover design: Diana Goodin

CONTENTS

Preface **5**

PART ONE — SPORT IN CULTURE

1. The Crisis in Sport **10**

• Jocks and Coaches • Profits and The Media • Sport and Health • Sport and Education • Sex and Sport • Sport and Humanism •

2. Jock Liberation and The Counter-Culture **28**

• Rise and Sweep of the Counterculture • Jock Lib and The Black Movement • Jock Lib and The Third World • Jock Lib and Women's Lib • Jock Lib and The Youth Culture • Whither the Counterculture •

3. Play, Game, and Sport **43**

• Play • Games • Sport • Play, Sport, and Work •

4. From Fun to Business: Historic Beginnings **61**

• The Agonistic Society: Greece • Bread and Circuses: Rome • The World of Camelot: The Middle Ages •

5. From Fun to Business: Sport in Modern Society **84**

• The Age of Self-Control: Puritanism and Anti-Sport • Puritanism and American Sport • Take-off and the Leisure Masses. •

PART TWO — SPORT AND SOCIAL ORGANIZATION

6. The Anthropology of Games **112**

• The Functions of Games • Latitude, Maintenance, and Cultural Complexity • Game Types and Child Training • Ascriptive and Achievement Games •

7. Contest and Civilization **138**

• Surplus and Civilization • Emulation in Trobriand Society • The Potlatch Syndrome • Ritual Spring Contests • Agon in Civilized Institutions • Agon in Political Life • Economic Life as a Game • The Sexes and The Generations • "High Culture" as Contest •

8. Sport and Social Power **154**

• Football and Ethnic Mobility • The Sociology of Ethnic Mobility • The Perils of Upward Mobility • The Athletic Subculture • Sport and Power—The Balance •

9. Social Character of The Different Sports **179**

• The Essence of The Game Is Individuality: Baseball • The Essence of The Game Is Intimidation: Football • The Essence of The Game Is Deception: Basketball • Soccer: The Game Is Football • Hockey: Game of The North • The Democratization of Tennis • Ultimate Self-Confrontation: Golf •

PART THREE — THE SOCIAL PSYCHOLOGY OF SPORT

10. Socialization: The Rules of The Game 208

• The Process of Socialization • Antagonistic Cooperation • Roles • Internalization • Game Rules and Life History • Constraint and Reciprocity • Varieties of Group Success • Cheating, Winning, and Socialization •

11. Enculturation: Sport and The Achieving Society 227

• Fairness, Skill, and Victory • Strategic Competence and Achievement • Good and Poor Competitors • Sex, Status, and Game Choice • Sport and The Rise of Capitalism • Achievement and The Sport Creed •

12. Violence in Sport: Catharsis or Reinforcement? 259

• Violence, Hostility, and Aggression • Evidence for Catharsis • Evidence for Reinforcement •

13. Self-Actualization: Play As Freedom 279

• The Fascination of Risk • Autotelic Experience and Flow •

14. Player and Spectator 300

• Agon, Self-Actualization, and Athlete • Agon, Self-Actualization, and Spectator • Self-Realization Through Identification • Are Sport Spectacles Corrupt? •

Postscript 315
Index 316

PREFACE

Man is God's plaything, and that is the best part of him. Therefore every man and woman should live life accordingly, and play the noblest games, and be of another mind from what they are at present . . .Life must be lived as play, playing certain games, making sacrifices, singing and dancing, and then a man will be able to propitiate the gods, and defend himself against his enemies, and win in the contest.

—*Plato,* **Laws**

You can deny, if you like, nearly all abstractions: justice, beauty, truth, goodness, mind, God. You can deny seriousness, but not play.

—*Johan Huizinga,* **Homo Ludens**

Playfulness and gamesmanship are not as trivial and nonserious as our puritan forebears opined, though they are ephemeral, postponable, and capable of much neglect. They can be forgotten when the urgencies of the group ethos or the group survival are given paramount value. Yet in play, and in its more immortal issue, art, each individual differentiates himself from his own entrapment and in so doing becomes, momentarily at least, a free spirit.

—*Brian Sutton-Smith,* **The Folkgames of Childhood**

The purpose of this book is to look at sport as one of our major social institutions—others are the family, economic life, politics, religion, education, science, healing, and art. We will try to see how sport reflects, and helps shape, the culture of which it is a part. We will also examine how sport reflects, and helps shape, the kind of people we are, in ours and in other societies.

Preface

The scientific study of sport is fairly new among social scientists. As one person put it: "An examination of the works of early historians would lead the reader to believe that individuals were born and they died, they earned a living, fought in wars, and elected other individuals to political office, **but they never played**." In recent years scholars and researchers have begun to give sport the attention previously given to other institutions. We now have physical educators, sociologists, psychologists, historians, anthropologists, and economists studying the relationships among sport, culture, and personality. In this book you are invited to explore, and add to, some of the things they have found.

This book is for people who are involved in sport as an institution—players and coaches, their families, owners, athletic directors, teachers of physical education, team physicians, trainers, managers, cheerleaders, sportswriters and other fans—who want to understand the role of sport in the whole social scene.

Academically, it is intended primarily for courses in sport sociology and also for the courses in sport history, in sport psychology, in the anthropology of sport, and in the social and cultural dimensions of physical education, that have developed recently to serve these people.

We begin with the "athletic revolution" that surfaced as part of the counter-culture in the mid-sixties, and promises radically to change sport as it now exists. We define the issues at stake. We examine the history of sport and its cross-cultural variation. We then explore its role in social organization and its social psychology. At the end we will examine some of the issues of the athletic revolution in the light of our study.

This book grew out of the course in Sport and Culture (now Sport and Society) that I have taught since 1973 at the University of Miami, first to students in our Honors Program, and then to general students, many of them athletes. I have built upon the many approaches that have been useful to me in my teaching:

- Academic sociology, as represented for example by Henry Edwards' delineation of "strains" in the social roles of people involved in sport.

- The anthropological description and analysis of games by John Roberts and Brian Sutton-Smith.

- The historical-cultural treatment as found in the works of Johan Huizinga, Roger Caillois, and John Rickards Betts.

• Treatment of sport by physical educators like Eleanor Metheny, Florence Stumpf Frederickson, and Jack Scott.

• Philosophical approaches like those of Paul Weiss, Howard Slusher, and George Leonard.

• The sociopsychological treatment of games by George Herbert Mead, Jean Piaget, Ervin Goffman, and Eric Berne.

• Sport psychology as exemplified by Bruce Ogilvie and Thomas Tutko's study of the "problem athlete" and Tutko's analysis of the win-at-any-cost psychology.

• The psychoanalytic approach as represented by Arnold Beisser's **The Madness in Sports**.

• Treatment of the sport business by economists like Roger Noll.

• Books by sportwriters like Jerry Izenberg, Neil Amdur, and Martin Ralbovsky.

• Accounts of their experience by sensitive and analytical sport figures like George Sauer, Dave Meggyesy, Dave Kopay, Bernie Parrish, Bob Cousy, Jim Bouton, and Bill Veeck.

Although this book's major focus is on sport in American society, which is where most readers will be, I have tried to induce a cosmopolitan sense of sport as a dimension of the whole human enterprise.

I want to express my particular gratitude to my former student, Gary Kusic, for whetting my interest in the subject through his research on Monongahela Valley athletes who escaped the steel mills; to my present colleague, Dr. Harry C. Mallios, our Director of Athletics, for encouraging me to develop this course and encouraging intelligent and articulate athletes to take it; and to student athletes and nonathletes, some of whom are quoted in these pages.

Donald W. Calhoun

PART ONE
SPORT IN CULTURE

CHAPTER 1
THE CRISIS IN SPORT

"The popularity of athletics, the growth of competition, and the rewards lavished on successful athletes completely changed the character of athletics. . .It was a change. . .from spontaneous to organized sport. The change brought with it both good and evil: the standard of performance was greatly improved, but athletics ceased to be pure recreation and something of the old. . .joy was lost."[1]

These words were not written about the crisis in sport in America in the 1970s. They were written about a crisis of the Olympic spirit in Greece in the sixth century B.C., but they could have been written today. Excessive competition, excessive rewards, the change from spontaneity to organization, the gain of skill and the loss of joy, have again "changed the character of athletics." History has repeated itself 25 centuries later. This is where we begin our book.

Very few people are really happy about the situation in sport today. There are, of course, some. In the semi-professional athletics that are called "amateur," there are a few large "winning" schools whose players, coaches, students, athletic associations, public relations officers, and alumni are fairly content (except on the rare occasions when they lose). In the frankly professional sphere, there are the fans (most of them powerless people) who get their thrills from identification with "our" Packers, Mets, Dodgers, Reds, Dolphins, Bruins, or 76ers. A small minority of very talented performers make it big with glory in the "amateurs" followed by dollars in the pros. TV networks enhance their public competitive image, if perhaps not their profit and loss accounts, by operating both amateur and professional sport as an entertainment business.

But dissent comes from more quarters than we would at first thought imagine.

"Jocks" and Coaches

First, athletes themselves—more than 95 percent of whom will **not** make it big in fame or fortune—when they have time, energy, and inspiration enough to think about it, resent being recruited as valuable flesh by agents who have sometimes been rather accurately described as pimps. They resent the collusion of "amateur" and "professional" athletic bodies that results in their being paid much less than they could make in an open market. They resent that what began for them as play has become a business in which they must win at any cost to themselves or their opponents. They resent the routine acceptance of "uppers," "downers," anabolic steroids, and playing when medically incapacitated for this purpose. They resent being treated like children—being told where they can live and eat, how they can cut their hair, what they can do in their spare time, what their politics can be, when (and with whom) they can sleep. If they are black, they may feel that a white world that gives them no other significant opportunities has oversold and exploited them on the very long chance that they might reach the top in sports.

These are hard times for coaches too. As Harry Edwards puts it, the coach's job combines "limited control with complete liability."[2] That is, a coach can lose (or win) a game for any number of reasons about which he can do nothing, but when next year's contracts are written (and for many weeks before) he will get all the blame (or credit). Under these circumstances, he is under job pressure to keep things in hand by appearing decisive and authoritative. Thus his job situation makes him very sensitive when players question his authority, as they have increasingly since the mid-sixties.

The coach's personality and personal background are apt to make such challenges more threatening. As a group, coaches are, in the words of sport psychologists Bruce Ogilvie and Thomas Tutko, "extremely conservative politically, socially, and attitudinally."[3] James Michener reports that of 60 prominent athletes he has known personally, 59 were Republicans and only Stan Musial a Democrat. "I have never so far heard of a coach who was a Democrat, although some of the Southwest Conference men may be so nominally."[4]

Job strains and personality may both make it very hard to live in the kind of atmosphere where a Tennessee coach with a 46-12-2 record nearly lost his job one year for winning only 7 of 12 games; where a small Ohio river town's high school coach had a defeat by the arch rival celebrated by a bullet that ripped through a window and lodged just above his baby's crib; where University of Miami coach Charlie Tate in the middle of a fair season had garbage dumped on his lawn and his wife received obscene phone calls; where Oklahoma coach Barry Switzer, in an unbeaten season, experienced severe pressure because some games were **close**. Add to these pressures some other conflicts that Edwards suggests. As a church or temple goer, a coach may find it hard to play dirty in order to win. As an adult responsible for youth, he may have to risk their safety or health on the field in order to keep his job. He may also be uncomfortable when his intellectual colleagues, whose jobs are not on the line day by day as his is sterotype him as a meathead who kicks other "dumb jocks" around. Under such conditions, it is not surprising that as early as 1969, **Sports Illustrated** published an article entitled "The Desperate Coach."[5] It may be that Ogilvie and Tutko were right in predicting that in the near future one third of our present coaches may not continue.

Profits and the Media

The promoters of amateur and pro sport aren't happy either. They have been brought up against a hard fact: spectator sports can no longer pay their own way locally. Since football ordinarily pays a large part of college athletic budgets, as football goes so go most other sport programs. Already in December 1962 **Fortune** magazine announced to the business community that college football is a losing business.[6] Of 200 colleges playing "marketable" football, only 30 or 40 were clearly in the black financially. Two main causes cited were the expense of recruiting squads for the two-platoon system that came in after World War II, and a loss of student interest, (this was **before** the student unrest of the mid-sixties). A decade later things were worse. According to NCAA figures, the total athletic budget for colleges of over 4000 students, which in 1960 was 60 million dollars, in 1965 had risen to 115 million, and in 1971-2 was 195 million.[7] The 1962 **Fortune** article estimated that it cost $400,000 to field a major football team. Today an estimate of a million dollars would be conservative. Faced with these rising costs, in the sixties 42 colleges droppped intercollegiate football.

In **Sports Illustrated** in 1971 Pat Ryan reported that two-thirds of all college athletic programs were losing money; even Ohio State, though in the black, was hurting; and loss of the 10 percent of athletic income derived from student fees was a serious threat. He spoke of the strain of athletics "keeping up with the Joneses" as it was described by Oregon State athletic director Jim Barrett: "If our major opponent hires another football assistant coach, we try to match them. If our major opponent has more football scholarships than we have, we try to catch up. If our major opponent has an athletic dormitory, we get out the hammer and nails. If our opponent shops for artificial turf, we start organizing a fund-raising campaign. This goes on and on."[8]

During the 1976 football season **Forbes** magazine described the state of the intercollegiate sport business: "College football as such has long been a powerful moneymaker. . .However, the margins are dropping and while many of the most powerful teams playing in big stadiums are still making money, there is less and less left over to cover the rest of the athletic department budget. Meanwhile, the cost of everything is rising. . . .The problem on everyone's mind is financing the red ink in the rest of the athletic budget. . .it looks like tough times ahead."[9]

Writing in 1973, Edwards predicted that intercollegiate sports as we know them may eventually join "panty raids" among collegiate legends. "It appears highly unlikely that sport will survive even the 1970s in its present form."[10] In the near future Edwards saw professional and big-time college sport continuing, inter-school sport almost disappearing in the major high schools, and being eliminated in favor of intramural programs in the non-big-time colleges. (I would guess this may happen by 2000, not 1980.)

The professionals, whom Edwards sees holding their own, are not doing so well either. At the end of 1975 the World Football League had folded and eight NFL teams finished in the red in spite of getting $1.2 million each for TV rights. 25 of the 28 major basketball teams had lost money. So had half the teams in the National Hockey League, which had tabled plans for expansion and was talking about dropping teams instead.[11]

If professional sport survives, along with big-league college programs, it will not be because it pays its own way as local spectator recreation. It will be as the tail of the kite of television entertainment. The TV industry, which played a large part in creating the crisis of organized sport, may bail it out.

The relationship between the television industry and the amateur and professional sport industry has been a mixed one. At first, in the 1940s and 1950s, TV undermined sport by posing this question: "Why pay good money to sit in the sun at the ballpark to watch the Local Yokuls when I can sit at home for free with a bottle of beer and see the national Game of the Week?" This question destroyed most of baseball's minor leagues, local boxing clubs, and small college football. Even the big leagues were not immune. The Cleveland Indians, a really outstanding team who televised most of their home games, lost 67 percent in home atttendance between 1948 and 1956. The Boston Braves, a good team who also televised most home games, dropped 81 percent between 1948 and 1952. They moved to Milwaukee, later to move again to Atlanta, in part because the virgin (to big league ball) South seemed to offer a much better television market than the already saturated Chicago-Milwaukee-Minneapolis area.

On the other hand, TV has also helped the sports business. It has created a nationwide and worldwide market for major and minor sports. The role of TV in publicizing sport has been most dramatic in the economically less developed countries. The Polish sport sociologist Andrzej Wohl says, "It is precisely television which in an unbelievably short time managed to transform people, who so far had been most indifferent in regard to sport, completely unaware of its role and significance, into its ardent adherents. Inhabitants of villages, who themselves had never practiced sport, express themselves, under the influence of television, in favor of their children going in for sport, fully approve the financing of the construction of sports facilities, declare their readiness to help with the building. These are not at all isolated statements, but have become a rule."[12]

Another eastern European country—Hungary—illustrated the diversity of influence that television can bring. In the 1960s, according to Foldesi Támasné, the spread of television brought about a decrease in "live" attendance at sport competitions. "Involvement in sport did not decrease unambiguously; it merely took a different shape. Television increased the number of fans and widened sport related knowledge of the population. It made telecast of sports popular with such strata of society (women, children, the aged) that, for different reasons had not previously seen "live" sports competitions; and brought such sports into the orbit of involvement of TV viewers that previously had not been popular in mass dimensions (e.g., figure skating, ice-hockey, car-races, etc.).[13] You will find it helpful to think of American parallels.

ABC staged the championship tourney that revived boxing after the promoters had removed their biggest drawing card by dethroning Muhammad Ali. CBS has been the "angel" for the NFL; the AFL came of age with NBC support; and ABC money has kept the NCAA football powers solvent. Today most big college athletic directors and owners of pro teams will agree that they would be helpless without TV contracts. However, he who pays the piper calls the tune: game schedules are arranged, timeouts are called, not for the players or the coaches or the spectators at hand, but for the convenience of network programming.

Who complains? The Minnesota Vikings, whose touchdown drive was stalled deep in Green Bay territory in 20 below zero weather by an official's timeout to allow a commercial. The players in the 1967 Superbowl game who had to repeat the second half kickoff because a commercial was on when the original kickoff took place. The fans who completely jammed NBC Broadcast Control in New York with protest calls when technicians mistakenly tuned off an NFL game and tuned in a children's program before the trailing team scored two touchdowns in the final minute to win. The churchgoers of Los Angeles when the National Basketball Association scheduled games at the church hour of 11 a.m. so that fans back east could see them at 2 in the afternoon.

Conversely, the irate fans who demonstrated at Belleview Baptist Church in Memphis when the local ABC station refused to cancel a weekly broadcast of services in order to carry the 1980 hockey game in which the American team won the Olympic gold medal. The admirers of basketball star John Havlicek in April 1978 when CBS, to meet a commitment at the Augusta Masters golf tournament, cut off Hondo's 9 point scoring burst in the last two minutes of his final game in Boston Garden, and with it the standing, thundering ovation by 15,000 people that marked the end of his 16 years of stardom. Lee Trevino who, on the 71st hole of a Florida golf tournament, was called to by a TV announcer from a booth above the putting surface: "Hey, Lee, we're in a commercial break. If you wait twenty seconds you can get your putt live on television." Trevino looked up, stuck out his tongue at the announcer, went ahead and three-putted hole 71 and then bogied hole 72 with another three putts.[14]

This messy marriage of stadium and tube doesn't seem to bother college and professional sports promoters very much. As typical capitalists, their attitude generally seems to be "Business is business, and if it isn't always a bed of roses—tough!" The TV magnates seem more disturbed. Tom Gallery, former sports director for NBC, voiced their complaint: "The pro football people have been driving so damned hard for a buck, they've driven the sponsors right out of sight with those high fees. It's killing the networks too, and I for one don't know how long it can last."[15] Contrary to some popular impressions, the networks generally lose money on their sport programs. Why, then, do they continue them? Landing a big sporting event, or series of events, boosts a network's image and helps it sell **other** programs. Roone Arledge of ABC says, "Having exclusive rights to the NFL or the World Series or the Army-Navy game is damned near like owning a space shot or the Pope's visit."[16]

William MacPhail, CBS sports director, said, "Sports is a kind of 'loss leader' [a publicized item sold below cost to draw customers to buy other merchandise]. For us, the rights have gotten so damned costly that we almost have to do sports as a public service and just forget about its making a profit."[17] In the "game" of business, like every other game, a big sport contract gives to TV executives and those all the way down the line the ego boost so important to Americans, the distinction of being "first." Also, in a world where reformers, including politicians, are on the necks of TV violence, pornography, and other errors, being on top in "good clean sport" helps purify a network's image. Network sport executives hope all critics will agree with Senator John Pastore, who in 1966 introduced a bill for complete federal regulation of television, but said, "Sports is one of the finest things television does. I have nothing but laudatory words for these programs. I feel strongly that sports makes up many of TV's finest hours."[18] It may be more than the public that is appeased. "We have a guilty conscience because of the general run of schlock we put over the air," said Jack Dolph, later American Basketball Association commissioner, when he was a CBS sports director. "Profit is the reason CBS is in business. But we have to balance that whole approach with our guilty consciences. So we have news. And so we have sports. It's that simple."[19]

Apart from the objectors to television's handling of sport, a good many fans have the sense that they are being ripped off. Escalated admission prices are hard to pay in an era of inflation. As is usual with inflated consumer prices, the easy answer is to overlook business profits and blame it all on high wages. Professional athletes used to be semi-illiterate refugees from farming, mill, and mining communities, who escaped more grinding poverty to become the legal and still poorly paid property of paternalistic sport owners who called the tune, financially and otherwise. Today's athletes may come from these communities, plus the urban ghetto, but many have been attached to a college or university on the way up and some of it has rubbed off. The organization of labor that spread after the Depression has come to include professional athletes, who now bargain collectively. Legal changes have given them an increased power to bargain individually as free agents. There are skilled lawyers to help and encourage collective and individual bargaining. A sport column by Bob Rubin in the **Miami Herald** is fairly representative of fan gripes at the excesses of this situation. Rubin sees a fuller and less one-sided picture than does the usual castigation of the greedy jock:

> *It's difficult to sleep at night knowing that Jim Palmer is forced to get along on $230,000 a year. . .Do you realize that the pittance the Orioles pay Palmer amounts to. . .a lousy $26.25 an hour, 24 hours a day, 365 days a year?. . .*
>
> *The bizarre thing is that Palmer truly is underpaid by the incredibly inflated standards of baseball salaries today. Far lesser talents are paid more.*
>
> *But that doesn't foster sympathy for Palmer. Instead it increases disgust over the excesses and inequities of an economic system that pays entertainers (including athletes) obscene amounts of money and it*

raises fundamental questions about the values of a society that created such a system. The more I hear of endless squabbling between whining owners and the athletes they have so badly spoiled, the less my interest in sports. It's insane for a man to earn millions to sing, dance, tell a joke, or pitch a baseball. . .Entertainers serve a purpose as diversions from life's daily grind, but their contributions to society are trivial compared to those of teachers, cops, librarians, firemen, research scientists, hospital workers, soldiers, etc.

So pay the jesters a decent wage, but not a fortune that could be used in so many more important ways. . .

The owners merit no sympathy. Despite their constant complaining and doomsaying over the average player salary rising from $22,000 in 1970 to a current $120,900, they are not paying anything they cannot afford. If they did, they would go out of business.

They're crying all the way to the bank. I bleed for them as much as I do for the .250 hitters they sign for the gross national product of Bolivia. . .[20]

Another unhappy group are some of the media workmen—sports writers and announcers with a journalistic conscience. As reporters, their job is theoretically to present an objective account of the events they cover. As media employees, they are actually PR men and women for the local team and for the sport industry. In the face of this, a John R. Tunis or Red Smith can be a top-flight journalist and social critic. Bil Gilbert can expose the use of drugs in sport.[21] Jerry Izenberg can explode the myth that a sporting contest is the pursuit of the Holy Grail.[22] Neil Amdur can argue the case for a maverick coach who practices democracy in football.[23] An editor like Dave Burgin can cover sport with fairness and honor in the San Francisco Bay area during the tumultuous era of the 1960s. Leonard Schecter, Robert Lipsyte, Joseph Durso, Sandy Padwe, and others may also dedicate their lives to telling the public the truth about the scene they report. But the strongest pressures, here as elsewhere, are to keep the boat unrocked.

Sport and Health

Also disturbed about the sport scene are those concerned with physical and emotional health—physicians, physical educators, psychiatrists, and the clergy. Few athletes, especially in contact sports, end their careers without some kind of permanent physical impairment. NCAA records show that an average of 28 players a year were directly killed in football from 1931 to 1975. In 1974, 86 out of 100 high school players could expect to be injured at least once during the season. (James Michener wonders what would be the reaction to high school physics if it were shown to have a record of killing 28 students a year and injuring 86 percent of its enrollees.)[24] Similarly, in the pros in 1975, a Stanford University study for the NFL estimated that 90 percent of players could expect to be injured before the Super Bowl was over. One-tenth of these injuries would finish the player for the season. The injury level is related to the way in which winning is put ahead of ordinary health standards. Under medical pressure, there has been some relaxation in the brutal late summer practices where for some time it was routine to vomit and finally collapse into bed, unable to eat. However, seriously injured players are still "shot up" with novocaine and sent back into action.

Novocaine is not the only drug that concerns the health professions. Jim Bouton says that half of the players in the American baseball league couldn't function without amphetamines (called "greenies" there)[25] and Chip Oliver guesses that half of the NFL would fall asleep in the third quarter if Pete Rozelle put a lock on the bottle of "speed" (called "rat turds" there).[26] In a class research project in the 1960s, Mike Mohler, a football player at the University of California, Berkeley, interviewed the whole team and found 48 percent using "speed" and 28 percent using weight-building anabolic steroids. In track, steroids are almost a "must" for success in the weight events and the decathlon. Commenting on the fact that one side effet of steroids is atrophy of the testicles, Paul Hoch sees an athletic future dominated by "plastic Supermen with no balls."[27]

Broken bodies in sport are not only a physical concern. To some in the healing professions, they are a symptom of psychological and spiritual problems. Players will kill themselves, slowly or suddenly, to win. Such urgency to win, they think, is among other things a poor preparation for the hard realitites of life. In every season, in every league, there must always be many more losers than winners. In the long run, for everyone, everything and everybody dear must be lost. How is a person brought up on the doctrine "winning is the only thing" to contend with that?

To some in the healing professions, the greatest problem in sport violence is that it dehumanizes both parties. Where violence is "the name of the game"—whether because one "loves to hit" or because one has to do it to carry out his assignment—one ceases to become a person, they say, and one's body becomes an instrument. The opponent also ceases to be a person and becomes an object to be removed. Both ways, people are turned into things.

The drug problem, from this standpoint, is similar. To "up" or "down" one's natural physiology, to artificially stimulate muscle development to win a game, turns one's body again into an instrument. As a human being one may wonder who, or what, it is that wins the coveted victory. One athlete told me: "I don't use drugs, because if I do great, I want to know that it was **I** that did it, and not bennies or steroids."

Beyond the effects on the athlete there is the problem of the impact of the sport system on the non-performer. For a century sport has become increasingly a form of spectator entertainment. It has increasingly enlisted a minority of performers selected for very atypical height and weight (this is obvious in football and basketball, but **Sports Illustrated** noted in 1977 that it is also becoming true in baseball). The physically typical person sits and watches. In the TV age he or she doesn't even have to walk from the parking lot to the stadium. What happens to these spectators? Since Hans Kraus reported in 1954 that six times as many American as European school children from comparable urban and suburban backgrounds had failed a battery of very simple muscular fitness tests—and suggested that the American habit of "spectating" might be one of the reasons[28]—this question has been of concern to many.

There is a stereotype of the athlete who overdevelops his heart, puts on weight after he ceases to be athletically active, and becomes a candidate for a heart attack. But a comparative study in 1956 did not show athletes to be significantly heavier than non-athletes in later life, although when active they had been. And strenuous athletic activity may develop alternative circulatory paths that can enable an ex-athlete to survive a blockage of normal blood flow to the heart muscle. The evidence is not all in, and many people have lived long with almost no exercise; but there is a good chance that the ex-jock with "athlete's heart" may outlive the spectator who watched him from the stands.

Another problem that bothers the health professions is the **kind** of sport that our athletic system encourages. It is the "minor" sport activities—walking, swimming, cycling, bowling, golf, and tennis doubles—that are most likely to help a person keep in shape over a long lifetime. Our emphasis on the "major" sports of baseball, football, basketball, and hockey stresses activities that (1) do not ordinarily enlist the physically typical person, and (2) for those who do participate will not continue beyond their youth. Relevant to this point is a 1970 study by Harvard anthropologists, who compared men who attended Harvard between 1880 and 1916 and had participated in major sports (baseball, football, crew, etc.) with those who had been in minor sports (fencing, golf, swimming, etc.). The minor sport athletes lived significantly longer than those in major sports (the difference was too large to have been due to chance factors).[29]

Neither health nor education is served by experiences like that of a senior football player who a few years ago explained to me why he had missed two weeks of my class. He had been sick with flu, which had not kept him from his daily spring practice. In the spring intrateam game, he was so sick that he threw up at the half. His coach held him out of the second half, but told him later that he could have done better if he had tried—presumably like another top player who had played the whole game with a severely congested chest.

Sport and Education

The impact of sport on education has concerned many people—academically serious students (including some athletes), teachers, administrators, and alumni. Two events symbolize what bothers them. In the fall of 1975 a professor at North Carolina State University was arrested for jogging on his own university's running track, in violation of security regulations that had been set up to protect secrecy of football practice for a big game. In the same year Yale University, in the middle of a $370 million endowment drive, lost a two million dollar bequest, and others, and a longtime recruiter resigned from the admissions committee "because a certain quarterback didn't get admitted."

Most educationally serious people would agree with one of the irate Yale alumni that athletics has a proper place in a balanced educational experience, that "all work and no play makes Jack a dull boy." But they do not believe that such balance means making a university a base for mass spectacles performed by semi-professionals who are students only secondarily and generally don't graduate. They do not think it requires turning the colleges into minor leagues that spare the professional promoters the salaries, recruiting costs, and other expenses of maintaining a "farm" system to secure and train players.

These critics applaud the fact that athletic ability enables some serious students, many from ethnic minorities, to go to college when they could otherwise not afford it. There are the Moe Bergs, Byron Whites, Bill Bradleys, Frank Ryans, Tom McMillens, Ted Hendrickses, and Pat Hadens, although in the total picture they are "token scholars" comparable to token blacks and token women in racial and chauvinist settings. Although the critics may not agree that training for professional athletics is a proper function at college, they may be glad that some students with no conventional academic interests can use college as a stepping-stone to a professional sport career. But they are not pleased when money that could have given a genuine **scholarship** to a serious and able and needy student is given to a non-student (however needy) to play ball.

They are also concerned about the possible damage to the career possibilities of the person on athletic "scholarship." Athletic departments pay lip-service to academic requirements to keep their players eligible, and the more conscientious departments actually get them graduated. But in actual fact there is no doubt where the real priority lies. Athletic performance comes first. The player (whose preoccupation with sport in high school has usually left him short in academic preparation) is advised into a program of courses he can handle. If he still has time, energy, and motivation, he studies after practice, film sessions, and other athletic responsibilities have been met. Sometimes he can't—he is just too tired. He attends class enough to get by and maintain his eligibility. If he doesn't have time to write assigned papers, there are other students or off-campus professional services that will provide them for a fee. So this athlete leaves college, graduated or not, having learned little outside his sport. "By the time I graduated," says ex-St. Louis Cardinals' linebacker Dave Meggyesy, "I knew it was next to impossible to be a legitimate student and a football player too. There is a clear conflict, and it is always resolved on the side of the athletic program."[30] The athlete has been "tracked," on the basis of his athletic ability, out of the chance of realizing other possibilities to which college could open him. Who knows how many potential physicians, scientists, lawyers, and teachers have been lost to society (and to themselves) because their intelligence and skill were focused very early on the football or baseball field or the basketball or tennis court?[31]

During the 1930s one of the outstanding football coaches of his time, Robert C. Zuppke of the University of Illinois, predicted that by the 1980s a "more sophisticated and secure" American public would reject the linkage of education with high-powered semi-professionalism, and let coaches get back to their proper job of building physical fitness and moral character.[32] (Again, we shall probably have to set this prediction back to at least the year 2000.) Fifty years after Zuppke, the educational critics of sport are not against "school spirit." But they, too, would rather have student group enthusiasm center around bona fide student activities, not the activities of non-students to whom their college's name happens to be attached.

Sex and Sport

In speaking of college semi-pros, I have used the pronoun "he." This is not entirely male chauvinism. As yet the "shes" in college sport have not been professionalized like the males. Whether they will be is part of another question.

Many members of both sexes are displeased with developments in sport, for opposite reasons. Female athletes, seeing women's liberation gaining in other areas, cannot accept second-class citizenship in the world of athletics. In high school, they are put off by the way in which girls are, for example, chased from gym floors when boys come along. They are offended by the way in which the major athletic events are dominated by males, while girls chosen as sex symbols lead the cheers, "relegated to the position of worshiping at an altar they can never really be part of."[33] In college, they are incensed when male teams routinely travel by plane while women have to scratch to get to their meets by car. They question the appropriateness of using women students as bait in athletic recruiting—the Gibson Girls (Kansas State), Gator Getters (University of Florida), Hurricane Honies (University of Miami). In the pros, women tennis players have sought "equal pay for equal work" by seceding from the men's tournaments and forming their own. (These have, incidentally, subsequently become as commercial as those for males.) Socially aware women athletes are conscious that organized sport is one of the strongholds of **machismo**. They are revolted by the kind of infantile attitudes toward females described in Jim Bouton's account of "beaver shooting" by big league baseball players: looking under women's skirts from dugouts, hanging on roof tops and fire escapes to play Peeping Tom.[34]

Women athletes must contend with the fact that for many people, sport does not fit their idea of a woman's role. The Polish sociologist Barbara Krawczyk is right in describing as outdated a statement made in 1913 by a Harvard physics professor:

> *Sport, in the form it exists at present, is nothing but a loss of time and often a pretext for flirtations. The only sports which. . .could best serve to develop the female body are simple household chores, which put all the muscles into motion. There is nothing more useful for the strengthening of the leg muscles and to avoid obesity, than often to run up and down stairs. The best means to develop the muscles of the chest and the small of the back is washing floors with both hands and in a kneeling position. Sweeping floors strengthens the muscles of the shoulder blades, carrying buckets is an excellent athletic exercise. A woman who is baking bread and kneading the dough achieves magnificent development of her upper limbs. An exercise worth recommendation, too, is laundering—an hour at the wash tub means more than an afternoon of playing tennis.*[35]

But many people today might agree with the 1932 opinion of a physical educator from Krawczyk's own country, who does not consider housework to be great physical training but says: "The road of sport for women should not be completely the same as that of sport for men. The different physical structure, different psyche and finally a different activity in life requires that sport should cultivate different virtues in the case of women. While physical education for men and sport as its superstructure should prepare them for constant intensive motor activity and make them capable of frequent maximum effort, physical education for women should rather be treated as a neutralizer for lack of movement and a monotonous mode of life and should thus prepare not for a maximum, but should require a normal minimum of physical effort."[36]

And there are still others everywhere who will be bewildered and disturbed as was the mother of a student at the Polish Academy of Physical Education, quoted by Krawczyk in 1965:

> *My mother was in principle against my going in for sport. . . .She was mainly concerned about the fact that sport is not the proper recreation for a girl. 'You are running around undressed on the sports field, together with boys, as if you had no shame at all.' . . . She would have preferred me sitting at home or being occupied with something else. . . And suddenly she found out that (it was) not enough that I was practicing sport, I even wanted to start sports studies. That was too much for her. If at least it would have been under her eyes she could have accepted it but to let me go to some other place, to live amidst athletes, far from home—oh, no. She was afraid that I would get spoiled in the world, that sport and freedom far from her maternal eye, would destroy me completely.*[37]

The sex issue in sport was brought to a head by Title IX of the Education Act of 1972, which forbids sex discrimination by federally funded organizations. The NCAA, the core of the male semipro sport establishments, put out practically a telephone book of argument against Title IX, contending that it would ruin college athletics. The NCAA was not concerned about women whose breasts might be injured if they came out for college football, which they are not likely to do. It was not worried about the possibility of mixed locker rooms, which for students used to co-ed dorms should pose no real problem, anyway. What did worry it was what might happen to "amateur" dollars. The male establishment was concerned that the cost of equalizing opportunities for women athletes might put an added drain on an already losing business. Underlying this anxiety was the fear that Title IX will undermine the male hero-female cheerleader syndrome and bring women as equals into a hitherto male world.

Sex equality in sport raises another issue that bothers thoughtful women and men alike. Until recently, sex discrimination has kept women from profiting by, and being exploited and brutalized by, the commercialization of sport. Will equal opportunity bring to women the same competitive "masculinization" already satirized in the business world by Norman Lear's All That Glitters? On the bizarre fringe, there is already in operation a semipro women's football league. In the mainstream (tennis especially) some very young women, like some very young men, are coming to take for granted the earning, in intense and widely publicized competition, of incomes that a few years ago were reserved for corporate executives.

In the fall of 1978 an Association of American Colleges Study[38] reported that in 1974 only 60 colleges offered athletic scholarships to women. "Today there are over 500." It also reported that the Department of Health, Education, and Welfare had set up a special task force to look into such matters as women's athletic scholarships, player recruitment, athletic association rules, contact sports and coaches' pay, "problems that have plagued the men, but not the women, for years. . . In a few short years the athletic scholarship has replaced the bake sale as the symbol of intercollegiate athletics for women. As a result, the nonfinancial problems of women's sports are now becoming harder to distinguish from those of the men's."[39]

Sport and Humanism

Another group who are unhappy about sport are people with humanistic values. This group includes some people from all the groups previously discussed.[40] Humanists feel strongly the gap between sport as it might be and sport as it is. They object particularly to three things in sport as presently organized—competition, exploitation, and violence.

They regret that where sport could be a channel for release, for self-actualization, an oasis in the desert of "real life," it reproduces and intensifies the merciless competition of a business civilization. In a world where labor with hand and brain is technically a "commodity," to be bought, used, and sold (where a **person** is economically a **thing**), humanists see the sport and legal establishments repeatedly affirming that the athlete is the property of his employer, to be merchandised like a side of beef, subject to the command of whoever "owns" him at the moment.

The humanists see sport, which could be a respite from the violence of the everyday life of street, factory, and office, in fact accentuating and glorifying this violence. (This is true not only of the contact sports—football, boxing, hockey—but also of the baseball pitcher throwing at the batter, the basketball player taking his opponent out under the basket, the "power" game that has taken over tennis.) While sport has sometimes been a vehicle for bringing ethnic minorities a success elsewhere denied them, it has, in the eyes of some spokesmen for these minorities, made use of their social and economic powerlessness to exploit them as a source of eager and underpaid labor.

"Winning is a reflection of national purpose." President Carter embraces speed skater Eric Heiden, winner of five Olympic gold medals. Courtesy of United Press International.

When the competitive urge expresses itself internationally in the struggle for national power and domination, the humanists see sport—which could bring people together as people to nonviolently test their skills against one another—serving instead as an arm of that national power. For example, they see President Ford's Commission on Olympic Sports asserting that "winning. . . is a reflection of our national spirit and purpose," and calling for a national sports authority, for which Cuba suggested a model, that would improve United States medal-winning in the Olympics.

* * * * * * *

In this first chapter, we started with the proposition that nobody is really happy about sport as it exists today. We have surveyed the feelings of players, of coaches, of sport promoters, of media people, of the healing professions, of educators, of women, of men, of humanists. What we have seen is a social system in a crisis that can't be blamed on individual villains, but of which all (or almost all) participants are at this point victims. The social system of sport is in turn part of a larger social system (our society) that is also in crisis. Chapter 2 deals with this relationship.

FOOTNOTES

[1]E. Norman Gardiner, **Greek Athletic Sports and Festivals**, reprint edition, Dubuque, Brown, 1979, 70.

[2]Harry Edwards, **Sociology of Sport**, Homewood, Ill., Dorsey, 1973.

[3]Bruce Ogilvie and Thomas Tutko, "Sports—If You Want to Build Character, Try Something Else," **Psychology Today**, October 1971.

[4]James A. Michener, **Sports in America**, New York, Random House, 1976, 264.

[5]John Underwood, "The Desperate Coach," **Sports Illustrated**, September 1, 8, 1969.

[6]Myles Jackson, "College Football Has Become a Losing Business," **Fortune** magazine, December 1962.

[7]Edwards, **op. cit.**, 288.

[8]Pat Ryan, "A Grim Run to Fiscal Daylight," **Sports Illustrated**, February 1, 1971, 19.

[9]**Forbes** magazine, Nov. 15, 1976, cited in George H. Hanford, "Controversies in College Sports," **Annals of the American Academy of Political and Social Science, 445**, September 1979, 74.

[10]Edwards, **op. cit.**, 316.

[11]Associated Press release, **Miami News**, Oct. 27, 1975, lc, 4c.

[12]Andrzej Wohl, "The Influence of the Scientific-Technical Revolution on the Shape of Sport and Perspectives of its Develoment," **International Review of Sport Sociology**, 10, 1, 1975, 30.

[13]Foldesi Tamásné, "Involvement in Sport and Watching of Sport Events of Workers at a Large Enterprise in Budapest," **International Review of Sport Sociology**, 14, 1, 1979, 62.

[14]Al Barkow, **Golf's Golden Grind: The History of the Tour**, New York, Harcourt, Brace, Jovanovich, 1974, 277.

[15]William O. Johnson, **Super Spectators And The Electric Lilliputians**, Boston, Little, Brown, 1971, 143.

[16]**Ibid.**, 55.

[17]**Ibid.**, 71.

[18]**Ibid.**, 72.

[19]**Ibid.**, 72-3.

[20]Bob Rubin, **Miami Herald**, Mar. 3, 1980, p. D1.

[21]Bil Gilbert, "Drugs in Sport," **Sports Illustrated**, June 23, June 30, July 7, 1969.

[22]Jerry Izenberg, **How Many Miles to Camelot? The All-American Sport Myth**, New York, Holt, Rinehart, and Winston, 1972.

[23]Neil Amdur, **The Fifth Down: Democracy and the Football Revolution**, New York, Coward, McCann, and Geoghegan, 1971.

[24]Michener, **op. cit.**, 85.

[25]Jim Bouton, **Ball Four** New York, Dell, 1971, 70.

[26]Chip Oliver, **High for the Game** New York, Morrow, 1971, 44.

[27]Paul Hoch, **Rip Off the Bi Game: The Exploitation of Sports by the Power Elite**, Garden City, N.Y., Doubleday, 1972, 125.

[28]Hans Kraus and Ruth P. Hirschland, "Minimum Physical Fitness Tests in School Children," **Research Quarterly**, 25, May 1954, 178-187.

[29]Anthony C. Polednak and Robert Damon, "College Athletes, Longevity, and Cause of Death," **Human Biology**, **42**, February 1970, 28-46.

[30]Dave Meggyesy, **Out of Their League**, Berkeley, Ramparts, 1970.

[31]One of my sources for this paragraph has been literally hundreds of research papers dealing with college athletes, written for my course in Sport and Culture at the University of Miami.

[32]Cited by Godfrey Sperling, Jr., The **Christian Science Monitor** News Service in **Louisville Courier-Journal**, October 26, 1975.

[33]**Toronto Telegram Weekly Magazine**, cited by Hoch, **op. cit.**, 154.

[34]Bouton, **op. cit.**, 36-38.

[35]Quoted in **Ruch** magazine, Warsaw, 1913, no. 10. Cited by Barbara Krawczyk, "The Social Role and Participation in Sport: Specific Social Features of Women's Sport," **International Review of Sport Sociology**, 8, 3-4, 1973, 48-49.

[36]W. Jonosza, "It Shouldn't Be Like This," **Start** magazine (Poland), No. 19, 1932, p. 2.

[37]Cited by Barbara Krawczyk, doctoral dissertation, Department of Social Sciences, University of Warsaw, 1965. Quoted in Krawczyk, **op. cit.**, 53.

[38]"Sports," Project on the Status and Education of Women, Association of American Colleges, no. 21, Fall 1978, Washington, D.C., p. 7.

[39]Hanford, "Controversies in College Sports," 77.

[40]One of the most moving statements I know of the humanist position on sport—and many of my students agree—is "The Souring of George Sauer," the explanation by a young man, son of a football coach and star of the 1969 New York Jets' upset Super Bowl champions, of why he retired from the game. See "The Souring of George Sauer," interview between Jack Scott and George Sauer, **Intellectual Digest**, December 1971.

CHAPTER 2
JOCK LIBERATION AND THE COUNTER-CULTURE

In May of 1970, at Notre Dame University, the football bastion of Middle America, ten football players petitioned Coach Ara Parseghian for permission to issue a statement registering concern about the murder of students at Kent State. That they should have asked an athletic coach before exercising their First Amendment rights said something about the athletic system. That they even dared to ask indicated that times were changing: five years before, said sportswriter Sandy Padwe, such a request would have been unthinkable.[1] No statement was issued, but concerned players were allowed to skip—and later make up—a spring practice session to attend a campus demonstration. These events at Notre Dame were one expression of a growing dissatisfaction with the athletic establishment and beyond it, with the social and political establishment.

The historic position of athletes was concisely put in 1932 by sociologist Willard Waller, "Athletes have the inevitable conservatism of the privileged classes, and they can be brought to take a stand for the established order."[2] Such a "stand" led Wisconsin football players in the 1930s to throw anti-ROTC protesters into Lake Mendota, and Columbia crewmen in 1968 to beat up student demonstrators. It made it possible for Paul Brechler, the

Berkeley athletic director during the agitated mid-sixties, to boast that California athletes had never been involved in political demonstration—meaning, says Jack Scott, that they had never participated except by attacking their demonstrating fellow students. The typical attitude of the athletic establishment toward its employees was capsulized in the reply of Texas coach Darrell Royal when Gary Shaw told him he had decided to quit football: "Don't you think that's our decision to make? I'll decide whether there's any need or not. . .We didn't put all that money into you to have you come tell me what you're going to do. **I** make those decisions. I expect you suited up tomorrow afternoon."[3]

But as the sixties moved toward the seventies, the traditional stance of jocks began to change. The defiant gesture of Tommie Smith and John Carlos on the victory stand at Mexico City in 1968 capped the Olympic Project for Human Rights. Shortly before this the Philadelphia Phillies, baseball team by threatening to forfeit, had forced cancellation of a game that league officials were determined to play on the day of Martin Luther King's funeral. In the fall of 1969 Harvard quarterback Frank Champi quit football after the second game of the season, protesting that "we're like pieces of machinery." In the same fall 14 members of the Wyoming football team faced—and got—suspension over the issue of wearing black armbands on the field to protest what they saw as racism at Brigham Young University. In 1970 Carlos Alvarez, all-American and pre-law honor student at the University of Florida, was instrumental in organizing an athletes' union. At a campus rally after Kent, he said of football: "If the sport doesn't change or bend a little, it might not last. I think the coaches will be made to change by kids coming up and not wanting to play under a lot of restrictions, where everything has to be done by the rules and you can't change the rules."[4] His quarterback, John Reeves, the nation's top passer in 1969, protested in 1970 that he felt "like a robot" because Coach Doug Dickey called all the plays. Alvarez and Reeves reflected the feeling expressed by Jim Calkins, computer science major and 1969 football captain at Berkeley, "The most degrading thing is being treated like a child. . .The attitude is that you're getting paid to play football, so you can't gripe. If that's the way they want it, fine. **But I say to them, you don't pay enough.**"[5] The University of Pennsylvania's leading ground gainer quit in the middle of the 1970 season. The wages for winning at any cost displeased 1970 Ohio State quarterback Rex Kern: "We probably make less than a dollar an hour. There are days when you simply don't want to do it."[6]

While the semi-professional "amateurs" were asserting themselves as persons, the open professionals began to pull the rug out from under a century-old system that made them economic chattels—the word chosen by Senator Sam Ervin in 1971 to describe the relationship of baseball, football, basketball, and hockey players to the "giant sports trusts." Since baseball emerged as the first modern professionalized game, the athlete has typically worked for a monopoly subject to no external control. He has had no freedom to choose who shall be his employer, through either individual or collective bargaining. He has characteristically entered his profession through a "draft" in which "competing" employers collaborate. Under a "reserve clause" his employer has had an indefinitely renewable option on his services. Thus the player has been subject to the arbitrary whims of coaches, managers, club owners, and sport commissioners. As Edward R. Garvey, former executive director of the National Football League Players' Association put it, "Because a player cannot quit but can be suspended without pay by the club owner or the Commissioner, he must obey all the rules and regulations of the club and the league, whether they be reasonable or unreasonable, or be denied employment in his profession."[7]

This monopolistic system has been challenged unsuccessfully in the courts since 1922. But in 1975 the United States Supreme Court, in **Radovich v. NFL**, held that all team sports except baseball were subject to the antitrust laws. In the late sixties and early seventies, player unions were organized. In 1972 major league baseball players went on strike, in 1974 the football players, and then in 1977 the NFL referees followed suit and in 1978 the baseball umpires. In 1975 a federal arbitrator (who wouldn't have been there except for the strength of the players' union) invalidated the baseball reserve clause and released a large number of veteran players as "free agents," able to sell their services to the highest bidder, just like any other employee in a capitalist economy. One outcome was that the average major league salary rose from $51,500 in 1976 to $96,000 in 1978 and $144,000 in 1980. While in 1972, $125,000 was a huge salary for a baseball player (more than Ted Williams, Joe Di Maggio, or Babe Ruth ever made), by 1980 it was below the major league average. At the same time, professional athletes in all sports got more control over their daily conditions of work.

Rise and Sweep of the Counterculture

The athletic revolution that peaked about 1970 was part of a cultural change described much earlier by the great Swiss psychologist Jean Piaget. Summarizing his empirical study of how children learn the rules of marbles, Piaget saw in individual development a transition from the very young child's unquestioning acceptance of parental authority to the later give-and-take of equal peers.[8] In society, as in the individual, Piaget saw the same transition from "constraint" (exemplified in Royal's statement to Shaw) to "reciprocity" (exemplified in Alvarez' prediction of a time when the "kids" would make their own rules).

In the twentieth century the long-run change described by Piaget has taken the form of conflict between an old, authoritarian culture and a new, democratic "counterculture," depicted by Theodore Roszak[9] and Philip Slater.[10] Although the fever of change reached its crisis in the 1960s, the countercultural revolution began much earlier. In **The Professional Soldier**[11] military sociologist Morris Janowitz spelled out a gradual democratization during the twentieth century in the most authoritarian of human organizations (the military):

> *A change 'from authoritarian domination to greater reliance on manipulation, persuasion, and group consensus.'*
>
> *A tendency of professional military men to develop 'more and more of the skills and orientations common to civilian administrators and civilian leaders.'*
>
> *Recruitment of officers from a 'broader base, more representative of the population as a whole.'*
>
> *A tendency to select more creative and innovative, even unconventional people for top positions (not the ranks).*
>
> *A weakening of traditional military images and concepts of honor.*[12]

In the factory, the heart of modern bureaucratic centralization, we have heard since the middle of the century that authoritarian methods are less efficient (as well as less humane) than participation by workers in decision-making. A classic research in the 1930s by Fritz Roethlisberger and William J. Dickson showed that the most important element in factory productivity was not formal authority but work-group morale.[13] In **The Human Problems of an Industrial Civilization,**[14] Elton Mayo made the case for "human relations in industry." Under the leadership of behavioral scientists like Rensis Likert,[15] more and more businessmen have tried "human relations" as a way of increasing profits. In 1968 Warren Bennis and Philip Slater proclaimed that "democracy is inevitable" because it is the form of organization best suited to advanced industry.[16]

Changes in the army and the factory have been long-run trends of reform within our cultural Establishment. But the counterculture has challenged that Establishment head-on. It has been a movement by two majorities and a number of minorities.

The first majority is the previously colonial peoples of the world. The South (primarily Latin America and Africa) has confronted the North (primarily Europe and North America). The South is also called the Third World, and is predominantly non-white (or at least non-Anglo Saxon). The liberation of the Third World began around the beginning of the twentieth century with the final breakup of the Spanish empire. It continued with the dissolution, in two World Wars and later, of the German, Dutch, and British empires. Since World War II, the Third World has become a powerful force in international politics, so that the South has become a factor to be contended with along with the East and West. For the first time in history, the majority of the human race now has a voice.

The other majority cuts another way. Throughout history, in the dominant civilizations of East and West, women have been second-class citizens. Females have been subordinate in economic and political life, in the home, in school, church, and temple, and in every branch of experience. The French and American revolutions, proclaiming the rights of man, opened the door for insistence on the rights of women. The Industrial Revolution brought the possibility of economic independence. Machinery made the sheer physical strength of males less important. Contraceptive techniques promised to give women, for the first time, control over their own bodies. The collapse of empire before the onslaught of Third World forces added momentum to the erosion of masculine chauvinism everywhere.

Women's liberation has reached a peak since about 1960, but it had vocal advocates like Mary Wollstonecraft in the early nineteenth century and John Stuart and Harriet Mill in the Victorian era. It has followed a general upward curve since the time of the Mills, two high points being the passage of female suffrage in 1920, and the Civil Rights Act of 1964. Passage of the Equal Rights Amendment, though now bitterly fought, is in the long run (by 2000 at the very latest) inevitable.

Around 1960 the Third World revolution erupted in the United States in the form of an uprising of the black minority. The linkage was expressed in a complaint I used to hear at the time around the black college where I then taught: "All Africa will be freed before I can get a lousy cup of coffee." Sparked primarily by the active non-violence of Martin Luther King, Jr., and his followers, the black movement so revolutionized the American scene that things that were unbelievable in the 1950s (such as blacks eating in "respectable" Southern restaurants) were taken for granted by the generation coming of age in the 1970s. (Directly on the "jock lib" scene, in 1977 one could see black football players at the University of Mississippi—which they could not have even entered fifteeen years earlier—hugging each other on the field while predominantly white spectators cheered them to an upset of Notre Dame.)

Four centuries of genocidal policy toward America's worst-treated racial minority, which began with the philosophy that "the only good Indian is a dead Indian," and continued with concentration on reservations, led in the countercultural period to refusal to accept second-class status for the red man (and woman). The oil crisis beginning in 1973 revealed, ironically, that location of large reserves of oil on Indian lands might give American Indians the kind of economic power wielded internationally by the OPEC nations—provided the historic pattern of robbing them of their resources is not repeated once more.

On one more forefront of cultural change, another exponent of nonviolent direct action, Cesar Chavez, during the sixties organized and gave voice to the last unorganized mass of American laborers, the predominantly Latin migrant and stationary farm workers. As was King in his attitude toward certain "black power" leaders, Chavez was countercultural in discouraging anti-Anglo racism.

The cause of these minorities had much appeal for a generation of youth raised under a nuclear umbrella constructed by their parents, resentful of being processed in educational factories into raw material for vast bureaucracies or, as an alternative, being conscripted to fight a Third World nation in a jungle. All these things made the sixties a decade of resistance to the educational and military and economic machines, and of support for rising minorities at home and the rising majority abroad.

The counterculture has embraced three other self-conscious and militant minorities: the elderly, the handicapped, and the gay. The Social Security Act of 1935 recognized the fact that in an urban industrial society older people can no longer expect to contribute to and be supported economically by their children's families. As the population boom that began with World War II tapered off and the percentage of "senior citizens" in the population increased, the elderly became another militant pressure group. In 1978 we were on the way to eliminating mandatory retirement. As health measures have increasingly made possible the survival of physically handicapped people, and as the Vietnam war added visible and vocal young people to their numbers, the less-than-able-bodied became another effective minority. In 1973 the Rehabilitation Act extended to physically and emotionally disabled people the protection granted to women and racial minorities under the Civil Rights Act.

Homosexuals, despite their distinguished achievements throughout history, are like women and blacks and the disabled in having been denied equal rights in employment and otherwise. Gays suffered a severe local defeat in 1977 when Miami citizens refused to guarantee their civil rights. Gay rights have not been written into national law, as have those of women, ethnic minorities, and the handicapped. However, in general the sixties and seventies have brought growing recognition of the right of sexual preference.

As I suggested earlier, the whole counterculture is much more than a matter of certain militant interest groups. It goes back to the basic trend from authoritarianism to reciprocity described by Piaget. It involves a fundamental questioning of the whole foundation of bureaucratic industrial society.

We need to understand this to understand "jock liberation" as well as to understand any other part of the counterculture. The basic question raised by the counterculture is one of human exploitation. This is not a loaded "dirty word," but simply refers to the situation where people are regarded as mere instruments for the profit, power, or physical gratification of others rather than as persons with value in themselves. Who is guilty of this exploitation? There are exploiters who are white, black, yellow, Gentile, Jew, male, female, young, old, middleaged, athletes, intellectuals, physically disabled and physically able bodied people. The counterculture opposes exploitation of, or by, any of these.

Slater has outlined in detail how the counterculture differs from our traditional culture.[17] I shall illustrate in the field of sport.

(1) **The counterculture gives preference to human rights over property rights.** In sport, this has led to challenge of the sport law that has made an athlete a piece of property, to be "sold" at will or depreciated on a corporate tax return.

(2) **The counterculture puts human needs above technical requirements.** If artificial turf is, for example, easier to maintain at the cost of more injuries to players, the counterculture will opt for natural grass.

(3) **The counterculture stresses cooperation over competition.** For the philosophy of winning at any cost, it substitutes the joy of group effort regardless of the final score.

(4) **For the counterculture, sexuality has priority over violence.** In sport, for example, it would prefer to see players spending the night before a game with their wives or girlfriends, rather than in psyching up masculine group hatred for the "enemy."

(5) **The counterculture favors distribution over concentration.** For this reason, it would favor the suggestions of football players Dave Meggyesy[18] and Bernie Parish[19] that sport franchises should be owned by players and fans rather than businessmen.

(6) **The counterculture puts the consumer ahead of the producer.** Here, for example, it would oppose dragging baseball players and spectators out in Arctic clothing on October nights to fit the World Series to the requirements of TV sponsors.

(7) **For the counterculture, means are more important than ends.** It would concur with Grantland Rice's familiar slogan, "It's not whether you won or lost but how you played the game."

(8) **The counterculture prefers openness to secrecy.** If it became dominant, there would be no practice sessions protected by armed guards at Ohio State and perhaps other big time athletic factories.

(9) **In the world of counterculture, personal expression is more important than social reforms.** It would recognize the need for fundamental changes in the sport Establishment, but they would always be aimed at the

personal growth and development of participants.

(10) **The counterculture stresses gratification over striving.** Here again, it would try to make sport fun for players and spectators rather than a device for becoming Number One.

(11) **It puts communal love above Oedipal love.** Here it would favor the democracy through which football coach George Davis had his players pick their starting line-ups,[20] over the love-hate father-fixation manipulated by coaches like Vince Lombardi.[21]

The athletic revolution is part of the long-run historical movement from constraint to reciprocity. More immediately, it is an expression of the specific countercultural movements that are struggling for their identity.

Jock Lib and the Black Movement

More than anything else, jock liberation is an outgrowth of the black liberation movement. In 1970, white California football captain Jim Calkins, previously quoted, said "You see so many black athletes speaking out now. But the white players are gutless. They don't want to take a stand. They are so entrenched in the system and so full of all this super-patriotic stuff."[22] While other careers were barred to blacks, athletics became an area where it was possible for a black to get ahead in money and recognition. Black hopes for upward mobility still are to a large extent "tracked" into the sport and entertainment business. As always, "rising expectations" lead to discontent: revolutions occur not when people are at rock bottom, rather when they are on their way up, **but not fast enough.** Contrary to popular stereotypes, most black athletes are generally more disciplined, more punctual, more organized, and more respectful of authority than their white brothers. The main reason is that all their eggs are all in one basket, so they have more to lose. But when they have suffered discrimination in this one avenue to "success," or even the same kind of mistreatment accorded white athletes, the more perceptive blacks have been more likely to rebel. Leaders among black athletes have taken care of their own personal interests and struggled for those of black athletes in general, but the outstanding personalities among them—the Jackie Robinsons, the Bill Russells, the Curt Floods, the Arthur Ashes, the Abdul-Jabbars, the Roberto Clementes, the Pelés—have been humanists identified with all athletes and with all people.

Jock Lib and the Third World

The athletic revolution has been clearly related to the rise of the Third World. The connection between anticolonialism and sport is indicated strongly in a study of African athletes published in 1978 by a Soviet sport sociologist and one from Ruanda. The research, which covered 12 countries in central Africa, showed the top motive for participation "To bring fame to one's own country, heighten its prestige." This motive ranked ahead of becoming a champion, achieving popularity, and avoiding boredom and isolation. The authors interpret: "From our point of view this is explained by two causes. Firstly, the social spirit of the population in the African countries which have freed themselves from the colonial yoke, connected with awareness of victory over the colonizers and the feeling of national pride and the striving to achieve rapidly economic and cultural independence. Secondly, the polled individuals are top-class athletes, striving to defend in the best possible manner the honor of their nation."[23]

These developments brought to a head a cultural conflict at least two centuries old, J. A. Adedeji writes that in Nigeria, for example, native games and sports beginning in babyhood formerly played an important part in the preparation of young people for adult life.[24] Examples were rope and tree climbing, swimming, archery, spear throwing, sword bearing, canoeing, fishing, swimming. Youths from various ethnic groups embarked on a program of socializing their peer group with activities that were peculiar to them. . . The youths who were hero worshipers often chose their heroes among the skillful performers and emulated them. This served as a great incentive that kept them training all the year round.[25] During the 18th and 19th centuries colonial administration, military officers, and especially missionaries (in the case of Nigeria, the British) assumed that the native culture, including native sport, was mere savagery and an obstacle to westernization and Christianization. "Youths who had been emancipated from their villages and ancestral gods and lived at boy's quarters with their expatriate masters played more important games like football, cricket, and net ball and adopted their value system. These youths in the course of time viewed their traditional values as obstacles to full participation in the imported sports and games."[26] In time, they discovered that their masters didn't really want them to participate in western sports. "European clubs hardly accepted Nigerians to play games with them. Nigerians were not allowed access to the swimming pools and other games."[27]

We may say that the way in which native youth finally took the white man's games and with them won Olympic medals and national self-respect was a typical case of the way in which colonial peoples have used the institutions of their colonizers to undermine and eventually eliminate their power.

(The Christian religion and university education have also been so used.)

The threatened Olympic boycott of 1968 (against South Africa and Rhodesia) and the actual boycott of 1976 (against New Zealand) have focused a protest against three forces that are actually one: (1) the international big power dominated military-political Establishment (mainly the USSR and the USA), (2) the international big power dominated athletic Establishment (mainly the national and international Olympic committees), and (3) the intranational and international racism of both.

The 1968 Olympic Project for Human Rights began as a black American protest, spread to other non-white teams and, especially after the suspension of John Carlos and Tommie Smith for their "black power" gesture on the victor's stand, drew in white competitors. Martin Jellinghaus, after winning a bronze medal in the 1600 meter relay race, said of the Olympic Project for Human Rights insignia that he wore, "I am wearing this medal because I feel solidarity not only for them as persons, but for the movement, the human rights movement."[28] Veteran Olympic hammer thrower Hal Connolly threatened to withdraw from the games after the suspension of Carlos and Smith, and the white Harvard crew supported the human rights movement throughout.

The 1976 boycott, in which 18 black nations, led by Tanzania, actually withdrew from the games was, as Erich Segal put it, an effort to dramatize racism by leaving the games a "white Olympics." The issue was again South Africa, although the immediate target was New Zealand, which had sent a rugby team to play in the blacklisted land of **apartheid**. The African athletes seemed to feel that New Zealand should have followed the lead of India, which in 1974 had withdrawn from Davis Cup tennis competition in protest against the presence of South Africa, and Mexico, which had withdrawn in 1975 and 1976. That New Zealand played rugby in South Africa is not surprising in view of the fact that the two countries had long-standing athletic ties, and that New Zealand practiced her own variety of **apartheid** against her native Maori minority, barring them from rugby, cricket, track and field, golf, tennis, weightlifting, and volleyball. The 18 teams left in protest against the refusal of the International Olympic Committee to bar New Zealand from the games. As Segal suggested, their departure, which made them inconspicuous by their absence, was probably less effective than might have been another Smith-Carlos type gesture in Montreal.

The 1976 games also brought up the question of Taiwan, whose relationship to the counterculture is ambiguous. Established by Chiang Kai-shek as an anti-communist stronghold after his 1949 defeat by Mao Tse-tung, for three and a half decades Taiwan has been used by, and has used, the western powers in the Cold War game. Thus it was strange that in the world of international sport it should have been Taiwanese boys who came to Williamsport, Pa., for the Little League baseball championship, and from

1971 through 1974 virtually annihilated the American opposition at their own national game. Following this, in a typical Establishment-type gesture, the Little League board announced that the Little League world series would henceforth be a United States series. The decision was, however, revoked before the 1976 championship, and the Taiwanese came back to win again.

Although the official national sympathies of the Third World powers have been Maoist and anti-Taiwan, it is hard to imagine that the ordinary people of the deveolping nations, if they knew of some of these events, did not feel some of the same kind of glee with which they greeted an "uppity" black man's domination of heavyweight boxing. Whatever the common people of the world may have felt, in 1976 the Taiwanese Olympic team was barely permitted to appear, but only under the banner of Taiwan, not as the representative of China—which they, and probably most of the western political and athletic Establishment wished.

Jock Lib and Women's Lib

In sport as elsewhere, the greatest victims of discrimination are women. This is best exemplified in the colleges. Intercollegiate sport is almost entirely male-provided mass entertainment, sold in a market that demands the three Vs—Violence, Velocity, and Victory. Even in non-contact sports like baseball, tennis, and golf, women can't throw a ball 95 miles an hour, blast the "big" serve, whale the ball off the tee like men. Here, as in track and field, their smaller size and lighter musculature make their product less salable to the old culture. Even when a contest between women may be more skillful, the blasting males will generally get the audience. In any sport, on a 1 to 10 scale, the males are likely to rank toward 10 in power-speed-skill, and the women to rank toward 1. In the old culture, with its emphasis on top performance, and its impatience with anything less, a one-sided tensionless match between a 9 and a 10 is likely to outdraw a tensely contested match between a 2 and a 3. Thus Arthur Ashe, who knew race discrimination, could defend lower pay for touring women tennis pros, "Only three or four women draw fans to a tourney, so why do we have to split our money with them?"[29]

In the colleges, emphasis on Violence, Velocity, and Victory leaves women's athletic budgets only a small fraction of the budgets for men. At the University of Miami in 1977 the total women's athletic budget—for softball, volleyball, basketball, tennis, swimming, and golf—equalled the salary of the male football coach. James Michener describes a state university with a student body 50 percent female in which less than eight-tenths of one percent of a $3,900,000 athletic budget was spent for women. Under such circumstances, it is not suprising that women athletes who are aware of what is going on are not very friendly toward the athletic Establishment.

In 1970, the year with which I began this chapter, women players threatened to boycott Jack Kramer's Pacific Southwest tennis tournament, because of the discrimination in allocation of prize money defended by Ashe. In considerable part because of Billie Jean King, an activist in the women's movement, they were successful in organizing their own tournaments. Ironically, as Paul Hoch points out, "soon the women's tournies became every bit as commercialized as the men's."[30] The makers of Virginia Slims cigarettes capitalized by sponsoring five of the tournaments and were able to cash in on women's liberationist sentiment by marketing a cigarette created especially for women with the slogan, "you've come a long way baby."[31]

In the same year, Patricia Palinkas, as a placekick holder for her husband, became the first woman in pro football. In the early seventies a women's semipro football league was formed. Women broke in as horse race jockeys and ran in the Boston Marathon. A woman became a minor league baseball umpire, in spite of fears that a female umpire might be subjected to "unladylike" language. By court order a young woman was placed on high school ski and cross country teams in Hopkins, Minnesota. The state of New Jersey ruled that sexual segregation must be eliminated in public schools in football, baseball, basketball, and wrestling (traditionally boys' sports) and also in the traditionally girls' sports of softball, field hockey, and lacrosse. The United States government revised the Little League charter to allow girls to play, and replaced the stated goal of "manhood" with citizenship and sportsmanship.

Title IX of the Education Act of 1972, which abolished sex discrimination in federally funded institutions, brought women into a basic collision with the athletic Establishment. Although athletic programs are only one aspect of Title IX, the most intense opposition came from the NCAA, which claimed that equal athletic rights in colleges would destroy the intercollegiate athletic entertainment industry, which it represents. To understand the intensity of the collision we must understand that not only profit, but **machismo**, is at stake. As everyone knows who is aware of how little girls and little boys are brought up, playing physical games to win is the core of "virility" in our society. Thus sport is a "no woman's land," and should, it is felt, be kept that way. The emotional collision is even wider than this. Extensive psychological testing has shown that those with machismo are likely to be politically conservative, rigid, dogmatic, and authoritarian—with antipathy to everything for which the counterculture stands.

So great is the economic and psychological stake of the athletic Establishment that it is unlikely that we shall see real athletic equality for college women during the twentieth century. The central rationalization will be the fact that college athletics is not primarily either fun or student health but a profitable industry. A straw in the wind: Michener, after describing a 1 percent allocation for women as "outrageous," says he would find acceptable a university athletic budget split of 77 percent for men and 23 percent for women.

Jock Lib and the Youth Culture

Most athletes, amateur and professional, of whatever race, sex, or nationality, are under 30. So they belong to the youth culture. At a time when that culture has changed—in lifestyle, hair, dress, speech, politics—this is a very important fact, which sociologist Harry Edwards has analyzed well.[32]

Like all people, the athlete wishes to be thought well of by his peers. Traditionally, he has been highly regarded, while at the same time his career and personal identity have been tied up with the social and political status quo. All this was possible as long as there was no serious conflict between the youth culture and the Establishment. However, as the "apathetic generation" of the 1950s became the "involved generation" of the 1960s and gave rise to significant numbers of hippies, yippies, zippies, and New Leftists, things became more difficult for the athlete. While the followers of the counterculture were a minority of youth, they were a vocal one, and received a great deal of media coverage. When dissenters were an insignificant and powerless minority, the athlete could simply ignore them or dismiss them as unrealistic, fanatical, and subversive. In an extreme, he might attack them verbally or physically. But when counterculture hair styles, dress, lifestyle, and political views began to be admired and imitated by large numbers of young people, the athlete could no longer ignore, dismiss, or attack them. Neither could he be comfortable as the crewcut, square, uncritical jock. He began to look at his culture, at himself, and at his role in his culture. As a result, even some of the descriptions of the athlete offered by people as knowledgeable as Jack Scott and Harry Edwards as late as the early 1970s are regarded by some of my students in the late seventies as outdated stereotypes.

Coach Woody Hayes, as far to the "right" athletically as Edwards is to the "left," agreed in 1973: "Players living in dorms are exposed to the attitudes of other students. It's bound to rub off. They'll listen to their peer group. They've done it with long hair and in other dress ares. There will be influence in time in discipline, too."[33]

Interesting in this connection is a study reported by Brian M. Petrie in 1977 comparing the social and political attitudes of jocks and nonathletes at the University of Western Ontario.[34] Although this is a Canadian school, all three major U.S. TV networks are received there, and the campus newspaper used material from the U.S. student "underground." So Petrie "hypothesized that there would be little variation in patterns of political orientations among students of the two societies."

The result: there were no significant differences in attitudes between athletes and nonathletes at Western Ontario. "The athletes, however, were more liberal than their nonathletic peers in their rejection of the idea that physical attacks against radical demonstrators were justified (only 3 percent of the athletes agreed with the item as against 13 percent of the nonathletes)."

Whither the Counterculture?

What will happen in the future to the counterculture, and to the athletic revolution as a part of it? Some people see the decade of the sixties as an explosion that has run its course, a temporary outburst of utopian idealism by people who a decade later had mellowed and come to their senses. They anticipate that in a longer run things will return to "normal." In the light of our overview in this chapter, this does not to me seem likely.

Evidence that the countercultural aspects of the athletic revolution did not quite end with the sixties was the forced withdrawal of South Africa from the Davis Cup Tennis play in April, 1978, following major protests at Newport Beach and Forest Hills in 1976 and a March 1978 demonstration at the Vanderbilt University gym that reduced attendance for the matches between the United States vs. South Africa to 75 people, a number smaller than that of the protesters outside. Of this Al Campora, wounded in 1970 at Kent, said, "I thought that State had the most hated gym in the world, but now I guess Vanderbilt does."[35]

The counterculture has roots at least as old as our bicentennial. The sixties were a decade when many different areas of "rising expectations" came to maturity simultaneously, and became too much for the old culture to contain or satisfy. In the pattern by which societies change, peaks like this do not continue forever. They are followed by periods in which social gains born in the fever of crisis are slowly consolidated and expanded. In the counterculture in general, and in the athletic revolution in particular, this is what I think has happened in the seventies and will continue to happen at least until the end of the century.

FOOTNOTES

[1]Sandy Padwe, "Big Time College Football is on the Skids," **Look**, Sept. 22, 1970.

[2]Willard Waller, **The Sociology of Teaching**, New York, Russell and Russell, 1961, 116.

[3]Gary Shaw, **Meat on the Hoof: The Hidden World of Texas Football** New York, Dell, 1972, 267.

[4]Padwe, **op. cit.**, 67.

[5]Jack Scott, **The Athletic Revolution**, New York, Free Press, 1971, 165, n.

[6]Padwe, **op. cit.**, 69.

[7]Edward R. Garvey, "From Chattel to Employee: The Athlete's Quest for Freedom and Dignity," **Annals of the American Academy of Political and Social Science**, 445, September 1979, 93.

[8]Jean Piaget, **The Moral Judgment of the Child**, New York, Free Press, 1948.

[9]Theodore Roszak, **The Making of a Counter Culture**, Garden City, N.Y., Doubleday, 1969, and **Where the Wasteland Ends**, Garden City, N.Y., Doubleday, 1972.

[10]Philip E. Slater, **The Pursuit of Loneliness**, Boston, Beacon, 1970.

[11]Morris Janowitz, **The Professional Soldier: A Social and Political Portrait**, New York, Free Press, 1960.

[12]Summary from Donald W. Calhoun, **Persons-in-Groups: A Humanistic Social Psychology**, New York, Harper & Row, 1976, Chapter 13, "Bureaucracy," 297.

[13]Fritz Roethlisberger and William J. Dickson, **Management and the Worker**, Cambridge, Mass., Harvard, 1947.

[14]Cambridge, Harvard, 1946.

[15]Rensis Likert, **The Human Organization**, New York, McGraw Hill, 1967.

[16]Warren G. Bennis and Philip E. Slater, **The Temporary Society**, New York, Harper & Row, 1968.

[17]Slater, **op. cit.**, 100.

[18]Dave Meggyesy, **Out of Their League**, Berkeley, Ramparts, 1970.

[19]"The franchises," says Parrish, "should be owned by municipal corporations legally tied to the stadium authorities, having public common-stock ownership,. . .A formula could be worked out to pay the players a percentage of the total income. Then the profits after expenses could be earmarked for revitalization of the inner cities—improved wages for police, firemen, teachers, and other civil servants; upgrading of city and county hospitals; and care for the aged, to name a few recipients." Bernie Parrish, **They Call It a Game**, New York, New American Library, 1972, 290.

[20]Neil Amdur, **The Fifth Down: Democracy and the American Football Revolution**, New York, Coward, McCann, Geoghegan, 1971.

[21]See George Plimpton and Bill Curry, "The Green Bay Monster, **Quest, 1977**, March-April, 1977.

[22]Scott, **op. cit.**, 165, n.

[23]A. M. Maksimento and Antoine Barushimana, "Attitude Towards Sport Activity of Top-Class Athletes of Central Africa," **International Review of Sport Sociology**, 13, 2, 1978, 43.

[24]J. A. Adedeji, "Social and Cultural Conflicts in Sport and Games in Developing Countries," **International Review of Sport and Sociology**, 14, 1, 1979, 81-88.

[25]**Ibid.**, 85.

[26]**Ibid.**, 86.

[27]**Ibid.**

[28]Quoted in Paul Hoch, **Rip Off the Big Game: The Exploitation of Sports by the Power Elite**, Garden City, N.Y., Doubleday, 1972, 173.

[29]Hoch, **op. cit.**, 159.

[30]**Ibid.**, 160.

[31]**Ibid.**

[32]Harry Edwards, **Sociology of Sport**, Homewood, Ill., Dorsey, 1973, 179-182.

[33]Cited in **I.S.S.S. Newsletter**, Oberlin, Ohio, December 1973, 9.

[34]Brian M. Petrie, "Examination of a Stereotype: Athletes as Conservatives," **International Review of Sport Sociology**, 12, 3, 1977, 51-62.

[35]**Seven Days**, April 21, 1978, 10.

CHAPTER 3
PLAY, GAME, AND SPORT

To understand the athletic revolution, we will need to examine critically the role of sport in the whole program of human activity. In any scientific investigation, we must first stake out the areas of behavior we are going to study (the technical word is to **delimit**—establish the limits). In this book we are going to analyze **play**, **games**, and **sport**—their relationship to each other and their part in the total pattern of culture.

There is no absolutely right definition for anything. What we must ask of a definition is that it (1) delimit clearly what we are going to talk about, (2) be consistent with the way people have staked out the area in the past, and (3) be stated so as to indicate the kind of observations and manipulations that will test whatever statements we may make about the phenomena.

Play

The athletic revolution asks pointed questions about the meaning of human play. To think about these questions we will need to ask what play is. Most people who study the subject these days refer to the book **Homo Ludens** ("man, the player") by the Dutch cultural historian Johan

Huizinga,[1] which his colleague Roger Caillois has described as "the most important work in the philosophy of history in our century." Play is, to Huizinga, not a domain of behavior sharply set apart from all other human activity. It is, rather, a way in which we can follow any kind of human interest. To use a metaphor from music which Huizinga does not employ, play is a "key" in which we can perform any kind of activity—art, music, business, politics, religion, science, love, or even war.

What, then, is the key of play? The clue is **fun**. "It is precisely this fun-element that characterizes the essence of play."[2] Huizinga said that "the **fun** of playing resists all analysis and logical interpretation." However, Brian Sutton-Smith, a psychologist of child development, in 1972 pointed to two elements in fun: When people play, they set aside the pressure of the ordinary rules that govern their non-play life. At the same time they set up a new set of guidelines for their play.

The player substitutes his own conventions and his own urgencies for those of society and nature. . . This mixture of lowered tension in external relations and induced arousal within the novel restraints is probably the emphoric state we call fun.[3]

What the player experiences is a sense of being possessed. He is under the control of forces that at times he himself can scarcely control, yet the pretense quality of the game means that he can control them.[4]

The very complex interplay between the natural order and the play order may be clarified by three game situations where the two conflict. These are suggested by Bernard Suits.[5]

1. Given an oval running track surrounding an infield, the commonsense way to reach the finish line is to cut across the infield. But the runner in a track meet, in order to win, follows the rules of the race around the oval. The play order supersedes the natural order.
2. Given a long mowed strip with eighteen metal holes, the commonsense way to get the ball successively into the holes would be to walk and drop it in each turn. But the golfer instead hits the ball with a set of headed sticks made to specifications. The play order again supersedes the natural order.
3. A driver in a cross-country race sees a child wander on to the road ahead of him. Everyday commonsense tells him to leave the road. The rules of the game tell him to keep going. He goes into the ditch, the child is saved, and he loses the race. The natural order has superseded the play order.

Or consider an example suggested by the Soviet sport sociologist I. N. Ponomarev—a high jumper who can clear 7 feet in competition (play order) might have trouble going over a 5' 6" solid wall or barbed fence when pursued by a maniac (natural order).

In distinguishing between the demands of everyday life and the special demands set up by the rules of play, Sutton-Smith was following the lead given by Huizinga's earlier analysis in which he had outlined the characteristics of play:

(1) *Play is a voluntary activity. . . By this quality of freedom alone, play marks itself off from the course of the natural process. It is something added thereto and spread over it like a flowering, an ornament, a garment.*

(2) *Play is. . . a stepping out of "real life" into a temporary sphere of activity with a disposition all of its own. It stands outside the immediate satisfaction of wants and appetites, as a temporary activity satisfying in itself and ending there. . . an intermezzo,* an **interlude** *in our daily lives.*

(3) *Play is distinct from "ordinary life" both as to locality and duration. . . . It is "played out" within certain limits of time and place. It contains its own course and meaning. The arena, the card-table, the magic circle, the temple, the stage, the screen, the tennis-court, the court of justice. . . all are temporary worlds within the ordinary world, dedicated to the performances of an act apart.*

(4) *Inside the play-ground, an absolute and peculiar order reigns. . . Into an imperfect world and into the confusion of life, play brings a temporary, a limited, perfection.*

(5) *Play is "tense". . . a testing of the player's prowess: his courage, tenacity, resouces and last but not least, his spiritual powers—his "fairness"; because, despite his ardent desire to win, he must still stick to the rules of the game." [Also: "Prestige for past victories counts for naught; the need for proving oneself is ever demanded anew. The attractiveness of sport lies in its genuine element of surprise, which can be capitalized on but not twisted out of shape by political demands."—Henry Morton,* **Soviet Sport**, New York, Macmillan, 1963]

(6) *All play has rules. They determine what "holds" in the temporary world circumscribed by play. The rules of a game are absolutely binding and allow no doubt . . . Indeed, as soon as the rules are transgressed the whole play-world collapses. The game is over.*

(7) *A play-community generally tends to become permanent . . . The feeling of being "apart together" in an exceptional situation . . .*

of mutually withdrawing from the rest of the world and rejecting the usual norms, retains its magic beyond the duration of the individual game. The club pertains to play as the hat to the head.[6]

In summary, "play is a voluntary activity or occupation exercised within certain fixed rules of time and place, according to rules freely accepted but absolutely binding, having its aim in itself, and accompanied by a feeling of tension, joy, and the consciousness that this is "different" from "ordinary life."[7]

Jean Piaget, the Swiss psychologist whose studies of children's games are world-famous, agrees with Huizinga that play is not an isolated function, but "is in reality one of the aspects of any activity (like imagination in respect to thought)."[8] Like Sutton-Smith he finds play to be "distinguishable by a modification of the conditions of equilibrium between reality and the ego."[9] He also names the characteristics that are generally said to distinguish play from non-play:[10]

(1) "Play is an end in itself [autotelic], whereas work and other non-ludic behaviors involve an aim not contained in the activity as such."

(2) Ludic activity is distinguished by "the spontaneity of play, as opposed to the compulsion of work."

(3) "Play is an activity 'for pleasure,' while serious activity is directed towards a useful result irrespective of its pleasurable character."

(4) "Play is considered to be devoid of organized structure."

(5) In play, the inescapable real-life conflict between individual freedom and social restrictions is either absent or transposed so as to give an acceptable solution.

(6) Play is characterized by "overmotivation"—an extra unnecessary "twist," such as drawing figures with the broom while sweeping a floor.

Piaget's "extra twist" leads to what anthropologist Stephen Miller thinks is the essence of play—"galumphing." The word may not sound very coldly scientific, but it conveys the spirit of "fun." In ordinary life, we are under pressure to behave efficiently and economically, to seek the shortest and easiest means to our goals. Galumphing, on the other hand, is "a patterned, voluntary elaboration or complication. . . where the pattern is not under the dominant control of goals."[11] Play, as compared with ordinary life, is "a crooked line to the end." The most economical route from first to third base would take one through the pitcher's mound, but the rules of the game require that one detour by way of second base. One wastes time and energy to avoid stepping on the cracks in the sidewalk, but that is the nature of galumphing. Miller would suggest that in a world where we get tired of being structured to take the shortest route to our goals, we deliberately structure activities that take the long way around—and here is the fun.

Another important dissection of play, which is useful to our understanding of sport, is performed by the French sociologist Roger Caillois in his book, **Man, Play, and Games.**[12] Caillois distinguishes four main categories of play.

The first is **contest**, struggle. To this Caillois gives the Greek name **agon** (related to the English word "agony"). Forms of agon are competitive games, economic competition, competitive advertising, and competitive examinations. The adjective describing such activities is **agonistic**.

The second form is **chance** or luck (which Caillois calls **alea**, after the Latin word for dice). Here the player, instead of summoning his energies for an agonistic struggle, lets go and submits to fate, chance, the Universe, God. Examples are craps, poker, bingo, roulette, parimutuel betting, state lotteries.

A third major type of play Caillois calls **mimicry**. This includes the imitative behavior of animals, role-taking by children, drama, hero-worship, the wearing of uniforms, and ceremonial etiquette.

Here we find ritual, which uses regularly repeated dramatic performances to portray and symbolize wider group experiences and conflicts of which the individual's life is a part. It is important that throughout history spectator sport has often been, and today still often is, a ritual dramatic spectacle, a "morality play" in which the athletes represent the forces of good clashing with the forces of evil.

The fourth form is **vertigo** (which Caillois names **ilinx**, from the Latin word for "whirlpool"). It includes swinging, ecstatic dancing, speed on skis, in cars, motorcycles, and boats, carnival rides, mountain climbing, alcohol and drugs, tightrope walking. Today we might add such activities as rock music and skydiving.

Caillois summarizes his four forms of play in this way:

> *In* **agon**, *the player relies only on himself and bends all his efforts to do his best; in* **alea**, *he relies on everything except himself and he surrenders to forces that elude him; in* **mimicry**, *he imagines that he is other than he really is and invents a fictitious universe;* **ilinx**, *the fourth fundamental tendency, is an answer to one's need to feel the body's stability and equilibrium momentarily destroyed, to escape the tyranny of perception, and to overcome awareness.*[13]

Caillois' analysis of play contains another distinction relevant to the questions raised by the athletic revolution. This is the difference between impulse and control—between the kind of spontaneous unreflective turbulence and self-expression found in the play of children, for which he uses the word paidiá (child's play); and the tendency to adapt play to "arbitrary imperative, and deliberately hindering conventions," which he describes by the Latin word for play, **ludus** (adjective, **ludic**).

The distinction between the two modes of play is so central to the basic issues raised in this book that it may be well to illustrate each mode very specifically with examples that are close enough to everyone's experience to "ring a bell." First, **ludus** as delineated in Harold Garfinkel's statement of the basic rules of tick-tack-toe:

> *Play is conducted on a three by three matrix by two players who move alternatively. The first player makes a mark in one of the unoccupied cells. The second player, in his turn, places his mark in one of the remaining cells. And so on. The term "ticktacktoe player" refers to a person who seeks to act in compliance. . . .*[14]

Then, John Bowman's description of adult paidiá:

> *Five women are walking along the edge of a large embankment. They stop momentarily and look at one another. One person remarks: "I used to love to roll down hills." Without comment, one of the other persons in the group flings herself to the ground and rolls down the hill. Everyone begins to laugh and three of the remaining four roll down the hill also. Upon reaching the bottom all laugh hysterically for several minutes with tears coming to several of the women's eyes.*[15]

Bowman's illustration suggests what may be the most important thing in distinguishing paidiá (just fun) from **ludus** (organized play): the presence of smiling and laughter in **paidiá**, their absence in **ludus**.

Any act of play falls somewhere on a continuum (a continuous gradation) between spontaneity (paidiá) and conventionality (ludus). This continuum runs through all four forms of play, as shown in Table 3.1.

Some students of play have emphasized that it is a form of communication through group make-believe related to metaphor in language.[16] An example of a metaphor is "Richard is a lion." This is a paradoxical statement: "A is like B and is also not like B." Richard is courageous, like a lion, but unlike a lion, he has no tail. Similarly, in children's play a broom ridden by a child is like a horse but known not to be a horse. A piece of clay is molded like a cake but not eaten because it is known not really to be a cake. Linda, as her mother, talks to Linda, who is not her mother, and as not-mother-

Linda, she also talks back. Much of the importance of play comes from the paradox of play as a metaphor of life: "The play order is and is not the natural order." The ball game is just a game, but when "my" team wins on the field I feel myself more of a champion in real life. The ugly witch that I, as a child, destroy vicariously in a fairy tale is not my frustrating mother, and yet in removing a menacing parent figure I reduce some of the pain of being a "mere" child.

Table 3.1 The Dimensions of Play

	AGON (COMPETITION)	ALEA (CHANCE)	MIMICRY (PRETENSE)	ILINX (VERTIGO)
PAIDIA	races combats etc. athletics } not regulated	*comptines* heads or tails betting roulette	childish imitation masks costumes theatre	children's swings merry-go-round teeter-totter waltz outdoor sports skiing mountain-climbing
noise agitation laughter dance hoop solitaire games of patience crossword puzzles	boxing fencing football checkers chess	lotteries compounded or parlayed		
LUDUS				

Note: In each vertical column, the games are classified very approximately in such order that the *paidia* element constantly decreases, while the *ludus* element constantly increases.

Source—Roger Caillois, "The Structure and Classification of Games," **Diogenes, 12,** Winter 1955, page 75.

Games

When we move from play in general to games and then to sport, the organized, ludic element becomes more prominent. The unorganized amusements, pastimes and hobbies of children and adults contain much of the unstructured, spontaneous "turbulence and self-expression" of **paidia**. Examples of such pastimes and amusements are bicycle riding, horseback riding, climbing, swimming, fishing, kite-flying, throwing snowballs, skiing, tobogganing, hiking, and ice- and roller-skating. Hobbies include such early rural activities as play with leaves, flowers, grass and nuts; and cooking, sewing, knitting, playing with tools, machinery, model aeroplanes, and stamp and coin collecting. Also among the pre-game play activities—especially of young girls—are "central person games" (chasing games with an It figure) in which "a central player has an arbitrarily game-granted status that allows her to dictate the course of the action, while the other players attempt to escape, or dispossess the central person of her power."[17]

Compared with these less structured play activities—out of which it may have grown—a game is "a play activity which has explicit rules, specified or understood goals. . ., the element of opposition or contest, recognizable boundaries in time and sometimes in space, and a sequence of actions which is essentially 'repeatable' every time the game is played."[18]

The contest may be between two individuals, between two teams, between an individual and a group, as in "central person" games, between an individual or team and inanimate nature (as in running rapids or mountain climbing), between a person or group and animate nature (as in hunting, fishing or bull-fighting), or between an individual or team and an ideal standard. As well as between or among people, contest may take place within an individual, as between a child and an imaginary companion, or between one's present and past performance. It may also be a struggle between two animals (as in a horse race or cockfight), or between a real and an artificial animal (as in a greyhound race against a mechanical rabbit).

In their anthropological study of games in different cultures, John M. Roberts and his colleagues have distinguished three major forms of games: games of **physical skill**, whose outcome depends upon the physical abilities of the players; games of **strategy**, which involve a series of moves each representing a choice among alternatives; and games of **chance**, which are determined by either non-rational guesses or the behavior of a mechanical device.[19] Pure examples of the three types are weight lifting, chess, and craps. A prize fight or a marathon race is also a fairly pure example of a physical skill game. Chess, the Japanese board game **go**, or the simple universal game tick tack toe are fairly pure strategy games. High card win and roulette are other examples of pure chance. There are important combinations of the three types—physical skill with secondary reliance on strategy (as in baseball, football, basketball, and tennis); physical skill combined with chance (example: musical chairs); games of strategy and chance (such as bridge and poker); combinations of physical skill, strategy, and chance (example: the child's game of "steal the bacon").

Of the three major forms of games, physical skill games are the most widespread among the human race and were probably the first to develop historically. For illustration, in her study of a simple Eskimo hunting people, anthropologist Lynn Ager reports that of 39 games played by children, 25 were games of physical skill.[20]

Roberts has also found that the three types of games are related to different kinds of cultural problems. Physical skill games are in part training for mastery of the natural environment. Chance games are ways of mastering uncertainty; they are most common among peoples who have a hazardous and unpredictable existence. They are almost absent among the simplest peoples, and grow in number and complexity as societies become more complex economically and technically and more stratified socially. We shall examine this and related research in Chapter Six.

A distinction fundamental to the problems raised by the athletic revolution comes from the mathematical study of games of strategy, which we know as "game theory." The distinction is between zero-sum games and non-zero-sum games. In zero-sum games, the winner's gains are equal to the loser's losses. It is impossible for both to win, or for both to lose. Examples are tick tack toe, checkers, chess, bridge, most competitive sports as now organized, war, a "rating" contest between two networks, and a "price war" between two corporations. In non-zero-sum games, everybody can win, or lose. An example of an "everybody win" situation is the unique way in which basketball is played by some Navaho Indians, who enjoy the game intensely but don't keep score. There have been attempts to develop "noncompetitive" forms of the major sports, which would really make them non-zero-sum games.

A zero-sum view of athletic competition is Vince Lombardi's famous slogan: "Winning is not the most important thing—it's the only thing." An example of a non-zero-sum view is Grantland Rice's equally famous slogan: "It's not whether you won or lost, but how you played the game." A good deal of the disappointment of athletes with the current sport scene lies in the fact that they have a non-zero-sum view of athletic competition, whereas many coaches, fans, and alumni have a zero-sum view. The question at issue is whether there can be non-zero-sum competition. It is the same issue as is involved when businessmen caught in a cut-throat competitive rat race long for a brotherly competition that would not be to the death.

Sport

With the rise of sport we reach the ultimate in the organization and formalization of play. "A game," says philosopher Paul Weiss, "is an occurence; a sport is a pattern."[21]

"Sport," in modern history, has meant two essentially different things: a badge of status for rural gentlemen, and professionalized entertainment for mass leisure in an urban industrial society.

Thomas Jefferson, a political democrat but still a Virginia aristocrat, expressed the difference when he said that "games played with a ball stamp no character on the mind."[22] Only a horse and gun, he felt, can do that. The directors of the nineteenth century British Henley Regatta expressed the same distinction when they excluded from participation any person who was "by trade or employment a mechanic, artisan, or labourer."[23]

Sport as a gentleman's activity is primarily British. Neither Jefferson nor most British gentlemen would have approved the cruder of the "blood sports" that appealed to many Englishmen—"setting dogs to bait and kill chained bears. . . and pitting against one another gamecocks whose spurs where shod with steel."[24] But British gentlemen did approve and practice a related blood sport, "pursuing with hounds the lone fox until he forfeited his life to the snarling pack." And Jefferson "thoroughly enjoyed. . . .being in at the death of a fox."[25] Transplanted to the United States, sport took such forms as horse racing, fox hunting, horse shows, the breeding of dogs, polo, and yacht racing (cricket did not quite transplant). These survived to some extent into the twentieth century, as sport historian John Rickards Betts tells us:

> *Even at the turn of the century society still remained in control of the leading tennis and golf associations; fox hunting prevailed among eastern and southern families; many continued to flock to Newport, Saratoga, and other resorts; horse shows remained a notable event on the social calendar; . . . yachting remained essentially an aristocratic monopoly; racquets and squash were played only by the metropolitan elite; and polo showed no signs of being vulgarized by the masses.*[26]

However, with the shortening of the work week from about 70 hours to about 35 in the past hundred years, gentlemen's sport has given way to commercial sport. This is a fairly modern development, which originated in England. Its main characteristics are (1) continuity, (2) division of roles, (3) dynamic interaction with an audience, and (4) a supporting sport Establishment. Commercial sport usually involves pure physical skill games, or games of physical skill mixed with strategy.

Huizinga, we will remember, spoke of how play activity tends to establish the playing group as a permanent community. "The great ball-games require the existence of permanent teams, and herein lies the starting point of modern sport."[27] English football legendarily grew out of the kicking of the skulls of dead Viking enemies. This led before the twelfth century to the game of Dane's Head, in which an inflated pig bladder was kicked between two towns with the village greens as goals. It was in the nineteenth century that rugby and cricket became organized sports involving permanent teams. Huizinga names conditions in English life that made it the scene for the development of modern sport:

> *Local self-government encouraged the spirit of association and solidarity. The absence of obligatory military training favored the occasion for, and the need of, physical exercise. The peculiar form of education tended to work in the same direction and finally the geography of the country and the nature of the terrain, on the whole flat and, in the ubiquitous commons, offering the most perfect playing-fields that could be devised, were of the greatest importance. Thus England became the cradle and focus of modern sporting life.*[28]

Organized sport was first a creation of the British middle class. This class, says Peter McIntosh, "rose to a position of political power and social influence on the crest of the Industrial Revolution. They shaped their games and sports to a large extent at the Public Schools."[29] These were "railway schools" like Marlborough College, where middle class young men came via the new railway system, hoping to emulate the upper class boys who went by horse and coach to Eton, Harrow, and Winchester. Sport came to the working class when the work week was reduced, as by the introduction of the Saturday half-holiday in industrial Birmingham, and the introduction of the 9 hour day between 1869 and 1873.

Organized sport, like the industrial society that gave it birth, involves a sharply marked specialization of roles. There are team games without this differentiation—for instance, the children's games of cowboys and Indians and cops and robbers. The team game of buzkashi, a kind of mounted football played in Afghanistan by riders with the carcass of a beheaded calf on a quarter-mile field has teams up to 100 in number but without the assignment of roles which appears in soccer, rugby, or polo. The early English Dane's Head, although played by teams from town to town, apparently did not have positions and roles allocated as in modern English football.

Sport also includes dynamic interaction between players and spectators who identify with their efforts. The great cultural historian Lewis Mumford defines sports as organized play in which the spectator is more important than the performer, and in which the game loses a large part of its meaning if there is no audience.

Finally, the players are related not only to the audience but to an institutionalized "sport order" which includes sporting goods manufacturers, sport clubs, national and international governing bodies for amateurs and professionals, publishers of sport magazines, and the personnel of the media that cover sports.

Play, Sport, and Work

The complex technical organization of sport as an Establishment led Huizinga to ask a fundamental question that many athletes are asking: Is sport play? Reviewing a century of modern sport, Huizinga said, "In the case of sport we have an activity nominally known as play but raised to such a pitch of technical organization and scientific thoroughness that the play-spirit is threatened with extinction.[30]

In this chapter we have analyzed play as an area of behavior that includes games, which in turn include sport. We have treated sport as a subdivision of play. Three sociologists of sport question whether this is the case. Heinz Meyer says, "Sport is to be seen as a phenomenon that, although it started its development from play, contrasts with play, especially because of the regulations set up for competitions and of the control of records; these accents are, of course, ...already there in play; but they got a new stress in the British movement of sport and they dominate sport of nowadays in such a way that the relationship to play is no longer to be seen."[31] Harry Edwards lists a number of characteristics in which sport differs from pure play.[32] Sport is less spontaneous and less under the individual participant's control. Formal roles and responsibilities play a larger part. Sport is less separated from the pressures of daily life. The participant's goals are no longer derived from the activity but from outside it. Sport's extreme seriousness demands a greater proportion of his time and attention. He is required to exert himself beyond the point where his activity is interesting or refreshing. Edwards says that "there is *no* overlap at all between play and sport [italics his]." Allen Sack is less dogmatic, but he does ask whether sport is really play or work.[33] He points out that commercial sport fails to meet three of Huizinga's main standards for play. "Professional games. . . inasmuch as they (1) involve activity that participants are obliged to perform, (2) are oriented to the pragmatic concerns of everyday life, and (3) are pursued for profit or material gain, share almost nothing in common with play."[34] He suggests that "upon hearing the final gun that ends his game the professional athlete is likely to experience feelings of relief as is any other worker when a whistle ends his working day."

Reality requires us, Sack feels, to locate different activities on a continuum from play to work. Dancing, riding a bicycle, sexual intercourse, riding a merry-go-round, camping, mountain climbing, when not competitive or institutionalized, are non-sport play. Small college football may be close to the play end of the continuum. Big time college football is close to work. Pro football is work. The boxed analysis (and justification) of the socialist "amateur" by Polish sport sociologist Barbara Krawczyk points up some of the problems and dynamics of the play-work continuum.

The Socialist "Amateur"

Without completely losing its qualities of play, i.e., voluntary, spontaneous activity, though based on rules and norms, which is a source of joy and a change in normal life, sport simultaneously accepts features of work, i.e., activity whose aim is the achievement of useful, socially accepted values, such as the results of a sport contest. The 19th century ideology of sport as play, a magnificent youthful adventure, sounds ambiguous in confrontation with the situation, in which the result ceases to be exclusively the competitor's own business, being transformed into a desired value which is produced with the expenditure of enormous organizational, training, and financial efforts. In the socialist system a top-class athlete today takes advantage of social privileges, has at his disposal free time to train, has a guarantee of good financial conditions, a coach and equipment, free of charge. The basis for taking advantage of these privileges is talent and work, honest effort and the accepted results of this effort, which can be socially verified. The athlete (is) granted privileges not only to enjoy pleasant experiences, but also to supply such experiences to the community he represents, through his behavior, attitudes and fight, in exchange for the chance he has been given to develop his talent, the chances for promotions, fame, and social recognition.

. . . The process of the transformation of sport from selfless play to activity which has the features of useful work and is socially important does not spontaneously signify the degradation of sport competition. Just the opposite; it gives it new symbolic meaning and values.—Barbara Krawczyk, "The Social Origin and Ambivalent Character of the Ideology of Amateur Sport," **International Review of Sport Sociology**, 12, 3, 1977, 46-47.

A related continuum is put forward by Michael Salter.[35] At one end is play, which involves a message, "this is play," is voluntary in nature, has rewards that are intrinsic rather than extrinsic, and is fun. In the center of the continuum are three kinds of games: the ludic game, where the spirit of play prevails; the sport, where the spirit of play and the will to win are in balance; and athletics, where winning is paramount. At the far end from play is the **terminal contest**, where winning is **all** that counts, and any means are justifiable. The pure terminal contest is war; among sports, the gladiator games were as good an example as any.

Figure 3.1 Play-Game Continuum

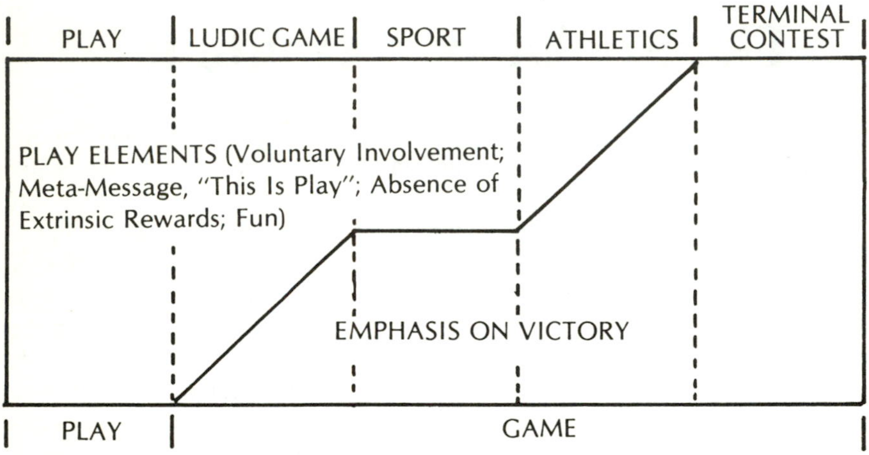

Source—Modified from Figure 2 in Michael A. Salter, "Play in Ritual: An Ethnohistorical Overview of Native North America," in Play and Culture, ed. Helen B. Schwartzman, West Point, N.Y., Leisure Press, 1980, p. 72

Kent Pearson, an Australian sociologist, has made a helpful distinction between two stages in what he calls the "athleticization of play"—play-sport and athletic-sport.[36] Play-sport remains essentially informal. Athletic-sport is more competitive, has more systematic techniques for developing skill, and tends to become bureaucratically organized like big business, big government, and the military. In Australia Pearson finds a contrast between surf life saving (an organized athletic-sport) and surf board riding (still essentially a non-competitive, informal play form). "Surf life saving is a highly organized competitive sport covering four main areas of competition: (1) rescue and resuscitation, (2) beach events (including sprint running, beach flags, etc.), (3) boat events and (4) small craft events (board and ski racing)."[37] On the contrary, "although surfboard riding has developed as a competitive sport, for the vast majority of . . . in Australia and New Zealand surf board riding is a sport providing 'challenge' in a natural environment and the opportunity for self-expression.''[38]

Table 3.2 summarizes the essential differences between the two sport forms.

Table 3.2 Some Dimensions of Contrast Between Play-Sport and Athletic-Sport

	Play-Sport	Athletic-Sport
Degree of Organizational Complexity	**Low**	**High**
Coherence of Central Values and Norms	**May be Low or High**	**High**
Rationalization of Techniques Geared to the achievement of precisely specified performance outcomes	**Low**	**High**
Emphasis on qualitative aspects of performance. . . (Process rather than product)	**High**	**Low**
Importance of (formal) social competition	**Low**	**High**
Complexity and specificity of formal game rules	**Low**	**High**

Source—Kent Pearson, ''The Institutionalization of Sport Forms,'' **International Journal of Sport Sociology**, 14, 1, 1979, Table I, p. 52.

Pearson outlines the conditions that promote one form or the other. Athletic-sport is more likely to develop when participants must cooperate in order for the event to take place; when there are clear-cut criteria for victory by individuals or teams; when man-made sport settings (field arenas, tracks, swimming pools, etc.) are important, and require organization for building and management, and regulation of sport activity; when science and technology are applied to the development of game skills; and when there are commercial sponsors. On the contrary, activities are likely to remain play-sports when organization is not necessary, competition is not important, the sport can be pursued in areas (like the ocean) that are easily accessible and don't have to be fabricated, improvements in equipment are worked out by enthusiasts themselves rather than by commercial equipment-makers, and when the participants value informal fun and resist organization.

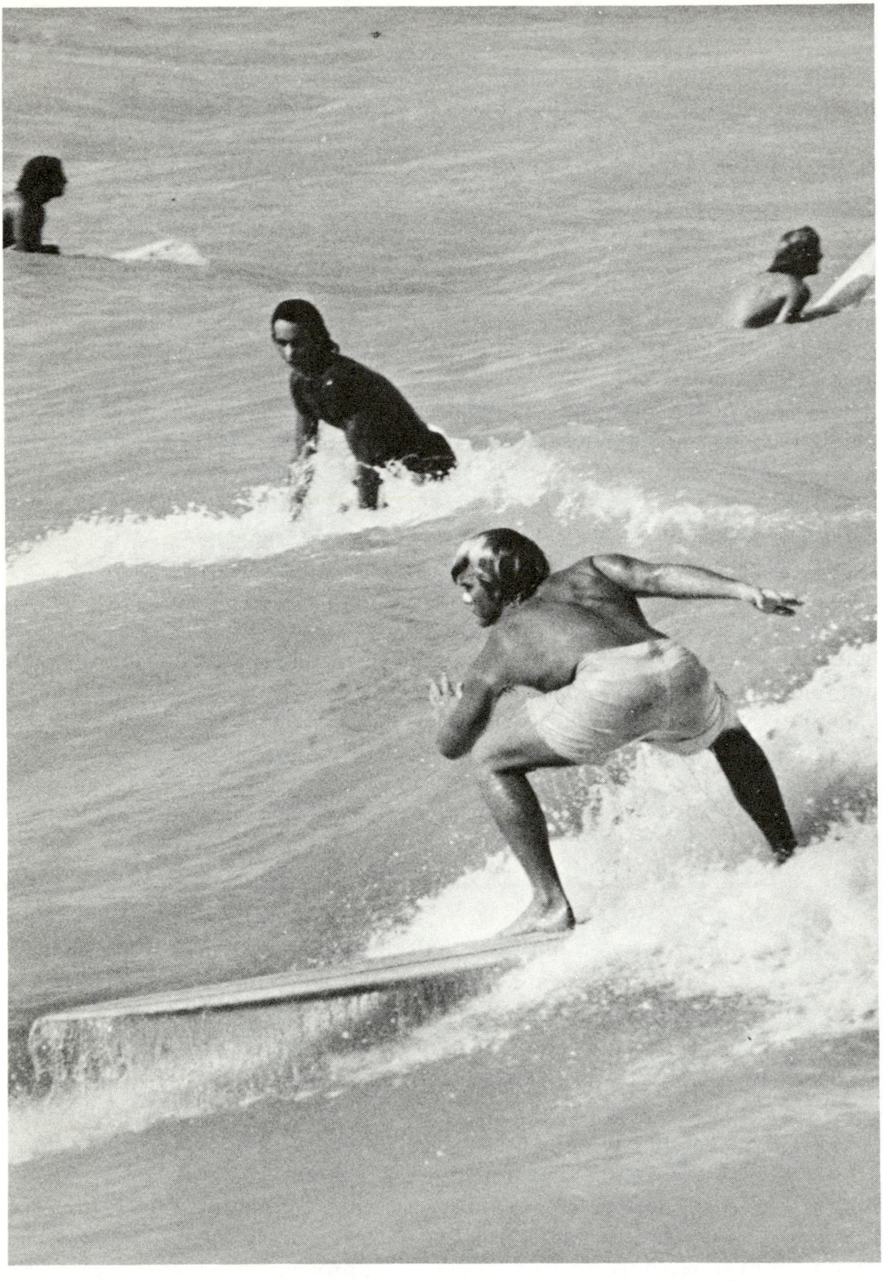

Surfboard riding is a play-sport providing challenge in a natural environment and the opportunity for self-expression. Photo by Dick Kassan, courtesy of Miami Beach Visitor and Convention Authority.

Ordinary fishing and hunting, I would think, are still essentially play-sports (despite the presence of the gun lobby); organized fox hunting, long central to British upper-class recreation, is more of an athletic-sport. Volleyball, when I was a boy, was almost always a "pick-up" play-sport. Today it has been organized as an athletic sport—a half-mile from my home, Miami-Dade Community College has organized competitive volleyball teams, as does the University of Miami. Frisbee, which would seem a natural play-sport, is today in transition—there are already organized competitive contests. Sky-diving, mountain climbing, hang-gliding, hot-air ballooning, and surf swimming are, I think, still play-sports. Pearson's example of a play-sport—surf board riding—is no longer play, as he suggests when it is sponsored by soft drink companies or when it is organized for TV production and beamed around the globe by Wide World of Sports.

We shall develop this whole question further in Chapters four and five.

FOOTNOTES

[1]Johan Huizinga, **Homo Ludens: A Study of the Play Element in Culture**, Boston, Beacon, 4th paperback printing, 1964.

[2]**Ibid.**, 3.

[3]Brian Sutton-Smith, **The Folkgames of Children**, Austin, University of Texas Press for the American Folklore Society, 1972, Introduction, xiii, xv.

[4]Elliott Avedon and Brian Sutton-Smith, **The Study of Games**, New York, Wiley, 1971, 439.

[5]Bernard Suits, "What is a Game?" Philosophy of Science, 34, 1967, 148-156.

[6]Huizinga, **op. cit.**, 7, 8-9, 9-10, 10, 11, 11-12. The enumeration is mine.

[7]**Ibid.**, 28.

[8]Jean Piaget, **Play, Dreams and Imitation in Childhood**, tr. C. Gattegno and F. M. Hodgson, New York, Norton, 1962, 147.

[9]**Ibid.**, 150.

[10]**Ibid.**, 147-150.

[11]Stephen Miller, "Ends, Means, and Galumphing: Some Leitmotifs of Play," **American Anthropologist, 75**, 92.

[12]New York, Free Press, 1961.

[13]Roger Caillois, "The Structure and Classification of Games," **Diogenes, 12**, Winter 1955, 74.

[14]Harold Garfinkel, cited in John R. Bowman, "The Organization of Spontaneous Adult Social Play," in **Play: Anthropological Perspectives**, ed. Michael A. Salter, 1977 Proceedings of the Association for the Anthropological Study of Play, West Point, N.Y., Leisure Press, 1978, 272.

[15]Bowman, op. cit., 144.

[16]For example, Gregory Bateson, "A Theory of Play and Fantasy," in Bateson, **Steps to an Ecology of Mind: Collected Essays in Anthropology, Psychiatry, Evolution, and Epistemology**, San Francisco, Chandler, 1972, 177-193, and Helen B. Schwartzman, "Children's Use of Metaphor in Imaginative Play Events," **Newsletter of the Association for the Anthropological Study of Play**, 6, no. 2, Fall 1979, 11-18.

[17]Avedon and Sutton-Smith, **The Study of Games, op. cit.**, 404.

[18]Lynn Price Ager, "The Reflection of Cultural Values in Eskimo Children's Games," in **The Study of Play: Problems and Prospects**, Proceedings of the First Annual Meeting of the Association of The Anthropological Study of Play, ed., David F. Lancy and B. Allan Tindall, West Point, N.Y., Leisure Press, 1976, 80.

[19]See:

John M. Roberts, Malcolm J. Arth, and Robert R. Bush, "Games in Culture," **American Anthropologist, 61**, June 1959, 595-605.

John M. Roberts and Brian Sutton-Smith, "Cross-Cultural Correlates of Games of Chance," **Behavior Science Notes, 3** 1966, 131-144.

Roberts and Sutton-Smith, "The Cross-Cultural and Psychological Study of Games," in Günther Lüschen, ed., **The Cross-Cultural Analysis of Games**, Champaign, Ill., Stipes, 1970, 100-108.

[20]Ager, **op. cit.**, 82.

[21]Paul Weiss, **Sport: A Philosophical Inquiry**, Carbondale: Southern Illinois University Press, 1969.

[22]Letter to Peter Carr, cited in Dixon Wecter, **The Saga of American Society: A Record of Social Aspirations, 1607-1937**, New York, Scribner's, 1937, 428.

[23]Peter C. McIntosh, **Sport in Society**, London, Watts, 1971, 36.

[24]Ralph H. Gabriel, preface to John Allen Krout, **Annals of American Sport**, vol. 15 of **The Pageant of America: A Pictorial History of the United States**, ed. by Gabriel, New Haven, Yale, 1929, 2.

[25]Foster Rhea Dulles, **America Learns to Play: A History of Popular Recreation, 1607-1940**, New York, Appleton-Century-Crofts, 1940, 61.

[26]John Rickards Betts, **America's Sporting Heritage, 1850-1950**, Reading, Mass., Addison-Wesley, 1974, 61.

[27]Huizinga, **op. cit.**, 196.

[28]**Ibid.**, 197.

[29]McIntosh, **op. cit.**, 6.

[30]Huizinga, **op. cit.**, 199.

[31]Heinz Meyer, "Puritanism and Physical Training: Ideological and Political Accents in the Christian Interpretation of Sport," **International Review of Sport Sociology**, 8, 1, 1973, 48-49.

[32]Harry Edwards, **Sociology of Sport**, Homewood, Ill., Dorsey, 1973, 59.

[33]Allen L. Sack, "Sport: Play or Work?," **Studies in the Anthropology of Play**, Proceedings of the Second Annual Meeting of the Association for the Anthropological Study of Play, West Point, N.Y., Leisure Press, 1977.

[34]**Ibid.**, 190-191.

[35]Michael A. Salter, "Play in Ritual: An Ethnohistorical Overview of Native North America," **Play and Culture**, ed., Helen B. Schwartzman, 1978 Proceedings of the Association for the Anthropological Study of Play, West Point, N.Y., Leisure Press, 1980, 70-82.

[36]Kent Pearson, "The Institutionalization of Sport Forms," **International Review of Sport Sociology, 14**, 1, 1979, 51-60

[37]**Ibid.**, 53

[38]**Ibid.**

CHAPTER 4 FROM FUN TO BUSINESS: HISTORIC BEGINNINGS

I personally feel that football as a sport is really a game, and I feel that as a game it should be enjoyed by players for the "worth" of the game and not its "goal." The "goal" is to **win** *and to win at all costs makes the "worth" decrease. This turns the game into a business and you shouldn't mix business with pleasure.*

Arnito Muskat
University of Miami student,
1976

The history of sport is the story of transition from amateurism to professionalism. The **amateur** is a **lover**. The word is derived from the first and simplest verb many beginning Latin students learn—**amo** (I love).

Although the transition away from amateurism has been taking place since the beginning of sport, it can be illustrated by a contrast which spans the recent period in which it has moved most rapidly.

The contrast begins in 1937, my last year as a college undergraduate in South Carolina. My school had a good small college football team, recruited for the most part from the regular student body. It was made up primarily of students who happened to play football, not of football players who happened to be registered for classes. That is, our players were genuine amateurs, not semi-professionals. If an excellent football player chose our college, we were not unhappy, and our coaches and alumni did actively seek such athletes. There was an occasional player from New York, New Jersey, or Pennsylvania, but our roster listed mostly addresses in South Carolina or the immediately adjoining states.

Not only were our players amateurs, but they were fairly unspecialized. They played one-platoon football, with each man alternating between offense and defense. Eleven men ordinarily played most of a game, with occasional individual spot substitutions to spell an injured or exhausted player, or to let a benchwarmer get experience. If a man was replaced by a substitute, the rules forbade him to return again in the same quarter. The nearest thing to "platooning" might occur when a new unit of eleven two-way players would start the second half or come in toward the end of a lopsided victory. In several games that year, eleven of our men played all sixty minutes. There were a few members of the team who played through about half the games without substitution.

Lest we think this was just small-college stuff, in bigger-time football eleven Yale men had in 1934 played all sixty minutes of their traditional "big" game with Princeton. On the same level, the one-platoon system produced such incidents as occurred in the sensational 1946 Notre Dame tie with Army, when the great Irish offensive quarterback Johnny Lujack saved the game in his role as defensive safety man by bringing a touchdown-bent Army back down in an open field.

To illustrate the personal quality of this unspecialized amateurism I can remember our tough, talented, no-nonsense all-state end who several times wept openly when he ran to the sidelines in front of the stands after being replaced because of injury or exhaustion.

Today, if football at my Alma Mater had been able (as it was not) to survive the increasing specialization and professionalization which followed World War II, instead of a traveling squad of about thirty part-time student athletes, we would probably travel with at least forty players from many of the fifty states, a large number on athletic scholarship. Instead of taking their classroom licks along with the rest of the student body, these semi-pros would be kept eligible by tutors through specially arranged programs of not-too-demanding courses. Where my college generation of athletes were kings of the campus, today's might be looked down on as "dumb jocks" enjoying a free four-year ride. Instead of being ready to go both ways, on offense and defense these players would then be divided into offensive and defensive specialists, and then subdivided into offensive running specialists, offensive passing specialists, defensive specialists against the run, and against the pass, specialists in punting, placekicking, holding for the placekick, kicking off, returning kickoffs, covering punts, returning punts, and so on. If our all-state end could return rejuvenated today, rather than giving and weeping for old Erskine, he would probably be calculating his chances in the pro draft. If he could look back and compare the two situations, forty years apart, he might say, as do some of my students, remembering their high school athletic years: "That was fun, but now it's a business."

He would be commenting on the development of trends that had already been summarized during his sophomore year in high school, when the Carnegie Foundation published in 1929 a comprehensive report on American college athletics:[1]

1. The extreme development of competitive games in the colleges has reached the secondary schools. The college athlete begins his athletic career before he goes to college. . .
2. Once in college, the student who goes in for competitive sports. . finds himself under a pressure, hard to resist, to give his whole time and thought to his athletic career. No college boy training for a major team can have much time for thought or study. . . .
3. The college athlete, often a boy from a modest home, finds himself suddenly a most important man in the college life. He begins to live on a scale never before imagined. . . When he drops back to a scale of living such as his own means can afford, the result is sometimes disastrous. . . .
4. He works (for it is work, not play) under paid professional coaches whose business it is to develop the boy to be an effective unit in a team. . . .
5. Inter-collegiate athletics are highly competitive. Each college or university longs for a winning team. A system of recruiting and subsidizing has grown up. . . . The system is demoralizing and corrupt, alike for the boy who takes the money and for the agent who arranges it. . . .
6. In the matter of competitive athletics the college alumnus has in the main played a sorry role. It is one thing for the "old grad" to go back and coach the boys of his college as at Oxford or Cambridge. . . . It is quite another thing for an American college graduate to pay money to high school boys. . . in order to enlist their services for a college team. . . .
7. There can be no doubt that athletics, if well conducted, may be made to contribute significantly to the physical health of students. . . . However. . . . under the present system of conducting athletics, too few students benefit and too many incur positive harm. Moreover, certain widespread athletic practices. . . actually jeopardize the physical health of the participants. . . .

8. For many games the strict organization and the tendency to commercialize the sport have taken the joy out of the game. In football, great numbers of boys do not play football, as in English schools and colleges, for the fun of it. A few play intensely. The great body of students are onlookers. . . .
9. The blaze of publicity in which the college athlete lives is a demoralizing influence for the boy himself and no less so for his college.

Any who doubt that college athletics is big business should review some statistics cited by Neil Amdur, sport columnist for the **New York Times**. They show the relationship between football records and alumni contributions to selected academic institutions.[2]

The University of Georgia:

Year	Record	Contributions
1961	3-7	$130,000.00
1962	3-4-3	168,000.00
1963	4-5-1	172,000.00
1964	6-3-1	185,000.00
1965	7-4	173,000.00
1966	10-1	211,000.00

Ohio State University:

1962	6-3	$762,834.00
1963	5-3-1	627,737.00
1964	7-2	744,908.00
1965	7-2	1,247,698.00
1966	4-5	762,236.00
1967	6-3	1,353,799.00

The University of Missouri:

1956	4-5-1	$ 57,792.68
1957	5-4-1	157,790.94
1958	5-4-1	418,746.72
1959	6-5	227,409.03
1960	10-1	442,445.77
1961	7-2-1	288,307.55

"Every college graduate likes to see his school doing well in football," said one alumni director. "It gives him a chance to flaunt his school ring at cocktail parties and it makes for Monday conversation at the office. If he's at a school that has been down in football for years and suddenly makes it big, it's a bonus."[3]

Amdur's most impressive figures come from smaller schools. Amherst won the Little Three football championship from 1959 through 1966 in every season except two, 1961 and 1966. Alumni contributions increased every season except two, 1961 and 1966. Wilkes College in Wilkes-Barre, Pa., had these won-lost and contribution records:

1961	1-6	$6,917
1962	3-4	9,512
1963	3-5	14,589
1964	1-6	24,745
1965	7-1	29,924
1966	8-0	83,801

There are different ways of interpreting such data: (1) football victories may induce alumnni contributions, (2) alumni contributions may promote athletic success, or (3) both victories and contributions may be due to other factors. But some of Amdur's correlations are striking.

A different example of the development of professionalized competitive sport—in this case without the extreme commercialism of American sport—is the career of the "martial art" of judo, analyzed by B. C. and J. M. Goodger. As developed in Japan under the influence of Dr. Jigoro Kano in the late nineteenth century, judo was a "civilized" form of the more violent jiu-jitsu, stressing **jita kyoei** ("self-perfection and mutual benefit and welfare") and **seiryoku-zenyo** ("maximum efficiency"). "Self-perfection was to be combined with an awareness of the benefit of others; the individual was to be of service to the world while developing his own capacities, physical and spiritual."[4] Judo was primarily a middle-class art. It was Japanese. It was sometimes associated with the study of zen. Foreigners would study in Japan, live there, even marry Japanese women while seeking to absorb its cultural background.

After World War II, "international competition became a major focal concern in Judo." Before this time "international matches tended to be occasional, ad hoc 'friendly' affairs," but European championships were inaugurated in 1951, World championships and National Team Championships in 1956, and in 1964 judo was included in the Olympic Games.

These developments meant the proliferation of rules and regulations, administered by bureaucracies. By contrast with its original self-improvement goals, successful judo became competitive medal-winning. It was taken up by the mass media, and rules were frequently changed, as in other sports, to enhance spectator appeal. Successful performance came to be thought of in terms of scientific analysis of movement rather than of insight and special knowledge. Development of judo as a sport led to the employment as coaches and referees of a number of fairly low-grade players who were not thoroughly grounded students of judo, but technicians. Recruitment of working-class performers "toughened" judo. The judo specialist who formerly went to Japan to soak up the judo culture was replaced by the international star who visits Japan for a short period to "sharpen up" or get a "good hard practice" for the European championships. Like the senior British judo player, he may feel he could train as well at home: "Just because the Japanese take up Rugby, I wouldn't encourage their players to eat steak and kidney pudding."[5]

In their 1977 study the Goodgers wrote:

> *The focal concern is almost exclusively national, and, even more, international competition. Whereas in previous stages most participants tended to view contests as an aspect of judo that contributed to the educational and developmental end of judo practice, competition would now appear to be an end in itself. Weight training and running have been incorporated into the schedules of most judo players. The esoteric and philosophical components of previous stages tend to be dismissed as mumbo-jumbo. . . Thus, judo training and practice is now viewed in mainly instrumental terms, as a preparation for contest rather than as mental and physical training of essentially intrinsic value. . .and the moral significance of the training situation is more 'secular' and more typical of Western amateur sport in general.*[6]

How did organized sport come to turn against the spirit of play? An answer will lead us on an excursion into the historical origins of modern sport. This will take us into the main influences that have shaped our whole modern western society. Our first roots we shall find in the role of agonistic contest in ancient Greece, which gave us, among other things, the Olympic Games. Then we shall look at the public spectacles that united and pacified the Roman masses. From here we shall give notice to the courtly tournaments of the medieval nobility, and to what Huizinga called the "unbuttoned" play of the medieval common people. Next we shall see the spirit of fun and play beseiged and suppressed by the Puritan stress on sobriety and work. We shall see then how this severe ethic gave rise to economic expansion, which in turn provided the leisure and affluence that made possible modern mass sport.

The Agonistic Society: Greece

Just after the 1980 Olympics it is hard to forget that one of the sources of contemporary sport lies in the agonistic tradition of ancient Greece—in "the serious contests that formed the core of Greek social life."[7] Homer, in the early days of Greece, memorialized the urge "always to be the best and to excel others." The beginnings of the agonistic tradition, over a thousand years before Christ, are described by Huizinga in this way:

> *Our point of departure must be an almost childlike play-sense expressing itself in various play-forms, some serious, some playful, but all allowing the innate human need of rhythm, harmony, change, alternating contrast and climax, etc., to unfold in full richness. Coupled with this play-sense is a spirit that strives for honor, dignity, superiority, and beauty. Magic and mystery, heroic longing, the forebodings of music, sculpture and logic all seek form and expression in noble play. A later generation will call the age that knew such aspirations "heroic."*[8]

Aristotle, a member of this "later generation," said, "Men crave honor in order to persuade themselves of their own worth, their virtue. They aspire to be honored by persons of judgment and in virtue of their real value."[9]

Central to the way of life of Greece were **agon** (contest), **agonia** (death struggle or fear), both related to **agora** (a gathering—the name of the central meeting-ground in Athens and other Greek cities). In these public events one sought to express or establish his **arete** (personal virtue or excellence), a concept related to **aristos** (superior), the quality of "aristocracy."

"The Greeks," says Huizinga again, "used to stage contests in anything that offered the bare possibility of a fight."[10] Alexander the Great celebrated the death of a hero by a musical and gymnastic **agon** in which prizes were given to the heaviest drinkers. Thirty-five of the contestants died during this **agon**. The winner, along with five others, survived to die shortly afterward. The Greeks, whose sculpture preserves their admiration for the male body, also held beauty contests for men at their festivals, along with competitions in singing, and in keeping awake. There were "slanging matches" in which people would strive to insult and "put down" one another. One of the outcomes of these slanging matches was political satire—Greek political life, like ours, rested to a large extent on ability to "put down" an opponent. As with us, the courts of law had the same agonistic quality—courtroom eloquence was a more sophisticated slanging match. Another outcome of these slanging matches may have been poetry (**iambos**, the root of the word **iambic** for one of the basic verse forms, originally meant "derision"). Greek philosophy may have originated in competitions in solving riddles. Greek drama, both tragic and comic, was composed for public competitions, especially the feast of Dionysius. "The whole public reacted to the subtleties of style and expression, sharing the tension of the contest like a crowd at a football match."[11]

In the Greek quest for excellence, the most admired figure was the athlete (from the word **athlos**—prize—which united the concepts of contest, struggle, exercise, exertion, endurance, and suffering). In the **Odyssey**, Homer said, "There is no greater glory for a man as long as he lives than that which he wins by his own hands and feet."[12] "We must not," says the cultural historian Will Durant, "think of the average Greek as a student and lover of Aeschylus or Plato; rather, like the typical Briton, or American, he was interested in sport, and his favored athletes were his earthly gods."[13]

On one occasion the record shows that a general returning from a military triumph was welcomed home "like an athlete." Even military invasion could not stop athletic competition. On the history-making day when a handful of Greeks turned back Xerxes' army at Thermopylae, thousands watched the games at Olympia. A Persian exclaimed to his general: "Good heavens! What manner of men are these against whom you have brought us to fight?—men who contend with one another not for money but for honor!"[14]

Greek games were private, municipal, and national (Panhellenic). A relief (flat) sculpture in Athens shows a wrestling match on one side, a field hockey game on the other. Bareback riding, swimming, throwing and dodging missiles when mounted, were not only spectator sports but common activities. The Greeks, like us, had ball games—in Sparta the word for **youth** also meant **ballplayer**. A short description by Antiphanes of a star player in a game four centuries before Christ reads like a modern sports page. In this game a team tried to throw the ball over or through the other team until one side was driven back over its goal line. Here is the star: "When he got the ball, he delighted to give it to one player while dodging another; he knocked it away from one and urged on another with noisy cries. Outside, a long pass, beyond him, overhead, a short pass."[15]

The oldest of the Panhellenic games began at Olympia in 776 B.C. (the first definite date in Greek history), and took place every four years.

We have seen Durant describe Greek athletes as "earthly gods." This could, in a way, be said of the feeling of many people today about their sports heroes. But there is a difference. The Olympic games were a formally religious festival for all of Greece. The Olympic enclosure was a sacred area, with shrines which were open all year and in which the fires were never allowed to die out. Although Greek towns and states were almost constantly quarreling, hostilities were suspended during the month when athletes and spectators traveled to and from Olympia "under the protection of tradition and the watchful eyes of the gods."[16] For these religious rites the participants were required to dedicate themselves intensely. All had to swear that they had been in training during the ten months before coming to Olympia. Once there, they followed strict programs of exercise and diet. "There were hot and cold baths; steam and vapor baths. . . drying rooms, restrooms and luxuries that few modern athletic plants can boast."[17] At one time in the early Olympics the training table diet consisted entirely of fresh cheese and water.

Durant paints graphically the color of the Grecian Olympics, obviously a scene of both fun and business, something like an ancient Disney World:

"We picture the pilgrims and athletes starting out from distant cities, a month ahead of time, to come together at the games. It was a fair as well as a festival; the plain was covered not only with the tents that sheltered the visitors from the July heat, but with the booths where a thousand concessionaries exposed for sale everything from wine and fruit to horses and statuary, while acrobats and conjurers performed their tricks for the crowd. Some juggled balls in the air, others performed marvels of agility and skill, others ate fire or swallowed swords: modes of amusement, like forms of superstition, enjoy a reverend antiquity. Famous orators like Gorgias, famous sophists like Hippias, perhaps famous writers like Herodotus, delivered addresses or recitations from the porticoes of the temple of Zeus. It was a special holiday for men, since married women were not allowed to attend the festival; these had their own games at the feast of Hera. Manander summed up such a scene in five words: 'crowd, market, aerobats, amusements, thieves.'"[18]

The competition lasted five days. Forty-five thousand spectators typically stayed in the stadium all day, battling heat, thirst, and insects. Hats were forbidden and the water was usually bad. All contestants, who must be freeborn Greeks, were naked, except sometimes for a loincloth.

One of the featured events was boxing, with blows confined to the head, no rule against hitting a man when he was down, no classification of boxers by weight. There were no rounds and no rests and bouts lasted until one gave up or was beaten down. Eventually boxing was combined with wrestling in a game called **pankration** ("contest of all powers"). Here biting and gouging and even kicking in the stomach were allowed. The brutality is suggested by the case of one winner who "struck so ferociously with straight extended fingers and strong sharp nails that he pierced the flesh of his adversary and dragged out his bowels."[19] There were footraces, one of four hundred yards, another for 2 2/3 miles, and a third an armed race in which the runners carried heavy shields.

The main Olympic contest was the pentathlon—five events designed to test a man's all-around skill. The victor had to win three events out of the five: a long jump, holding weights, from a standing start; throwing a twelve-pound discus of stone or iron; the javelin throw; wrestling; and a final sprint race the length of the stadium—about two hundred yards.

The culminating event of the games was the chariot races in the hippodrome below the stadium. In a typical race ten chariots, each drawn by four horses, had to run 23 laps of a course with posts which must be rounded at each end. So, as in a modern auto speedway race, "accidents were the chief thrill of the game." In one race, out of forty chariots that started, one finished the race.

In the sixth century B.C. Greek athletics was at its peak. There were established also the Pythian games at Delphi, in honor of Apollo, the Isthmian games at Corinth, and games in honor of Zeus at Nemea. In these later games contests were added in music, pottery, poetry, sculpture, painting, choral singing, oratory, and drama. These influenced the whole development of the arts in Greece.

Together, the games formed a **periodos**, or cycle: every Greek athlete's ambition was to win the "quadruple crown" at Olympia, Delphi, Corinth, and Nemea.

Victorious athletes were intensely popular. Cities voted them substantial sums of money on their return. Some became generals. So idolized were they that the philosophers complained jealously. Their names were written into history: by the later Greek historians, time was designated by Olympiads, each named after the victor in the stadium sprint.

Although the Olympics were an all-Greek festival, they did not include **all** Greeks. Women were not allowed in the early games as participants, and married women were excluded from the stadium. At one time a dramatic event occurred when the father of a runner, Pisodorous, died during the training period. The runner's mother took over the training and attended the games in disguise. When Pisodorus won, she was understandably so elated that she could no longer conceal herself. The penalty for such an invasion of a male event called for her to be thrown off a huge rock to her death, but the penalty was not enforced. Finally, women were admitted as spectators and eventually as contestants. In the 128th games in 264 B.C. the chariot race for pairs of colts was won by Belisiche, a Macedonian woman.

Within four centuries after the beginning of the Olympics in 776 B.C., Greek athletics went through the same kind of change which modern sport has undergone. Writing in 1910 in the most thorough book researched on the Greek Olympics, E. Norman Gardiner saw this lesson in Greek sport: "The nemesis of excess in athletics is specialization, specialization begets professionalism and professionalism is the death of true sport."[20]

The original Olympic ideal had been the well-rounded development of the body, primarily as a preparation for national self-defense; this included **aidos**, the disciplined self-control of the sportsman. The early Olympic athlete was an amateur. He ate the simple nourishing vegetarian diet of the Greek farmer or villager: figs, cheese, porridge, meal cakes.

But in the sixth century B.C.,

> *There is a point in any sport or game where it becomes over-developed, and competition too severe for it to serve the true purpose*

> *of providing exercise or recreation for the many. It becomes the monopoloy of the few who can afford the time or money to acquire excellence, while the rest, despairing of any true measure of success, prefer the role of spectators. When the rewards of success are sufficient, there arises a professional class, and when professionalism is once established, the amateur can no longer compete with the professional.*[21]

If we want a specific date, we might place the beginning of professionalism in the year 594 B.C. when Solon promised that any Athenian winning at Olympia would receive 100 drachma (the value of 100 oxen).

By the fifth century B.C. the amateur sportsman had been replaced by the specialist, in the hands of a professional trainer. The well-rounded development of the body gave way to intensive preparation to win a particular event. In the 80th Olympiad (456 B.C.) a meat diet was introduced to provide bulk for the boxing and wrestling which were highly favored. This change, says Gardiner, "created an artificial distinction between the life of the athlete and the life of the ordinary man." Thucydides reported that the "ordinary man" had become a passive spectator. Hippocrates of Cos, whose oath is now taken by all physicians, lamented that specialization was creating an unhealthy one-sided development. Plato, who himself had won in wrestling at Delphi, Corinth, Nemea, and possibly Olympia, in his **Republic** did not include athletics in the preparation of youth to defend his ideal state. Euripides in the play **Autolycus** said: "Of all the countless evils throughout Hellas, there is none worse than the race of athletes. . . . I blame the custom of the Hellenes who gather together to watch these men, honoring a useless pleasure."[22] In 388 B.C. a low point in commercialization was reached when Eulopos was caught bribing opponents to lose to him in the 98th Olympic boxing competition.

Bread and Circuses: Rome

As the Panhellenic games expressed and symbolized the glory that was Greece, says Durant, so the spectacles in her Colosseum expressed and symbolized the **vain**-glory that was Rome.

For almost five hundred years following the assassination of Julius Caesar in 44 B.C., the Roman empire extended, over the larger part of the known world that Caeser had conquered, the largest and most widespread period of peace and affluence that the world had known. Rome preserved the solid culture of the Greek poets, philosophers, and sculptors, and added to it. But her talent was engineering and administration, her chief qualities

Discobolos

The contrast between the early magnificent discus thrower (Discobolos by Myron) and the later paunchy Olympic performer (Farnese Heracles by Glycon, after original by Lysippus) dramatizes the degeneration of the Greek athletic idea. Courtesy of The Bettman Archive.

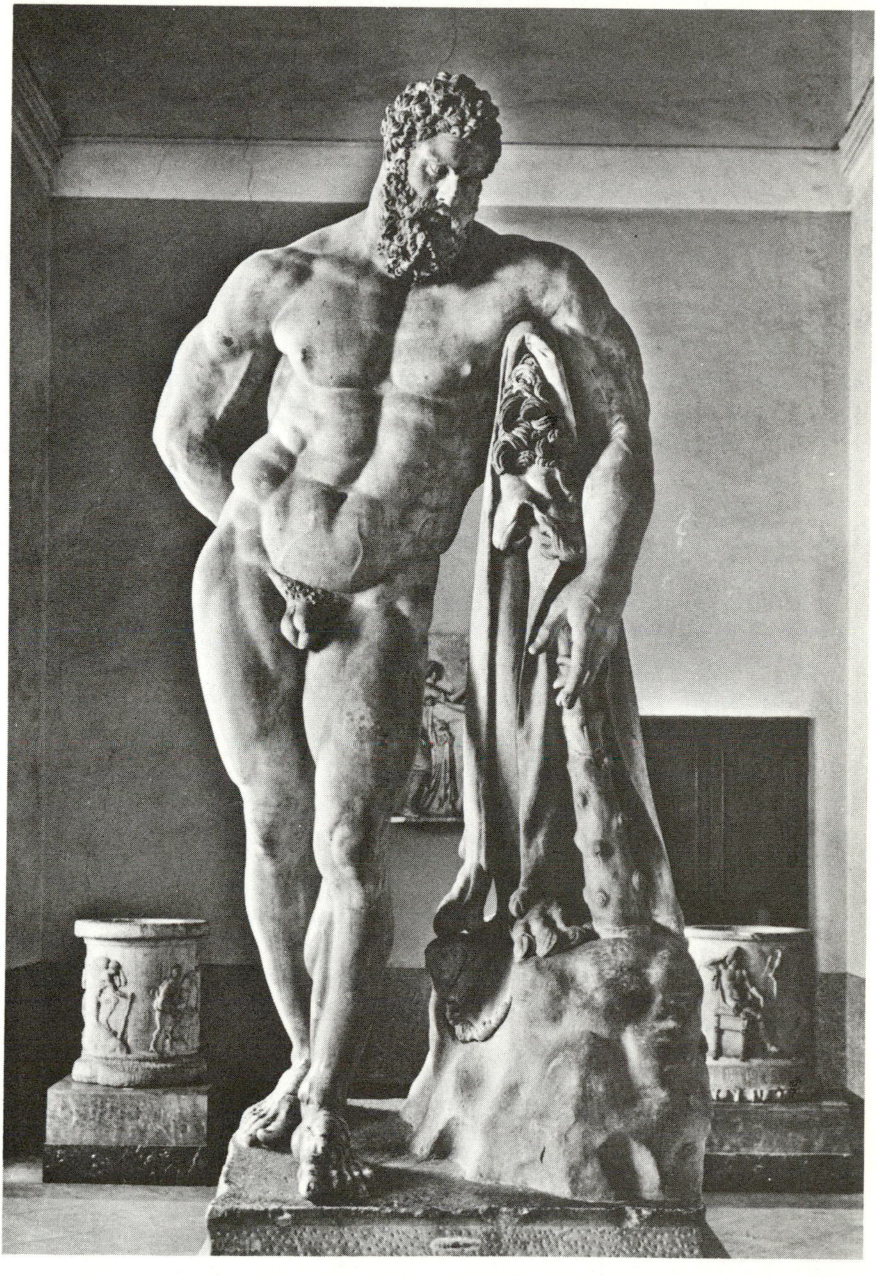

Farnese Heracles

affluence and power. Public spectacles and games were a central part of the life of the Empire. Anxious to spread the power and affluence of Rome, emperors built cities to the very edge of the desert, and each one of them had an amphitheater for the entertainment of the people. As the Empire declined, this public entertainment became more important to its life.

Let us look at sport in Rome in the first century after the birth of Christ. There were in the Roman year seventy-six religious festival days celebrated by **ludi**—about two thirds by plays and other shows (Caillois' ''mimicry'') and the other third by games in the circus, stadium, or amphitheater (**agon**).

In a stadium, there were typically wrestling and boxing matches and foot races, mainly by professionals and aliens. The masses of people found simple athletics dull compared to the boxing matches in which huge Greeks fought with gloves reinforced at the knuckles by a thick iron band. The Roman populace was ''turned on'' by action which resembled the fictional encounter in Virgil's **Aenead**:

> *Then the son of Auchises brought out hide gloves of equal weight, and bound the hands of the antagonists. . . Each took his stand, poised on tiptoe and raising one arm. . . Drawing their heads back from the blows they spar, hand against hand. They aim many hard blows, pummeling each other's sides and chests, ears and brows and cheeks, making the air resound with their strokes. . . Entellus puts for his right, Dares slips aside in a nimble dodge. . . Entellus furiously drives Dares headlong over the arena, redoubling his blows, now with the right hand, now with the left. . . Then Aeneas put an end to the fray, Dares' mates led him to the ships with his knees shaking, his head swaying from side to side, his mouth spitting teeth and blood.*[23]

At the Circus Maximus there were races, either by horses and jockeys, or chariot races such as we saw at Olympia.

At the Hippodrome

> *On the appointed day 180,000 men and women moved in festive colors to the enormous hippodrome. Enthusiasm rose to a mania. Excited partisans smelled the dung of the animals to assure themselves that the horses of their favorite drivers had been properly fed. The spectators passed by the shops and brothels that lined the outer walls; they filed through hundreds of entrances and sorted themselves out with the sweat of anxiety into the great horseshoe of seats. Vendors sold them cushions, for the seats were mostly of hard wood, and the program would last all day. Senators and other dignitaries had*

special seats of marble, ornamented with bronze. Behind the imperial box was a suite of luxurious rooms, where the emperor and his family might eat, drink, rest, bathe, and sleep. Gambling was feverish and fortunes passed from hand to hand as the day advanced. . . The usual length of a chariot race was seven circuits, about five miles. The test of skill lay in making the turns at the goals as swiftly and sharply as safety would allow; collisions were frequent there, and chariots, and animals mingled in fascinated tragedy. As the horses or chariots clattered to the final post the hypnotized audience rose like a swelling sea, gesticulated, waved handkerchiefs, shouted and prayed, groaned and cursed, or exalted in almost supernatural ecstasy. The applause that greeted the winner could be heard far beyond the limits of the city.
—*Will Durant,* **Caesar and Christ**, Part III of **The Story of Civilization**, New York: Simon and Schuster, 1944, 382-383.

The most colossal Roman sport was the **naumachia**, a sham naval battle in a flooded area, or artificial lake, in which captives or condemned criminals reenacted historical naval engagements until they had killed off each other. The victors, if they pleased the audience, might be granted freedom.

The most famous Roman games were the fights involving animals and gladiators in the Colosseum. There were events such as a contest between a bull and a man. But what really turned on the Roman audiences were the fights by pairs or masses of armed men. Augustus gave eight spectacles in which a total of 10,000 men took part. Attendants prodded fallen gladiators with iron rods to make sure they were dead, and if they were not, killed them with mallet blows on the head.

The combatants were war captives, disobedient slaves, or condemned criminals. The criminals came from all parts of the Empire: murder, robbery, arson, sacrilege, or mutiny might lead one to be sentenced to a gladiatorial career. This could happen even to knights and senators. The gladiators were trained in gladiatorial schools, of which there were four in Rome, several others in Italy, and one in Alexandria. On entering a school one swore "to suffer himself to be whipped with rock, burned with fire, and killed with steel."[24]

A gladiator who fought very hard might be freed immediately. If he just survived, he might have to fight again and again on other holidays.

It is hard to believe that not all the "athletes" were displeased with their work:

Some were elated with victories and thought of their prowess rather than their peril; some complained that they were not allowed to fight often enough. . . They had the stimulus and consolation of fame; their names were daubed by admirers on public walls; women fell in love with them, poets sang of them, painters portrayed them, sculptors carved for posterity their iron biceps and terrifying frowns.[25]

Prominent Romans found many justifications for the gladiatorial spectacles. The gladiators' crimes had been serious, they said, and the spectacles would deter the audience from making the same mistakes. And was not the chance of life in the Colosseum more merciful than sure and sudden execution? In any case, what was shed was only **vilis sanguis**—the blood of common men.

Others, like the philosopher Seneca, were not impressed by such arguments. He dropped into the games one day at noon when most of the spectators had gone to lunch, and reported:

I came home more greedy, more cruel and inhuman, because I have been among human beings. By chance I attended a midday exhibition, expecting some fun, wit, and relaxation. . .whereby men's eyes may have respite from the slaughter of their fellow men. But it was quite the contrary. . . These noon fighters are sent out with no armor of any kind; they are exposed to blows at all points, and no one ever strikes in vain. . . In the morning they throw men to the lions; at noon they throw them to the spectators. The crowd demands that the victor who has slain his opponent shall face the man who will slay him in turn; and the last conqueror is reserved for another butchering. . . This sort of thing goes on while the stands are nearly empty. . . Man, a sacred thing to man, is killed for sport and merriment.[26]

Seneca's reaction reminds us of the way some people feel about the brutality and violence of some of our contemporary sports. By examining why these spectacles were important to Rome, we may throw some light on our own times. (Whether they are right or not, some people think that we are now living in a period similar to the decline and fall of Rome. Also, some of my football players refer to themselves as "gladiators".)

For one thing, Roman sport was a way of keeping the masses of people busy and amused, and thereby keeping down rebellion. In the affluent society, the Roman working class called for a share of **panem et circenses**—bread and circuses: free food and engrossing spectacles in the circular arena in which they could forget their own suffering by seeing others suffer.

Furthermore, for the upper classes in an affluent society, sponsorship of sport was a form of "conspicuous consumption." "During the first centuries of the Empire thousands of citizens from all quarters competed in the funding and donating of halls, baths, theaters, in the mass distribution of food, in the institution or equipping of new games, all of which was recorded for posterity in boastful inscriptions."[27] Huizinga calls this the "potlatch spirit," referring to the tradition of Kwakiutl Indians, known to all beginning sociology and anthropology students, in which chiefs contended in a public competition (potlatch) to see who could display or destroy the most wealth.

More than this, the sporting festivals gave meaning to life and fostered a patriotic identification with the Roman state:

> *A modern ear is inclined to detect in this cry (for* **panem et circenses***) little more than the demand of the unemployed proletariat for the dole and free cinema tickets. But it had a deeper significance. Roman society could not live without games. They were as necessary to its existence as bread—for they were holy games and the people's right to them was a holy right. Their basic function lay not merely in celebrating such prosperity as the community had already won for itself, but in fortifying it and ensuring future prosperity by means of ritual.*[28]

Another oustanding cultural historian, Lewis Mumford, related Roman sport to a broader setting which includes us:

> *Play in one form or another is found in every human society and among a great many animal species: but sport in the sense of a mass spectacle, with death to add to the underlying excitement, comes into existence when a population has been drilled and regimented and depressed to such an extent that it needs at least a vicarious participation in difficult feats of strength or skill or heroism in order to sustain its waning life sense. The demand for circuses, and when the milder spectacles are insufficiently life-arousing, the demand for sadistic exploits and finally for blood is characteristic of civilizations that are losing their grip: Rome under the Caesars, Mexico at the time of Montezuma, Germany under the Nazis. These forms of surrogate manliness and bravado are the surest sign of a collective impotence and a pervasive death wish. The dangerous symptoms of that ultimate decay one finds everywhere today in machine civilization under the guise of mass sport.*[29]

The World of Camelot: The Middle Ages

Those who saw one of the most popular musical romances of our time ("Camelot," with Vanessa Redgrave, Richard Harris, and Franco Nero) will know what the veteran sports writer Jerry Izenberg meant when he wrote in 1972 of his ex-semipro baseball player father:

> *Sports were the biggest single thing in my old man's life, because everything was always clear-cut. There were good guys and bad guys, and sometimes the bad guys played dirty, but that was part of it, too. That's the way I grew up, and when I became a sports writer for money. . ., I still thought of the whole thing as a kind of wall-to-wall Camelot. . . Well, it's not, and it never really was. . .*[30]

To pick up our continuity: The period from the fall of Rome to about 1300 we call the Middle Ages, its way of life "medieval." In 455 A.D. Rome, the center of the most developed urban culture yet known, was sacked for ten days by Vandals from the north. The next five centuries saw the European remnants of the Graeco-Roman-Christian civilization repeatedly overswept by invading Arabs, Germans, Vikings, Hungarians from the north and east. Beginning about the year 1000, Europe finally stabilized around a new type of political and economic organization called feudalism, of which the Camelot myth was an important part.

The work of feudalism was twofold. First, it was to master nature. "At the beginning of the Middle Ages," Durant says, "the greater part of Europe's soil was untilled and unpeopled forest and waste, at their end the Continent had been won for civilization."[31] The peasants of Europe had "drained marshes, raised dykes, cleared woods and canals, cut roads, built homes, advanced the frontier of civilization, and won the battle between jungle and man."[32] To do this it was necessary that order be maintained—against invading hordes and against fighting among neighbors. For these purposes there was no longer the Roman government which had built aqueducts and amphitheaters, no longer the imperial army which had enforced the **pax Romana** (Roman peace). So there arose a new form of structure based not upon the sovereignty of a central state, but upon private contracts between individuals. A powerful person would grant land to another as a fief or **feudum** (note the origin of "feudal") and agree to protect his "vassal" in exchange for the vassal's military service. "Imagine," says a historian writing of the period, "a society in which the governmental authority of the state, as we know it, has almost completely disappeared. . .

There, instead of one central government that all must answer to, hundreds of little 'governmental' organizations come into being, each virtually an independent territory, though vaguely connected by a kind of feudal hierarchy or network of personal agreements among the local 'governments'."[33] Each fief was organized economically in the form of a manor, an agricultural estate, on which worked a peasantry composed of serfs, free landholders, and semi-free people called villeins. Everyone's station in life, from the lord of the manor down to the serf, was ascribed by his birth. Each had hereditary rights and obligations. In the absence of central government, the widest unifying force was the church. This saw the feudal arrangement as part of a larger plan:

> *Society, like the human body, is an organism composed of different members. Each member has his own function, prayer, or defense or merchandizing, or tilling the soil. Within classes there must be equality. . .Between classes there must be inequality, for otherwise a class cannot perform its function or. . . enjoy its rights. Peasants must not encroach on those above them. Lords must not despoil peasants.*[34]

A central part of the medieval pattern, very important to the traditions of sport, was **chivalry**—the code of conduct for the mounted vassal warrior called the knight, toward his lord, toward his fellow-knights, toward women, and toward the church. The term comes from the Latin word for horse, **caballus** (related to the French **cheval** and the English **cavalry** and **cavalier**). The chivalric code was extremely important to security in the society I have described. The knight did not attack a wounded man. He kept his word (**parole**) which was good enough to free him when he was captured in battle and held for ransom. In a world where men were often away at war and left women at home, the knight was pledged to honor and protect them. Out of this idealized protectiveness grew the concept of romantic love—which was more often for a mistress than for a wife. The knight was to fight when necessary in defense of the church and of the needy. All this was the Camelot ideal, although in fact "more knights looked for damsels *to* distress than *in* distress and churches to raid than to aid."[35] (Italics mine.)

Chivalry was very important in maintaining the class structure of society. It set the lords and knights off from the peasants, who had no obligation to be chivalrous, and also from the merchants of the towns which had survived the decline of the Roman empire. By the late thirteenth century, chivalry had solidified into a very elaborate system of ideals and rituals. "By emphasis on observance of the chivalric code and way of life the nobility thought it could best preserve its social status, indeed its very identity. . . against the . . . upstart merchants."[36] There is a parallel in the way in which the Southern landed aristocracy in the United States preserved a "medieval" code of chivalry against a rising urban and industrial society before and since the Civil War.

> *Behind the formal structure of feudalism, the feudal picture is not merely one of serfdom, illiteracy, exploitation, and violence, but as truly a scene of lusty peasants clearing the wilderness; of men colorful and vigorous in language, love, and war; of knights pledged to honor and service, seeking adventure and fame rather than comfort and security, and scorning danger, death, and hell; women patiently toiling and breeding in peasant cottages, and titled ladies mingling the tenderest prayers to the virgin with the bold freedom of a sensuous poetry and courtly love.*[37]

Where did sport come in? First, what Huizinga calls the "joyous and unbuttoned play of the people."[38] On Sundays and holidays, after Mass,

> *the peasant sang and danced, and forgot in hearty rustic laughter the dour burden of sermon and farm. Ale was cheap, speech was free and profane, and love tales of womankind mingled with the awesome legends of the saints. Rough games of football, hockey, and wrestling, and weight throwing pitted man against man, and village against village. Cock fighting and bull baiting flourished, and hilarity reached its height when, within a closed circle, two blindfolded men, armed with cudgels, tried to kill a goose or a pig. Sometimes of an evening, peasants visited one another, played indoor games and drank. . .*[39]

Almost everybody swam. In the north, in the winter, skating was about as common. All classes practiced archery, although later it became an upper class pastime. Hunting had its practical as well as its sportive aspects: medieval Paris, for example, was sometimes invaded by wolves. The fields of peasants would sometimes be trampled down by hunting nobles, who had no doubt about their right to enter. Only the working classes fished—this had not yet become a leisure class game. Ice hockey is recorded in Ireland as early as the second century A.D. Tennis (named from the cry, "**tenez!**" [hold!], of server to receiver) was introduced from Moslem areas and was popular in France. In England it attracted large crowds in theaters and in the open air. A Turkish historian of the twelfth century describes a form of polo played with corded racquets and resembling lacrosse. A medieval writer tells of football as "an abominable game wherein young people propel a huge ball not by throwing it into the air but by striking and rolling it along the ground, not with their hands but with their feet."[40] Gardiner believes that the game came to England from China by way of Italy.[41]

"Planned spectacles," says Durant, "were a vital part of medieval life: church processions, political parades, guild celebrations, filled the streets with banners, floats, wax saints, fat merchants, and military bands."[42] One of the distinctive public spectacles, central to the Camelot myth, was the tournament. Tournaments had their highest popularity in France (the original home of Lancelot du Lac, the successful suitor for the favor of Queen Guenivere at Camelot), beginning about the tenth century. They were held in connection with an important symbolic public event, such as the ordination of a knight, a royal marriage, or the visit of a king.

Heralds would be sent around to announce the tournament. Knights would come to the tournament town, hang their armor in their windows, and post their coat-of-arms in public places where they could be examined. Anyone who challenged a knight's participation could lodge his protest with the tournament officials. If the challenge was upheld, the knight was disqualified, and thereafter had a "blot on his scutcheon" (shield). The tournament town had some of the carnival quality of Olympia (and Disneyland): "To the excited gathering came horse dealers to equip the knight, haberdashers to clothe him and his horse in fit array, moneylenders to ransom the fallen, fortunetellers, acrobats, mimes, troubadors and trouvéres, wandering scholars, women of loose morals, ladies of high degree. The whole occasion was a festival of song and dance, trysts and brawls, and wild betting on the contests."[43]

The event itself might last about one day or as long as about a week. It took place in the "lists": the town square would be partly enclosed by stands and balconies for the richer spectators. The commoners would stand on foot around the field. All the knights would enter, to the fanfare of opening music, before the first engagement.

In a man-to-man event, the **joust** or tilt, the mounted knights would approach each other with their lances extended, at top speed. When one or both were knocked off their mounts, the tilt would continue on foot until one was **hors de combat** (disabled or killed), or one quit, or the king or lord called a halt. A tournament consisted of a large number of such tilts, in which the knights vied for the favor of the lords, and ladies.

The feature of the tournament was the **tourney**, a mock battle by masses of knights, usually with blunted weapons. This might be very bloody: in a tourney at Neuss in 1240, about sixty knights were killed. The tourney was a miniature war. Prisoners were taken, and could be held for ransom. At the end of the tournament the victors and the nobles celebrated by feasting, singing, and dancing. The successful knights heard songs and poems composed in their honor, and were kissed by beautiful ladies.

The Church tried repeatedly to ban tournaments but, along with the feasts and poems and kisses, "the knights loved money even more than war."[44] We are reminded of professional athletes in Greece and Rome, and today, by the legend of a knight who "protested the Church's condemnation of tournaments on the ground that if effective, it would end his only means of livelihood."[45]

FOOTNOTES

[1]Howard J. Savage, Harold W. Bentley, John T. McGovern, and Dean F. Smiley, **American College Athletics**, New York, The Carnegie Foundation for the Advancement of Teaching, 1929, xiv, xv, 157.

[2]Neil Amdur, **The Fifth Down: American Democracy and the Football Revolution**, New York, Dell, 1971, 126-129.

[3]**Ibid.**, 126.

[4]B. C. Goodger and J. M. Goodger, "Judo in the Light of Theory and Sociological Research," **International Review of Sport Sociology**, 12, 2, 1977, 10.

[5]**Ibid.**, 24.

[6]**Ibid.**, 24, 25.

[7]Huizinga, **Homo Ludens: A Study of the Play Element in Culture**, Boston, Beacon, 1964, 48.

[8]**Ibid.**, 73.

[9]**Nicomachean Ethics.**

[10]Huizinga, **op. cit.**, 73.

[11]**Ibid.**, 145.

[12]Homer, **Odyssey**, tr. A. T. Murray, viii, 146.

[13]Will Durant, **The Life of Greece**, Part II of **The Story of Civilization**, New York, Simon and Schuster, 1939, 211.

[14]Herodotus, **History**, London, 1862, viii, 26.

[15]E. N. Gardiner, **Athletics of the Ancient World**, Oxford, 1930, 234.

[16]John Kieran and Arthur Daley, **The Story of the Olympic Games: 776 B.C. to 1972**, rev. ed., Philadelphia, Lippincott, 1973, 14.

[17]**Ibid.**, 14-15.

[18]Durant, **op. cit.**, 213.

[19]Pausanius, **Description of Greece**, London, 1886, viii, 40. Cited in **ibid.**, 215.

[20]E. Norman Gardiner, **Greek Athletic Sports and Festivals**, reprint edition, Dubuque, Brown, 1970, 122.

[21]**Ibid.**, 130.

[22]**Ibid.**, 132.

[23]Virgil, **Aenead**, v., 362f.

[24]L.Friedlander, **Roman Life and Manners Under the Roman Empire**, London, 1928, **ii**, 49.

[25]Will Durant, **Caesaer and Christ**, Part III of **The Story of Civilization**, New York: Simon and Schuster, 1944, 386.

[26]Seneca, **Epistles**, 7, 95.

[27]Huizinga, **op. cit.**, 178.
[28]**Ibid.**, 177.
[29]Lewis Mumford, **Technics and Civilization**, New York: Harcourt Brace Jovanovich, 1934, 303.
[30]Jerry Izenberg, **How Many Miles to Camelot? The All-American Sports Myth**, New York, Holt, Rinehart & Winston, 1972, 2.
[31]Will Durant, **The Age of Faith**, Part IV of **The Story of Civilization**, New York, Simon and Schuster, 1950, 559-560.
[32]**Ibid.**, 579.
[33]Deano J. Geanakoplos, in **Western Civilization: Paleolithic Man to the Emergence of Economic Powers**, gen. ed. William L. Langer, New York, Harper and Row and American Heritage, 1968, 389-390.
[34]R. H. Tawney, **Religion and the Rise of Capitalism**, Baltimore, Penguin, 1947, 27-28.
[35]Geanokoplos, **op. cit.**, 603.
[36]**Ibid.**, 602.
[37]Durant, **The Age of Faith**, 578-579.
[38]Huizinga, **op. cit.**, 179.
[39]Durant, **The Age of Faith**, 559.
[40]G. G. Coulton, **Medieval Panorama**, New York, Norton, 1974, 83.
[41]E. N. Gardiner, **Athletics of the Ancient World**, Oxford, 1930, 238.
[42]Durant, **The Age of Faith**, 839.
[43]**Ibid.**, 573.
[44]**Ibid.**, 574.
[45]E. Prestage, **Chivalry**, New York, Knopf, 1928, 75.

CHAPTER 5 FROM FUN TO BUSINESS: SPORT IN MODERN SOCIETY

The Age of Self-Control: Puritanism and Anti-Sport

On August 22, 1926, at Shibe Park, the Philadelphia Athletics beat the Chicago White Sox 3-2 behind the pitching of the great Lefty Grove. The game was a memorable event, not particularly because of the brilliance of Grove, but because it was the first Sunday baseball game in the history of Philadelphia.[1]

"The Puritan Sabbath," says Winton Solberg, "exerted a powerful influence on the life of the American people from the time of the initial settlements until well into the twentieth century. . . At stake was not simply the religious observance of a stated day of the week, but a whole way of life involving man's relations with God and the entire realm of work and play."[2]

The roots of the Puritan way of life take us back to sixteenth century Europe, and especially England.

Between the fourteenth and the eighteenth centuries the Middle Ages became the modern world. Much as the landed aristocracy tried to hold on with the myth of Camelot, power nevertheless moved to the craftsmen, merchants, and bankers of the towns and cities. An economy based on land gave way to one based on money. Science began to replace traditional faith as the method for handling reality. First in Italy and later in western Europe, economic power shifted to the **bourgeoisie**, the townsmen or burghers (note the French suffix—**bourg** and the English—**burg**,—**berg**, —**burgh**, and—**bergh**). Voyages of discovery expanded the known world and the market for trade. The feudal system was replaced by new national states. Political power shifted from the lords to the "commoners" (again, mainly the townsmen) in England in sixteenth and seventeenth century political revolutions, in France in the eighteenth.

Preserved Smith, the historian of the Reformation, summed up how this began: "Such a change in man's environment and habits as the world has rarely seen took place in the generation that reached early manhood in the year 1500. In the span of a single life. . . men discovered not in metaphor but in sober fact, a new heaven and a new earth. In those days masses of men began to read many books, multiplied by the new art of printing. In those days immortal artists shot the world through with a matchless radiance of color and meaning. In those days Vasco da Gama and Columbus and Magellan opened the watery ways to new lands beyond the seven seas. In those days Copernicus established the momentous truth that the earth was but a tiny planet spinning around a vastly greater sun. In those days war in large part accomplished the economic shift from medieval guild to modern production by capital and wages. In those days wealth was piled up in the coffers of the merchants, and a new power was given to the life of the individual, of the nation, and of the third estate (the bourgeoisie). In those days the monarchy of the Roman church was broken, and large portions of her dominions seceded to form new organizations governed by other powers and animated by a different spirit."[3]

Of all the revolutionary developments that ushered in the modern era, none was more important for society and for sport than was the last change named by Smith—the Protestant Reformation. We shall need to examine the "different spirit" which it brought to the world.

The Reformation was a religious revolution within the church that had grown up in the centuries after the life of Jesus. It was a protest (hence the name Protestant) against a power organization that had made itself the sole authority in religious matters and insisted that only through it could a person be related to God. The main thrust of Protestantism was its insistence on the direct relationship and responsibility of the individual to God.

The "spirit" that animated Protestantism was most clearly expressed in the sixteenth century by John Calvin in Geneva, by the Reformed church in the Netherlands, by the Presbyterians in Scotland, and by the Puritans in England and later in New England. It was the spirit of the self-conscious, dedicated individual who felt a personal responsibility to live righteously before his God, and to persuade and if necessary force others to live the same way. As Mrs. Storm Jameson says in her book **The Decline of Merry England**, "Every form of human activity should be dedicated to one single end, the self-perfection of man, whereby he purges himself of sin and may win Paradise."[4]

In England the intensity and single-mindedness of this dedication led their enemies to label such Protestants by the mocking term "Puritan." The Puritan tended to regard himself as an instrument for doing God's work in the world, and to see only two proper activities—work and worship. In this "Puritan ethic" there was no place for activity which did not have a high purpose but was just enjoyable in itself. The Puritan felt bound to keep under control his strong desires for fun and pleasure.

Puritanism was an intensely controlled channeling of human energies which had two sides. It was repressive. Smith, a thorough scholar of the Reformation, says that Puritanism "has been justly blamed for a certain narrowness in its hostility or indifference, to art and refinement." Puritanism was also liberating. Smith also says that "politically, it favored the growth of self-reliance, self-control and a sense of personal worth that made democracy possible and necessary."[5] It also favored economic individualism. Crane Brinton, in **A History of Western Morals**, says that the Protestant ethic took the **agon** (formal contest, combat) into the world of business, where it "began to take economic channels that were to lead to the Napoleon of Industry."[6] It stimulated scientific progress: two-thirds of the original Royal Society of scientists were Puritans.

A Dutch Protestant writer, Abraham Kuyper, interprets what happened in the Netherlands:

> *Scarcely had Calvinism been firmly established in the Netherlands for a quarter of a century when there was a rustling of life in all directions, and an indomitable energy was fermenting in every department of human activity, and their commerce and trade, their handicrafts and industry, their agriculture and horticulture, their art and science flourished with a brilliancy previously unknown, and imparted a new impulse for an entirely new development of life, to the whole of Western Europe.*[7]

In his 1906 work, **The Protestant Ethic and The Spirit of Capitalism,**[8] Max Weber contended that the spirit of the individual dedicating himself to God without intercession by the church was also the spirit of capitalist individualism breaking free of feudal restrictions. He gave evidence that capitalism in its early days had grown most successfully in Protestant areas. Fifty years later a psychologist, David C. McClelland, showed statistically that in the twentieth century Protestant nations led Catholic nations in economic development, measured in terms of per capita consumption of electric power.[9]

What does all this have to do with sport? The Puritan era was an age of anti-sport. Weber says: "Sport was accepted if it served a rational purpose, that of recreation necessary for physical efficiency. But as a means for the spontaneous expression of undisciplined impulses, it was under suspicion."[10] In the **agon** for God and for political and economic individualism, there is no place for **agon** in the pagan Greek sense or in the romantic Camelot sense.

Let us look at the world into which the Protestant ethic came and how it changed that world. The sixteenth century poet Edmund Spenser spoke of pre-Puritan England in this way:

> *Then our age was in its prime. . .*
> *A very merry, dancing, drinking,*
> *Laughing, quaffing, and unthinking*
> *Time.*[11]

Describing "England in the Fifteenth Century" Durant says:

> *Amusements ranged from checkers and chess, backgammon and dice, to fishing and hunting, archery and jousts. Playing cards reached England toward the end of the fifteenth century. . . Dancing and music were as popular as gambling. . . Men played tennis, handball, bowls, quoits; they wrestled and boxed, set cocks to fighting, baited bears and bulls. . . Kings and nobles kept jugglers, jesters, and buffoons; and a Lord of Misrule, appointed by the king or queen, superintended the sports and revels of Christmas tide. . . Women moved freely among men everywhere: drank in taverns, rode to the hounds, hunted with falcons, and distracted the spectators from the contestants at tournaments.*[12]

In France Francois Rabelais filled a whole chapter listing games, and in the Netherlands Bruegel showed about a hundred games in a single painting. "Never," says Preserved Smith, "has the theater been more popular."[13] In Paris alone there were 250 tennis courts. Even the Protestant reformer Martin Luther approved of dancing as a way of bringing young people together, and the Protestant leader Melancthon still danced when he was in his forties.[14] Calvin himself, from whom Puritanism sprang, "bade his followers play harmonious games like bowling or quoits, and enjoy wine in moderation."[15] The Scottish Calvinist John Knox once found Calvin himself bowling on the Sabbath.[16]

But when Protestantism came to power—as it did under the dictatorships of Calvin at Geneva in the mid-1500s and Oliver Cromwell in England in the mid-1600s—it "turned with all its force against one thing: the spontaneous enjoyment of life and all that it had to offer."[17]

The Council at Geneva arranged yearly visits to every home to question the members on whether they had engaged in any forbidden activities: gambling, card-playing, profanity, drunkenness, dancing; whether they had sung irreligious or indecent songs, or been excessive in their dress or entertainment; whether they had worn colors of clothes prohibited by law, used more than the legal number of dishes at a meal, worn jewelry or lace, or piled their hair too high. They were not questioned about their habits at the theater, because eventually even religious plays were forbidden.[18]

In England, "dancing, profane singing, wakes, revels, wrestling, shootings, leapings, ringings of bells, church-ales, may-poles, all. . . were thrown. . . upon the rubbish heap."[19] The Puritans illegalized betting, made adultery a capital crime, ordered all Maypoles cut down, attacked both plays in the palaces of nobles and wrestling matches and dancing by ordinary people on village greens. They attacked puppet shows, horseracing, and bearbaiting. The historian Macaulay, who was too anti-Puritan to be a fair judge, claimed "the Puritan hated bearbaiting, not because it gave pain to the bear, but because it gave pleasure to the spectators."[20] The theater was closed. "The playhouses where to be dismantled, the spectators fined, the actors whipped. . . "[21] In Stratford-on-Avon the Puritan town government closed the theater while Shakespeare was still living there during his last years.[22] Greek statues were to be "cleaned up" by the chisels of Puritan stonemasons. Even pictures of Jesus and the Virgin Mary in the royal collection were to be burned, presumably as a protest against Catholic Virgin-worship.

Very important for the future development of sport was the way in which the Puritans discouraged any spontaneous or free activity on Sundays or holidays. "They were strict observers of the Sabbath," says Brinton, "because they felt strongly that the Catholics from whom they were revolting had profaned the Sabbath by letting all sorts of worldly activities go on then, making it what in English is now called a holiday, instead of making it what God intended it to be, a holy day."[23] Before Charles I lost his throne and his head to the Puritans, he and his father James I had specifically fought them on this issue by issuing the Book of Sports which legalized a number of Sunday amusements outside of church hours. "When shall the common people," James had argued, "have leave to exercise, if not upon the Sundays and Holy-Days, seeing that they must apply their labour and win their living in their working days?. . .If these times were taken from them, the meaner sort who labour hard all the week should have no recreations at all to refresh their spirits. . . "[24]

"The feudal and monarchical forces," says Weber, "protected the pleasure seekers against the rising middle-class morality."[25] In his history of sport "from Elizabeth to Anne", Dennis Brailsford spelled this relationship out a little more:

> *Much of the early Stuart encouragement of popular sporting activities was not given on account of the benefits seen in the sports themselves, but for social, religious, or political motives, associated with the fact that those whom the crown increasingly recognized as its opponents had become identified with a negative, restrictive attitude towards games. The simple principle of opposition suggested encouragement to the people's play, while this encouragement seemed, at the same time, a useful means of propaganda on behalf of the established order.*[26]

One example may have been Robert Dover's organization of the Cotswold Games in the western English hills in 1612 in an effort to blend upper class sport and rural folk games in an anti-Puritan revival of the Olympics. It was a deliberate attempt, says Peter McIntosh, to "bring together two patterns of sporting activity, the popular and the courtly, and thereby to preserve the existing social system against Puritan attack."[27]

When the Puritans won militarily and politically, the "Cotswold Games survived only as a local and unimportant celebration."

The other side of this may have been, as Foster Dulles suggests, that "the Puritans resented the amusements of the wealthy, leisured classes, making a moral isue of their discontent. These two influences, spiritual reform and economic envy, can never by disentangled."[28]

In power, the Puritans had the Book of Sports publicly burned by the common hangman.

Solberg has analyzed the reasons behind the Puritan aversion to sport. Some non-Puritans would have accepted some of them. (James I, who issued the **Book of Sports**, held that football was "meeter for laming than for making able the users thereof.")

(1) To the Puritan, sport was "essentially frivolous." A person's chief duty was to glorify God through work in a chosen calling. "Work was serious, earnest, a material necessity. . . . Play was entirely different."[29]

(2) Sports and games had to take place outside the full six-day working week that was then customary, so they fell on the Sabbath. "Even innocent diversions such as running, jumping, stoolball [an ancestor of baseball], . . . marbles, archery, hunting, and fishing were devilish pastimes because they lured people away from church and kept them from spending the entire day in spiritual edification. . . The player ran the risk of forgetting his religious duties by abandoning hiself to the rapture generated by exhilarating physical exercise and sportive competition."[30]

(3) Furthermore, some sports were brutal. Brailsford says ". . . if Puritanism often allied itself with those forces that were restricting leisure

A Puritan tract laments the supposedly true story of eight young men who fell through the ice and drowned after a scuffle in a Sabbath football game. Courtesy of the Houghton Library, Harvard University.

activities, it also. . . supported the gradual civilizing of many sporting pursuits. . . The Puritan tradition has been a considerable force in reducing barbarity and crudity in sport.''[31] Cockfighting and the baiting of bears and bulls were widely popular sports that cruelly exploited animals. Of the Sunday game of football, a critic wrote during the reign of Queen Elizabeth:

For as concerning football playing: I protest with you, it may rather be called a friendly kind of fight, than a play or recreation. A bloody and murdering practice, than a fellowly sport or pastime. For, doth not everyone lie in wait for his adversary, seeking to overthrow him and to [pitch] him on his nose, though it be upon hard stones, in ditch or dale, in valley or hill, or whatever place it be, he careth not so he have him down. By this means, sometimes their necks are broken, sometimes their backs, sometimes one part thrust out of joint, sometimes another, sometimes the nose guts out with blood, sometimes their eyes start out. . . Is this murdering play an exercise for the Sabbath day; is this a Christian dealing for one brother to maim and hurt another?[32]

The football described is not modern soccer or rugby, or American football (which the description might conceivably fit fairly well), but a mass struggle like the ancient Dane's Head, played by hordes of young men who sought to propel an inflated bladder across country from one village green to another.

(4) Sport encouraged gambling, a way of ''getting something for nothing'' that was contrary to the Puritan ethic of hard and serious work. ''Elizabethans enjoyed betting on athletic contests—bowling, pitching the bar, and the like.''[33]

(5) Sporting events attracted crowds whose behavior violated the Puritan's ideal of how a person should behave on the Sabbath, or any other day. ''Sunday recreations provided an opportunity for rogues and ruffians to practice trickery and deceit. Permit Sabbath recreations, and what followed was sexual immorality, crime, drinking and gambling, brutal sports, quarreling and brawling, scenes of wild disorder.''[34]

Heinz Meyer, a West German sport sociologist, insists further that sport and the Puritan religion are two total and incompatible ways of life. Although Puritanism supported physical training as a way of keeping the body fit for work, its real goal was not the happiness and well-being of the body but the salvation of the soul. Not so with sport:

Sport. . . has a certain demand and totality of its own, it is a way of life with its own horizon of values. Sportsmanship, a mingling of healthy and beautiful corporeality, acceptance of life, modernity, and a bit of fairness has been established as an important value in our culture. Sportsmanship understood that way is a genuinely profane phenomenon, an unreligious form of mastering and widening existence and of enjoying it. Seen from a Christian point of view this activates shallow worldliness. The demand to use the time meaningfully to reach salvation is not obeyed, time is spent in self-sufficient distraction. And the Christian demands of modesty and altruism are antagonistic to the striving for success, a maximum of proficiency and beating other competitors. About sport there is something essentially heathen.[35]

Thus, says Meyer, the emperor Theodosius was logical in A.D. 395 when he banned the Olympic games along with other heathen sports three years after making Christianity the state religion. So also were the Puritans consistent.

In 1644 the Puritan Parliament declared December 25th a day of fasting in which people would do penance for their previous celebrations on Christmas.[36] The Puritans not only thought the Catholics had allowed holy days to be misused. They also felt that they had had too many of them, and reduced the number. Karl Marx once observed that by eliminating many Catholic holidays the Protestants made it possible to do more work and make more profit. According to the calculations of one speaker in Parliament in 1715, it cost Catholic France six million pounds a year (at today's exchange rates about twelve million dollars) to have fifty more holy days than did Protestant England.[37]

So far as sport is concerned, Puritanism gave to the developing western world the two heritages I described earlier: (1) its serious, disciplined, dedicated view of lifechanneled energy into the mastery of nature and of economic want, thus setting the stage for the increase of leisure and affluence, and (2) it cast a pall over all activities, including sport, that appeared to divert energy away from this goal.

But, in the long run, not from sport in the modern sense, perhaps. It is interesting that sport sociologist Gunther Luschen has found the Protestant "work ethic" most productive also of success in sport, as indicated by his study of the religious backgrounds of Olympic winners.[38] By this standard the United States should be the most successful nation in sport, it would seem. However, in a paper on "The Role of Competitive Sports in Different Societies,"[39] P. Seppanen argues that it is modern socialism that today best embodies the Puritan work ethic and so should best promote sport success. Our next section will give us some basis for judging this question.

Puritanism and American Sport

The Puritan attitude toward sport crossed the Atlantic with the settlement of America. "While the Puritans were not always opposed to sports and recreation as such," said Solberg, "for all practical purposes this appeared to be the case, because they feared and prohibited recreations and entertainments that touched the irrational springs of man's nature, those that catered to the sensual appetites, and those that took place on the Lord's Day. Hence Sabbatarianism suppressed the sportive, playful, and aesthetic element in American culture in the formative years."[40]

The Book of Sports (1618) was a main factor behind the emigration of Puritans like John Cotton and Thomas Hooker. The settlement at Plymouth (1620) followed James' declaration by two years. Historian John Allen Krout says, "Dancing, running, jumping, and kindred sports of the village green were associated with profanation of the Sabbath. . . Had the leaders of Plymouth, Salem, and Boston been in Parliament in 1643 they would have voted with the majority that all copies of the **Book of Sports** be seized and burned."[41] There was more to this than transplanted English prejudices. "Fighting Indians, clearing new lands, and building towns," says John Rickards Betts, historian of American sport, "allowed little time for most colonists to devote to merry-making. Only after two centuries of settlement in the New World was sport to emerge as an important institution in American life."[42]

Puritanism was strongest on the rural frontier and among the Anglo-Saxon population, and began to weaken with the development of towns and cities and their settlement by non-WASP immigrants (like the Germans, with their tradition of Sunday picnicking and beer-drinking). Although Betts says that in the 1820s and 1850s "in both the frontier town and the eastern city there was a decline in religious restraint and in Puritan orthodoxy,"[43] as late as the 1900 Olympics these feelings were still so strong that 8 of 13 University of Pennsylvania athletes refused to participate on the Sabbath. In 1906, when the Chicago White Sox beat the Cubs in the World Series, a local minister who was a baseball fan lamented: "It is a shame and disgrace to any community as enlightened and civilized as Chicago that Sunday baseball should be tolerated and indulged in, not only by professionals, but by boys and young men in general, many of the better classes."[44] "Blue laws" against Sunday sport were on the statute books of all states except California as late as 1915. Pennsylvania, in spite of being a strongly urban state with a large immigrant population, tried to enforce into the 1930s the 1794 statute against "worldly employment" on the Sabbath. In 1927 in

Commonwealth v. the American Baseball Club of Philadelphia, the judge declared in support of the blue law: "We cannot imagine. . . anything more worldly and irreligious in the way of employment than the playing of professional baseball as it is played today. Christianity is part of the common law of Pennsylvania, and its people are Christian people. Sunday is the holy day among Christians. No one, we think, would contend that professional baseball partakes in any way of the nature of holiness."[45]

How the Puritan ethic wavered in the balance with other forces is illustrated by the fact that at about the same time, while the very conservative churchman Daniel Poling and the liberal John Haynes both opposed commercialized sport, Bishop Manning planned a Sport Bay (window) in the Episcopal Cathedral of St. John the Divine in New York City, saying, "Not only does religion not frown upon sport, but encourages and sympathizes with it and gives it an important place in the temple of God."[46] Similarly, in their famous community study of Muncie, Indiana, in 1925, Robert and Helen Lynd found Sunday baseball still condemned by the churches and many other people while golf courses and gun clubs were open.[47] Several states, including Pennsylvania and Alabama, solved the rural-urban conflict by laws that left Sunday codes up to local option. Thus Philadelphia got legal baseball, and Birmingham, Montgomery, and Mobile got Sunday movies, baseball, and tennis, all in strongly Sabbatarian states.

Take-off and the Leisure Masses

On the last lap of our historical journey, it will be helpful to look at one of our most important tools for understanding how our modern world has developed. This is Walt Rostow's analysis of the stages of economic growth.[48]

Looking back at how we have arrived at our contemporary urban industrial world, Rostow outlines five phases of development:

(1) **The traditional society,** *in which one generation essentially repeats the last. Feudal society is an example. Most of the primitive cultures studied by anthropologists also are. Ancient Greece is perhaps another case: in his book* **The Idea of Progress,**[49] *J. E. Bury tells us that the Greeks did not have the idea of progressive growth.*

(2) **The preconditions for take-off,** *in which a traditional society is changing in ways which will make it ready for economic*

progress. The sixteenth century as described earlier by Preserved Smith was such a period.

(3) **Economic take-off,** *in which the conditions for economic growth, especially investment in machinery, accelerate strongly. This happened in England about 1775, in the United States after 1850, in Japan and Russia about 1880 to 1890.*

(4) **The drive to maturity,** *in which investment in capital equipment, at first confined to a small part of the economy, spreads to include all activities. This happened in the United States in the three generations following the Civil War.*

(5) **The age of high mass consumption,** *where the earlier investment in productive equipment pays off in a spread of consumer affluence. The United States was the first country to reach this stage, in the 1920s, followed by Japan and western Europe in the 1950s, and the Soviet Union in the 1960s.*

These five stages begin with dire need, of the kind which has gripped most human beings since the beginning of history, and still does. Then there is a period of intense hard work and saving, dominated by a Puritan ethic, which builds up the equipment for mastering need. Finally concentration on production gives way to an emphasis on consumption of goods and services, including sport.

The rise of sport in the modern sense coincided, in time and place, with the world's most spectacular burst of industrial take-off, in the late nineteenth century United States. John Rickards Betts summarizes concisely what happened:

Manufacturers, seeking cheap labor, encouraged immigration; factories were most efficiently run in larger towns and cities; urban masses, missing the rural pleasures of hunting and fishing, were won to the support of commercialized entertainment and spectator sports; the emergence of a commerical aristocracy and a laboring class resulted in distinctions every bit as strong in sport as in other social matters; and the urgency of physical exercise as life became more sedentary was easily recognized.[50]

Only when the first fierce struggle against the wilderness was won," says John Allen Krout, "did a few in the older communities find wealth and leisure which enabled them to introduce to the New World such sports and pastimes as intrigued the nobility and gentry of Europe."[51] But sport also had roots in the struggle itself. Hunting was a necessary way of getting a living, but a cooperative venture with elements of a game. Also, "on each successive frontier barn raisings, log rollings, plowing bees and corn huskings were ventures which developed into sporting tests of strength and skill so dear to the heart of the pioneer. In them were matured those elements of competition and cooperation essential in the development of modern organized sport. . . One can see the settlers. . . testing marksmanship with bow and arrow as well as matchlock, comparing strength in wrestling and throwing the bar and competing with each other for supremacy in running and jumping."[52]

Before 1850, the leisure classes had followed the traditional upper class pastimes of fox hunting and horseracing. There had been some general interest in rowing, running, prizefighting, cricket, and fencing. But horseracing was the only organized sport that really turned people on. After the middle of the century, masses of city dwellers needed escape or diversion from the routine of factory and office. They also had time and income to afford it. "During the years which passed from the close of the Civil War to the end of the century were laid in America the foundations of the new era of sport. . . British sport was primarily a phase of the life of the upper classes; in America the appearance of baseball at the very beginning of the athletic era signified a mass movement affecting all groups of the population."[53]

City dwellers, with workday hours cut, a half-Saturday holiday, and sometimes two-week summer vacations, were trapped in the city with as yet no parks and no access to the country. They found a substitute for the activity of pioneers: "A people whose attitude was greatly influenced by the traditions of a pioneering frontier life felt restless under city restraints. Until they found the escape value of sports for themselves, they eagerly took the next best thing. If they could not play or compete, they could at least get the thrill of vicarious participation by cheering on their favorites from a grandstand."[54]

Table 5.1 shows the transition from play to work in seven American sports. R. T. Furst points out that five of the sports were professionalized in the years from 1895 to 1903.[55] This commercialization coincided, he says, with a burst in the application of new bureaucratic methods for maximizing industrial profit. (It was, for example, the period when industrial and financial concentration was colliding with anti-trust laws that sought to check it.)

I cannot stress too much how new a thing is leisure for the majority of people. Life for most human beings has always been work, work, work to survive—and still is in most places. Before America's mid-nineteenth century take-off, we could speak of the leisured minority and their sports, as did Thorstein Veblen in his famous classic, **The Theory of the Leisure Class.**[56] But it was only with industrialism that there arose, as Gregory Stone points out,[57] alongside the leisure class, the "leisure masses," who furnish the market for spectator sport.

Table 5.1 Commercialization of Major American Sports

	Baseball	Football	Hockey	Basketball	Golf	Tennis	Bowling
Play	1831-1945 (14 years)	1874-1882 (8 years)	1855-1875 (20 years)	———	1779-1786 (7 years)	1874-1881 (7 years)	1825-1875 (50 years)
Game	1845-1869 (24 years)	1882-1895 (13 years)	1875-1903 (28 years)	1891-1898 (7 years)	1786-1894 (108 years)	1881-1926 (45 years)	1875-1895 (20 years)
Work	1869-1970 (101 years)	1895-1970 (75 years)	1903-1970 (67 years)	1898-1970 (72 years)	1894-1970 (76 years)	1926-1970 (44 years)	1895-1970 (75 years)

Source: R. T. Furst, "Social Change and the Commercialization of Professional Sports," International Review of Sport Sociology, 6, 1971, p. 157.

This leisure was accompanied by the fact that from the seventeenth century to the nineteenth, the Puritan ethic had weakened. This made it possible for Sunday in the industrial cities to be again a day of games.

Another way in which industrialism fostered mass sport was by advances in transportation and communication. Before 1860 the railroad and steamboat began to bring spectators long distances to horse and trotting races, regattas, cycling races, track and field events, and prize fights. The first intercollegiate rowing race, between Harvard and Yale in 1852, was sponsored by the Boston, Concord, and Montreal railway.[58] In 1869 a "jerky little engine steamed out of Princeton" to Rutgers for the first intercollegiate football game. The outstanding 1870 Harvard baseball team went by rail on an extended tour, winning a majority of games against both amateurs and professionals. After the formation of the National Baseball League, an advertisement in the 1886 Spalding Official Baseball Guide told dramatically of the role of the railroad in the development of organized baseball: "The cities that have representative clubs contesting for the championship pennant this year are Chicago, Boston, New York, Washington, Kansas City, Detroit, Saint Louis, and Philadelphia. All of these cities are joined together by the Michigan Central Railroad. This road has enjoyed almost a monopoly of Baseball travel in former years."[59]

The technology of communication vastly expanded the number of people involved in sporting events. "The expansion of sporting news. . . ," says Betts, "was directly related to the more general use of telegraphy, which made possible instantaneous reporting of ball games, horse races, prize fights, yachting regattas, and other events. Box scores, betting odds, and all kinds of messages were relayed from one city to another, and by 1870 daily reports were published in many metropolitan papers."[60]

A popular magazine of the time tells graphically what telegraph communication meant to the American sport lover. When Harvard rowed in England against Oxford in a famous 1869 race, "the result was flashed through the Atlantic cable to reach New York about a quarter past one, while the news reached the Pacific Coast about nine o'clock, enabling many of the San Franciscans to. . . swallow defeat with their coffee."[61] The Sullivan-Kilrain fight in New Orleans in 1889 was covered by reporters from "every prominent journal in the Union," and Western Union had fifty operators to handle 208,000 words of special news dispatches.[62]

In 1887 big league baseball scores were wired to every large city inning by inning, and were often posted on a board by telegraph operators at saloons as a special attraction. Before TV or even radio transmission had become familiar, the Associated Press wired the 1916 Brooklyn-Boston World Series on a single 26,000 mile circuit to all of its lease wire members.

These developments foreshadowed the changes in the sporting market which the sociologically oriented jurist Jerome Frank dramatized in the

1948 Gardella case testing the reserve clause in baseball contracts. The federal court refused jurisdiction in the case on the ground that baseball had been held by the Supreme Court in 1922 not to be interstate commerce, since a game and its audience were always confined to a single state. This might have been true in 1922, said Frank, but in 1948 this precedent had been sociologically outdated by radio and television, which had created an audience that knew no state lines.[63]

Another technological advance central to sport as we now know it was the electric light. In 1883, although Madison Square Garden had installed some electric lights, fans at the Sullivan-Slade heavyweight boxing championship had to battle both cigar smoke and gaslight fumes. Ten years later the Chicago **Daily Tribune** reported, "Now men travel to great boxing contests in vestibule limited trains. They sleep at the best hotels. . . and when the time for the contest arrives, they find themselves in a grand, brilliantly lighted arena."[64] The late nineteenth century made indoor night sport possible. A third of the way through the twentieth century the outdoor night game began to become commonplace, thus expanding the range of the sport business.

By 1905 James Bryce, the British historian of America, said of the "passion for looking at and reading about the athletic scene":

> *It occupies the minds not only of the youth at the universities but also of their parents and of the general public. Baseball matches and football matches elicit an interest greater than any other public events except the Presidential election and that comes only once in four years. The interest in one of the great contests, such as those which draw forty thousand spectators to the great "Stadium" recently erected at Cambridge, Massachusetts, appears to pervade nearly all classes more than does any "sportive event" in Great Britain. The American love of excitement and love of competition has seized upon these games.*[65]

Now let us analyze some of the characteristics of modern sport as it has developed since our industrial take-off.

Sport is at the same time an escape from modern industrialism and an expression of it. First of all, team sports are a part of the industrial society. Frontiersmen (and women) and settled farmers practiced spontaneous cooperation in barn raisings and husking bees, but these did not involve a continuous assignment of specialized roles, as do organized team sports. These reflect the organization of industry. Historian Ralph Gabriel says of early nineteenth century sport, "The few sports of the time were those emphasizing individual skill (hunting, fishing, and horse racing). Americans were not yet ready to submit to the discipline of team play."[66]

The fan who crowds into a stadium or sits glued to his TV set is experiencing a release from the stress of his daily factory or office job and is at the same time the consumer of a commodity mass-produced for profit. What does it do for him? Obviously, satisfies to some degree his desire for fun, as defined in Chapter Three. Also, it provides catharsis in two senses. As Sutton-Smith pointed out, the world of sport can upset the hierarchy of ordinary life, so that the chronic loser becomes a winner. Also, especially in the violent sports, the fan can, through his team, discharge some of the hostility built up by social frustration. Even in a non-contact sport like tennis, he can identify with the overpowering "big game"' which has taken over the sport in recent years.

Furthermore, in a mobile urban world where most people have few close long-standing ties, sport gives a sense of roots. "The sports pages," says Stone, "provide some confirmation that there is a continuity in the events and affairs of the larger society. . . reassurance that is not possible from following current events, the continuity of which is not readily discernible for many readers. . . Team loyalties formed in adolescence and maintained through adulthood may serve to remind one, in a nostalgic way, that there are areas of comfortable stability in life—that some things are permanent amid the harassing interruptions and transitions of daily experience."[67] James Reston says, "Sports in America are a unifying force, and a counter to the confusion about the vagueness and the complexity of our cities, our races, and in this long-haired age, even the confusion between our sexes."[68]

But there are those who see these as misleading escapes. Writing of the relationship of Japaneses sport to business enterprise, Takaaki Niwi says that for two reasons the typical modern worker feels alienated from his work. First, in advanced capitalism he works for a large business enterprise whose profits go to someone else. Second, mass technology and industrial organizatioin are so vast that he feels overwhelmed. Sport partially relieves the problem, and at the same time intensifies it:

> *We can discover many worthy and significant aspects in sport today, as a leisure activity connected with the healthy body and mind, etc., but sport is in fact performing the role of channeling a person's attention away from the solution of these alienation problems. When the masses become enthusiastic about sport and its basic appeal, they gradually forget their uneasiness and dissatisfaction which is based on the condition of society. This means that the greater the effect of sport on the unhappy psychological condition of the individuals, the more the individual is divorced from the solution of the problems of social reality.*[69]

As Stone has put it, **play has tended to give way to display, the game to**

the spectacle. The spectacle is distinguished from the game by the overwhelming way in which the spectators outnumber the players. It is also distinguished by the predictability of the outcome. Related to this is the degree of personal expression by the player. The purest example of the predictable spectacle is the staged drama of professional wrestling, with its good guys and bad guys, each playing his (her) part. A pure example of the unpredictability of the game is the "spectacular play" in which the player "outdoes himself," makes the "impossible catch." Another example of the contrast: The Super Bowl, which reached stature with the startling 1969 upset of the Colts by the Jets, has in the opinion of many people degenerated into a much-ballyhooed but unexciting and predictable spectacle. Stone feels that the trend toward display is unhealthy. He would probably agree with Lewis Mumford: "Sport, which began originally, perhaps, as a spontaneous reaction against the machine, has become one of the mass duties of the machine age. It is part of that universal regimentation of life—for the sake of private profit or nationalistic exploit—from which its excitement provides a temporary and only a superficial release. Sport has turned out, in short, to be one of the least effective reactions against the machine.[70]

Spectatoritis has not taken over completely. "In the first forty years of the twentieth century," says Dulles, "there was a far greater increase in the number who played than in those who watched."[71] The early years of the century brought a "progressive" movement, from Theodore Roosevelt to Woodrow Wilson, that shifted some of the benefits of industrialism from the few to the masses. A part of this was the development of city parks and playgrounds. Religious organizations, schools, and ethnic athletic clubs promoted games for youth as an antidote to crime and delinquency. There was another surge in opportunities for participant play during the 1920s. The automobile took people to urban and suburban recreational facilities and national parks. Under the New Deal of the Depression years, the federal Works Progress Administration (WPA) spent half a billion dollars constructing 3700 recreational buildings, 881 parks, 1500 athletic fields, 440 swimming pools, 3500 tennis courts, 123 golf courses, and 28 miles of ski trails.[72] In 1940 Dulles estimated that the number of people swimming annually at municipal beaches and pools (200 million) was almost as large as the total yearly attendance at all spectator sports. An observation in the 1950s by social historian Frederick Lewis Allen suggests the democratization of a traditionally elite sport: "A street was being torn up for repairs and while the workmen were standing waiting for the arrival of new equipment, one of them, who had in his hands an iron rod presumably used for prying off manhole covers, was enjoying a little relaxation. I looked twice to see what he was doing with that rod. He was practising a graceful golf stroke."[73] After the 1954 study by Hans Kraus showing American children trailing Europeans shockingly in basic physical skills,[74] there was a wide surge of concern for physical fitness. Jogging was one of the outcomes. A 1978 survey of TV sport viewers by Opinion Research Corporation showed that three-fourths had played organized sports at some time in their lives and nine-tenths had engaged in unorganized sports.[75] Other surveys reported in the late seventies showed 60 million roller skaters, 30 million tennis players, 14 million skiers, a million or more gymnasts, 22 million bowlers, 15 million bicyclists, 20 million joggers, and 40 million walking for exercise.[76]

Modern sport embraces three classes of participants: the genuine amateur, the formal "amateur," and the frank professional. It arose, as we have seen, from two sources—the stylized activity of the leisure classes, and the occasional "unbuttoned play" of the laboring class which, as Paul Hoch says, was "most of the time worked so brutally that it simply would not have had the time or energy to engage in sports activity."[77] With the rise of the "leisure masses," we continued to have some people, rich and poor, doing their own thing for fun (genuine amateurs). We also developed a class of specialists who played for the entertainment of others. In addition there arose a group of people who were nominally amateurs but actually were unpaid or underpaid professionals. This included the players of the "gentlemen's sports" like tennis and golf, the college athlete, and Olympic performers and aspirants. Stone points out some important and paradoxical facts about these three groups. The sports that are "played" are professional (baseball, football, hockey, tennis, golf). "Precisely those sports that are 'played' have become work in America. Here is the matrix of professional athletics." The sports that are amateur (hunting, fishing, archery, bowling, skiing, yachting) are not "played" and are not work. They are mostly upper class pastimes with the exception of bowling, which is mainly lower class. Summarizing the paradoxical situation, Stone says, "In the United States, sports that were once work are never played, but these engage the "players"—the amateurs. Sports that were never work are always played, and these engage the workers—the professionals.[78] The formally amateur sports—intercollegiate athletics and the "gentlemen's games"—are mainly feeders for frank professionalism.

The Japanese sociologist Sadao Morikawa has analyzed systematically the "self-contradiction of amateur sport":[79]

"First of all, amateur sport can exist only by relying upon the results of other people's labor, because it cannot be used as means for earning one's livelihood. . .

"Secondly, the emphasis on amateur sport gives rise to a contradiction that works against (its) development. . . because of the difficulty in combining sports life and work to earn a livelihood.

"This contradiction, thirdly, creates a tendency that amateur athletes either abandon amateur sport or turn into professionals.

"Fourthly, under such circumstances, the efforts to maintain amateur sport strengthen the "parasitic" character of amateur sport. . . (We can easily understand this phenomenon by observing the present conditions of the so-called amateur sportsmen belonging to companies and universities.)

"Fifthly, universal characteristics of modern sport promote the popularization of sport, but for the working people who are lacking in physical and economic conditions, amateur sport transforms itself into the sport to 'be seen.' Consequently, the growing popularity of amateur sport paves the way to professional sport.

"Sixthly, the unbalanced development and dual structure of sport. . . brings about too much emphasis on rewards and victory on the one hand, while prize money and reward as its compensation become a problem. This narrows the distinction between amateur and professional sport, bringing the crisis of the existence of amateurism to the surface. . ."

As a business, professional sport exercises an influence far beyond its actual size. All of the people employed in amusement, recreation, and related services in 1960 made up eight-tenths of one percent of the whole labor force. In 1964 only one worker in ten thousand was a professional athlete.[80] Roger Noll, a Brookings Institution economist who is sometimes called the Ralph Nader of the sports industry, says that professional sports is about half the size of the canned soup industry. Senator Sam Ervin, in Senate hearings on the industry, said that it is about equal in size to pork and beans. Sociologist Harry Edwards calculates that in 1970 there were 500 industrial corporations each of which had gross sales greater than all 24 major league baseball clubs combined.[81] Paul Hoch, who streses the domination of sport by the "power elite," estimates the total American sports budget at $25 billion a year (which is only about 2 percent of the Gross National Product.)[82]

Yet we would be way off base if we took these cold statistics as a measure of the importance of sport on the American scene. About a third of the population of the United States (63 million) saw one game of the 1971 World Series on television and a third (65 million) again saw the 1972 Super Bowl Game. "Intercollegiate athletics," said George Hanford, Senior Vice President of the College Board, in 1979, "are big business. Five years ago it was estimated that inter-collegiate athletics consumed about 1% of the ($30 billion) budget for higher education in the United States.' That came to $300 million or so, at a time when $3 million was a high sports budget. Today, with the budgets for athletic programs at some institutions approaching $5 million, the intercollegiate athletic enterprise could be approaching the half billion dollar mark."[83]

These figures bring us closer to the remarkable proportion of space which the 1971 **New York Times Encyclopedic Almanac** gave to sport among other American activities: religion, 21 pages; science, 18 pages; education, 27 pages; medicine and public health, 21 pages; foreign affairs and national security, 37 pages; **and sport, 93 pages.**[84]

Sport is intimately related to social stratification and social mobility. For one thing, athletics has been a way for **minority group** members to get up in the world. The idea that first interested me in the sociology of sport was the 1948 analysis by George Saxon of young men of southern and eastern European extraction who used athletics to escape the coal mines and steel mills of the Monongahela Valley.[85] David Riesman and Reuel Denney have traced the democratization of American football. Before 1890, All-America teams were almost entirely Anglo-Saxon. Gradually the German, Irish, Jews, and Poles began to break in. "By 1927, names like Casey, Kipke, Oosterbaan, Koppisch, Garbisch, and Friedman were appearing with as much frequency as names like Channing, Adams, and Ames in the 1890s."[86] My 1937 college team, with which I started Chapter four, was still about 90 percent WASP. Since the Riesman-Denney and Saxon studies, the whole All-America picture has been changed by the rising prominence of black athletes. How prominent blacks have become is indicated by the fact that in 1979, while blacks made up only 1½ percent of college enrollments, they received 6 percent of athletic grant money.

However, opportunity is for only a minority. For every Joe Namath rising to fame from Beaver Falls, Pa., Jack Scott suggests, there are hundreds of ex-athletes drowning their faded hopes in the taverns of the Monongahela Valley. Dr. Roscoe Brown of the New York University Institute of Afro-American Affairs says, "Black youngsters pour too much time and energy into sports. They're deluded and seduced by the athletic flesh peddlers, used for public amusement—and discarded."[87]

Also, at the same time that new ethnic groups have entered the lower echelons of sport, control has continuously passed to a minority with capital. Professional baseball teams were first run by the players. But then financial promoters took over. College athletics were also first run by the athletes. But early in the twentieth century control passed to professional coaches, athletic administration, and alumni.

A dramatic statistical illustration of how "money speaks" in professional sport is the history of the Boston Red Sox after they were taken over by millionaire Tom Yawkey. In my boyhood, the Red Sox were habitually eighth in an eight-team league. Then this happened, as reported by two economists: From 1922 to 1932, before Yawkey, the Sox had a winning average of .359, and their average place in the eight-team league was 7.66. From 1933 to 1970, after Yawkey, their winning average was .522, their average place-finish 4.39.[88]

The concentration of control in sport is enhanced by what economist Walter Nolte has called its "peculiar economics." Organized management has generally fought labor organization by glorifying the right of the worker to bargain freely as an individual (as in so-called "right to work" laws). But in organized sport, neither collective bargaining nor free individual bargaining is really legitimate.

As Gary Shaw implied in the title of his book on Texas football, the athlete in our culture is "meat on the hoof," a piece of property.The capitalist society, in theory, is a system where one sells his assets, including his labor power, on a competitive market to the highest bidder. But organized sport has not been this kind of competitive market. Rather than competing freely for athletic labor power, the businessmen in the different sports have combined to establish procedures that prevent free competition for players. One such procedure is the "draft," whereby prospective professionals are assigned to teams. Another is the "reserve clause," which binds an athlete, once he signs a professional contract, to play for his team until he retires or his services are traded or "sold" to another team.

The reserve clause, in one form or another, has been the basis for all major professional sport in the United States. As early as 1922, in the case of the upstart Federal baseball league, such restriction of competition was attacked as a violation of the Sherman Anti-Trust Act. The Federal league charged the American and National leagues with moving into Federal league towns and buying up teams so as to kill off competition. Players Gardella in the 1940s, Toolson in 1953, and Flood in 1971 charged the major baseball leagues with conspiracy in restraint of trade. In 1962 the American Football league sued the National Football league for monopolizing the player pool. But in 1966 both leagues saw the advantage of combining and secured a special act of Congress protecting them against possible anti-trust suits. In 1971 the National Basketball Association and the American Basketball Association tried to do the same thing, but players got a special Senate hearing and finally won damages in court for the harm done them by the reserve clause. These basketball players, football player Yazoo Smith in 1968, and baseball pitcher Andy Messersmith in 1975, were instrumental in breaking down the reserve clause and leaving players free, under stipulated conditions, to sell their services as "free agents" to the highest bidder. So, about 60 years after the Federal league suit, 30 years after Danny Gardello's challenge of commissioner "Happy" Chandler, and a decade after Curt Flood's historic suit, jocks have succeeded in bringing a measure of free competition into the athletic marketplace. A "free agent" is not "meat on the hoof," but those athletes who cannot qualify still remain subject to drafts and reserve clauses.

Restriction of competition is not limited to frankly professional sport. The administrative limitations by the NCAA on athlete recruitment, says sport writer Bil Gilbert, "are essentially for the benefit of NCAA members, not the athlete. Substantially, they are monopolistic in intent, designed to minimize competition for the services of athletes. It is a 'restraint of trade' arrangement.''[89] Gilbert says that if the NCAA were serious about abuses in recruiting athletes, perhaps the simplest answer would be to ''abolish all the restraining regulations, and permit schools to select athletes on a highest-bidder basis.'' He thinks that such ''free enterprise'' would leave only a few schools able to hire athletes and force the rest to use student walk-ons.

The status of the athlete as property is dramatically reflected in the fact that his (her) value can be depreciated by an employer for tax purposes. An individual or corporation with property that loses value over time can deduct in any year the value lost by that property in that year. Bill Veeck cites the case of the 1966 transfer of the Milwaukee Braves to Atlanta as an example of how depreciation works. The cost of the Braves to their new owners was six million dollars, of which $50,000 was the price of the franchise. The rest, more than 99 percent, was the value of the players held as property. Assuming that they had an average life of 10 years in baseball (an optimistic assumption), the owners could claim $600,000 depreciation annually over a ten-year period. If the club made money, this could reduce its taxable net earnings. If it did not earn money, the depreciation could be used to reduce taxable net earnings from any other enterprises owned by the management. Veeck says that when one buys an athletic team, what he buys is essentially **the right to depreciate**. Clearly one can depreciate only property that he owns, not the services of freely contracting persons.

The position of the run-of-the-mill professional athlete is still that of a property in the entertainment business, where one is usually, as Phil Donahue put it in citing his own history, at the arbitrary power of people who can terminate you with a pregnant wife and an overdue car payment on a whim that comes to them while shaving.[90]

Another aspect that counteracts democracy in sport is the fact, pointed out by Stone, that the occupational structure of sport is an inverted pyramid, narrower at its base than at the top. ''Those engaged first hand in the production of the. . . game or the match constitute a minority within the industrial complex, while those engaged in the administration, promotion, and servicing of the prodution constitute a sizeable majority.''[91] This inverted pyramid is similar to the situation on college campuses: a major complaint of organized university teachers is the way in which the upper administrative levels have expanded at the expense of the teaching base.

Finally, the structure of organized athletics may not only raise false hopes of climbing to affluence and glory. It may also positively keep down young people who might climb the ladder. In an interview about why he quit football, former all-pro wide receiver George Sauer suggests that the concentration of energy and attention on a sport career that is encouraged by athletic scholarships may actually narrow the opportunity of young athletes of working class origin by putting all their eggs in the basket of athletic ambition.[92] Thus a bright and athletically gifted student who could become a doctor, lawyer, businessman, or scientist may be prevented by his athletic scholarship from really exploring these possibilities. "If you are black and can play some ball," says Harry Edwards, "your chances are infinitely greater of gaining access to a college education than if you have only limited athletic ability, but have the potential for a significant intellectual contribution to society."[93] Our elementary and secondary schools have been criticized for "tracking" working class students into repeating the careers of their parents, while their middle and upper class peers are tracked into college preparatory programs. Athletic scholarships may continue this tracking on the college and university level.

We shall explore the whole relationship of sport to social stratification at greater length in Chapter eight.

FOOTNOTES

[1]Information courtesy of Tom Danazo, Sports Department, **Philadelphia Bulletin.**

[2]Winton U. Solberg, **Redeem the Time: The Puritan Sabbath in Early America**, Cambridge, Mass., Harvard, 1977, ix, 3.

[3]Preserved Smith, **The History of the Reformation**, New York, Harcourt Brace Jovanovich, 1920, 3-4.

[4]Storm Jameson, **The Decline of Merry England**, Indianapolis, Bobbs Merrill, 1930, 18.

[5]Smith, **op. cit.**, 345.

[6]Crane Brinton, **A History of Western Morals**, New York, Harcourt Brace Jovanovich, 1959, 222.

[7]Abraham Kuyper, **Calvinism**, Grand Rapids, Eerdman, 1931, 73.

[8]Trans. by Talcott Parsons, New York, Scribner, 1958.

[9]David C. McClelland, **The Achieving Society**, New York, VanNostrand Rinehold, 1961.

[10]Weber, **op. cit.**, 167.

[11]Jameson, **op. cit.**, 15.

[12]Will Durant, **The Reformation**, Part VI of **The Story of Civilization**, New York, Simon and Schuster, 1957, 115.

[13]Smith, **op. cit.**, 500.

[14]**Ibid.**

[15]Durant, **The Reformation**, 477.

[16]Foster Rhea Dulles, **America Learns to Play: A History of Popular Recreation 1607-1940**, New York, Appleton-Century, 1940.

[17]Weber, **op. cit**, 166.

[18]Durant, **The Reformation**, 474.

[19]Jameson, **op. cit**, 20-21.

[20]Thomas Babington Macaulay, **The History of England from the Accession of James the Second**, London, Longmans, Green, Reader, and Dyer, 1871, 79.

[21]**Ibid.**

[22]Weber, **op. cit.**, 169, n.

[23]Brinton, **op. cit.**, 225.

[24]"The King's Majesties Declaration to his Subjects, concerning Lawfull Sports to Be Used," in S. R. Gardiner, ed., **The Constitutional Documents of the Puritan Revolution**, 1625-1660, 2nd enlarged and revised edition, Oxford, Clarendon, 1899, 99, 101.

[25]Weber, **op. cit.**, 167.

[26]Dennis Brailsford, **Sport and Society: Elizabeth to Anne**, Toronto, University of Toronto Press, 1969, 107.

[27]Peter C. McIntosh, "An Historical View of Society and Social Control, **International Review of Sport Sociology**, 6, 1971, 10.

[28]Foster Rhea Dulles, **America Learns to Play: A History of Popular Recreation, 1607-1940**, New York, Appleton-Century-Crofts, 1940, 3.

[29]Solberg, **op. cit.**, 49.

[30]**Ibid.**, 49-50.

[31]Brailsford, **op. cit.**, 156.

[32]Philip Stubbes, **The Anatomy of Abuses**, London, Richard Jones, 1583; reprint, New York, Da Capo, 1972, original unpaged.

[33]Solberg, **op. cit.** 50.

[34]**ibid.**, 51.

[35]Heinz Meyer, "Puritanism and Physical Training: Ideological and Political Accents in the Christian Interpretation of Sport," **International Review of Sport Sociology**, 8, 1, 1973, 49.

[36]Macaulay, **op. cit.**, 79.

[37]Jameson, **op. cit.**, 22.

[38]Günther Lüschen, "The Interdependence of Sport and Culture," **International Review of Sport Sociology**, 2, 1967, 127-141.

[39]Presented at the World Congress of Sociology, Varnia, Bulgaria, 1970.

[40]Solberg, **op. cit.**, 301.

[41]John Allen Krout, **Annals of American Sport**, vol. xv of **The Pageant of America: A Pictorial History of the United States**, ed. Ralph H. Gabriel, New Haven, Yale, 1929, 10.

[42]John Rickards Betts, **America's Sporting Heritage: 1850-1950**, Reading, Mass., Addison-Wesley, 1974, 5.

[43]**Ibid.**, 28.

[44]John Roach Stanton, in **Chicago Daily Tribune**, Oct. 15, 1906.

[45]cited in **Literary Digest**, July 30, 1927, 28.

[46]**New York Times**, Jan. 7, 1926, 27.

[47]Robert and Helen Lynd, **Middletown**, Harcourt, Brace, Jovanovich, 1963.

[48]Walt W. Rostow, **The Stages of Economic Growth**, New York, Norton, 1962, paper.

[49]New York: Dover, 1955.

[50]John Rickards Betts, "The Technological Revolution and the Rise of Sport, 1850-1900," **Mississippi Valley Historical Review, 40**, 1953, 231-232.

[51]John Allen Krout, **Annals of American Sport, op. cit.**, 9.

[52]**Ibid.**, 9, 11.

[53]Ralph H. Gabriel, preface to Krout, **op. cit.**, 3.

[54]Foster Rhea Dulles, **America Learns to Play**, etc., 137.

[55]R. T. Furst, "Social Change and the Commercialization of Professional Sports," **International Review of Sport Sociology**, 6, 1971, 153-173.

[56]New York: Macmillan, 1899.

[57]Gregory P. Stone, "American Sports: Play and Display," in Eric Dunning, ed., **The Sociology of Sport**, London, Cass, 1972, 46-65. Reprinted in John T. Talamini and Charles Hunt Page, eds., **Sport and Society: An Anthology**, Boston, Little Brown, 1973, 65-85.

[58]Robert F. Kelley, **American Rowing: Its Background and Traditions**, New York, Putnam, 1932.

[59]**Spalding's Official BaseBall Guide**, New York, 1886, Appendix.

[60]Betts, "The Technological Revolution and the Rise of Sport," **op. cit.**

[61]**Frank Leslie's Illustrated Newspaper, 29**, Sept. 28, 1969, 2.

[62]New Orleans **Daily Picayune**, July 10, 1889.

[63]Judge Jerome Frank in **Gardella v. Chandler**, Second Federal Circuit Court of Appeals, 1948.

[64]September 8, 1892.

[65]James Bryce, "America Revisited: The Chances of a Quarter-Century," **Outlook, 79**, Mar. 25, 1905, 738-739.

[66]Gabriel, **op. cit.**, 3.

[67]Stone, **op. cit.**, 73.

[68]**Minneapolis Tribune**, October 11, 1966, p. 6. Cited, **Ibid.**, 73, n.

[69]Takaaki Niwi, "The Function of Sport in Society (With Special Reference to Sport in Japanese Business Enterprise)," **International Review of Sport Sociology**, 8, 1, 1973, 55.

[70]Lewis Mumford, **Technics and Civilization**,, New York, Harcourt, Brace, Jovanovich, 1963, 303-305, 307.

[71]Dulles, **op. cit.**, 349.

[72]**Ibid.**

[73]Frederick Lewis Allen, "The Big Change", **Harper's Magazine, 201**, October 1950, 145-160.

[74]Hans Kraus and Ruth P. Hirschland, "Minimum Physical Fitness Tests in School Children," **Research Quarterly**, **25**, 178-187.

[75]**TV Guide**, August 19, 1978, p. 3.

[76]Larry Eldridge, "Changing Values in Sports," **Christian Science Monitor**, August 10, 1978, p. 12.

[77]Paul Hoch, **Rip Off the Big Game: The Exploitation of Sports by the Power Elite**, Garden City, N. Y. Doubleday, 1972, 32.

[78]Stone, **op. cit.**, 72.

[79]Sadao Morikawa, "Amateurism—Yesterday, Today and Tomorrow," **International Review of Sport Sociology**, 12, 2, 1977, 64-65.

[80]Stone, **op. cit.**, 68-69.

[81]Harry Edwards, **Sociology of Sport**, Homewood, Ill., Dorsey, 1973, 277.

[82]Hoch, **op. cit.**, 48.

[83]George H. Hanford, "Controversies in College Sports," **Annals of the American Academy of Political and Social Science, 445**, Sept. 1979, 73.

[84]Charles H. Page, "The Mounting Interest in Sport," in Talamini and Page, **op. cit.**, 4.

[85]George Saxon, "Immigrant Culture in a Stratfield Economy," **Modern Review**, February, 1948. Available in Don Calhoun **et al**, eds. **Personality, Work, Community: An Introduction to Social Science, 2nd revised edition**, Philadelphia, Lippincott, 1961, 309-315.

[86]David Riesman and Reuel Denney, "Football in America: A Study in Cultural Diffusion," American Quarterly, 3, 1951, 309-325.

[87]Quoted in **The Killer Instinct**, by Bob Cousy with James Devaney, New York, Random House, 1975, 85.

[88]James Quirk and Mohamed El Hodiri, "The Economic Theory of a Professional Sports League," in Roger W. Noll, ed., **Government and the Sports Business**, Washington, Brookings, 1974, 42, n.

[89]Bil Gilbert, "What Counselors Need to Know About College and Pro Sports." **Phi Delta Kappan**, October 1974, 124.

[90]Phil Donahue to Tom Brokaw, NBC "Today" show, February 29, 1980.

[91]Stone, **op. cit.**, 69.

[92]The Souring of George Sauer," interview by Jack Scott, **Intellectual Digest**, December, 1971.

[93]Harry Edwards, "Sport Within the Veil: The Triumphs, Tragedies, and Challenges of Afro-American Involvement," **Annals of the American Academy of Political and Social Science, 445**, September 1979, 122.

PART TWO

SPORT AND SOCIAL ORGANIZATION

CHAPTER 6 THE ANTHROPOLOGY OF GAMES

In Chapters 4 and 5 we related the crisis in sport to the development of modern sport in the perspective of time. These chapters were essentially the social history of sport. Chapter 6 will add the perspective of space. It will be primarily the cultural anthropology of sport.

The Functions of Games

Anthropology has contributed in many ways to our understanding of technically advanced societies, but its distinctive contribution has been through study of preliterate (sometimes called "primitive") cultures. Although play, games, and sport have not been given as much attention by anthropologists as have other aspects of preliterate cultures, some researchers have always held with the great Robert Lowie that an accurate account of a boys' game on stilts is as significant as a report of Tahitian priests' explanation of the origin of the world. For example, as early as 1829, although some scholars, then as now, believed that primitive man was too busy for games and that only with leisure and civilization were games invented, William Ellis reported of the Society and Sandwich Islands of Polynesia that "their games were numerous and diversified and were often affairs of national importance."[1] In 1879 the British anthropologist Edward B. Tylor wrote for the **Fortnightly Review** an article on "The History of Games." One of the biggest controversies in anthropology at that time centered around the close similarity between the backgammon-type game **patolli**, played by the Aztecs of Mexico, and the Hindu Indian game of **pachisi**. Tylor held that two games with so many similarities could not have been invented independently by Hindus and Aztecs, but that **pachisi** must at some early time have been carried across the Pacific, then to become **patolli**. Other anthropologists supported the idea of independent invention against the "diffusion" theory. One of them was Stewart Culin, who around the beginning of the twentieth century published a book on games in Korea, China, and Japan; studied the play of boys in Brooklyn; and prepared for the Bureau of American Ethnology an 800-page study of the games of the North American Indians. In this last book a colleague wrote: "The popular notion that games are trivial in nature. . . soon gave way, under the well-conducted studies of Mr. Culin, to an adequte appreciation of their importance as an integral part of human culture."[3]

Research in Mexico also brought to light the fascinating story of **pok-ta-pok**, the longest-surviving game in the history of the western hemisphere. During and after the great Mayan civilization, from about 700 to 1765 A.D., there was played on stone courts from Guatemala to Arizona this team game whose objective was to put through a fixed stone ring one of the first rubber balls known to sport. Because of the ring, pok-ta-pok has been called a forerunner of basketball, but the ball could be struck only with buttocks and knees, not with hands, or with feet (as in soccer). William A. Goellner, who visited archaelogical sites in Mexico and Guatemala to research pok-ta-pok while a graduate student in physical education, points out that the game was very central to the cultural and religious life of the Mayan civilization. He also relates how pok-ta-pok, first a game for amateurs, became so popular that it underwent the same professionalization and corruption that have visited ancient Greek and contemporary American sport.[4]

In the later years of the twentieth century there has been a revival of interest in the anthropology of play. Physical educators Frederick Cozens and Florence Stumpf Frederickson have reported anthropological findings to their colleagues, urging them to see their work as an aspect of culture.[5] Developmental psychologist Brian Sutton-Smith has performed extensive field research on games in his native New Zealand and elsewhere, and has also edited collections of studies by other scientists.[6] John M. Roberts and others have used modern statistical techniques to interpret the data on play,

Mayan ball court at Chichén Itzá, Yucatan. Courtesy of Peabody Museum, Harvard University. Photograph by Carnegie Institute of Washington.

Stone ring fallen from the wall of the Chichén Itzá pok-ta-pok court. Courtesy of Peabody Museum, Harvard University. Photograph by Carnegie Institute of Washington.

games, and sport as reported in anthropological field work. In the 1970s research on play was officially recognized as a specialty in the field of anthropology, and there was formed an Association for the Anthropological Study of Play. What does the anthropology of games tell us? The main premise of anthropology is that the nature and meaning of anything depends on the total cultural situation in which it occurs.

Three illustrations may clarify this.

One is the play of the Tununak villagers of Nelson island, Alaska. Struggling to keep alive in a harsh environment, these Eskimos learned early that everyone's survival depended on everyone else. So they developed a very strong noncompetitive group morale. This affected the games they borrowed from the outside world. Lynn Ager, the first anthropologist to visit Nelson island, says, "The kind of competition I saw was one in which everyone tried to do his best but not at anyone else's expense."[7] Specifically, these Eskimos enjoyed a "non-winning" game of marbles, a test of skill in which each player came with one marble and left with the same marble. The children tried the "winning" game in which one player takes all the marbles, but didn't seem to care for it.

A similar case of a non-winning game is **paro paro** ("little fish"), a water game played by young girls among the Motu people of New Guinea. The game involves two circles of players in the water, one inside the other. The inner group tries to penetrate the outer circle by swimming under water, and the outer group sings, beats the water, and uses body blocks to prevent them. The cultural background is that the Motu, like the Tunanak villagers, have very hard conditions of survival. For them too it is urgent to cooperate to survive, and this fact colors their games. Annette Rosenstiel, an anthropologist who has studied the Motu, points out that in **paro paro** excellence is sought and admired and thus swimming skill is developed, but nobody "wins." "The games are non-competitive. . . No prizes are awarded."[8]

A third illustration is the game of tag as played by the Mescalero Apache Indians of New Mexico. Claire Farrer distinguishes two characteristics of the Apache culture. People spontaneously have much more body contact than do Anglo-Americans. Also, circles are a very basic feature of the culture. Houses are circular. Meetings are circular. Tribal decisions are made by consensus. "The circle pattern is egalitarian as is the society. No one is the obvious leader in a circle."[9] Dances are circular. And tag-games are circular, played by three to eight children while they circle clockwise on a jungle gym. "I've never," says Farrer, "seen tag played on the ground." The circling tag-players are also in close physical contact, very unlike those in the Anglo-American game, where each person runs on the ground in a straight line by himself or herself and is apart in his own private space until he is tagged.

Games must be understood in terms of the **function** they perform for people in their particular cultural setting. The most general statements we can make about the games of children and of adults that anthropologists have studied are two: (1) Games are a form of what Sutton-Smith calls "buffered" cultural learning. That is, in games children model, and adults reinforce in symbolic and therefore safe form, the activities and attitudes important in their cultures. These may be patterns now existing, or patterns that existed in the past. For example, chess is a "buffered" model of war: "Two players direct a conflict between two armies of equal strength upon a field of battle, circumscribed in extent and affording no advantage of ground to either side."[10] (2) Games are also a form of emotional expression similar to folk tales, music, drama, and painting. They are **fun**, as we saw it defined by Huizinga and Sutton-Smith in Chapter 3, and they are also **catharsis**, in the sense that that they are a safe theater for "getting off" the frustrations developed by living in a culture.

Thus games have both a modeling and an expressive function. Let us look at some concrete examples from anthropological research.

In the historic culture of Samoa, physical educator Helen Dunlap reported to her colleagues games, sports, dancing, and other vigorous recreational activities had these functions:

(1) They were forms of social intercourse that strengthened group unity.

(2) They were socially approved ways of expressing rivalry and gaining prestige and honor.

(3) They provided outlets for the emotions generated by such life crises as birth, marriage, and death.

(4) They strengthened people's relationships to their gods. For example, through symbolic fights tribal members could display devotion to their deities. Also, erotic dancing might stimulate and please the gods as it stimulated humans.

(5) Games trained for participation in adult society. Rivalry in fishing and pigeon netting were preparation for very important economic activities.

(6) In games people learned such war skills as disc and stick throwing, spear throwing and parrying, and fighting with clubs.They also developed strength and endurance that served them well in war.[11]

Maxwell Howell, Charles Dodge, and Robert Howell generalized for sport historians in a 1975 article about the function of play in four preliterate societies: Melanesians, Polynesians, Eskimos, and the aborigines (blackfellows) of Australia:

(1) **Economic** training, as in the Australian game of spearing the disc, Polynesian games of stilts, Melanesian canoe contests, and Eskimo sealing games.

(2) A **political** (or military) function, exemplified by boomerang tourneys in Australia, boxing matches in Polynesia, the Melanesian game of "cross-

ing the bridge," and the Eskimo tug-of-war.

(3) **Domestic** functions, as in playing at marriage among the Australians, Melanesian courting games, and Eskimo doll play.

(4) A function of unification through **ceremony**—examples, the corroboree among the Australian aborigines, pitching discs among the Polynesians, Melanesian dancing, and Eskimo drum-playing.

(5) **Social** gratifications ("fun"?): mud-sliding in Australia, juggling in Polynesia, finger-games in Melanesia, Eskimo ball games.[12]

Summarizing the functions of games among the Maori of New Zealand, who were until recently in the stone age, Cozens and Frederickson see them as playing these roles in that culture:

(1) training for war

(2) acquiring skill and grace

(3) contributing to economic efficiency

(4) a fundamental part of recreational life

(5) a means of promoting tribal loyalty and solidarity

(6) an outlet for healthy competitive urges in a culture organized for cooperation rather than competition.[13]

Frederickson gives a dramatic example of the range of functions a single sport activity can have. Wrestling competition, one of the oldest sports, can be:

(a) a way of settling the boundaries of rice fields (Phillipines) or villages (Cook Islands).

(b) a part of the tribal initiation rites at puberty (Cook Islands).

(c) a way of selecting a mate (Nigeria).

(d) a demonstration of a chief's power and prestige (Hawaii).

(e) a way of securing a successful harvest (ancient Japan).[14]

An important treatment of the role of games in culture is Michael Salter's discussion of the part played by games in rituals connected with crucial events in the lives of the northeast American Indians from the Saint Lawrence River to Louisiana at the time of settlement by the white man.[15] The main critical events Salter discusses are fertility of crops, control of weather, illness, and death. The rituals were related to supernatural beings, who were thanked or supplicated by feasts, dances, taboos, and ceremonies of purification. Associated with these rites were games—archery contests, pole-climbing, foot races, wrestling, handball, football, lacrosse, dice games, guessing games, hide-and-seek, tug-of-war. Each game was a contest symbolizing a struggle between elemental forces—good and bad weather, fertility and famine, illness and health, life and death. The successful playing out of the athletic contest was supposed to win the favor of, or give help to, supernatural forces or beings in these very life-important natural struggles—for the falling of needed rain, the fertility of crops or game, the healing of an illness, the freeing of a dead person's spirit. Thus, on the principle of "like begets like," the successful playing of the game was believed to give a "homeopathic reinforcement" to the forces favorable to human beings. Salter diagrams the process in Figure 6.1. With issues so central to the very life of a people at stake, it is not surprising that intense competition was encouraged by gambling and prizes, and that in terms of Salter's play-game continuum (see Figure 3.1), these ritual games were often much closer to "terminal contest" than to "fun." "It is hard," says Salter, "to imagine a. . . message 'This is play' being transmitted between the participants of a game-rite designed to ward-off an epidemic of smallpox." We shall return to this "homeopathic" function of games in Chapter 7.

Figure 6.1 Basic Mechanism Underlying a Ritual Game Among North American Indians

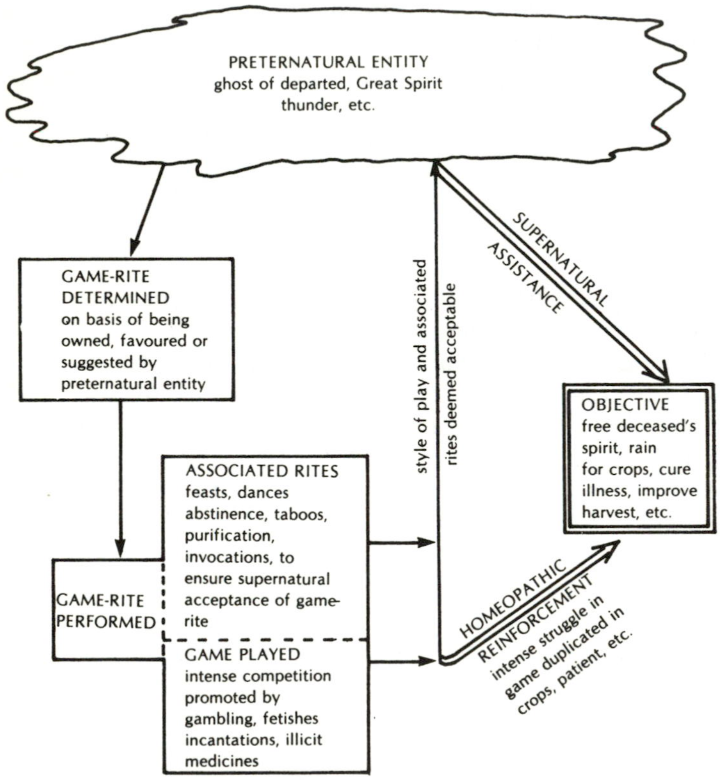

Source—Michael A. Salter, "Play in Ritual: An Ethnohistorical Overview of Native North America," in **Play and Culture**, ed. Helen B. Schwartzman, West Point, N.Y. Leisure Press, 1980, Figure 3. p. 80.

Latitude, Maintenance, and Cultural Complexity

These examples of the cultural function of games will give us background for examining the studies conducted by Roberts and others, using cross-cultural data collected under the direction of John Peter Murdock.[16] In the mid-twentieth century Yale anthropologists, under Murdock's leadership, gathered together and classified data on a number of topics gathered by major anthropological investigations up to that time. These were collected in the Cross-Cultural Survey Files and the Human Relations Area files. Using these files, Roberts, Sutton-Smith, and other colleagues proceeded to correlate different kinds of game behavior with different environmental and cultural conditions. They asked how the type and frequency of games played by different peoples have been related to favorableness or harshness of surroundings, to geography and climate, to methods of food-getting, levels of technical development and political organization, way of bringing up children, and concepts of the supernatural.

Roberts defines games as organized play involving (1) competition, (2) two or more sides, (3) criteria for determining an outcome, and (4) agreed-upon rules. A basis for this research was the distinction, which we saw in Chapter 3, of three kinds of games: games of physical skill (pure examples, weight-lifting and a marathon race), games of strategy (pure examples, chess and the Japanese board game "go"). Other games are mixtures of types: our major sports—baseball, football, basketball, hockey—for example, mix sheer physical skill with strategy and some luck. (For an excellent account of football as strategy that makes it sound much like chess, see Kyle Rote and Jack Winter's **The Language of Pro Football.**[17])

Which types of games occur most frequently? In a sample of 50 cultures selected from the files, 44 had games of physical skill, 19 had games of chance, 19 had games of strategy, and 5, surprisingly, had no games at all. Roberts feels that, historically, physical skill games, being the simplest type, generally originated first, followed by games of chance, and then, in more complex societies, by the more involved games of strategy.

We have looked at some of the general functions that games perform in culture. How do the functions performed by the three types of games differ? Each is primarily concerned with mastery of a certain aspect of the environment. Physical skill games are concerned with mastering the physical world and oneself. Games of chance involve mastery of the supernatural. Games of strategy train for, and express, mastery of the social order.

How is each type of game shaped by the physical and social environment? To answer, we must establish a framework for looking at this environment.

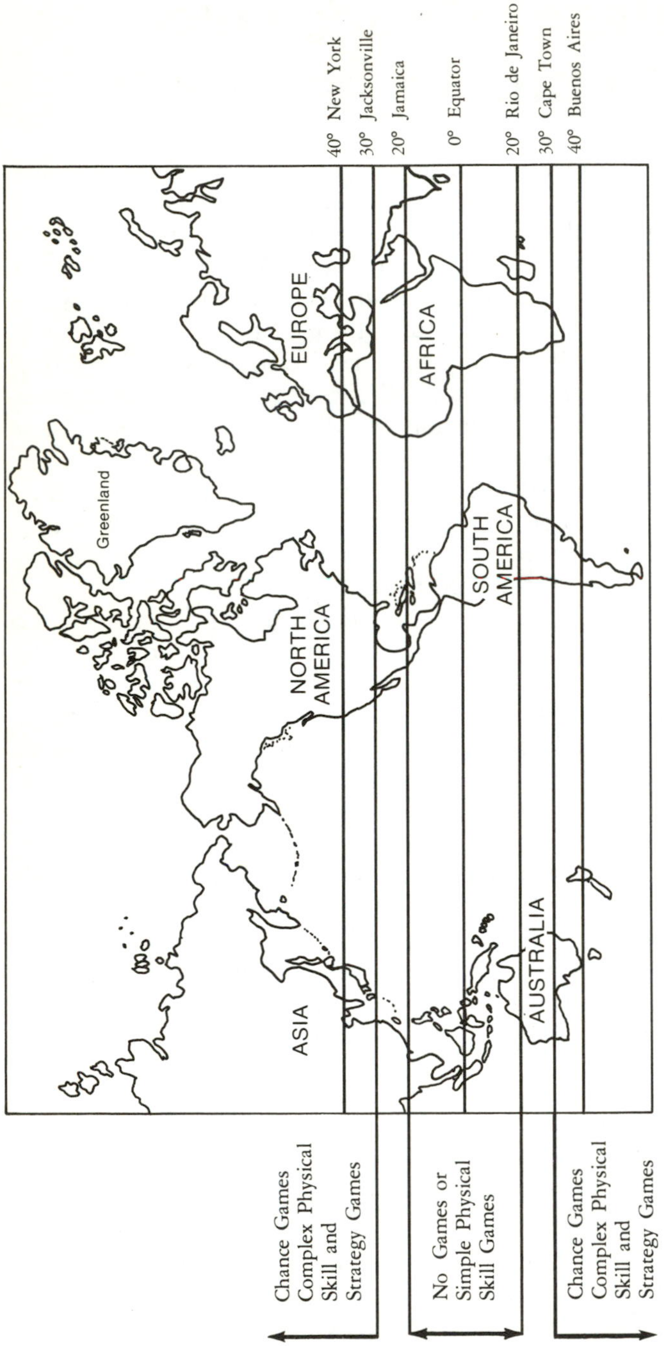

Distribution of games of physical skill, chance, and strategy is related to distance from the equator.

We shall prepare to locate societies and their games on a geographical and on a maintenance axis.

Physically, all societies that exist and have existed are situated somewhere on the surface of the globe. Let us establish some points of reference. In the northern hemisphere, 20 degrees from the equator is approximately the latitude of the island of Jamaica; 30 degrees the latitude of Jacksonville, Florida; and New York City is about 40 degrees north. South of the equator, Rio de Janeiro is about 20 degrees south; Cape Town, South Africa and Santiago, Chile about 30 degrees; and Buenos Aires about 40 degrees.

Culturally, all societies now and in the past have maintained themselves in one of several ways. The earliest stage, which still exists in some part of the world, is **hunting and gathering**. Among now-living peoples, the Bushmen of South Africa, the aborigines of Australia, the Tierra del Fuegans of Patagonia, and some Eskimos are still hunters and gatherers. Having no metal tools, they are still classified as Stone Age people. Around 7000 B.C. a revolution in food-getting took place. Since then it has occurred all over the world, and is still taking place. The collection of wild plants and animals gave way to their domestication in **agricultural** and **pastoral** societies. The Old Testament Hebrews are a classic example of a pastoral people. The Pueblo Indians of the southwest United States are a typical settled agricultural society. The transition from hunting and gathering to settlement was accompanied by a number of changes. Metal tools, such as the plough, replaced stone implements, thereby making possible more productive technology. Whereas hunting and gathering tribes usually had no sharp social distinctions and very simple government, settled peoples developed social classes and a political state. They developed slavery, war, industry, art, philosophy, science, leisure for the classes and eventually for the masses, and "conspicuous consumption."

How, now, are the three types of games related to the geographic and maintenance axes?

In terms of latitude, as we move from the tropics toward the poles, we find greater cultural complexity. In historic times (approximately from the agricultural revolution on) scholars have noted that, beginning in areas with an annual mean temperature of about 70 degrees, the center of civilization has moved to areas with an annual mean of about 50 degrees. This "coldward course of civilization" may be related to lower tropical and subtropical energy levels due to heat and poorer protein in the diet. In keeping with this, it is in the cooler areas of the earth that we find the more complex games.

Within 20 degrees of the equator are located cultures with no games, or with a few simple physical skill games (hitting, throwing and catching, hopping, jumping, running, swimming, sailing). Cultures farther away are likely to have a wider variety of physical skill games. Of 23 cultures within 20 degrees of the equator, only 5 had as many as 5 different physical skill games. Of 24 cultures beyond the 20th parallel (north of Jamaica or south of Rio) 16 had 5 or more physical skill games.

As the climate gets cooler, there are also likely to be more games of chance. Chance games typically occur beyond the 30th parallel (north of Jacksonville and south of Santiago). This fits with the correlation between physical skill and chance games—where there are few games of physical skill there are also few games of chance, and vice versa. Of 30 cultures with fewer than 5 physical skill games, only 4 had games of chance. Of 19 cultures possessing 5 or more games of physical skill, 15 did have chance games. In the northerly areas we are also likely to find the most advanced form of game—games of strategy—and especially those games of physical skill and strategy that carry us toward modern sport.

The coldward course of civilization suggests that latitude and maintenance are not unrelated "independent variables." However, let us now shift our focus to the relationship between game types and maintenance patterns.

First, the rare cultures without games. We must remember that these have no games as "game" was defined earlier. This in no way means that these people do not play or that they have no individual or group pastimes for their unoccupied moments. The no-game cultures are tropical, mainly in South America and Australia. They have a fairly undeveloped political organization and no stratification into classes.[18]

The cultures with only simple physical games are quite similar to the no-game cultures. They differ in that women and men are more likely to be segregated, and separate "nuclear" families of mother, father, and children appear along with the three-generation "extended" family. This separation may require more individual male self-reliance in hunting and fighting, for which games like spear-throwing and archery are a preparation.

Games of chance, which are a symbolic way of handling supernatural forces, are likely to occur where the environment is harsh and anxiety-provoking and there is a great deal of personal and social uncertainty. As compared with the no-game and the simple physical game cultures, chance game cultures are farther from the equator, are colder, and have greater seasonal change. People typically live in small nomadic groups without fixed settlements, and maintain themselves by hunting, fishing, and gathering. Their food supply is insecure and food shortages are common. Warfare is frequent. Premarital sexuality is typically tabooed, and people are likely to experience sexual anxiety and personal self-doubt. With such environmental, social, and personal uncertainty, it is not surprising that people will welcome supernatural help. The cross-cultural files show that people with chance games are likely to believe that the gods are friendly and easily influenced. In short, people play chance games where life is too hard for their scientific and technical skills and they believe that it can be managed by playing games with the fates. Chance games are practice in "a way of making up one's mind with the help of a benevolent Fate."[19] Also success in games of chance may strengthen people to endure hardship in hope of a more fortunate future.

Games of strategy, symbolizing mastery of the social environment, are related to social complexity—large agriculturally-based settlement, advanced technology, stratification of social classes, and political complexity.

Of the societies with strategy games that were studied, 4 were classified as nomadic (wandering), semi-nomadic or semi-sedentary; 35 were sedentary (settled). Table 6.1 spells out the relationship between strategy games and maintenance patterns in greater detail. It is clear that the development of intensive farming is the point at which games of strategy become prominent.

Technical development in agriculture is likely to be accompanied by other kinds of technical maturity. Only three cultures with strategy games were without pottery, and most had weaving and leather work. Working in metal was highly correlated: of 42 cultures with metal work, 31 had strategy games and 11 did not; of 59 who did not work in metal, only one had games of strategy. All of these factors are highly related to size of community, which Table 6.2 shows is also directly correlated with strategy games.

Of cultures with high political integration and social stratification, 12 had strategy games and 3 did not; of cultures where both political integration and social stratification were low, 3 had strategy games and 13 had none. Anthropological examples of high political integration are the Hottentots and Dahomians of Africa, the Aztecs of Central America, the Kwakiutl Indians of the Pacific Northwest, and the Polynesians. All of these, although preliterate, developed a political state. Examples of low political organization are the Melanesians, the Samoans, the Hopi Indians, and the African Bushmen. All have simple, more informal methods of group control.

What is meant by "political integration" should be made clearer by Table 6.3, which deals with the number of political levels above the local community. (Example: the resident of Coral Gables, Florida is subject, beyond the city of Coral Gables, to the governments of Metropolitan Dade county, the state of Florida, the United States, and the United Nations, a total of four "jurisdictions beyond the local community.") The table shows dramatically that the greater the number of jurisdictional levels the more likely it is that the community will have games of strategy.

Societies with complex technical and political development are likely to believe in strong (often monotheistic) supernatural beings ("high gods"). (An example would be the contrast between the Old Testament Hebrews and the Canaanite tribes they displaced in their conquest of Israel.) So it is in keeping with the other correlates of games that of 36 tribes with games of strategy, 29 had high gods.

Table 6.1 Games of Strategy and Intensity of Cultivation

Method of Maintenance	**Strategy Present**	**Strategy Absent**
No agriculture	2	32
Gardens	0	14
Casual agriculture	1	6
Extensive agriculture	13	33
Intensive agriculture	13	7
With irrigation		
Permanent intensively cultivated fields	12	3

Source—
John M. Roberts, Brian Sutton-Smith, and Adam Kendon, "Strategy in Games and Folk Tales," **Journal of Social Psychology, 61**, 1963, Table 1, p. 186.

Table 6.2 Games of Strategy and Mean Size of Local Community

	Games of Strategy	
Mean Size of Local Community	**Present**	**Absent**
50 or less	1	18
50-59	1	10
100-199	7	10
200-399	5	3
400-1000	3	4
1000+	2	0
Towns up to 50,000	5	1
Towns of more than 50,000	11	0

Source—
John M. Roberts, Brian Sutton-Smith, and Adam Kendon, "Strategy in Games and Folk Tales," **Journal of Social Psychology, 61**, 1963, Table 3, p. 188.

Table 6.3 Jurisdictional Levels and Strategy Games

Levels Beyond Local Community	**0**	**1**	**2**	**3**	**4**
Games of Strategy Absent	66	26	2	0	0
Games of Strategy Present	5	10	14	9	4

Source—
John M. Roberts, Brian Sutton-Smith, and Adam Kendon, "Strategy in Games and Folk Tales," **Journal of Social Psychology, 61**, 1963, p. 188.

These findings on the relationship of game complexity to cultural complexity are paralleled by the work in which anthropologist Alan Lomax has related dance forms to levels of cultural development.[20] Through "choreometrics" Lomax has identified three forms of dance in terms of their dominant pattern of movement—linear (one-dimensional), curvilinear (two-dimensional), and spiral (three-dimensional). The simplest linear dances are found in the economically simplest Stone Age hunting-gathering cultures. Dances become circular with the use of metal tools. Dance pattern follows work pattern: stone and wood tools are too breakable for any but the simplest straight-line stroke but metal edges make possible sweeping cutting movements. Spiral dances are typical of pre-industrial states with irrigation and social stratification. (Eighty percent of the cultures with metal have two-dimensional dances; 80 percent of the irrigation cultures have spiral dances.)

Lomax has found a similar relationship between cultural complexity and another element in dance—use of the torso as a single unit or as multiple units. The American square dance, most American Indian dances, and the folk dances of Scotland and Ireland typically move the torso as one piece. The hula, the twist, and the belly dance are examples of a multi-unit dance. As with forms of games, single- and multi-unit dance are distributed according to both geography and cultural charcteristics. Single-unit dances are typically found among hunters and gatherers, multi-unit forms among people who practice agriculture and keep herds. Dances in cold climates tend to be single-unit. Multi-unit dance is generally tropical—African, Polynesian, Caribbean. (An exception Lomax found is some Hungarian folk dances where the women swing their hips. This is explained by another principle: Multi-unit dance is correlated with the status of women, and among these Hungarians the woman typically shares work in the fields with men, rather than staying in the house.)

Game Types and Child Training

The different types of games appear to be associated with different themes that run through each culture. Since every society "enculturates" its young members to perform in the socially accepted manner, these themes appear in the early training of children. The three main themes are obedience, responsibility, and achievement. Examples of **obedience** are the behavior of the old-fashioned woman who promised to "love, honor, and obey" her husband; the behavior typically expected of soldiers by the military; and the behavior expected of athletes by the authoritarian coach for whom they would "run through a brick wall" if so told. The child who is to be "seen and not heard" is being prepared for this kind of response. **Responsibility** is obedience with somewhat more flexibility and original initiative. The farm boy who was brought up to assume certain "chores" as part of the teamwork of the family enterprise is an example. Although women have traditionally been expected to obey their husbands, in real life they have performed highly responsible roles as mothers and wives, for which doll-playing and helping with cooking and housekeeping as young children have prepared them. As modern women are aware, this responsibility training is different from training for **achievement**, which basically involves performance that is distinctive and outstanding. An example of achievement training is the familiar one of the Jewish boy who is pushed by his family and relatives into becoming a doctor or lawyer. It should not surprise us that in our culture women and economically lower-class people are customarily trained for obedience and responsibility, while males and middle-class people generally are trained for achievement. (Even the middle-class Jewish girl, while not often encouraged to **become** a doctor, may be prepared to "move on up" by **marrying** one.)

In their anthropological study relating games to child-training, Roberts and Sutton-Smith selected 56 societies from the Yale Cross Cultural Survey and Human Relations Area files. Then they scored these societies on obedience, responsibility, and achievement, using a scale developed by Bacon, Barry, and Child.[21]

Table 6.4 Chance Games and Frequency of Reward for Responsibility

Responsibility Score	Games of Chance	No Games of Chance
Above median	18	8
Below median	9	18

Based on John M. Roberts and Brian Sutton-Smith, "Child Training and Game Involvement," **Ethnology, 1**, April 1962, Table 3.

Table 6.5 Strategy Games and Frequency of Reward for Obedience

Obedience Score	Games of Strategy	No Games of Strategy
Above median	12	7
Below median	5	26

Based on John M. Roberts and Brian Sutton-Smith, "Child Training and Game Involvement," **Ethnology, 1** April 1962, Table 2.

Table 6.6 Physical Skill Games (including combined Physical Skill and Strategy) and Frequency of Reward for Achievement

Achievement Score	9 or more Games **of Physical Skill**	8 or fewer Games **of Physical Skill**
Above median	14	4
Below median	7	19

Based on John M. Roberts and Brian Sutton-Smith, "Child Training and Game Involvement," **Ethnology, 1**, April 1962, Table 4.

What did they find? In a sentence, "strategy is associated with obedience and not with responsibility or achievement, chance with responsibility and not with obedience, and physical skill with achievement and not with obedience and responsibility."[22]

Games of **chance** are typically found in societies that train their children for responsibility. Comparing scores for responsibility in societies that had chance games with those lacking them, the researchers found that chance game cultures scored above the average (median) in frequency of reward for responsible behavior much more often than did cultures without games of chance (see Table 6.4). You will remember that cultures with chance games typically experience uncertain and unpredictable life conditions, where these games are devices for enlisting supernatural help. In these difficult circumstances, it makes sense that children should be trained for responsibility (which is more flexible) rather than for unthinking obedience ("theirs not to reason why"). Where life demands novel decisions, they must be trained to make them, although finally they may run out of options and call on the gods.

Games of **strategy** are found typically associated with training for obedience. Cultures with strategy games scored above the median in frequency of reward for obedience more frequently than did cultures that did not have these games (see Table 6.5). You will recall that strategy games appear in complex societies. These typically require that people mesh their activities into complex ongoing patterns in which they give and take orders. Strategy games are microcosms (miniature models) of this kind of pattern.[23] In the complex strategy game culture, childhood training to obey prepares for both games and "real life."

Societies emphasizing acheivement typically have many games of **physical skill**. "Games of physical skill appear to be a direct. . . representation of achievement." As we saw earlier, there are cultures with no games, even of physical skill, but they are rare. So Table 6.6, unlike the two previous tables, shows not **presence** or **absence** of physical skill games, but the **number** of these games. It also includes games that combine physical skill and strategy.

In addition to the cross-cultural correlations, the Roberts and Sutton-Smith theory receives interesting support from George Rich's case study of Icelandic children.[24] The situation of Iceland is severe and isolated. Back to the days of the Scandinavian sagas, says Rich, Icelanders have had "a pragmatic, achievement-oriented individualistic world-view made to fit in a rugged environment." Today,

> *If we compare Iceland with 18 of the world's most technologically advanced societies, Iceland ranks 8th in overall per capita consumption: this amongst societies that far surpass Iceland in natural wealth.*[25] *Such an achievement has not occurred as a product of fateful and favorable circumstances, such as an abundance of easily exploitable resources, or a good proximity to the hub of the Industrial Revolution. Rather, in spite of severe environmental limitation, six centuries of foreign domination, and the need to import virtually everything but fish, potatoes, and wool, the Icelanders have achieved what they have only with talent, perseverance, and a strong national will, translated along the way into personal motivation to achieve and get ahead.*[26]

This drive is clearly related to parental training: "As though Icelanders have acquired their system from a guide to independence training, there is . . . a low emphasis on parental authority and obedience. Icelandic parents are notably unauthoritarian, unrestrictive, and generally unconcerned with obedience, as we conceive it. Doting, restrictive, or dominant parents are considered potentially detrimental to the development of sound character in children."[27] As in other cultures where the struggle with nature is hard, the need for individuality is blended with "strong emphasis on the value of sociability, on the value of affiliating with others, and of establishing enduring friendships." Asked to describe the ideal child, Icelandic parents emphasized sociability, talent, and independence, **in that order**.

Now what about the play activities of these Icelandic kids? Rich administered to about 75 percent of the children between 8 and 12 in a northern Icelandic village scales rating the games they preferred and those in which they actually participated. Here comes the test of the Roberts and Sutton-Smith theory. On the basis of this hypotheses, says Rich, "I could anticipate the following: (1) that the children would show a predominant interest in games of skill, reflecting the strong emphasis placed on independence and achievement training; (2) that with the moderate concern for responsibility training, games of chance would figure only moderately in the preference and involvement patterns of the children; (3) that with the

The Icelandic environment is isolated and severe. Above, aerial view of the volcanic island of Surtsey which rose from the ocean about 1970. Below, Akureyri, the principal town in the north of Iceland. Copyright by Eddafoto, Reykjavik, Iceland. Reprinted by permission.

negligible concern for obedience, and with the laxity of training in this area, games of strategy would be unimportant.[28]

The results? 283 children preferred physical skill games, 7 preferred chance games, and, in spite of the fact that chess is a national board game for adults (probably ideal for long cold winter evenings), no child listed a strategy game as a favorite. A difference as large as this would occur by chance alone less frequently than one time in a thousand ($p < .001$).

In keeping, however, with the cultural emphasis on sociability, the physical games chosen are typically group games "in which the individual players must assert themselves as individuals and simultaneously monitor and incorporate the roles and needs of others in a cooperative enterprise." This, says Rich, is crucially important "in a society where the inordinate emphasis on independence and individualism might be socially pathological unless monitored by a counter-emphasis on sociability."[29]

We find two kinds of cultural situations in which physical skill is combined with achievement: very simple societies that have only games of physical skill; and very complex societies that combine physical skill with strategy. The complex societies are also likely to have other games of chance and strategy.

Simple achievement societies are those where survival depends on the mastery of basic physical skills necessary for food-getting. Physical skill games are practice for survival. Those who succeed in this practice are honored by their peers; those who fail tend to lose status.

We touched earlier upon the Alaskan Eskimo village of Tununak. As this village existed before 1945, out of 39 recorded games, 25 were games of physical skill. There were no chance or strategy games. The only non-physical games were those that Eifermann, the Israeli student of children's play, has called "memory-attention games." To understand all this, we must know of these Tununak Eskimos that "the overwhelming fact of their lives, that their very survival depends on a hunter's ability to find, kill, and retrieve game, has dominated every aspect of their culture."[30] Lynn Ager's explanation of the function of the memory-attention games describes also the main function of achievement in the physical skill games: "A good memory. . . was a valuable personal asset in a hunting culture, for it is of positive survival value to remember one's own experiences in emergencies, the experiences of others in similar situations, to remember landmarks on an almost featureless terrain, to remember animal habits which enable one to predict their behavior. Remembering helps the hunter and may even save his life."[31] Skills achieved in physical skill games may do the same.

The Motu of New Guinea, also mentioned earlier, live under equally hard conditions. The rainfall is low, the soil shallow and infertile. Thus the Motu depend on hunting and fishing, which are done on a cooperative, community-wide basis, with established rules for distributing the catch so that everyone eats. Of greatest importance is the annual **hiri**, a trading expedition of several hundred miles to exchange thousands of pots, made by the Motu, for sago, a starch food, and wood, which is essential for the outrigger canoes (lakatoi) that are their main source of water transportation.

Under these conditions, it is not surprising that the Motu children can swim before they can walk, that the girls begin to play **paro paro** (the two-circle swimming game previously described), and the boys early in life build and race miniature outrigger canoes. Also, "at eight to twelve years of age, boys are already adept at handling the fish spear, using a toy spear about two-thirds the size of the adult spear. Thus, when they are ready to accompany their fathers on hunting and fishing expeditions, the small boys have already acquired those characteristics of fearlessness, poise, and visual and muscular coordination which will be necessary during their entire adult life."[32]

These purely physical skill games of simple achievement societies are quite different from the competitive sports into which games of physical skill and strategy often turn in the more complex achievement cultures. There, instead of learning skills for the common welfare, children of the same age may be trained by their elders to throw baseballs at each other's heads. Roberts and Sutton-Smith may be right in suggesting that, by contrast with those whose achievement is a gratifying means of common survival, "perhaps persons who play games (of physical skill and strategy) are in conflict about real achievement and use the simulated achievement of games to assuage their anxiety."[33] Here it may be time to go deeper into the development of the modern-day achievement culture. In doing so, I shall relate our anthropological discussion to the revolutionary world changes described in Chapter 5, in terms of some ideas developed by Sutton-Smith and David Riesman.

Ascriptive and Achievement Games

The changes that have taken place since the time of Oliver Cromwell (1599-1658) can be summarized in a very few basic concepts: capitalism, Puritanism, nationalism, machine technology, urbanization, population explosion, shift from extended to nuclear family, development of competitive sport. These developments have transformed the western world and touched most of the "economically underdeveloped" cultures traditionally studied by anthropologists. The old culture survives primarily in the economically developing world and in lower socioeconomic groups in the modernized nations. The new culture centers in the middle class in both—or in those who aspire to be middle class.

Sutton-Smith, taking terms from the sociologists, sees the transition as a change from a society where status is ascribed by birth (an "ascriptive" society) to one where it is achieved during one's lifetime. There has been, he thinks, a corresponding change in play and games.[34] Riesman sees a shift from a "tradition-directed" to an "inner-directed" society, which has lately been threatened by a tendency to "other-direction."[35] The term "tradition-directed" does not require explanation. The "inner-directed" society is essentially the world of the Puritan conscience as described in Chapter 5, where every person's course is determined not by the past but by an "inner gyroscope" that steers his direction. People in the more recent "other directed" society are steered by a psychological radar sense that tunes them into what their neighbors want them to be and do.

In the ascriptive culture, as described by Sutton-Smith, childhood is not a period of learning the skill for responsible or achieving behavior. It is rather a number of unformed years that one lives through before being dumped very early into the adult world, to repeat the career of one's parents and their parents before them. If anything is learned, it is how to fit into one's ascribed role by obeying first one's parents and then the social powers-that-be. According to Philippe Aries, "in the Middle Ages, at the beginning of modern times, and for a long time after that in the lower classes, children were mixed with adults as soon as they were considered capable of doing without their mothers or nannies, not long after a tardy weaning (in other words, at about the age of seven). They immediately went straight into the community of men, sharing in the work and play of their companions, old and young alike."[36] In other words, in the ascriptive culture, there was not the peer group that stands apart from the adult world in a changing society and bridges the gap to that world.

So the play of childhood is dominated by obedience and imitation. The child in the ascriptive culture was described by Freud: "Mimicry is the child's best art and the driving motive of most of his games. A child's ambition aims far less at excelling his equals than at mimicking the grown-ups."[37]

Sutton-Smith describes the situation this way:

> *. . . About the age of two and three years [children] imitate the activities of their adults. But their imitative play is not imaginative. They use realistic toy representations (rather than improvised ones) to imitate in very circumscribed ways the behavior of their parents. If they play together it is normally in terms of one child*

> *bossing the others. When the others refuse to be subordinate, the play breaks down. Or the play is in parallel terms in which each child with the same toy does the same thing. . . They cannot readily shift to something else, or improvise without the toy. Their spoken language tends to be power oriented or manipulative of others (bring me this, take that away). . . Laughter is aggressive and has a ridiculing function.*[38]

Sutton-Smith uses the present tense because this summary is based primarily on Sara Smilansky's recent work in Israel. Observing that the Oriental (Sephardic) Jewish children, who are socioeconomically disadvantaged as compared with the children of European (Ashkenazic) origin, lag seriously in their school work, Smilansky decided to use sociodramatic play ". . . to teach the child full utilization of his scattered experiences, knowledge, and vocabulary in an imaginative combination, to develop in him the ability of positive interaction, and to broaden his concepts through the interaction with coplayers, peers, and adults."[39] But she ran up against a brick wall—she discovered that these children "*do not participate in sociodramatic play at all*," [italics Smilansky's] in the sense of imaginatively "taking the role of the other" rather than mechanically imitating parents. She found that 69 percent of the privileged children engaged in no spontaneous play at all. Twenty percent of each group spontaneously imitated adults. Seventy-nine percent of the privileged (European) group engaged in imaginative sociodramatic play, as compared with 11 percent of the underprivileged (Asiatic) group.

We may compare a report from England showing that when children begin fantasying imaginary playmates, middle class mothers are typically glad to see this development of imaginative powers, while working class parents are likely to worry about their children's mental health.[40]

Another significant class comparison is reported by Henry S. Maas between two clubs of working class and middle class adolescent boys in the United States.[41]

The working class boys carried over into their group life their relationship with their parents: group leaders, as well as adult advisors, were seen as authoritarian parent figures. This attitude was ambivalent—the parent figure in the group was the object of both admiration and hostility. By contrast, the middle class clubs regarded group leaders and adult advisors more as equals.

A dramatic case of an adolescent parent figure, from a different research report, was Doc, the leader of an Italian street gang studied by William F. Whyte.[42] A number of the gang were better bowlers, but in their games they could rarely beat Doc, the recognized group leader. This is a clear case of how ascriptive status can shape a competitive situation.

These findings are all supported by Geoffrey Watson's study of what middle class and working class parents found valuable in Little League baseball: "opportunity for more self-directed behavior for the middle class son, and more conforming behavior for the working class son."[43]

With respect to game types, the child's personal history tends to repeat social history. Sutton-Smith's study of the developmental psychology of children's games in New Zealand revealed that children typically begin with ascriptive games and end with achievement games. The earliest games are "central person" games that are "play representations of the relationships which children normally experience in their family life."[44] The central figure is a parent substitute. She or he may play a "limelight" role, of which Sutton-Smith gave as examples the game in which the group dances singing around Sally, "who is a-weeping," or Punchinello, the "funny fellow." In the "it" games of tag or hide-and-seek the group tried to avoid or outwit an aggressive central person. In "scapegoat" games the central figure is made a villain by the group. In games like King of the Mountain the group members attack and try to displace the central person. These ascriptive central person games, says Sutton-Smith, "are a symbolic bridge between the child's primary tie to his parents and his secondary ties to his peers." In these games the child learns to act out his conflicting attitudes of submission and rebellion toward parents in such a way as at the same time to become prepared for his cultural role.

At the age of ten or later, central person games typically give way to competitive team skill games. Two kinds of games serve as transitions from the ascriptive central person games to competitive team sports. One is individual games of physical skill—hopping, jumping, running, catching, marbles, tops. Another transitional type is the "pack against pack" contest without specialized individual roles. In our culture, cops and robbers and cowboys and Indians are examples. When individual skill contest and desultory pack contest give way to confrontation of organized teams before audiences, we have come all the way from ascriptive play to modern sport. "The competitive individual and team games are subordinate now to the main cultural concern with effective competition and the chance of victory."

Returning to Riesman, what it adds up to is that cultural modernization brings a transition from tradition-directed games that initiate and help perpetuate the status quo, to games that stress the inner direction of the achieving individual in an achieving society. In his New Zealand studies, Sutton-Smith saw this trend. He also saw two others.

One is the tendency of organized sport to take the place of all other games. Here, where the individual becomes submerged as a cog in a team bent on victory, we might say that inner-direction has been replaced by other-direction, personal achievement by strategy in combination with obedience. In American terms, the difference is between the boy quarterbacking a pickup football game and a Paul Brown calling all the shots from the bench,[45] or between sandlot baseball and coach Mike Maietta signaling every pitch as his Little League team wins the world championship.[46]

Nevertheless, recognizing this trend toward organization, Sutton-Smith disagrees with those who say that organized sport has reduced players to machines. In a follow-up study in New Zealand twenty years after his first research, he found less interest in formal team sports and more in informal activities like cycling and fishing. He still seems to believe in the possibility that the achievement culture will nourish in play the "autonomy" that Riesman also hopes for. Perhaps, Tununak and Motu-style, this will repeat the simple acheivement attained in physical skill games before they became entangled in the culture of strategy. Sutton-Smith suggests that the vogue of team sports may have been tied to the rise of upward-bound minorities, hinting that as the Irish, Polish, Latins, and now blacks are able to achieve recognition in areas other than organized sport, this sport will no longer be so important. "I don't suppose we should protest if sports cease to be a form of national mania and become recreations."[48]

FOOTNOTES

[1]**Polynesian Researches**, No. 1, London, Fisher, Son, and Jackson, 1829.

[2]Edward B. Tylor, "Backgammon Among the Aztecs," **Macmillan's Magazine**, London, **39**, 1878, 142-150. Reprinted in Brian Sutton-Smith, ed., **The Games of the Americas**, New York, Arno, 1976.

[3]Stewart Culin, **Games of the North American Indians**, Twenty-fourth Annual Report of the Bureau of American Ethnology, Washington, 1907, 39-40.

[4]William A. Goellner, "The Court Ball Game of the Aboriginal Mayas," **Research Quarterly**, **24**, May 1953, 147-168. Reprinted in Brian Sutton-Smith, ed., **op. cit.**

[5]Frederick W. Cizens and Florence Stumpf Frederickson, **Sports in America**, Chicago, University of Chicago Press, 1953.

[6]Brian Sutton-Smith, **The Folkgames of Children**, Austin, University of Texas Press for the American Folklore Society, 1971.

[7]Lynn Price Ager, "The Reflection of Cultural Values in Eskimo Children's Games," in **The Study of Play: Problems and Prospects**, Proceedings of the First Annual Meeting of the Association for the Anthropological Study of Play, eds., David F. Laney and B. Allan Tindall, West Point, N.Y., Leisure Press, 1976, 82.

[8]Annette Rosenstiel, "The Role of Traditional Games in the Process of Socialization Among the Motu of Papua, New Guinea," **Ibid.**, 55.

[9]Claire R. Farrer, "Play and Inter-Ethnic Communication," **Ibid.**, 89.

[10]H. J. R. Murray, **A History of Chess**, Oxford, Clarendon, 1913.

[11]Helen L. Dunlap, "Games, Sports, Dancing, and Other Vigorous Recreational Activities and Their Function in Samoan Culture," **Research Quarterly**, **22**, 1951, 298-311.

[12]Maxwell L. Howell, Charles Dodge, and Robert A. Howell, "Generalizations on Play in 'Primitive' Societies," **Journal of Sport History**, **2**, No. 2, 1975.

[13]Florence Stumpf [Frederickson] and Frederick W. Cozens, "Some Aspects of the Role of Games, Sports, and Recreational Activities in the Culture of Modern Primitive Peoples," **Research Quarterly, 18**, October 1947, 198-218.

[14]Florence Stumpf Frederickson, "Sports and the Cultures of Man," in Warren R. Johnson, ed., **Science and Medicine of Exercises and Sport**, New York, Harper & Row, 1960, pp. 633-646.

[15]Michael A. Salter, "Play in Ritual: An Ethnohistorical Overview of Native North America," in **Play and Culture**, ed. Helen B. Schwartzman, 1978 Proceedings of the Association for the Anthropological Study of Play, West Point, N.Y., Leisure Press, 1980, 70-82.

[16]The best-known report is "Games in Culture," by John M. Roberts, Malcolm J. Arth, and Robert R. Bush, **American Anthropologist, 61**, June 1959, 597-605.

[17]New York: Random House, 1966.

[18]John M. Roberts and Brian Sutton-Smith, "The Cross-Cultural and Psychological Study of Games," in Gunther Lunschen, ed., **the Cross-Cultural Analysis of Games**, Champaign, Ill., Stipes, 1970.

[19]**Ibid.**

[20]Alan Lomax, "Dance in Human History," a film available from the University of California Extension Media Center, Berkeley, California.

[21]M. Bacon, H. Barry III, and I. L. Child, "Rater's Instructions for Analysis of Socialization Practices With Respect to Dependence and Independence," mimeographed, 1952.

[22]John M. Roberts and Brian Sutton-Smith, "Child Training and Game Involvement," **Ethnology, 1**, April 1962, reprinted in Elliott M. Avedon and Brian Sutton-Smith, eds., **The Study of Games**, New York, Wiley, 1971, 474-475.

[23]See, again, Rote and Winter, **op. cit.**

[24]George W. Rich, Games and Values in Iceland," in **Play: Anthropological Perspectives**, ed. Michael A. Salter, 1977 Proceedings of the Association for the Anthropological Study of Play, West Point, N.Y.: Leisure Press, 1978, 113-126.

[25]Organization for Economic Cooperation and Development, **Economic Survey: Iceland**, Paris, 1973.

[26]Rich, **op. cit.**, 114.

[27]**Ibid.**, 115-116.

[28]**Ibid.**, 118.

[29]**Ibid.**, 124.

[30]Ager, **op. cit.**, 81.

[31]**Ibid.**, p. 82

[32]Rosenstiel, **op. cit.**, p. 55.

[33]Roberts and Sutton-Smith, "Child Training and Game Involvement," 481

[34]Brian Sutton-Smith, "The Two Cultures of Games," in Sutton-Smith, **The Folkgames of Children, op. cit.**

[35]David Riesman, **The Lonely Crowd**, New Haven, Yale University Press, 1950.

[36]Philippe Aries, **Centuries of Childhood**, tr. Robert Baldick, New York, Knopf, 1962, p. 411.

[37]Sigmund Freud, **Jokes and Their Relation to the Unconscious**, New York, Norton, 1963, p. 227.

[38]Sutton-Smith, "The Two Cultures of Games," p. 299.

[39]Sara Smilansky, **The Effects of Sociodramatic Play on Disadvantaged Preschool Children**, New York, Wiley, 1968, 3-4.

[40]**New York Times**, November 3, 1968, 97-99.

[41]Henry A. Maas, "The Role of Members in Clubs of Lower and Middle Class Adolescents," **Child Development Bulletin**, 25, 1954, 241-251.

[42]William F. Whyte, **Street Corner Society**, Chicago, University of Chicago Press, 1955.

[43]Geoffrey G. Watson, "Games, Socialization, and Parental Values: Social Class Differences in Parental Evaluation of Little League Baseball," **International Review of Sport Sociology**, 12, 1, 1977, 44.

[44]Brian Sutton-Smith, **The Games of New Zealand Children**, reprinted in **The Folkgames of Children, op. cit.**, 213.

[45]See Bernie Parrish, **They Call It a Game,** New York, Dial, 1971 by a Cleveland Browns' star who was a leader in player unionization.

[46]See Martin Ralbovsky, **Destiny's Darlings**, New York, Hawthorn, 1974, a follow-up twenty years later of the members of the 1954 Schenectady Little League world champions.

[47]Sutton-Smith, "The Two Cultures of Games," 309.

CHAPTER 7
CONTEST AND CIVILIZATION

There would be no civilization without winning, because winning is the epitome of group activity. The last man that sails down the Oletangy River will look at the ruins of that Ohio Stadium and say, "Well, what was it that prompted civilization to build that?" So many of the things that made ours a great civilization are the same things we see enacted in there on a Saturday afternoon.

—Football Coach Woody Hayes

In **Homo Ludens** Johan Huizinga contends that play has been the central factor in the development of civilization. "Culture arises in the form of play. . . it is played from the very beginning. In myth and ritual the great instinctive forces of modern life have their origin: law and order, commerce and profit, craft and art, poetry, wisdom, and science. All are rooted in the primeval soil of play."[1] The great historian would seem to agree with those advocates of sport who speak of its great "civilizing" influence. In this chapter we shall examine the relationship between play (particularly **agon)** and civilization.

Surplus and Civilization

By derivation, civilization (from the Latin word **civis**, city) is "citification." Historically it has been associated with two great bursts of urbanization—the first in Egypt, India and the Near East between about 5000 and

3000 B.C., and the second in Europe and America from about 1750 A.D. to the present. As we saw in Chapter 6, the key to the first burst, and to all civilization that has developed since then, has been the creation of an **economic surplus**. Through a change from hunting and gathering to a settled agricultural economy, and the application of the plough, food was made available well in excess of the needs of those producing it. This released people from the land to live in towns and cities and carry on business and industry. The civilization that ensued was a mixture of positive and negative qualities. People released from immediate economic need were able to devote themselves to the development of "high culture": music, poetry, literature, drama, the fine arts, science, philosophy. As the bare struggle for existence gave way to relative affluence, life became more graceful, generous, chivalrous, "civilized." Human beings came to be regarded and to regard themselves, not as mere instruments for production and reproduction, but as individual persons with identities capable of constant enrichment.

On the other hand, as the struggle against nature was modified, another struggle appeared in its place. Before a surplus and the beginnings of civilization, there may not have been much to go around but it was usually shared so that no one was hungry or otherwise needy. As people moved toward civilization, a minority began to appropriate the surplus produced by the majority. We can estimate the controlling minority at about 1 to 5 percent of the population. Present wealth distribution figures for the United States show somewhat less than 1 percent. In one form of this class domination, members of the majority were seized as slaves. There were also conflicts between minorities over control of the surplus: in addition to working in production, the majority were also enlisted in a new social institution called war.

All of these contradictory elements constituted, and still constitute, what we mean when we speak of civilization.

Where, now, did play and contest fit into this developing picture?

Emulation in Trobriand Society

First, let us look at the role of emulation (the striving to equal or surpass) in the life of the preliterate Trobriand islanders of southwest Melanesia as reported in Malinowski's famous 1922 study.[2] Along with fish they caught in the bays and open sea, the chief source of food for the Trobrianders was grown in their yam gardens. Here "healthy competition" was strong and played an important part in economic and social life. "A good garden worker in the Trobriands derives a direct prestige from the amount of labour he can do, and the size of the garden he can till. . . Men vie with one another in their speed, in their thoroughness, and in the weights they can lift, when bringing big poles to the garden, or carrying away the harvested yams."[3] After the harvest, each worker piled his yams for display under a small shelter of yam vine. Parties of natives would walk around comparing, criticising, and praising the best yields. In years when a good yield was likely, the chief might proclaim a competitive ceremonial **kayasa** display of yams, thereby increasing the straining to "achieve social distinction as a good gardener and a good worker in general." Trobriand competition was an "altruistic" competiton in the sense that three-fourths of the crop for which one worked so hard, and was honored, went to his relatives and to his chief. It was also part of a lifestyle that—compared with the aloofness and hostility of some neighboring people— was so open, friendly cooperative, and in the best sense "civilized," as to come to Malinowski "almost as a shock." Huizinga generalizes the significance of behavior like that of the Trobrianders:

> *From the life of childhood right up to the highest achievements of civilization one of the strongest incentives to perfection, both individual and social, is the desire to be praised and honored for one's excellence. In praising another each praises himself. We want to be honored for our virtues. We want the satisfaction of having done something well. Doing something well means doing it better than others. In order to excel one must prove one's excellence; in order to merit recognition, merit must be made manifest. Competition serves to give proof of superiority.*[4]

The Potlatch Syndrome

Malinowski's mention of "straining' in the special **kayasa** competititions suggests another kind of competitive display that was not so friendly and relaxed as that of the Trobriand islanders. This is the "potlatch" phenomenon traditionally found among the also preliterate Kwakiutl Indians of the Vancouver Island, British Columbia, and other Northwest Indian tribes from Puget Sound to Alaska.

Social position among the Kwakiutl was highly competitive, depending upon great wealth: the shells and etched copper sheets that served as money, cedar bark blankets, canoes, candlefish oil. It was not mere possession that counted, but competitive display. "We do not fight with weapons. We fight with property."[5] Every person of possible tribal importance, female or male, entered this competition as a child. Women made mats, baskets, and blankets for their men. There were two ways of claiming superiority over others. One could give lavishly of one's wealth, and if the receiver could not return with excessive interest (up to 100 percent) he was shamed. Or one could destroy one's property—burn one's candlefish oil or one's blankets, break up one's canoes or coppers, or kill his slaves. "The whole economic system of the Northwest Indians," says anthropologist Ruth Benedict, "was bent to the service of this obsession."[6] The most dramatic competitions were the **potlatches**, ceremonies offered by a tribal chief on the occasion of a marriage, birth, or death, a tatooing ceremony, a house raising, the coming to adolescence of a female, or as a challenge to the chief of another tribe. At the potlatch, the host chief was glorified by hymns sung by his retainers, which Benedict calls "unabashed megalomania":

> *I am the great chief who makes people ashamed. . . .*
>
> *Our chief makes people cover their faces by what he is continuously doing in this world, giving again and again oil feasts to all the tribes.*
>
> . . . .
>
> *Bring your counter of property, tribes, that he may try in vain to count the property that is to be given away by the great coppermaker, the chief.*[7]

In the potlatch, the chiefs vied in exhibiting their wealth through gifts of blankets, shells, coppers. The ultimate way of demonstrating superiority was to destroy one's wealth by fire. In one potlatch described to Benedict, the rival chief threw 7 canoes and 400 blankets on the host chief's fire in an attempt to put it out while his host poured valuable candlefish oil on the blaze to keep it alive. The roof of the host's house caught fire and the house was almost completely destroyed, while the host and his rival "kept their cool," continuing to throw more coppers, blankets and oil on the flame.[8]

Trobriand rivalry is not an **agon**; the potlatch is. While I used the term "healthy competition" to describe the Trobrianders, ritual display of yams, I think Benedict's terms "megalomania" and "obsession" better characterize the potlatch syndrome. Except for the name, the potlatch is not peculiar to the Northwest Indians. Like the Trobriand striving to excel in work, competitive display and destruction of possessions is a core type of human contest found in many cultures. Huizinga says, "Such competitions in unbridled liberality, with the frivolous destruction of one's own goods as the climax, are to be found all over the world." He believes that we should "regard the potlatch proper as the most highly developed form of a fundamental human need, which I would call playing for honor and glory."[9]

Comparable customs have been found in Greece, Rome, the old German culture, and in ancient China and India. There are similarities in the behavior of Cleopatra, going Mark Antony one better by dissolving her pearl in vinegar, and Philip of Burgundy, crowning a series of banquets given by his nobles by throwing a Gargantuan feast at which students ceremonially smashed the glassware.

In this chapter on contest and civilization it is significant that the Mahabharata, one of two great Asiatic Indian epics, depicts the world as a great dice game between the god Siva and his queen, and that Marcel Mauss, in his study of ritual gifts, says that "the Mahabharata is the story of a gigantic potlatch."[10]

The derivation of the word for the pre-Mohammedan Arabic equivalent of the potlatch, **mu'agāra**, shows the similarity: "to rival in glory by cutting up the feet of camels."[11] Huizinga thinks that this incident, recorded in an Egyptian newspaper, expresses the tradition of mu'agāra:

> *Two gypsies had a quarrel. In order to settle it they solemnly called the whole tribe together and then proceeded each one to kill his own sheep, after which they burned all the bank-notes they possessed. Finally, the man who saw that he was going to lose, immediately sold his six asses, so as to become victor after all by the proceeds. When he came home to fetch the asses his wife opposed the sale, whereupon he stabbed her."*[12]

Nor is the potlatch-mu'agāra syndrome found only in faraway times and places. "The manipulation of wealth on the Northwest Coast, says Benedict, "is clearly enough in many ways a parody of our own economic arrangements."[13] With probably no knowledge of the Kwakiutl, in 1889 the American sociologist Thorstein Veblen had described the "conspicuous consumption" and "conspicuous waste" that he saw making up so much of the life of the leisure class in western civilization. Writing in the middle of the United States' drive to affluence, Veblen spoke of how this conspicuous consumption and waste, which began with the leisure classes, was now being imitated by the rest of the people.

Ritual Spring Contests

A third core experience linking contest and civilization is human participation in divine struggles. To a person without modern scientific knowledge (and even to one with it) life and the world are mysterious and unpredictable. One mystery that is of life-and-death importance is the rotation of the seasons. Trees and plants bud into life in the spring, and are at their greenest and fullest in the summer. With autumn they begin to brown and die. The days get increasingly shorter, leaving the question: Will they ever get longer again? Will life return? In late December in the northern hemisphere (late June in the southern) the days are at their shortest and the nights their longest. The turning point has been reached. No wonder that this is the occasion for myths and rituals of rebirth. (We celebrate the birthday of Jesus on December 25 not because it is so recorded in the bureau of vital statistics at Bethlehem, but because this was the time of the pagan celebration of the winter solstice.)

For the study of sport and culture, the next turning point is the most important—the arrival of spring, with the return of fertility. With it comes the hard and uncertain task of bringing the year's food supply through to harvest. It is not strange that human beings, with limited powers, should project this as a struggle in which the gods are involved. The best known example is from the time and area where an economic surplus was first develped. The Egyptian sun god Osiris, who promoted fertility in plants and animals, was opposed by the god Set, who tried to block and undo his work, even to the point of murdering Osiris' son Horus. Preliterate peoples generally believe that by imitating or participating in the struggles of the gods they can influence the outcome, and thereby help themselves. So, at the festivals of spring, while the "good" gods were struggling to maintain fertility, the people would engage in contests—between villages, between sub-tribes, between women and men, between the married and the unmarried. "All these forms of contest," says Huizinga, "betray the connection with ritual over and over again by the constant belief that they are indispensable for the smooth running of the seasons, the ripening of crops, the prosperity of the whole year. . . Every victory represents, that is, realizes for the victor the triumph of the good powers over the bad, and at the same time the salvation of the group that effects it."[14]

A specific example of this "homeopathic reinforcement"will bring us to the threshold of sport. At the Egyptian Temple of Papremis, "more than a thousand" followers of Osiris would line up sone distance from the Temple, with an image of Osiris in a gilded box on a four-wheeled cart. Each man had a heavy wooden club. The object of the ceremony was to "rush" Osiris to and through the gates and door of the Temple. In the way stood an opposing array of priests, also armed with clubs. "There was hard fighting with clubs and heads were broken," but no lives lost.[15]

Here is a model of the "territorial" type of game—soccer, American football, hockey, lacrosse, basketball—with movement by a group, against opposition, toward a distant goal. First, we have the "team." H. I. Massingham suggest that peaceful conflict between teams arose in the ritual opposition of two parties who dramatized the conflict between departing winter and oncoming spring:

> *No sooner are we back in antiquity than we find it was the teams that made the game. Whenever it was played among peoples who. . . retained traces of the archaic culture which once overspread the world, we are made aware that it was a formal and sacred rite, conducted between two sections of the community. .. Out of this dualism rose the ball game which. . . was a ritualistic, spectacular exhibition of this dual grouping in action.*[16]

We have the teams, but what about the ball? In the fertility rite at the Temple of Paprimus there was no ball, but an object that served the purpose—the image of Osiris. In an earlier chapter I referred to the Afghan game of **buzkashi**, a polo-like contest in which the "ball" was the carcass of a calf or sheep. So a body, or image of one, can suffice. But it is an awkward object of contention. If one is going to play a territorial game, a head-shaped object is more practical than a whole body. Robert Henderson, in his book **Ball, Bat and Bishop**, feels that the ball originally represented the head of Osiris, or the sun (also a fertility symbol), or both.[17] In a fertility rite, which was often associated with a Saturnalia—a period of sexual license—, it could also have symbolized a testicle (note the double meaning of "ball").

Agon in Civilized Institutions

I have introduced three core elements that appear in human rivalry. Not all three are agonistic, especially if by **agon** we mean something close to **agonia** (agony). Trobriand-type emulation is the humane striving for excellence that underlies all contest. The potlatch and the territorial contest are the typically civilized forms of rivalry. The potlatch spirit is, as Huizinga says, the striving for honor, glory, and the sense of superiority. The territorial fertility ritual is the root of all those contests that mobilize intense group rivalry in what is conceived as a confrontation between light and darkness.

For the rest of this chapter, we shall see how these elements appear in the specific institutions of civilized society.

Agon in Political Life

First, law and order. Civilization is, at least in its highest forms, distinguished from savagery and barbarism by the "rule of law." An agreed-upon set of rules is supposed to supersede personal whim and force. The rules include procedures for ascertaining and dealing with violations. Disputes about the law originally were, and still are, settled by an **agon**, a fight within rules. "The winning as such," says Huizinga, "is for the archaic mind proof of truth and rightness."[18] The purest form of the judicial **agon** that we know about is the drumming-match as formerly practiced by the Greenland Eskimo. When two Eskimos had a difference, it was settled at a festive gathering of the clan or tribe at which, to the accompaniment of a drum, the opponents attacked each other through song and speech, with ridicule, satire, and pure slander. As in modern courtrooms, between sessions of mutual character assassination and sometimes physical abuse, the opponents might engage in friendly conversations. Like our litigation, the contest might go on as long as a period of years. At the end, the spectators decided which contestant had drummed the other down and therefore won the case. There was no idea of abstract justice: "this was the sole means of settling a dispute."[19]

In Java, law cases were formerly settled in an **adat**, in which skilled debaters poked little sticks into the ground for each "scoring" argument. The opponent with the most sticks was the winner. It took the ancient Greeks a long time, says Huizinga, to distinguish Dike (justice) from Tyche (chance) and Nemesis (vengeance). In the Middle Ages a typical form of trial was the Urteil (ordeal) in which ability to survive physical stress might be considered evidence of innocence. In England until 1571 civil suits could be settled by a ritualized personal battle, the last of which took place in that year at Westminster on a specially marked field sixty feet square. The courtroom today is a field of contest in many cases little removed from the drumming match or the **adat**. The trial is a typical game of strategy in which intimidation and deception are practiced within rules, and "justice" is a name given to the outcome.

Internal politics is also largely a game of strategy, in which it is more important to manipulate issues than to solve them. Marcel Granet found the ancient Chinese state related to the fertility contest: "The spirit of competition, which animated the men's societies or brotherhoods and set them against one another in the winter festivals in tournaments of dance and song comes at the beginning of the long line of development that led to State forms and institutions."[20] Research by a student of Huizinga showed that for about 200 years, debate in the British House of Commons has typically been "a continual match between the players whose object is to checkmate one another."[21] Of American politics Huizinga says, "Long before the two-party system had reduced itself to two gigantic teams whose political differences were hardly discernible to the outsider, electioneering in America had developed into a kind of national sport."[22] In the television age, it is a tactical spectator sport: report of the strategy and odds of a Presidential campaign is like nationwide coverage of a combined chess match, football game, and horse race.

International politics and diplomacy embody the braggadocio, magalomania, and obsessive self-aggrandizement that Benedict described in the potlatch. Huizinga's comment fits the traditional behavior of diplomats: "The potlatch spirit is akin to the thoughts and feelings of the adolescent."[23] That an international confrontation is a tactical game in which manipulation takes priority over solution is indicated by the sport metaphor in a **Christian Science Monitor** editorial on Prime Minister Menahem Begin's 1977 extension of social services to Arabs in Israeli-occupied territory: "Mr. Begin is proving to be a formidable leader and maneuverer. He is out front with the ball. The United States has yet to catch up."[24]

War, said the Prussian military theorist Clausewitz, is the continuation of diplomacy by other means. Another way of saying this is the definition of peace as "the period of cheating that comes between periods of fighting." As we saw earlier, war (as distinguished from angry personal fighting, ambush, raid, or punitive expedition) is a product of civilization. Organized, coordinated mass combat developed after the political state arose to enable a minority to protect its hold on the economic surplus, or to seize more. Except for the intermittent periods of mere "cheating," it has been the normal activity of nation states. It is the supreme form of physical skill-strategy game. As early as Old Testament day, it was a spectator sport: two contending military leaders say of their warriors, "Let the young men arise and play before us."[25] In the 1960s war was brought into American homes "in living color" along with Wide World of [other] Sports.

In the earliest civilizations war was a brutal and undisciplined affair. As waged, for example, by a Ghengis Khan, it was more savage than the worst behavior of preliterate "savages." Eventually war was "civilized." The chivalric code of the Middle Ages led to safeguards for prisoners and non-combatants, to an international law of war. "Chivalry," says Huizinga, "was one of the great stimulants of medieval civilization, . . . and one of the indispensable safeguards for the community of man."[26] War was brought under control as a game within rules. Sometimes, as in the "pitched" battle, these rules fitted our first definiton of play: combat was scheduled at a set time at a demarcated scene, like that of the judicial duel.

In the twentieth century the rules broke down and war became "total." With Coventry, Dresden, Auschwitz, and Hiroshima it ceased to be a "sporting" game. It still did remain a game in two senses. As I have said, media coverage makes it a spectator sport. For this, as Douglas MacArthur, Woody Hayes, and Max Rafferty have affirmed, athletics is an effective form of preparation and indoctrination. One of my football player students put the matter succinctly: "Football prepares young men for life, and life is war." War is also a game of the kind played in "game theory"—a sophisticated strategy game of dehumanized calculation in which abstractions ("casualties," "deterrence," "overkill") are manipulated as though no human beings were really present—a return to Genghis Khan with the twist of twentieth century computer technology. For this aspect the technically sophisticated coordination of football, with its detailed playbooks and pregame films on the "enemy," followed by telephonic calling of plays, may also be effective preparation.

Economic Life as a Game

What is true of politics is also true of economics. Consumptively, the civilized economy (the economy of economic surplus) has been a potlatch. Throughout most of civilization, only 1 to 5 percent of the population have been able to afford "conspicuous consumption" and "conspicuous waste." The rest of the people have had to be content to survive. With the coming of the "age of high mass consumption," an increasingly larger percentage of the population has got in on the show. Productively, a considerable part of human work has been motivated by Trobriand type emulation, and some still is. Pride in excellent craftsmanship, the striving to do one's best toward meeting human needs, were the motors of much economic activity until the rise of modern commercialism and industrialism. The best account of this is **Mutual Aid**, by Peter Kropotkin.[28] That this spirit of emulation is not impossible in the twentieth century is indicated by a speech made by a captain of industry in accepting an honorary degree from the Rotterdam Chamber of Commerce:

> *Ever since I entered the business it has been a race between the technicians and the sales department. One tried to produce so much that the sales department would never be able to sell it, while the other tried to sell so much that the technicians would never be able to keep pace. This race has always continued: sometimes one is ahead, sometimes the other. Neither my brother nor myself has regarded the business as a task, but always as a game, the spirit of which it has been our constant endeavor to implant in the younger staff.*[28]

However, as Kropotkin said, for the most part the economic life of industrial society is quite something else. Theoretically, market capitalism is a roulette wheel. This is clear for some when they "play" the stock market.

Insurance originated as a wager, and was referred to as "betting" as late as the seventeenth century. In a broader sense, profits in a capitalistic economy are theoretically a gambler's winning, as contrasted with the wages of management, which are the reward for hard and skilled work. This gamble is Caillois' **alea** (chance) (Table 3.1). But the productive and consumptive "rat race" is an **agon**, in which the vast majority lose, but both losers and winners suffer. In the race within the race, the agony of sport competition prepares a very few to win in the economy; the rest learn to lose. This is not peculiar to capitalism but to all modern industrial economies—the connection between victory and defeat in sport and victory and defeat in economic competition is just as true in the Soviet Union as here.

The Sexes and the Generations

The agonistic element is also found in the relationships within the family between the sexes and the generations. In the realm of sex, Huizinga says that while copulation itself is not play, the preliminary activities of "love play" are. In a wider sense, Kate Millett is certainly right in suggesting that, historically, relations between the sexes have been (and still essentially are) a political-economic strategy game in which the chief counters are (1) the male's ability to provide a livelihood, and (2) the female's ability to withhold her body.[29] In the future, since urban industrial society has taken away the male's monopoly on breadwinning, if relations between the sexes continue to be a game, the woman will in the nature of things hold the high card (her body). So males, having lost complete control over the paycheck, may have to stop playing games.

Industrial society has brought parent-child relationships within the realm of game-playing by breaking up the old patriarchal "extended" family and splitting childhood and adolescent peer groups away from the family group. Extremely rapid technical change has widened the "generation gap." Margaret Mead has said (I think with exaggeration) that "there are now no elders who know more than the young themselves about what the young are experiencing."[30] These changes have made relations between parents and children increasingly more of a strategy game in which parents try to perpetuate traditional cultural restrictions, especially on sexuality and independence, and youth seeks ways of avoiding or evading them. The generational game is especially manifest in education. The educational system serves mainly as a series of hurdles that stand between youth and admission to the jobs necessary for participating in the cultural potlatch, and the chief interest of most students is in "beating the game." A large part of the game is a matter of memorizing and regurgitating, for grades, information that the "players" (most students, and sometimes teachers) don't really understand, and in which they have little interest. An important part of the educational strategy game is the educational testing monopoly (or oligopoly) that sets up the major hurdles: SATs, College Boards, GREs, NTEs, LSATs, MCATs, and so on. For most students, the main objective is to learn the gimmicks necessary to win this hurdle race, and teachers are under pressure to make their courses practice sessions in hurdle-hopping.

"High Culture" as Contest

We come finally to the role of **agon** in the development of those "higher" cultural activities that grow out of economic surplus. It is reasonably clear that politics, which is the realm of power, is a contest. In a society that claims competition as the motor of economic life it is not hard to see the agonistic element there also. Kate Millett aside, the "war of the sexes" is a commonplace, as is the battle of the generations. But we are likely to think that the "high culture"—"refinement of thought, emotions, manners, taste, etc."[31] is above the agonistic hustle and bustle of more everyday life. Not at all. It is with the agonistic roots of drama, poetry and art, philosophy and science, that we shall now deal.

Although Caillois distinguishes drama from **agon**, without tension and conflict—between person and person, person and nature, person and inner self, person and Fate or god, god and god—there is no high drama (comedy, tragedy, or tragic comedy, for as Socrates said, all life is both and so should drama be). The territorial Osiris "game" at Papremis was a ritual religious drama, as were also the other spring fertility contests between villages, sub-tribes, women and men, married and unmarried—all **dramatic agon**. The circumstances as well as the content of drama have usually been antagonistic. The Greek dramatists composed their plays for competitions at the feast of Dionysius with "the whole public. . . sharing the tension of the contest like a crowd at a football match."[32] Production of drama is no less (and no more) agonistic today, with intense competition for Oscars, Emmys, Tonys, and on-Broadway runs.

"All poetry," according to the author of **Homo Ludens**, "is born of play: the sacred play of worship, the festive play of courtship, the martial play of the contest, the disputatious play of braggadacio, mockery and invective, the nimble play of wit and readiness."[33] Greek poetry also had its origin in ritual contests in which men and women "put one another down" at the feasts of Demeter and Dionysius. Some find in this "battle of the sexes" the original meaning of the word "iambos" (derision). (Students familiar with Shakespeare will recall that most of his plays are written in iambic pentameter verse form.) Derisive ritual chants gave rise to political satire. "Thus from an immemorial custom of ritual nature, iambic poetry became an instrument of public criticism."[34]

"In few human activities," says Huizinga "is competition more ingrained than in music."[35] He notes how easily musicians and followers of musicians fall into factions and cliques. In 1726, for example, all London society was lined up in competition between two Italian singers, with resultant catcalls and some actual fisticuffs. In the following century, there was a "lasting and embittered feud" between the followers of Wagner and those of Brahms. Were he alive in the late twentieth century, Huizinga could observe similar antagonisms between devotees of competing rock groups. In the arts of painting and sculpture, we have to note that in medieval Europe the "masterpiece" was originally the production marking successful completion of the competition that led to admission to the group of "masters."

Of all the elements in the high culture, we are least likely to think of philosophy and science as agonistic. Many people believe that philosophers and scientists are engaged in the "passionless pursuit of passionless knowledge." Historically, this has not generally been the case, and it seldom is today. Knowledge is power—over nature and over one's fellow-humans. Because it is the key to the unknown, we are likely to give to knowledge a magical or a sacred quality. So are we likely to do with those who possess it. The tribal medicine man, the priest, the scientist, have an aura, a "charisma," that gives them power in the strategy game of civilization.

It should not be surprising at this point that philosophy, like most of the high and low culture, arose in contest. "For archaic man, doing and daring are power, but knowing is magical power. . . Competitions in esoteric knowledge are deeply rooted in ritual and form an essential part of it.[36] Philosophy has always been polemic (from the Greek word **polemis**, war), rooted in dispute and argument. The earliest form was the riddle-contest, which school children still know very well, an **agon** whose object is to put down the other person by demonstrating his ignorance. In its earliest form this contest posed questions about the ultimate nature of the universe. These are embodied, for example, in the verses of the Indian religious classic, the Rig-Veda:

Who know it, and who shall declare where this Creation was born and whence it came?

. . . . . .

I ask you about the uttermost ends of the earth; I ask you, where is the navel of the earth? I ask you about the seed of the stallion; I ask you, where is the highest place of speech?[37]

The riddle-contest might be literally a matter of life and death. The early Greek poet Hesiod relates the myth of the wise men Chalcas and Mopsos. Chalcas had been told that he would die if he ever met a person wiser than himself. He encountered Mopsos, who engaged him in a riddle-contest and beat him. Chalcas either died of grief or killed himself, and his followers joined Mopsos.[38] Huizinga maps out the agonistic development of philosophy: "Gradual transitions lead from the sacred riddle-contest concerning the nature of things to the catch-question contest, with honor, possessions, or dear life at stake, and finally to the philosophical disputation."[39] By putting his philosophy in dialogue form, with Socrates as his spokesman, Plato reflected the agonistic nature of the search for truth. In fact, Socrates and Plato were considered by some to represent only a higher level of riddle-posing point scorers. Polemics readied a height in the medieval university, where "to beat your opponent by reason of the force of the work becomes a sport comparable with the profession of arms."[40] As a graduate of the University of Chicago, I can say that some circles in modern universities are not much different.

Science, which derives its conclusions by induction from carefully controlled observations, might seem very far removed from the potlatch and spring fertility rites. However, science is less often the objective pursuit of passionless knowledge than it is a passionate search, sometimes for verifiable truths, but very often for fame, position, money. Citing the expansion of knowledge in the seventeenth and eighteenth centuries, Huizinga says, "All knowledge is polemical by nature, and polemics cannot be divorced from agonistics. Epochs in which great new treasures of the mind come to light are generally periods of violent controversy."[41] The early American sociologist Lester F. Ward, originally a biologist, likened the progress of science to a prairie fire in which the line of the fire advances by catching up with licks of flame represent the creative pioneers, passionately riding unacceptable hypotheses that in the long run become parts of the accepted body of science. The "run" is usually long, because most scientists, like most people in general, are threatened by, and fight, discoveries that do not fit their view of the world. Copernicus' statement of the heliocentric theory of the universe, Harvey's discovery of the circulation of the blood, Semmelweis' experimental proof of the value of antisepsis, and the work of Freud and Wilhelm Reich on the sexual basis of psychological and social pathology, are all examples.

One thing common to all forms of the high culture—drama, poetry, music, visual and plastic art, philosophy, and science—is the tendency to form "schools," groups united by allegiance to an idea, style, or person, and intensely antagonistic to other schools. Here we are back at the fertility contests: each follower of an artistic, philosophical, or scientific school is likely to believe her/himself to be engaged in a mortal struggle between the forces of light and darkness.

Where do we arrive after our survey of the role of contest in civilization? At the end of **Homo Ludens**, Huizinga concludes:

> *Real civilization cannot exist in the absence of a certain play-element, for civilization presupposes limitation and mastery of the self, the ability not to confuse its own tendencies with the ultimate and highest goal, but to understand that it is enclosed within certain bounds freely accepted. . . True civilization will always demand fair play. Fair play is nothing less than good faith expressed in play terms.*[42]

Such a "true" or "real" civilization we have not seen yet. From the standpoint of this book, I think the civilization we have seen up to the present is most realistically described as **a many-dimensional game of strategy in which 1 to 5 percent of the population have dominated the other 95 to 99 percent within a system of rules that has ensured physical survival and certain minimal rights to most members of both parties.**

This may seem a dim and perhaps cynical view of the role of contest in the "high" and "low" aspects of the "culture of cities." This will be true only if we forget the first of our three types of striving for excellence—Trobriand-type emulation. Everywhere, behind the struggle and the manipulation, no matter how bizarrely twisted their strivings may become, people struggle to excel in overcoming scarcity, in cooperating with their fellows toward common human goals, in creating more of knowledge, wisdom, beauty, and goodness—the qualities that are in the best sense civilized.

FOOTNOTES

[1]Johan Huizinga, **Homo Ludens: A Study of the Play Element in Culture**, Boston, Beacon, 1964, 5.

[2]Bronislaw Malinowski, **Argonauts of the Western Pacific: An Account of Native Enterprise and Adventure in the Archipelagoes of Melanesian New Guinea**, New York, Dutton, 1950.

[3]**Ibid.**, 60-61.

[4]Huizinga, **op. cit.**, 63.

[5]Ruth Benedict, **Patterns of Culture**, Boston, Houghton Mifflin, 1934, 189.

[6]**Ibid.**, 193.

[7]**Ibid.**, 190.

[8]**Ibid.**, 199-200.

[9]Huizinga, **op. cit.**, 59, 62.

[10]**Essai sur le Don, L'Annee Sociologique**, 1923-1924, cited in Huizinga, **op. cit.**, 59.

[11]**Ibid.**, 59.

[12]**Ibid.**, 61.

[13]Benedict, **op. cit.**, 188.

[14]Huizinga, **op. cit.**, 56.

[15]Robert W. Hunderson, **Ball, Bat, and Bishop: The Origin of Ball Games**, New York, Rockport Press, 1947, 8-9.

[16]H. I. Massingham, "Origins of Ball Games," in **The Heritage of Man**, London, 1929, 208-227, cited in **ibid.**, 15.

[17]Henderson, **op. cit.**, 17-19.

[18]Huizinga, **op. cit.**, 81.

[19]**Ibid.**, 85.

[20]Marcel Granet, **Chinese Civilization**, London, Routledge, 1930, 204.

[21]Huizinga, **op. cit.**, 207.

[22]**Ibid.**

[23]**Ibid.**, 60.

[24]**Christian Science Monitor**, August 17, 1977, 32.

[25]Second Book of Samuel, ii, 14.

[26]Huizinga, **op. cit.**, 96.

[27]Peter A. Kropotkin, **Mutual Aid: A Factor in Evolution**, Boston, Porter Sargent, 1955.

[28]Cited in Huizinga, **op. cit.**, 200.

[29]Kate Millett, **Sexual Politics**, Garden City, N.Y., Doubleday, 1970.

[30]Margaret Mead, **Culture and Commitment: A Study of the Generation Gap**, Garden City, N.Y., Doubleday, 1970, 82.

[31]**Webster's New Twentieth Century Dictionary**, 2nd ed., New York, World, 1975, 444.

[32]Huizinga, **op. cit.**, 145.

[33]**Ibid.**, 129.

[34]**Ibid.**, 68.

[35]**Ibid.**, 163.

[36]**Ibid.**, 105.

[37]**Hymns of the Rig-Veda**, 10, 1.

[38]Hesiod, **Fragments**, 160.

[39]Huizinga, **op. cit.**, 113.

[40]**Ibid.**, 155.

[41]**Ibid.**, 156.

[42]**Ibid.**, 211.

CHAPTER 8 SPORT AND SOCIAL POWER

Chapter 7 concluded with the thought that the rewards of civilization are distributed very unequally. In Chapter 8 we will ask how organized sport affects the distribution of social power. Does it give significant opportunities to the powerless? Or does it strengthen the hold of those who have power? There are basically two views on this matter. One holds that sport is a significant way for those socially at the bottom to get up in the world. The other holds that sport reinforces the values by which those on the bottom are held down.

We can discuss the question most meaningfully by looking at the site of the most widely and highly organized sport activity—the United States. The basic fact with which to begin is that the culture of the United States has historically been dominated by male WASPs (White Anglo-Saxon Protestants). The specific question here will be: how has sport increased, or decreased, the power of male WASPs in American society?

Historically, sport in the United States has spread from the English-Scottish group that has historically been dominant, to include members of one after another non-WASP minority—Germans, Irish, Poles, Italians, Jews, and most recently, blacks and Latins. Before the Civil War, as we saw in Chapter 5, sport was primarily an upper-class game in the British tradition, centering around such activities as fox hunting and horse racing. The latter part of the nineteenth century was the period of industrial take-off, with rapid growth of cities, and immigration of eastern and southern Europeans who made up a large part of the labor force. Around the turn of the twentieth century, along with other industries, they began to move into sport, which had become a mass spectator business.

Football and Ethnic Mobility

An illustrative case is football. Allen Sack has written interestingly of the rise of Yale to football prominence over Harvard in the late nineteenth century.[1] Harvard football, played mainly by Anglo-Saxons from around Boston, was up to then a "gentlemen's" sport, in which excessive concern with winning was not quite proper. Yale, under the leadership of Walter Camp, with non-WASP players recruited from a much wider section of the country, played to win in a manner that in the British tradition was "unsporting," and beat Harvard 29 times in 33 years. In one year in the late 1890s, almost all the Harvard team came from near Boston, while Yale represented Connecticut, New York, Ohio, Illinios, Kansas, Virginia, and Arkansas. One of Yale's heroes, Pudge Heffelfinger, was in 1889 the first non-Anglo-Saxon to be named to the All-America team. Up to then the top gridiron jocks had names like Adams, Ames, and Channing.

The history of All-America teams from then to the present shows the ethnic shift, which was also a shift away from the Ivy League schools, and a shift away from players of New England origin. In 1889 and 1890, the team came entirely from Harvard, Yale, and Princeton. As the years went by, the team spread geographically to include these schools:

1891-5	Pennsylvania
1898	Chicago
1900	Columbia
1907	West Point, Cornell, Brown
1909	Michigan
1912	Wisconsin
1915	Pittsburgh
1916	Minnesota, Ohio State
1918	Nebraska[2]

Ethnically, after Heffelfinger broke the WASP monopoly, there came, from 1895 to 1924, Murphy (the first Irishman), Hershberger, Daly, Hagarty, Rafferty, Sheahin, Pierkarski (the first Pole), Bowditch, Eckersall, Hogan, McCormick, Ziegler, Schultz, Fish, Goebel, Tobin, Schillmiller, Hollenback, Fisher, Bomeister, Mulbetsch, Schlachter, Oliphant, Callahan, Allendinger, Stein, Schwab, Garbisch, Bedenk, Bjorkman, Stuhldreher, Koppisch. In the 1920s, there were Friedman and Luckman, in the 1930s Goldberg. The first black All-America player was William H. Lewis of Harvard, in 1892 and 1893, the next was Paul Robeson, in 1918. Although there were black professional baseball players in the late 1900s, and a black man finished fifth in the 1896 United States Open Golf tournament, it was not until Jackie Robinson broke the baseball barrier in 1947 that more than a few isolated blacks (like the early pro Fritz Pollard, Buddy Young at Illinois, Willis Ward at Michigan, and Marion Motley of the Cleveland Browns) appeared on the major football scene. Today blacks have superseded the previous minorities—Germans, Irish, Poles, Italians, Jews—and dominate football, basketball, and baseball, as well as boxing. The only significant non-black minority remaining are Latins in baseball.

In 1948, while the minorities in sport were still predominantly white, a refugee intellectual working as a coal loader wrote of the significance of sports for young men of eastern and southern European extraction in America's industrial areas. He saw athletics as a way out for those on the bottom of the heap:

> *The impossibility of attaining human goals in real life, in production and in social relations led to sublimation in the fanciful reflex world of sports. . . To the chosen few, athletics became a road to success. Individual ability could find expression in sporting events . . . to an extent not discoverable elsewhere in society. The worker no longer dreamed of being a capitalist; he wanted to be a football hero. . . Multi-syllabic Eastern European names became the means by which great universities were identified. . For every ten thousand who became aware of a shadowy Bertrand Russell [British philosopher] there could be ten million acutely aware of the diet and vital statistics of a Goldberg who could run back punts. But to become a Goldberg required only ability, to become a Russell required membership in another class.*[3]

Such was the way out, and up, for long-time football star George Blanda, who said of his childhood, "Hell, first thing you wanted to do was to escape the mines and that image of being a drunken, stupid, dirty Polish coal miner."[4] It was the way for the bus driver's son who got his best football offer from the University of Miami, "I've broken a leg, my nose, and my ass for this place, but at least I've gotten a degree. I won't have to drive a bus now." It was also the way for the other Miami football player who said:

> *Being from Pennsylvania, I have seen guys leave those steel mill and coal mining towns by athletics. Most of them understand life at a very early age. The reason is perfectly clear. They see their parents work themselves into the ground and don't want to end up that way. So, the only solution is to do well in college.*

It was also the way up for Gayle Sayers, who told high school students of his "escape": "I grew up there, I lived in the ghetto, but I never let the ghetto live in me."[5]

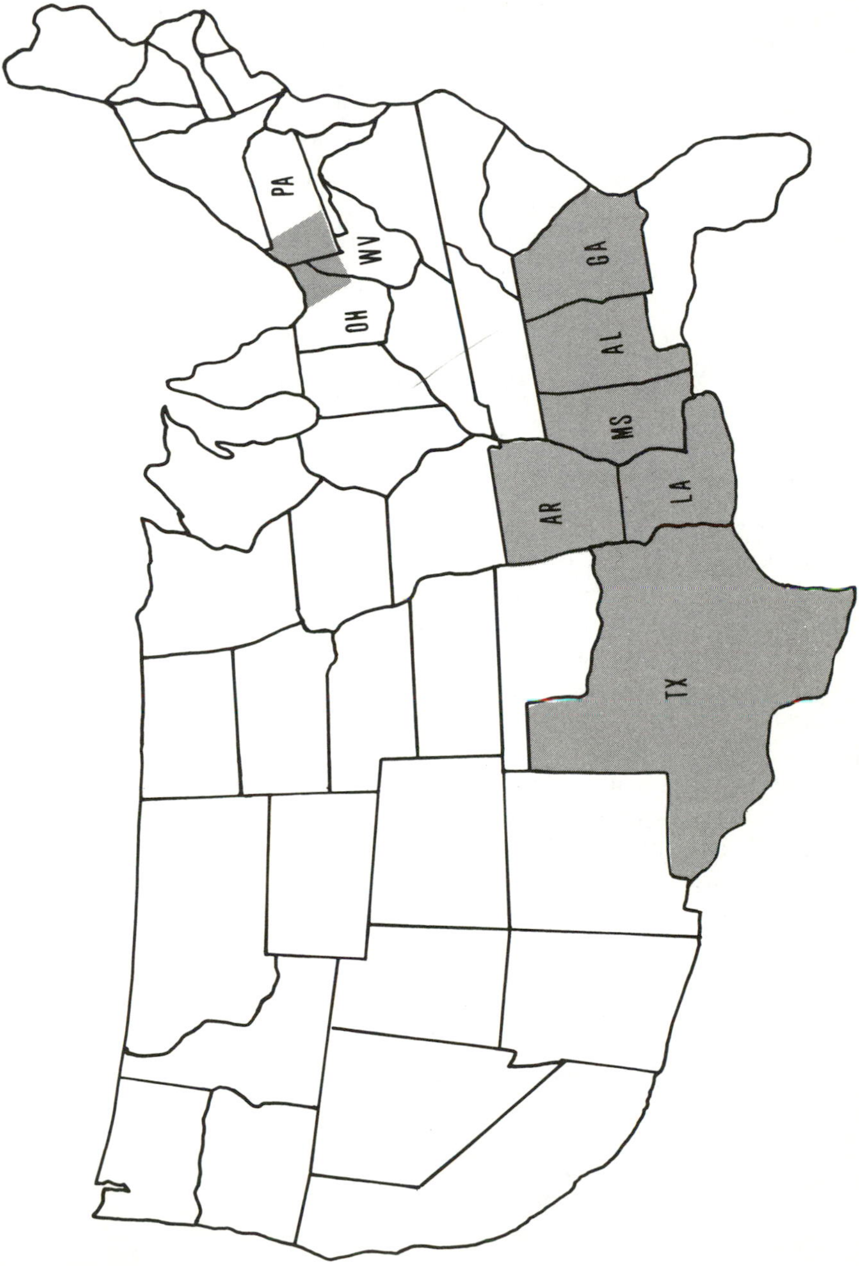

Football players came from the northern and coal-steel belt and the rural south. *Based on John F. Rooney,* **A Geography of American Sports,** *Reading, Mass., Addison-Wesley, 1974.*

I spoke earlier of a shift in the area from which athletes originate. John F. Rooney's **A Geography of American Sports**[6] shows two major areas from which football players come at present. One is a belt running from Johnstown, Pa., through the Pittsburgh area, across West Virginia, then to Cleveland. This area Saxon, the intellectual coal miner, described in 1948 as "a coal mining area where the degradation of modern society is epitomized by an enervating industrial complex."[7] The other area is the South from Georgia to Texas. James Michener explains this geography of athletic origins: "We don't find young people of promise from the advantaged states like Wisconsin, Iowa, Connecticut, and Oregon bothering with professional sports. They don't have to."[8]

The Sociology of Ethnic Mobility

Research by sport sociologists John Loy and Harry Webb throws further light on the upward mobility of athletes on the social ladder. Loy studied the social origins of 1021 Life Pass holders at the University of California at Los Angeles.[9] To be a Life Pass holder, one must have competed in college sport for 4 years and earned at least 3 varsity letters. Each Life Pass holder filled out a long questionnarie, and was scored in terms of a social status scale devised by Otis Dudley Duncan. Wrestlers, boxers, baseball and football players (three of these in contact sports) typically had lower-class fathers (Duncan scores of 43 to 49), and had themselves moved to the status of college graduates. Fencers, crewmen, ice hockey, cricket, tennis, and golf players typically had upper-class fathers to begin with (status scores of 60 to 74), so had nowhere to rise. Another measure was the percentage of athletes in different sports who had moved up from blue-collar backgrounds. The figures ran this way:[10]

Wrestling	48.1
Baseball	36.5
Football	34.6
Track	30.5
Soccer	26.3
Gymnastics	26.3
Basketball	16.4
Swimming	14.3
Tennis	13.3
Crew	10.4

Again, the wrestlers and baseball and football players had the greatest mobility. If the figures for basketball players with blue-collar figures seem low, this is probably because these figures cover all UCLA athletic history, most of which was before basketball became a sport mainly for ghetto graduates.

The percentages of those whose fathers had not finished high school again show football, wrestling, and baseball at the top:[11]

Football	51.59
Wrestling	49.99
Baseball	49.98
Track	43.30
Gymnastics	38.21
Basketball	37.38
Swimming	27.15
Tennis	25.19
Crew	23.87
Soccer	22.85

A "longitudinal" picture of mobility over an athlete's lifetime was given by comparing the status of the father's regular job with that of the son's first job after graduating and then with this present job:[12]

Status Scores

	Father's Main Job	Son's First Job	Son's Present Job
Wrestling	43	70	77
Football	48	63	74
Baseball	49	64	75
Soccer	51	74	79
Track	53	67	77
Basketball	57	69	77
Gymnastics	58	67	80
Crew	62	67	78
Swimming	63	67	78
Tennis	64	70	75

Again, the sports are in essentially the same order, but we have a more detailed view. Loy comments that "perhaps the most striking aspect. . . is the great degree of social mobility achieved by athletes whose parents had the lowest socio-economic status.[13]

Athletes had a surprising degree of academic success. About 44 percent had earned degrees beyond the bachelor's:[14]

Gymnastics	61.75%
Soccer	54.28
Wrestling	50.00
Track	45.79
Swimming	45.67
Basketball	43.91
Tennis	40.72
Baseball	37.11
Crew	29.85
Football	29.21

Another indicator of mobility was political preference. Since part preference is associated with social status (as one moves up in the world, he is more likely to be Republican), it is interesting that two groups with lower-class fathers had strong Republican preference (wrestlers 60.71%, football players 55.70%). In this connection, it is again relevant that Michener reports that of 60 athletes he has known well, only one was a Democrat, and that he knows no football coach who is a Democrat.[15]

The overall picture we get from the Life Pass study is that sport at UCLA, particularly the bodily contact sports, has offered a way up in the world to sons of lower-status parents. Another study, by Harry Webb, of 253 Michigan State athletes between 1958 and 1962, indicates that sport is not a significant way up for those at the very bottom of the ladder. He found Michigan State jocks drawn mainly from the middle three-fifths of the population. The United States Census classifies families in terms of five income groups from the top fifth (in 1960, over $9000) to the bottom fifth (in 1960, under $2800). Webb ranked his 253 athletes in terms of the fifth in which their family fell. The result: "Very few of the athletes come from [the] bottom fifth and not many of them come from the top fifth either. Athletes come. . . not from the poorest or the richest fifth, but from the middle income level."[16] The chance that the result could have occured by chance alone was less than one in a thousand ($p < .001$).

It was possible that individual sports (such as fencing, tennis, and golf) had loaded the results. To check this, Webb compared the income for families of 166 team sport athletes with the national distribution and found them, too, coming from the middle three-fifths. Again, the probability of chance was less than one in a thousand. Finally, calculating for 111 football players alone, he found them coming from the same middle three-fifths (again, $p < .001$).

Webb's results are reconciled somewhat with Loy's when we look at his classification of athletes in the major team sports (baseball, football, hockey, and basketball) in terms of their father's occupations. Close to three times as many major team sport athletes (65.6 percent) had fathers listed in "trades" or "labor," as had fathers who were listed as "professional," "technical," "clerical," or "sales" (23.2 percent). From Webb's Census data, we could judge that they were predominantly skilled or semiskilled rather than unskilled. His listing of sports in order of father's occupational status does not look very different from Loy's:[17]

1. Golf
2. Fencing
3. Tennis
4. Swimming
5. Baseball
6. Wrestling
7. Gymnastics
8. Track
9. Hockey
10. Football
11. Basketball

Webb's sample, active as athletes much later than most of Loy's, reflect the recent drop in the social origins of basketball players.

A Polish study shows that it is not only in the United States that sport serves as a ladder of upward mobility. Zbigniev Szot and Bogdan Jurkiewicz compared the social backgrounds of Polish gymnasts of the beginning level (first class), participants in the Polish national championships (national champion class) and participants in international competition (international champion class).[18] First, it was found that first class and national class gymnasts from intellectual families did better than those of working class origin. But, "this theses found no confirmation in the highest (international) class, where competitors of working class origin obtained results better. . . than their counterparts coming from the families of intellectuals." The reason? At the beginning, on the lower levels of competition, the white collar athletes have the advantage of not having to work to help support their families, and can go to school, where they have required physical education. But on the higher levels, the working class have started earlier, are helped by their experience in physical work, and are more strongly motivated. "Men who started to train gymnastics at the age of 10-12 years achieved the biggest success and they come from workers' families." Furthermore, for gymnasts of blue-collar origin there is "a possibility of promotion through practising of gymnastics which is greater than in the case of competitors from the families of intellectuals." Therefore, "they are more strongly committed to sport activitiy and show more perseverance in the difficult training for gymnastic exercises." I think that the factors of early beginning, physical work, and motivation outlined by the Polish sociologists would also help us understand why working-class Polish-American athletes and athletes from other ethnic minorities succeed in the American sport system.

The Perils of Upward Mobility

We have looked at what is true in the American dream of making it through athletics. Now what is false about it? I will start with two sociological researches, the first a group of uneducated athletes, the second a group of educated ones.

In a study of "the occupational culture of the boxer,"[19] S. Kerson Weinberg and Henry Arond found that boxers are typically uneducated. "A fighter with an education is a fighter who does not have to fight to live and he knows it. . . Only for a hungry fighter is it a decent gamble."[20] Boxers also come from ethnic minorities in areas of social disorganization, near the center of the city. There has been the ethnic succession typical of the bodily contact sports: "First Irish, then Jewish, then Italian, were most numerous among prominent boxers; now, Negroes."[21] Table 8.1, showing how ethnic groups ranked 1-2-3 in number of top fighters for a number of years, is as clear a picture of the ethnic athletic succession as we are likely to get.

Table 8.1 Rank Order of Number of Prominent Boxers of Various Ethnic Groups for Certain Years

	Rank 1	Rank 2	Rank 3
1909	Irish	German	English
1916	Irish	German	Italian
1928	Jewish	Italian	Irish
1936	Italian	Irish	Jewish
1948	Negro	Italian	Mexican

Source—S. Kirkson Weinberg and Henry Arond, "The Occupational Culture of the Boxer," **American Journal of Sociology, 57**, March, 1952, Table 1. Copyright © 1952 by the University of Chicago Press.

What happens in terms of social mobility? If a boxer is good, he may rise rapidly and early. But his decline is as spectacular as his rise. The tremendous physical beating boxers take, plus their tendency to squander their sudden earnings, plus their lack of non-boxing skills, is likely to make for an unhappy future.

Of ninety-five leading former boxers (i.e., champions and leading contenders), each of whom earned more than $100,000 during his ring career, eighteen were found to have remained in the sport as trainees or trainer-managers; two became wrestlers; twenty-six worked in, "fronted for," or owned taverns; two were liquor salesmen; eighteen had unskilled jobs, most commonly in the steel mills; six worked in gas stations; three were cab drivers; three had newsstands; two were janitors; three were bookies; three were associated with the race tracks . . .; and two were in business, one as a custom tailor.[22]

In 1975 Paul Dubois compared 160 athletes and 450 nonathletes who had graduated two years before from San Francisco, San Jose, and Hayward state universities.[23] On a social prestige scale developed by the National Opinion Research Center, he found no significant difference between the two groups. He also found no significant difference in annual income. He did find that team athletes had significantly higher job status ratings than individual sport athletes, perhaps because they were more sociable. In general Dubois said that his results "raise questions, especially for minority students, about whether they should put more time into academics and less into athletics. It's a myth that athletics is a steppingstone to success for most college athletes and students should know this."[24]

Athletes are likely to forget the tremendous odds against their individual success in sports. There are, of course, Joe Louis, Rocky Marciano, Muhammed Ali, Bronko Nagurski, O. J. Simpson, Henry Aaron, Carl Yastrzemski, Bill Russell, Bill Bradley, Kareem Abdul-Jabbar, Pancho Gonzales, Lee Trevino, Jimmy Conners. But 99 percent of athletes do not reach this kind of stardom.

In basketball, the current hope of black kids for exit from the ghetto, in 1974 there were 200,000 high school seniors and 5700 college seniors, of whom 211 were drafted and 55 signed.[25] Thus the men signed were 1 percent of the number of college seniors and 3/100 of one percent of the number of high school senior players. Of such chances Bob Cousy, a non-black who did make stardom, says,

Looking back, I'm amazed at how few individuals or teams ever make it in pro sports. Competition decrees that every year the losers outnumber the winners by twenty to one in the standings, by hundreds to one in the draft. Hating to lose as much as I do, I'm coming to realize that losing is the fate of almost everyone in one way or another, even those with talent, brains, and desire.[26]

In football, in the fall of 1968 there were 900,000 boys playing high school ball, and fewer than 30,000 college players.[27] Jack Scott, who himself was a jock on college football scholarship, says, "Schoolboys who spend four years of high school dreaming of collegiate gridiron glory are suddenly confronted by reality on graduation day. For every Broadway Joe Namath there are hundreds of sad, disillusioned men standing on street corners and sitting in the beer halls of Pennsylvania towns such as Scranton, Beaver Falls, and Altoona."[28]

In baseball, the other major sport, Department of Labor figures show millions of boys in Little League, 400,000 in high school ball and 25,000 college players, about 100 of whom will make it to the majors. "And just a handful of these will have a career that lasts as long as seven years."[29]

Thomas Tutko and William Bruns tell us, in summary, that as an avenue of upward mobility, the whole sports industry, which is only about half as big as the canned soup business, in 1975 fielded in six major team sports (football, basketball, hockey, baseball, tennis, and soccer) about 135 teams, with no more than 3500 active players, of whom no more than 1740 were starters.[30]

Harold Charnovsky, in his study of how baseball players see themselves, has stated very concisely the plight of the athletic failure: "Those who fall by the wayside represent a poignant study in disappointment and frustration, a failure to fulfill the American dream. The real tragedy lies not in their failure alone, for all men may fail, but in their failure after total commitment. They are unprepared to do anything else, despite baseball's claim that unsuccessful players are young enough to enter other fields."[31]

What happens when an athlete beats the tremendous odds and makes it to the top? First of all, he can anticipate only a few years of earning power before he is "over the hill" (in major league sports, about five). In those years he must earn his lifetime income, unless he is well enough known to cash in on his reputation in a big way while he is active or after he retires. When we consider that this is his lifetime income, the $140,000 per year earned by the average major league baseball player may not be so outlandish as it can seem to a college professor who compares it with his own mere $25,000. In addition to the brevity of the athlete's earning span, there is the risk. Apart from the fact that he is unlikely to retire from a bodily contact sport without some degree of permanent disability, the athlete's whole lifetime income is wagered on his chance of maintaining through his active career a high degree of health and efficiency in a body that was not constructed for the kinds of stresses that are routine in major sports. There is no lifetime income insurance to protect against what may happen when a running back's trick knee or a pitcher's arthritic elbow gives out (especially if he is a minor player).

Another problem of the athlete on the way up is **tracking**. This is the term among educators for the system by which students are channeled back into the occupational status of their parents. Athletic tracking closes out other opportunities for upward mobility that might be open. By his junior high school years, a prospective athlete has learned that his sport comes first, his schoolwork second. Thus he is shut out of the learning through which he might eventually become a businessman, scientist, physician, or lawyer. This tracking continues into college. Dave Meggyesy wrote of his experience at Syracuse University, "By the time I graduated, I knew it was next to impossible to be a legitimate student and a football player too. There is a clear conflict, and it is always resolved on the side of the athletic department."[32] This is essentially true for any major sport.

The Athletic Subculture

Beyond the economic gamble involved in sport as a career, there are for the professional (or "amateur") athlete the hazards of committing himself or herself to an athletic subculture that is essentially racist, sexist, nationalist, militarist, and anti-democratic.

Although they may disagree on details, outspoken critics and supporters agree that this is about where the sport subculture stands in the whole social scene. George Sauer, who said he loved football so much that he had to stop playing, told Jack Scott why:

> *I think football has come to look a bit like our country does at certain times. I think the same powers that keep a football player pretty much locked in place throughout his whole career are the same kind of powers that would tend to keep black and disadvantaged minorities, Mexican-Americans and Indians, locked in place. The ideology of football's power structure is pretty much the same as that of the nations's power structure.*[33]

Gary Shaw, another alumnus of University of Texas football, was equally pointed: "Football is the strongest remaining unquestioned remnant of an old culture, and the struggle to change its current form is no less than the conflict between an old culture and a new culture."[34]

Also from the South, which we have seen is a major supplier of athletic talent, Coach Pepper Rodgers of Georgia Tech saw essentially the same confrontation, but from a different point of view: "Football is exciting in the South because this is such a masculine-oriented country. The kids are brought up to consider it an honor and a privilege to play football. In a Southern high school you have to play football to be accepted as a man. It's like fighting for your country."[35]

Tom Hamilton, formerly coach at the United States Naval Academy, also saw his sport as a bastion of American values: "I think football is the greatest thing we have in education today. I wish every kid could get it; and I don't mind questioning and so forth, but if they are going to be responsible men, they have to learn to express their opinions and make their conduct in accord with the American system, and I say that's a pretty damn good system."[36]

Max Rafferty, another successful coach and once California Superintendent of Public Instruction, in 1969 drew a standing ovation from a meeting of California athletic directors with these ideas:

> *There are two great national institutions which simply cannot tolerate either internal dissension or external interference: our armed forces, and our interscholastic sports program. Both are of necessity benevolent dictatorships because by their very nature they cannot be otherwise. . . Your choice is simple: you can back up your coaches' authority to do with their teams what coaches have done for the last hundred years, or you can play a cowardly game of patty-cake with the activists and watch your sports program go down the drain with your own jobs going right along with it.*[27]

If my quotations seem loaded with football players and coaches, it is not because they represent the feelings of all people in all sports but because, as Gary Shaw said, football is the strongest example of the athletic subculture.

In recent years, sport has not been the most racist part of our society. In a sense, sport was ahead of the rest of the country in racial desegregation. The first black major league athletes in recent times were Marion Motley, fullback, and Bill Willis, linebacker, signed by the football Cleveland Browns in 1946, eight years before the Supreme Court desegregation of schools. The following year the baseball Brooklyn Dodgers signed Jackie Robinson, partly because owner Branch Rickey reasoned that if Motley and Willis had survived in a contact sport, Robinson could make it on the diamond. Four years later, and still three years before Brown *v.* Topeka, the first black major pro basketball player joined the N.B.A., helped by the fact that a white North Carolinian asked to be his roommate. Athletic desegregation has occurred, however, because it is good business. As soon as the Universities of Alabama and Mississippi became convinced that blacks could win games, these institutions—where George Wallace had personally barred the door to a black woman, and federal troops were necessary to admit a black man to graduate study—began to recruit them. But this does not mean that they were recruited as equals.

Racial attitudes, in the athletic subculture run all the way from baseball manager Alvin Dark's thoughtless remark about the deficiencies of Latin and black players to the feelings credited to Joe Namath by his militant black teammate Johnny Sample, "Joe doesn't have a prejudiced bone in his body. A white player can't say or do anything that is discriminatory in any way as long as Joe's around."[38]

Baseball statistics, for one thing, show blacks to be superior in performance to whites. From 1947 to 1973 (the period since Jackie Robinson broke in) "blacks and Latins have had significantly higher batting averages, doubles (with one exception), and stolen base rates than whites. Moreover, blacks have had consistently higher home run rates and slugging averages than both whites or Latins. . . Black and Latin pitchers have had a significantly higher percentage of victories, strikeouts per inning and lower (earned run averages) than whites."[39] In 1973 black hitters averaged 17 points above whites and in 1974, 14 points.

In any event, there is discrimination on and off the field. The most prevalent form of on-field discrimination is **stacking**. To get recruited, by pros or "amateurs," a black athlete must, in the first place, be outstanding. There is room on the bench for a white player of average talent, but not for a mediocre black. Once recruited, blacks are stacked in the non-central positions.

The most-quoted work on stacking is a 1970 study by John Loy and Joseph McElvogue.[40] These researchers started with the hypothesis that nonwhites would be segregated in the noncentral positions—the central positions being so located physically and also involving a high degree of interaction with other team members and frequent exercise of independent judgment. Loy and McElvogue studied the make-up of the teams in the National and American baseball and football leagues in 1968 to find out how positions were distributed racially. The central baseball positions were catcher, shortstop, and first, second, and third base. It was, of course, necessary to distinguish offensive and defensive units in football. Central offensive positions were quarterback, center, and guards; central defensive positions were (in the 4-3 system of linemen and linebackers then prevalent) the three linebackers.

That the central positions tend to be leadership posts is shown by Grusky's finding that in baseball a disproportionate number of catchers become managers (the catcher is the baseball "quarterback") and also by Gill and Perry's study of the 1973 University of Illinois women's intercollegiate softball team, in which the players rated catchers and infielders highest in team leadership.[42] Why not pitchers, whose position is also physically central? All three researchers seem to agree that pitchers don't have as much interaction with other team members as do catchers and infielders. They, and outfielders, tend to be in a "loner" situation.

Table 8.2 Whites and Blacks in Central and Noncentral Positions in the National and American Baseball League and the National and American Football Leagues, 1968

Baseball

Position	**White**	**Black**	**Total**
Central (Infield, including Catcher)	94	19	113
Noncentral (Outfield)	38	36	74
	132	55	187

($p < .0005$)

Football Offense

Position	**White**	**Black**	**Total**
Central (Quarterback, Center, Guards)	100	4	104
Noncentral (Others)	120	62	182
	220	66	286

($p < .0005$)

Football Defense

Position	**White**	**Black**	**Total**
Central (Linebackers)	72	6	78
Noncentral (Others)	120	88	208
	192	94	286

($p < .0005$)

Based on John W. Loy, Jr., and Joseph F. McElvogue, "Racial Segregation in American Sport," **International Review of Sport Sociology, 5** (1970), Table 1, p. 10, Table 2, p. 12, and Table 3, p. 13. Original data from **1968 Baseball Register; Official 1968 Autographed Yearbooks** of NFL and AFL; and J. Zanger, **Pro Football 1968**, New York, Pocket, 1968.

Loy and McElvogue's findings are summarized in Table 8.2, adapted and abbreviated from tables in their report. The results demonstrated racial segregation by position in baseball and football; none of them could have occurred by chance alone as many as five times in 10,000. Norman Yetman and Stanley Eitzen contended a couple of years later that stacking occurs in basketball as well, with guards (the playmakers) being typically white, and the forwards black.[43]

Blacks have generally competed with one another for the positions that require Supermasculine Menials (Eldridge Cleaver's term) who have speed, bulk and agility, while the positions that involve judgment and leadership have gone to whites. A typical case is the black quarterback who becomes a running back to leave the signal-calling post for a white man. Here again we see the athletic field duplicating the power structure of the outside world.

Why are black athletes stacked as they are, with the "central positions" predominantly white? The central positions involve roles with authority and control, demanding judgment. White players, coaches, and managers may feel out of place with a black in a command post. They may believe that he is incapable of filling such a demanding position. Blacks, having grown up in a prejudicial society, may share this belief and thus train for the noncentral positions. Marshall Medoff puts forward another reason why blacks may avoid them.[44] This is the cost of preparing themselves. Lacking objective data on cost of preparation for different positions, Medoff guessed that baseball positions would run in this order in terms of cost of training (the first the most expensive):

1. Pitchers and catchers
2. Second basemen, shortstops, and third basemen
3. First basemen
4. Outfielders

Players, managers, and sport writers whom Medoff surveyed generally agreed that this order is correct.

Which explanation fits the facts best—explanation in terms of prejudice, or explanation in terms of cost? Both fit the facts, says Medoff, if we look at the situation at any one particular time. But if we take a "longitudinal" view and look at changes over a period of time, he believes the economic explanation to be better. Table 8.3 shows that between 1960 and 1968 the proportion of blacks in major league baseball more than doubled for all central positions except catcher, where it increased slightly. The proportion of black pitchers **tripled**. Medoff believes that this was because of increases in black income in the 1970s which made blacks better able to afford training for the central positions. Could the increasing percentage of blacks in central positions be due to a decrease in prejudice? Medoff thinks not, and cites a writer on the economics of discrimination, who says that "discrimination has been relatively stable over time."[45] However, his source is a 1957 book, published almost a decade before the peak of the civil rights movement. I would say that the years 1960-1968 were marked by **both** increase in black income and decrease in white prejudice, both of which should be taken into account in explaining the increase of blacks in central positions in baseball. The same years, and the 1970s, have also been marked by an increasing number of black quarterbacks and I am sure, of basketball guards.

On-field stacking leads to off-field discrimination. As we saw, catchers are most likely to become baseball managers, and to be white. Those who hold central position, who are generally white, are more likely to land coaching, managerial, front office, or scouting jobs when their playing careers are over. Whites, whether in central positions or not, are more likely to be asked to endorse products. A black player may have to pay more for an apartment, if he can get one. He is likely to be able to make less money in an off-season job. While white players are picking up $1000 to $2000 for speaking appearances, a black player may have to settle for $100 dollar high school talks.

Table 8.3 Percent Distribution of White and Black Major League Baseball Players 1960, 1968

Playing Position	Percent Black 1960	Percent Black 1968
Pitcher	3	9
Catcher	11	12
Shortstop, Second and Third Base	11	23
First Base	17	40
Outfield	24	53

Source—Marshall Medoff, "Positional Segregation and Professional Baseball," **International Review of Sport Sociology**, 12, 1, 1977, Table 2, p. 53.

The most serious aspect of off-field discrimination is **social isolation**. Blacks are not recruited to become an integral part of a college or university body. At training tables, in recreation after practice and games, in casual campus and classroom contacts, blacks are likely to be found with blacks, and whites with whites. This is particularly true of heterosexual relations. Michener describes plainly the situation of the young black athlete, especially the man recruited to a predominantly white university, in an unfamiliar and distant place like Lincoln, Nebraska, Laramie, Wyoming, or Manhattan, Kansas:

> *The black athlete, cut off from black society of any kind, is supposed to spend four of his most virile years playing games for his university, and sitting alone in a room, forbidden to speak to any female. If he dares to do so, the whole weight of the athletic establishment falls on him; he is castigated verbally, threatened with the loss of his scholarship, demoted by his professors in class, and denied a starting position on the team where he is probably the best of the lot.*[46]

Michener cites a black University of Wyoming player who tried to date a white girl, whose cowboy brothers thereupon organized a posse to "gun down the nigger if he makes another move."

The athlete who hopes to move up in the world has also committed himself to an essentially military organization. For sport with the goal of winning at any cost **is** war. As we saw in Chapter 1, the coach is caught in an unbelievably tough bind—he is held completely responsible for winning or losing and , at the same time, he has no ultimate control in the game situation. So it is not surprising that he may be desperately fearful of any breach in his "authority." Rafferty is probably right that **in our culture** a "benevolent dictatorship" is necessary to win—George Davis, who compiled a 45-0 record while letting his high school players vote on their starting line-ups; and the Israeli army, which seems to combine democracy with efficiency, are not quite "of this world" so far as the American sport establishment is concerned. Michener says that, if he were a ghetto athlete, he would probably attach himself to the tough tyrannical type of coach as the one most likely to teach him the skills necessary for athletic success. But in terms of his social power, the athlete who does this is likely to be disqualifying himself for operating in anything other than an authoritarian establishment. In terms of our discussion in Chapter 6, he will be reinforced in his conditioning for obedience rather than achievement—especially since, as a black, he is likely to be tracked out of the "achievement" positions. As Michener also suggests, by committing himself to warring on his own race for the profit of whites, he becomes a poor "role model" for young blacks who are trying to establish their identity.

If sport may possibly be less racist than American life in general, it is probably more sexist. What anthropologist William Arens says of football is true of sport in general, "The game is a male preserve that manifests and symbolizes both the physical and cultural values of masculinity."[49] Reluctance to admit females as equals in this "preserve," plus fear of mounting expenses, was probably why the fiercest of all opposition to sex equality in education under Title IX came from the NCAA. I documented the inferior place of women in sport in Chapter 2. There are few sexual contrasts in American life sharper than that between female athletes who travel by private car and their male counterparts who travel by chartered plane.

Because of such conditions, relatively few females seek to use sport to travel the route from "rags to riches." (This explains why, in this chapter, I have generally referred to the upwardly mobile athlete as "he.") Another reason why women do not seek upward mobility through sport is that they are afraid it will be impossible to rise in athletics without losing their femininity and thus their ability to attract males. In 1977, for example, the coach of the University of Miami's two straight national championship women's swimming teams told my class that the big question that concerned his swimmers was whether they could win without training with weights, and whether they could use weights without being masculinized.

In terms of pure physiology, the woman athlete is not likely to develop bulging biceps or otherwise become masculine. But "femininity" and "masculinity" are more cultural than physiological. In the athletic subculture, and to an extent in our whole youth culture, the jock is properly a male, and the appropriate role for a female is that of a worshipful admirer of his feats. One particular type of admirer may share the stage, but not center stage—the cheerleader, who is preferably a busty and leggy sex object. However, black women can usually be athletic without being considered less sexually attractive.[50]

Female atletes who are concerned about the effect of sport participation on their feminine desirability can take heart from Hans Buhrmann and Robert Braton's study of girl athletes and nonathletes in a Canadian high school. The girl athletes were more popular with boys (as well as with teachers and with other girls) to a degree that could have occurred by chance less often than one time in a hundred ($p < .01$). Also, good athletes were better liked by all three groups than were poor athletes. It is also true that athletes were more often disliked than were nonathletes. In spite of the fact that Canadian communities don't generally support high school athletics as much as do those in the States, "it appears," the authors say, 'that visibility and being in the public eye does not only increase the positive aspects of status and recognition among peers, teachers, and the opposite sex, it also magnifies the chance of being disliked. . ."[51]

Sexism in sport divides the sexes in a way that in the long run decreases the power of males as well as that of females. Symbolic of this is the pregame sexual continence usually demanded of jocks. The anthropologist

Arens sees this as a version of a widespread primitive ritual of female-avoidance. For example, "the Cheyenne [Indian] feeling about male sexuality is that it is something to be husbanded and kept in reserve as a source of strength for the great crises of war."[52] In addition to this doubtful theory, pre-game abstinence serves to bind the male's allegiance more tightly to his male in-group. Jack Scott has made himself rather unpopular with the athletic Establishment by suggesting that many coaches are "latent homosexuals." Latent homosexuality (or anything latent) is hard to document, but it is clearly true that many coaches tend to make their own sex-group more vital than females for their players.

And football player George Sauer saw a healthy similarity in football to the naked wrestling of two young men described by D. H. Lawrence in **Women in Love**:

> *They became accustomed to each other's rhythm. They got a kind of mutual physical understanding. And then they had a real struggle. They seemed to drive their white flesh deeper and deeper against each other, as if they would work into a oneness. . . rapturously, intent and mindless at least, two essential white figures working into a tighter, closer oneness of struggle. . .*[53]

Dave Kopay, an NFL running back who was the first homosexual athlete to come out of the closet, sees football shot through with sexual symbolism:

> *The whole language of football is involved in sexual allusion. We were told to go out and 'fuck those guys'; to take that ball and 'stick it up their asses' or 'down their throats.' The coaches would yell, 'Knock their dicks off' or more often than that 'Knock their jocks off.' They'd say, 'Go out there and give it all you've got, a hundred and ten percent, shoot your wad.' You controlled their line and 'Knocked 'em into submission.'*
>
> *Over the years I've seen many a coach get emotionally aroused when he was diagramming a particular play into an imaginary hole on the blackboard. His face red, his voice roaring, he would show the ball carrier how he wanted him to 'stick it in the hole.' "*[54]

"The sexual allusions," says Kopay, "help explain the player's passionate attachment to the game." Pointing out that hugging and hand-holding, and ass-patting in public are, among males, peculiar to football players, Kopay sees these and other physical expressions as not necessarily homosexual, but as a positive and healthy (and otherwise repressed) demonstration of closeness.

Alabama coach Bear Bryant also spoke of, and rejected, the sexual connotation of the jock community, "I don't like you and you don't like me. Cause likin' leads to lovin' and lovin' leads to fuckin' and you don't fuck the Bear."[55]

Kopay's fellow-author says that the mystery about football is not how a man like Kopay could come out of such a super-masculine society as a homosexual, but "how could any man come through it as purely heterosexual after spending so much time idealizing and worshipping the male body while denigrating and ridiculing the female."[56]

In the male athletic culture, a female tends to become a dehumanized sex object. How this degrades both sexes is shown by Jim Bouton's description of the ballplayer's pastime of "beaver shooting" ("beaver" being female pubic hair): crawling under the seating of stadiums "so that to the tune of the Star-Spangled Banner an entire baseball club of clean-cut American boys would be looking up the skirt of some female."[57] Dave Meggyesy, a happily married man, reports that to football players he knew, a female was typically a "cunt" or a "piece of ass." One sad case he related is that of a married player, returning from a road trip, who said, "I'm really going to punish my old lady tonight. Put the wood to her. Make her suffer."[58] In terms of power, a male who reduces a female to a "cunt" at the same time psychologically reduces himself to a **schmuck** (the translation of the Yiddish is "prick"—a creature totally identified with his penis). He does this when, as Meggyesy's own case shows, the most important thing in maintaining one's own identity in the face of the athletic and non-athletic Establishment is the love of a woman whom a man regards as a person.

The most spectacular example of the athletic male subculture is the ritualized "super-masculine" behavior associated with British Rugby clubs, described by the sociologists Sheard and Dunning. Rugby is middle and upper class football, historically associated with the prestigious boys' "public schools"—Rugby, Eaton, Harrow, etc. "In Britain players of (Rugby Union football) have gained a reputation for regularly violating a number of taboos, especially those regarding violence, physical contact, nakedness, obscenity, drunkenness, and the treatment of property. Taboo-breaking of this kind tends to take a highly ritualized form. It has come to form an integral part of the subculture that has grown up and around the rugby game. One of its functions is that of providing an avenue of satisfaction for the players in addition to the game itself."[59] Examples of the subculture: roaring drunkenness is part of the tradition, accompanied by obscene songs that normally put down women and homosexuals. In a bar or in the bus after a match, a player may stage a ritual strip-tease, or he may be forcibly stripped and his body, especially his genitals, smeared with vaseline and shoe polish. In one case of a post-match strip, the player was carried naked past women students at a university bar. Property may be stolen or deliberately destroyed. Unlike the lower-class violence that may occur on "football specials'' after a soccer match, or unlike the super-macho behavior that used to be associated with the culture of the American pool hall, this violation of recognized standards is not considered hooliganism, but is accepted with the attitude that ''the old boys will be boys.''

Now why this stereotyped wild behavior on the part of young British ''gentlemen''? Sheard and Dunning see it as an assertion of ''masculinity'' in the face of doubt about one's male sex role. With the development of industry in the nineteenth century, these sociologists say the British gentleman or would-be gentleman lost the outlet for physical expression that he had previously, and substituted the physical inertia of an office existence. His grandfather, who had been able to ''ride to hounds,'' for example, could thus assert his role as a male. Now the middle or upper-class youth could assert it, not so much in the rugby contest itself but in the ritualized extracurricular ''masculine'' subculture. Also, the sex role of these young males was questioned from another quarter. Females of their class were becoming emancipated. ''The balance of power between the sexes is now beginning to veer toward a more egalitarian form of relationship. . . One of the principal initial responses of many men as the attack from women first began to be mounted was to withdraw into the all-male culture and celebrate its values. In them the singing of obscene songs which symbolically expressed their masculinitiy in a virulent form, men's fear of women, and their simultaneous dependence on them, became one of the central elements in the club subculture.'' Furthermore, in this male ''preserve'' where the strongest ties are to other males, homosexuality is to be feared. (In the segregated male public schools from which rugby sprang it was quite common. And ''even the game situation, where the players grasp each other in a hot sticky mass, their heads between each other's thighs, has become the butt for frequent jokes.'') Thus ''queers'' are reviled and mocked, along with women.

Sheard and Dunning tell us that the excesses of the rugby clubs have declined in recent years. This, they say, is in part because rugby has become more competitive and the men want to be in shape. But it is also because the ''new woman'' wants a man's life to be centered on her, not on the ''old boys.'' Rugby clubs are breaking down and admitting wives and other women friends. ''It appears likely that the old style rugby player will become just an historical curiosity.'' So, perhaps, on this side of the Atlantic, may the macho American athlete.[60]

Sport and Power—the Balance

It is doubtful whether, on balance, organized sport in any way significantly changes the distribution of social power. It does enable a few gifted people to attain wealth and fame. It does enable a somewhat larger number to move a notch or two up the socioeconomic ladder. But it gives large or smaller rewards to the winners at the price of raising and smashing false hopes in the vast majority of losers, meanwhile exploiting these dreams for corporate profit. Even the winners may be "tracked" out of significant contributions they could have made in the mainstream of human achievement. Organized sport teaches underprivileged people to submit to unquestioned authority, while setting them at each other's throats in a minor form of warfare. It widens the polarization of the sexes into sadistic male and passive female. By calling its activities "masculine," it enhances some males's sense of virility at the expense of females, and therefore at their own expense.

FOOTNOTES

[1]Allen L. Sack, "Yale 29, Harvard 4: The Professionalization of American Football," **Quest** January 1973, 24-32.

[2]Hanford Powel, Jr., **Walter Camp**, Boston, Little, Brown, 1926, Appendix A.

[3]George Saxon, "Immigrant Culture in a Stratified Economy," **Monthly Review**, February 1948, reprinted in Don Calhoun **et al**, eds., **Personality, Work, Community: An Introduction to Social Science**, 3rd ed., Philadelphia, Lippincott, 1961, 314.

[4]Quoted in Michael Novak, **The Joy of Sports**, New York, Basic, 1976, 14.

[5]Quoted in Jerry Izenberg, **How Many Miles to Camelot? The All-American Sports Myth**, New York, Holt, 1972, 212.

[6]John F. Rooney, **A Geography of American Sports**, Reading, Mass., Addison-Wesley, 1974.

[7]Saxon, **op. cit.** 314.

[8]James A. Michener, **Sports in America**, New York, Random House, 1976, 243.

[9]John W. Loy, Jr., "The Study of Sport and Social Mobility," in Gerald S. Kenyon, ed., **Sociology of Sport**, Chicago, Athletic Institute, 1969, 101-119.

[10]**Ibid.**, Table 2, p. 114.

[11]**Ibid.**, Table 3, p. 114.

[12]**Ibid.**, Table 4, p. 115.

[13]**Ibid.**, 115.

[14]**Ibid.**, Table 5, p. 116.

[15]Michener, **op. cit.**

[16]Harry Webb, "Reaction to Loy" in Kenyon, **op. cit.**, 124.

[17]**Ibid.**, 127.

[18]Zbigniew Szot and Bogdan Jurkiewicz, "An Attempt at Defining the Influence of Selected Factors Exerted on Results in Sport and Gymnastics," **International Review of Sport Sociology**, 14, 2(1979), 73-82.

[19]S. Kirson Weinberg and Henry Arond, "The Occupational Culture of the Boxer," **American Journal of Sociology, 57**, 1952, 460-469.

[20]**Ring Magazine**, July 1950, 45, cited by Weinberg and Arond.

[21]Weinberg and Arond, 460.

[22]**Ibid.**

[23]**Miami Herald**, September 8, 1976, p. 6F.

[24]**Ibid.**

[25]Thomas Tutko and William Bruns, **Winning is Everything, and Other American Myths,** New York, Macmillan, 1976, 126.

[26]Bob Cousy with John Devaney, **The Killer Instinct**, New York, Random House, 1975, 173.

[27]**Sports Illustrated**, September 29, 1969, 9.

[28]Jack Scott, **The Athletic Revolution**, New York, Free Press, 1971, 179.

[29]Tutko and Bruns, **op. cit.**, 126.

[30]**Ibid.**

[31]Harold Charnovsky, "The Major League Professional Baseball Player: Self-Conception Versus the Popular Image," **International Review of Sport Sociology**, 3, 1968, 41, n.

[32]Dave Meggyesy, **Out of Their League**, Berkeley, Ramparts, 1970, 44.

[33]Scott, **op. cit.**, 121-122.

[34]Gary Shaw, **Meat on the Hoof: The Hidden World of Texas Football**, New York, Dell, 1972, 282.

[35]Quoted in Tutko and Bruns, **op. cit.**, 66.

[36]Quoted in Neil Amdur, **The Fifth Down: Democracy and the Football Revolution**, New York, Coward, McCann, and Geoghegan, 1971, 30.

[37]Scott, **op. cit.**, 14, 21.

[38]Johnny Sample, with Fred J. Hamilton and Sonny Schwartz, **Confessions of a Dirty Ballplayer**, New York, Dial, 1970, 264.

[39]Wilbert Marcellus Leonard, II, "An Extension of the Black-Latin-White Report," **International Review of Sport Sociology**, 12, 3, 1977, 92.

[40]John W. Loy, Jr., and Joseph F. McElvogue, "Racial Segregation in American Sport," **International Review of Sport Sociology**

[41]Oscar Grusky, "The Effect of Formal Structure on Managerial Recruitment," **Sociometry**, 26, 1963, 345-353.

[42]Diane L. Gill and Jean L. Perry, "A Case Study of Leadership in Women's Intercollegiate Softball," **International Review of Sport Sociology**, 14, 2, 1979, 83-91.

[43]Norman R. Yetman and D. Stanley Eitzen, "Black Americans in Sports: Unequal Opportunities for Equal Abilities," **Civil Rights Digest**, August 1972.

[44]Marshall Medoff, "Positional Segregation and Professional Baseball," **International Review of Sport Sociology**, 12, 1, 1977, 49-56.

[45]**Ibid.**, 54.

[46]James A. Michener, **Sports in America**, New York, Random House, 1976, 161.

[47]Amdur, **op. cit.**

[48]Warren G. Bennis and Philip E. Slater, **The Temporary Society**, New York, Harper and Row, 1968, 5-6.

[49]William Arens, "The Great American Football Ritual," **Natural History**, October 1975, 77.

[50]For discussion, see Harry Edwards, **Sociology of Sport**, Homewood, Ill., Dorsey, 1973, 233.

[51]Hans G. Buhrmann and Robert D. Bratton, "Athletic Participation and Status of Alberta High School Girls," **International Review of Sport Sociology**, 12, 1, 1977, 65.

[52]Arens, **op. cit.**, 79.

[53]George Sauer, quoted in **Washington Star**, May 21, 1972.

[54]David Kopay and Perry Deane Young, **The David Kopay Story**, New York, Arbor House, 1977, 53.

[55]Quoted, **ibid.**

[56]**Ibid.**, 51.

[57]Jim Bouton, **Ball Four**, New York, Dell, 1971, 36.

[58]Meggyesy, **op. cit.**

[59]K. G. Sheard and E. G. Dunning, "The Rugby Football Club as a Type of Male 'Preserve': Some Sociological Notes", **International Review of Sport Sociology**, 8, 3-4, 1973, 5-6.

[60]In a paper published in 1980, John Sherry tells us that the rugby subculture has been transplanted to the American midwest (John F. Sherry, Jr., "Verbal Aggression in Rugby Rituals" in **Play and Culture,** ed. Helen B. Schwartzman, 1978 Proceedings of the Association for the Anthropological Study of Play, West Point, N.Y., Leisure Press, 1980, 139-150). Sherry details vigorously how the ritualized aggressive obscenity depicted by Sheard and Dunning looks in a United States setting. (There are, in fact, women's rugger clubs with their own brand of obscenity.) But he does not tell us exactly where, in what areas or what schools, this American rugby subculture is found. Nor does he analyze as convincingly as do Sheard and Dunning what the rugger's bizarre behavior does for him (or her) in this cultural situation.

CHAPTER 9 SOCIAL CHARACTER OF THE DIFFERENT SPORTS

In Chapter 8 we examined how sport is related to the whole pattern of social power. Organized sport, although it is an Establishment with a certain common ideology and organization, is not a monolithic unity. It is, so to speak, a federation of different sport activities, each of which has its own special relationship to the whole social structure. In this chapter we shall look at the different social functions of the specific sports.

As a beginning, let's examine four basic characteristics in terms of which we can distinguish the separate sports. There are territorial and non-territorial sports, time-bound and non time-bound sports, bodily contact and non-contact sports, striking and non-striking sports.

The territorial sports are variations of the Papremis spring fertility rites, involving movement in territory, against opposition, toward a goal: soccer, American football, basketball, hockey, lacrosse, polo. All have a fundamentally warlike relationship to space. Other sports also occur physically in space, but do not have the same warlike relationship to territorial goals: baseball, tennis, golf, swimming, track and field competitions. George Grella describes dramatically the difference between the territoriality of football and the non-territoriality of baseball: "The winning team in baseball, because of the shape of its field, cannot acquire territory, operating instead in a realm beyond spatial measurement. . . No other game opens rather than encloses space. If the stands were removed from the football field, the game would still be conducted within its dreary box; if baseball's outfield bleachers were removed, the game could continue its space across the land. . . "[1]

Some games are timed by the clock: all the territorial sports, also track and swimming events. If Lewis Mumford is right (and I think he is) in describing the clock as the basic machine of industrial civilization, then these time-bound sports are part of the industrial complex: those who watch the clock in their working hours also watch it in their recreation. Baseball, tennis, and golf are non time-bound as they are non space-bound. Their duration is determined by factors other than the running of a clock. In baseball, three outs add up to an inning, nine innings to a game. There is no such thing as a tie, so a game could go on forever. In tennis, points add to game, games to set, sets to match. Before the tie-breaker (an invention of, or for, the clock-conscious television industry) a tennis match could also theoretically continue to eternity. Of both games, as contrasted with the time-bound sports, what Grella says of baseball is probably true: "The game succeeds in creating a temporary timelessness."[2]

The chief sports in which bodily contact plays a fundamental and legal role are boxing, football, and hockey. Between these and the clearly non-contact sports are those, like basketball, soccer, and lacrosse, which formally outlaw contact but actually allow much of it by officials' interpretation. Whether or not bodily contact sport is a throwback to our pre-human ancestry, it is clearly a throwback to the pre-industrial days before brain (human or electronic) took the place of sheer brawn.

Finally, some games (baseball, tennis, golf, hockey, polo) feature the striking of a ball with some kind of stick. The other territorial games, track and field, and swimming, do not. Some see the hand-eye coordination involved in the striking games as a preparation for industrial activity.

Now, further into the particular sports. Leonard Koppett, in an excellent book on the social context of basketball, has described the essence of the game as deception.[3] I shall use Koppett's terminology in analyzing first our three major American spectator sports.

The Essence of the Game Is Individuality: Baseball

Baseball, the "grand old American game," is best seen, I think, as an expression of nineteenth century rural Yankee individualism. Michael Novak contrasts the key player in football with the star in baseball:

> *When Bart Starr completed a pass for the Green Bay Packers, all the Packers could be said to share the deed; one man alone is quite helpless. When Joe Di Maggio stepped to the plate in Yankee Stadium, with his unforgettable stance and fluid swing, Di Maggio stood in spotlighted solitude and none of his teammates could act in his behalf. Football is corporate, baseball is an association of individuals, . . . often taciturn, plying each his special craft, collaborating, but at each crucial point facing events alone, solving the mathematical possibilities of each task in the reflective quiet of his own hunches, instincts, and lightning moves.*[4]

Describing the drama of Ted Williams' final game at Fenway Park in Boston, novelist John Updike also speaks of baseball's individualism: "Of all team sports, baseball, with its graceful intermittencies of action, its immense and tranquil field sparsely settled with poised men in white, seems to me best suited to accommodate, and be ornamented by, a loner. It is essentially a lonely game."[5]

Grella points out that where each individual stands alone, each is also individually accountable: "Every player is potentially responsible for victory or defeat; just as his triumphs are visible to all, so are his mistakes. He cannot hide an error in a mass of struggling bodies or commit it in some obscure corner of the field, for it is there in the open for everyone to see."[6]

David Voigt, in a historian's reflection on baseball's relationship to American culture, suggests the peculiarly American type of hero that this game of personal accountability has produced.[7] The hero is a man of the people: Babe Ruth, a refugee from an orphan asylum; Shoeless Joe Jackson, an illiterate Carolina country boy playing the outfield in his bare feet; Lou Gehrig, home-loving son of an immigrant German steelworker; Bob Feller, an Iowa farm kid; Joe Di Maggio, an Italian-American batting genius who also married the nation's sex symbol; Mickey Mantle, another country boy from Oklahoma; and in the post-Vietnam era, socially conscious Tom Seaver with his lovely wife—as David Halberstam suggests, a Mr. and Mrs. America for the 1970s.[8] The hero has a nickname to give him the common touch. He is unselfish, strong but not a bully, manly, salty, earthy, a lover of his country.

He is also imperfect, like his fans, confronted with their own lonely tasks. Grella remarks that in baseball's legends it is the mistakes or bonehead plays that have been remembered the longest—Fred Merkle's failure to touch a base, Fred Snodgrass' muff of a crucial outfield fly, Mickey Owen's passed ball on a third strike. The flaw is sometimes of behavior or character: Ty Cobb's almost psychopathically vicious disposition; Babe

Ruth's gargantuan appetite for hot dogs, booze, and women; Hack Wilson rising above an almost constant hangover to hit 56 home runs and drive in 190 runs (still a record) in a season.The baseball hero also suffers: Iron Man Gehrig played over 2000 consecutive games and practically died in harness before he reached 40. Di Maggio patrolled the outfield with bone spurs and Mantle with osteomyelitis. Pete Reiser beat his brains against outfield fences. Jackie Robinson played brilliant and dedicated baseball when every day was an encounter with the stress of racial hatred and finally succumbed prematurely to diseases of stress—diabetes and hypertension. Sandy Koufax set strikeout records over the excruciating pain of an arthritic elbow.

Baseball is fundamentally a rural sport. The first recorded case of a baseball game played under essentially modern rules took place in June 1846 in a part of Hoboken, New Jersey, called the Elysian Fields. Grella thinks it is not accidental that baseball is mythically associated with Cooperstown (where it did **not** originate)—the town named after the novelist of the frontier who created such heroes as Hawkeye, Deerslayer, Pathfinder, and Leatherstocking, and where Natty Bumppo (a great

Baseball was played on Boston Common in 1834, years before it was supposedly invented by Abner Doubleday at Cooperstown. Courtesy of Racquet & Tennis Club.

baseball name, Grella thinks) roamed the hills. Novak says that although baseball's commercial centers are urban, its players are typically small-town boys, a large percentage from the South. Although blacks and Latins today play a large part, I think Novak is right in describing baseball as symbolically white and Protestant. "In baseball, the form of Anglo-American culture, especially rural culture, is perfectly reflected."[9] He points out that whereas a black basketball coach is easily accepted, to most people a black baseball manager just seems out of place. Voigt remarks that although baseball is played well in Latin America and Japan, it is not really the same game. Using David Riesman's terms, I think we can describe baseball as the game of "inner-directed" nineteenth century American values, oriented to individual achievement and personal responsibility. Novak sees it as playing an important role in the civilization of the nation: "It is a triumph of law over the lawless spirit. . . that so civilized, orderly, and lawful a game could have arisen from the plains, the Southlands, and the eastern cities of the nineteenth century, when the frontier and badlands still loomed upon the horizon."[10]

In the late twentieth century, baseball is not too well adapted to the television age. "Timing and waiting are of the essence," says William O. Johnson, "with the entire field in suspense waiting on the performance of a single player. By contrast, football, basketball, and hockey are games in which many events occur simultaneously, with the entire team involved at the same time. With the advent of TV, such isolation of the individual performance as occurs in baseball became unacceptable. . . Baseball is a game that was designed to be played on a sunny afternoon at Wrigley Field in the 1920s, not on a 21-inch screen."[11]

However, before we write its epitaph, we should note some points baseball has for our time. Novak says, "Baseball is an antidote to the national passion for bigness. It is a slow, careful, judicious game."[12] It is also an antidote to the excessive passion for rationality. Baseball is, or was until it came to terms with the twentieth century, a zany game. None of what Grella calls the "improbabilities of baseball history" could occur in the world of organized football, or organized basketball, or especially in the world of corporate business: three Dodgers occupying third base on the same play; a World Series being decided by **two** ground balls hitting a pebble and bouncing over the head of 18 year old Freddie Lindstrom; the holder of the all-time highest batting average starting his career playing for the Bloomer Girls; Bill Veeck sending a midget to bat; Wilbert Robertson, Dodger manager, trying to catch a grapefruit tossed from an airplane by one of his players; Giant manager John McGraw warming up the non-playing Charles Victory Faust before every game of three pennant-winning seasons because a fortune teller had said the Giants couldn't win without him.

In a world of territorial push, the symbolism of baseball's spatial arrangement is also important. As Grella points out, baseball is "the one arena of American life where you can go home again. The diamond. . . is merely an arrangement of bases, small islands of security in the perilous avenues leading from and toward home; most of the diamond is dangerous territory, with only three small spots where a man can be safe."[13] Novak sees the same symbolism against the background of frontier America:

One dusts off the sacred 'home,' starting place, Keystone, source and touchstone of triumph: those who cross it most often. . . carry off the victory. 'Around the world' is the myth: batter after batter trying to nudge forward his predecessors in this most American of games until the whole universe is circled, base by base, and runners can come 'home'. One imagines Yankee Clipper ships blown silently across the sparkling sea, sails creaking in the wind, the sound of wood, the silence and isolation of each sailor at his post, encircling the world for trade.[14]

Finally baseball is, as Grella says, the American rite of spring, of life and hope, as no other game is, especially not football, the game of autumn and dying life: "It is. . . the Summer Game, played by the Boys of Summer, an ongoing celebratory dance in the golden season. Its limits in time are April and October, including our happiest months. Even in cold climates we know that if Opening Day has come, spring cannot be far behind."[15]

The Name of the Game Is Intimidation: Football

Football is for the late twentieth century. It is another kind of characteristically American game, which has actually been accepted by nobody except the inhabitants of the United States and Canada.

J. H. Duthie points up the significance of American football for our century by contrasting its appeal with that of Olympic sports:

The individual events of the early Olympics Games. . . spotlight, in face of the inevitability of individual defeat and death, the importance of human force, speed, strength, cunning, and individual skill. The strong-man-alone was exalted. . . Olympic contest events, like running, jumping, wrestling down an opponent or throwing outdated weight objects are forms which retain their enormous emotional appeal because they demonstrably have no technological significance for today. They clearly educe nothing but the consciousness of what it means to be human, to strive, to wrestle, to impose our will for a short period on obdurate nature. . . Individual contest has an appeal deeper and more real than much of our everyday work life. Modern men, dwarfed by the technology they have created, still thrill to athletic events glorifying the energy and achievements of the single individual.[16]

On the contrary, American football does not transcend technological society; it **is** technological society:

Players disappeared to be replaced. . . by specialists with narrowly defined duties and clear-cut responsibilities. Carefully calculated tactics planned by squads of non-playing experts and educated officials who are measurement specialists provided quantifiable achievements denoted in exact intervals of space and time. Above all the submission of the individual as a shift worker to be called on and dismissed as required is mandated. American football, in which specialists in defense oppose an equally specialized offensive unit at all times, provides the most highly evolved athletic metaphor of a technological society.[17]

Clearly American football has nineteenth century roots. My student Mark Melzer has written very imaginatively about these. He likens the game to the nineteenth century American passion for land. "Football is a game of land, ownership, and possession." In neither hockey nor basketball does one capture or lose land. In them penalties are imposed against individuals, but football teams are penalized by taking away territory. Although computerization may have changed techniques and strategies, the basic nineteenth century motif is still there:

Nothing illustrates more the 'Manifest Destiny' of Americans than the game of football. Americans have always felt we must push our borders further and further west. We need more land. Our early settlers let no barrier stop their inexhaustible push forward. We conquered mountains, valleys, rivers, Indians, and you name it, all for that precious earth. And Americans stopped at no cost to gain this land, whether it meant breaking treaties with the Indians, deceiving Mexicans, or just out and out war. In football we also see this factor. Football is a game of deception; you try to fake or fool the opponent. Yet if that doesn't work you can always use brute force. The need for more land, the deception, the spirit, and the technological advancement, all factors evident in the game, provide us with an interesting insight into our own culture and heritage.[18]

Like baseball, football does have a place in the cycle of seasons. Historically, it has been intimately associated with the fall harvest rite—Thanksgiving. If, however, it has any of the spiritual quality of humble gratitude that characterized that Pilgrim holiday, it is the thankfulness of Anglo invaders for having been allowed to capture and survive in Indian territory. Novak believes that football, teaching that violence is the ultimate human reality, has a more pessimistic view of human possibilities than baseball's springtime view (I agree). He holds that the football view is the more realistic view (I disagree).

Anthropologist William Arens begins his analysis of "the great American football ritual": "Violence is one of our society's most obvious traits, and its expression in football, where bodily contact and territorial intrusion are essential, clearly accounts for part of the game's appeal."[19] But only part of it. "Football's violence is expressed within the framework of teamwork, specialization, mechanization, and variation, and this combination accounts for its appeal."[20] Conrad Dobler, a college political science major, described in 1977 (whether rightly or not) as "pro football's dirtiest player," on his NFL personnel form put this essence of twentieth century football in one sentence, "It is still the only sport where there is controlled violence mixed with careful technical planning."[21] Another of my students, Patricia Edelman, sees this product of two centuries as "cut along the lines of the American grain, savage, violent, militaristic in its meticulous organization, moralistic in its celebration of performance and high purpose, remorseless in the contempt for failure and its adulation of success." "The game," she says, "is ideally suited for television; the barrage of cameras, the zoom shots and the instant replays reveal subtleties the fan in the stadium could not see, and penetrate the hand-offs, traps, pile-ons, wedges, and other concentrations that obscure the action."[22]

In terms of social appeal, Novak describes football as "the immigrant myth and the corporate myth." As we saw in Chapter 8, football in this century is typically played by escapees from one or another lower middle class urban ghetto. Whereas baseball has typically been played by rural WASPs, football is promoted and watched mainly by urban middle class spiritual WASPs, already arrived or on their way up the corporate ladder. "Baseball and bowling. . . appeal to the less educated and the older segments of the population while both college and pro football appeal to the better educated and middle aged."[23]

The Football Fan - 1903

Writing on the psychology of football in the early days of the modern game (1903), a professional psychologist, G. T. W. Patrick, described his observation of football in this way:

In this game more than in any other there is a reversion to aboriginal manners. The game is more brutal, that is, more primitive than others. The lively chase for goal, the rude physical shock of the heavy opposing teams, and the scrimmage-like, melée character of the collisions awaken our deep-seated slumbering instincts. By inner imitation the spectators themselves participate in the game and at the same time give unrestrained expression to their emotions. If at a great football game one will watch the spectators instead of the players, he will see at once that the people before him are not his associates of the school, the library, the office, the shop, the street, or the factory. The inhibition of emotional expression is the characteristic of modern civilized man. The spectators at an exciting football game no longer attempt to restrain emotional expression. They shout and yell, blow horns and dance, swing their arms about and stamp, throw their hats in air and snatch off their neighbors' hats, howl and gesticulate, little realizing how foreign this is to their wonted behavior or how odd it would look at their places of work.

—G. T. W. Patrick, "The Psychology of Football," **American Journal of Psychology, 14**, 1903, 116.

Novak puts it together this way: "Football is preeminently the sport of the new white collar and professional class, of the statesmen, bureau chiefs, managers, executives, ad men, consultants, professors, journalists, engineers, technicians, pilots, air traffic controllers, secret service men, insurance agents, managers of retail chains, bank officers, and investment analysts. . . But football is also the liturgy of the working class, the immigrants, the rednecks."[24]

The preference of middle class people for football poses a problem in explanation. Common sense tells us that working class people are generally more violent and less restrained than the middle class. Scientific research shows that middle class children, in growing up, typically learn to suppress and repress emotional expression more than do working class children. On this basis we should expect the working class to prefer the violence of football and the middle class to prefer the greater restraint of baseball. The opposite is in fact the case. Why? Sociologist Harry Edwards says that people prefer aggressive sports in proportion to their "degree of active involvement in the mainstream of American life."[25] Those who are pushing aggressively, and somewhat successfully, to get ahead of their fellow humans easily identify with the aggression of football. They are likely to claim that "baseball is too slow." We will note that the middle class, upward bound in the "mainstream of American life," are not **playing** football, they are just enthusiastically watching those not in the mainstream ("the working class, the immigrants, the rednecks") beat **their** brains out.

As a strategy game, football's peculiar kind of territoriality places it in the same category as chess, which we have seen is a board model of war. "Basketball," says Novak, "is continuous action, but football is played as a set piece like chess. In chess, opponents alternate single moves."[26] There is, however, a difference. Carrying out the moves in their playbooks, football players are sometimes called pawns, and in a sense are. But they are also alive. The chess player (the coach) can plan his moves, but he cannot execute them. Execution depends basically on the ability of his players to intimidate the opposing pawns. Here is the essence of football.

The Essence of the Game Is Deception: Basketball

Comparing games to musical forms, Novak tells us that baseball is like chamber music. Vivaldi, he says, though not a right fielder for the Mets, should be: the name is right, and his style, "slow, pastoral, each instrument distinct, intensely grasped," penetrates the whole spirit of the game. Football is like Ravel's Bolero or Beethoven's Fifth Symphony: "football games build like symphonies to climatic resolution." And "basketball is jazz: improvisatory, free, individualistic, corporate, sweaty, exulting, screeching, torrid, explosive, exquisitely designed for letting first the trumpet, then the sax, then the drummer, then the trombone soar away in virtuoso excellence."[27]

Basketball shares with jazz the quality of improvisation. It is improvisatory by contrast with baseball and football, both of which involve set plays. For this reason basketball is much easier for the television or radio broadcaster than for the newspaper sports writer—for who can report a jam session in print? For the same reason, fans rarely remember specific plays, or even specific games, as they do with baseball or football. Basketball is also improvisatory by comparison with non-set play games like soccer and hockey, the "field" sports that it much resembles. The difference is that the world of basketball is three-dimensional (the goal is off the ground) whereas the goal in soccer and hockey is bound to the earth (or ice). The symbol of the difference is the jump shot (which made contemporary basketball), where one can improvise in many ways while airborne. The dunk, which doesn't require that one be 6:10, or even 6:2, further "verticalized" basketball. When basketball was limited to the earthbound set shot, with feet on the ground, the scores, although not like those in soccer and hockey, were abysmally low by today's standards (I can remember 23-21 college games). Of course, the 24 second rule, requiring a team to shoot or surrender the ball, also played a part in skyrocketing scores.

The two men who first advanced improvisation in basketball were white sons of immigrants—Angelo Luisetti and Bob Cousy. Luisetti's one-handed shot changed the world of the two-handed "set." Cousy, who became ambidexterous by constant practice carrying books, opening doors, turning keys, and eventually dribbling, passing, and shooting left-handed, in turn rescued basketball from a rigidity imposed by Luisetti's one-handed shot. "Cousy saved pro basketball," said a veteran. "Until he came along, the game followed a rigid pattern. It was the practice of every team to work the ball into the giant pivot man and he turned around and hooked a basket. Cousy changed all that. The fans ate up his razzle-dazzle."[28] Koppett says it was Cousy who brought **style** to basketball—**how** one does it is as important as the result.

Jazz, improvisation, style embody the essence of basketball—deception. Basketball, says Koppett, is the game of the poker face. A large part of the game consists of a feint with a hip here, a feint with a shoulder there, a look or a head movement in the wrong direction, fake passes, false dribbles, fake breaks toward the basket, fake shots. "Three or four times under the basket a man may pump before he actually lets go."[29] Deliberately invented in the late nineteenth century by a Christian clergyman to promote the physical well-being of young men in winter months, basketball was intended to provide sport without the bodily contact of football, and in the process to develop moral values. A hundred years later, the game maintains its legal barriers against physical contact, although the interpretation of them would probably shock the Rev. James Naismith. He would also probably be shocked to learn that in the eyes of an astute observer like Koppett, the basketball player is the supreme con artist in sport, and basketball tends to recruit players and spectators who have (or would like to have) a talent for deceiving their fellow humans.

Basketball is an art form, and is increasingly becoming a black art form. Teams are becoming more black, and audiences are becoming more black. In Chicago and Philadelphia basketball crowds tend to be black, while the whites watch hockey. Basketball is also played well by whites in the rural midwest, Novak reminds us, but it is a different game, "a game of the head, solid, deliberate, strategic, grinding"[30]—no jazz. Black basketball is "put-on." Although the first great put-on artist was Cousy, the term is a black term, central to the black experience. "Like the stories and legends of black literature, the hero does not let his antagonist guess his intentions; he strings him along, he keeps his inner life to himself until the decisive moment."[31] In brief, he puts on the Man, Uncle Charlie. Thus, the game symbolizes the centuries-old struggle for black identity. "Available records of life among black slaves," says Edwards, "indicate that a slave's wits were more important to insuring his longevity than physical prowess."[32] Surviving black work songs embody the same put-on of the Man. As much as the physical grace that stacks blacks in the forward positions, this is the quality that basketball celebrates. What does this celebration, by athlete and audience, do for black social power? Novak sees it as a positive affirmation of black identity. Others believe that it siphons black energies off into symbolic gratification and away from fulfillment in the mainstream of social and economic life.

Edgar Freidenberg sees another dimension of deception in basketball. This is violation as an accepted part of game tactics. To Friedenberg, basketball is a caricature of "our legalism and the intricate web of regulations among which we live and on which we climb."[33] In other games, actions that are illegal are generally dangerous or disrupt the game, and so are usually avoided. But in basketball, one does not observe the rules, but rationally balances the penalties of violation against the advantages to be gained. The deliberate and open tactical foul is, I think, unique to basketball. The coach, says Friedenberg, manipulates rule violations much as a businessman manipulates the Internal Revenue Code. Thus, while the player is putting on his opponents on the floor (a typically black move), the coach is calculating how profitably to break the law (a typically middle class move). Moral lessons are being learned that Naismith never dreamed of. We can see what Friedenberg meant by calling basketball "an abstract parody of American middle-class life."

A final comparison of our three major spectator sports:

Several factors make basketball more democratic and communal than either baseball or football. The smaller size of teams and the fluidity and unpredictability of play make impossible the benevolent despotism of the playbook football coach or baseball manager. The physical arrangement of the basketball arena brings the crowd much closer to the actions of players and officials. What Grella says of baseball is even truer of basketball—it is impossible to hide or avoid accountability for one's actions. Another democratizing and humanizing factor is that, in basketball, players engage almost naked, not in violent collision, but in intimate physical contact. Compare baseball, where Grella speaks of "the odd uniform, with its high stockings and knickers, the collarless shirts and boys' caps, all of it not very far removed from the uniforms of the Currier and Ives illustrations, a vestigial survival of what must have been gentlemen's leisure wear a century ago."[34] On compare the Superman appearance of the football player, for whom "the donning of the required items results in an enlarged head and shoulders and a narrowed waist, with the lower torso poured into skintight pants accented only by a metal codpiece."[35] By contrast, the basketball player is about as close as one can be, in a public team spectacle in our culture, to the nudity required of the Greek Olympic athlete.

Putting everything together, if one were to ask for a model for baseball, it would be nineteenth century capitalist individualism. A model for football would be twentieth century totalitarianism. A model for basketball might be the communes of the 1960s or earlier. It is not mere coincidence that the best example, at this writing, of a basketball player who combines individual brilliance with team dedication is Bill Walton, whose political convictions are democratic socialist.

Soccer: The Game Is Football

"When the dribbler wants to elude a defender and change direction, he must do so by faking with his legs and feet without losing control of the ball. Three things are really happening at once—the dribbler is controlling the ball, faking, and changing direction, all with the same part of the body. There is no move in baseball, football, or basketball which demands as much from one part of the body at the same time, because control of the ball in these sports comes primarily from the hands."[36]

Thus, Chuck Cascio describes the essence of soccer. In the United States, baseball, football and basketball (which, as Cascio says, are all forms of **hand** ball) are the overwhelmingly most popular spectator sports. But not so in the world as a whole. Kyle Rote, Jr., a former student of theology and the law, and probably the best known soccer player born in the United States, estimates that there are about 250 million soccer players in the world.[37] This would mean that about one human being out of 20 plays soccer. Even in the United States Pelé, with his three-year contract with the New York Cosmos, was the highest paid athlete in history. Cascio says that he is better known throughout the world than Larry Csonka, Johnny Bench, Wilt Chamberlain, Gerald Ford, Carol Burnett, and Frank Sinatra. Among Americans, only Ali might compare. The World Cup, unlike the so-called World Series in baseball, is a global event. "The contests," says Cascio, "become part of a national movement, a country rallying behind a team involved in a war fought with feet and a ball."[38]

Soccer, although popular in Britain, Germany, Holland, Italy, Hungary, and the Soviet Union, is primarily a game of the southern hemisphere. It is played on big green fields, which can be as large as 130 yards long and 100 wide, on which a player can run 7 to 12 miles in the course of a game. Novak describes it as "an almost total commitment to fluid form, to kinesis, to the patterns in motion of a unit of runners."[39] Periodically, the fluidity is interrupted, or intensified, by bursts of action. Soccer, says

Novak, lacks the physical aggression and the tactical control of small, detailed activities that mark the major sports in the United States. As our opening quote emphasized, soccer is a game of the feet as contrasted with the hand games of the northern hemisphere. **Homo Faber** (man the maker) has built the northern hemisphere, says Novak, with manual dexterity and manufacture (from the Latin **manus**, hand). So we might say that soccer is basically a Third World game. It makes sense that, in the days when manufacture was transforming England, the event occurred that is recorded on a commemorative stone at Rugby: "William Webb Ellis, with a fine disregard for the rules of the game, first took the ball in his arms and ran with it, thus originating the distinctive feature of the Rugby game." This manipulation (again, **manus**) began the series of events that finally ended with the transformation of soccer into American "football." In soccer, in the upper body, the head takes the place of the hand as an instrument of propulsion: "Good headers use the neck and head like a baseball player uses the wrist and hand. The wrist snaps the hand to provide force. In soccer, the neck snaps the head with much the same effect."[40]

Despite the trend to American football, soccer has also been here in the United States, but not as an American game. Baseball was fitted to the space of rural pastures, and basketball could be played wherever there was a barn to which to attach a peach basket. Soccer was played mainly by urban immigrants—German, Irish, Italian, and Polish immigrants in New England, New York City, and Pennsylvania, who attached themselves to clubs or teams sponsored by businesses like Bethlehem Steel, J. P. Coats Thread Company, American Woolen, and Interborough Rapid Transit. It was also played in the Ivy League colleges, but not in the heartland. In 1913 there was formed an amateur United States Football Association, but it was not until after the 1966 World Cup Games in England brought films of 32 matches that had drawn 1½ million people and grossed $7 million that United States promoters became seriously interested in soccer. The outcome was the formation of two pro leagues, which merged to form the North American Soccer League. At first the member cities imported whole foreign teams, who had in fact a soccer vacation with pay in their home off-season.

A ten-year contract with CBS did bring the game into middle America, and Pelé boosted attendance wherever he played, although it tended to drop back to normal afterwards. Individual imported players still make up the largest and the best part of the teams. However, the United States has developed a few native stars like Kyle Rote, Jr., and Bob Rigby. In 1975 the United States Soccer Federation estimated that there were 600,000 boys **and girls** playing soccer in the United States.[41] There were probably about 50,000 young players around Dallas (Rote's home town), 35,000 around St. Louis, and 40,000 in Washington, D.C.-Maryland-Virginia area. St. Louis University, Howard, Penn State, Clemson, and several smaller schools have

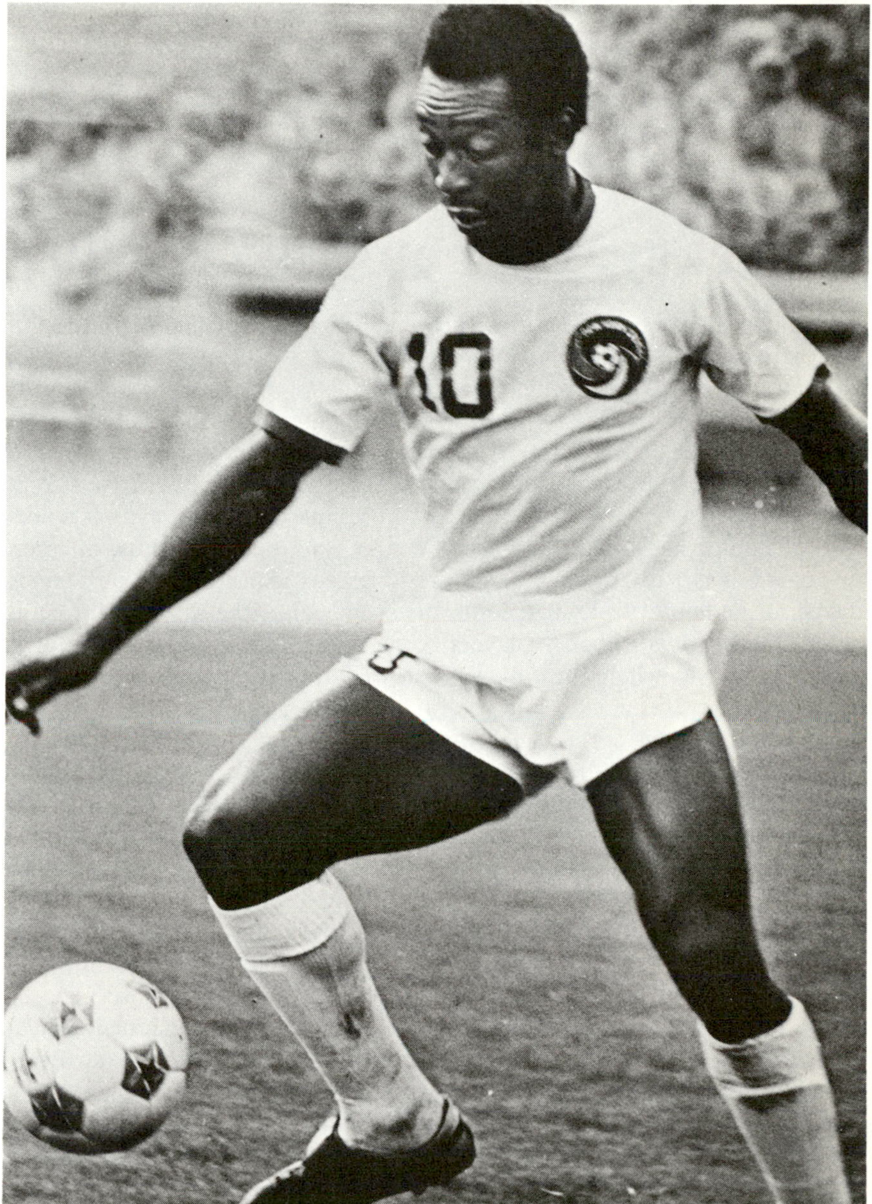

The Brazilian Football star Pele was the highest paid athlete in history and may be the best known person in the world. Courtesy of the New York Cosmos Soccer Club.

excellent soccer teams. The St. Louis Stars professional team, rooted in an area of soccer enthusiasm, was predominantly United States born, many locally recruited. However, in an age of manipulative technocracy, world-style football may be expected to have a hard time rooting itself in the American heartland and attaining the appeal of its somewhat illegitimate, but hand-oriented, violent, tightly coordinated, and authoritarian American grandchild.

Hockey: Game of the North

Hockey is a game of the north. It can technically be played in Miami, but it is native to the sub-arctic, where people live a profound confrontation with nature, where the ground is frozen solid six feet deep half of the year, where in winter blizzards are routine and a temperature of zero Fahrenheit is "warm," where there is ice on lakes in June and the possibility of frost in August. (Having grown up in the relative warmth of southern New York state, and having later taught four years in Minnesota, I can say that no one who has not experienced a sub-arctic winter can understand how different in quality it is.) Living in the sub-arctic breeds expectation of extremes, develops the habit of physical endurance, and raises the threshold to pain.

On this continent hockey players come typically from sub-arctic farms and small towns, where the only way out of this routine confrontation with nature is to go to the city, and the only way to the city for some may be hockey. I think this is the background against which we must understand the fact that hockey is the most violent of team games, the only team game where fighting is taken for granted, a game where collisions are so violent that part of a trainer's standard equipment are forceps to loosen swallowed tongues, where a team may carry a player with no real talent other than the capacity for mayhem.

Its native climate shapes the medium of the game and, therefore, the game experience. On skates on ice, players can reach velocities of up to 30 miles an hour, which no other sport approaches. By contrast with soccer, which he calls graceful, flowing, evasive, and quietly impassioned, Novak describes hockey as swift, physical, brutal, and violent.[42] The swiftness given by its icy medium lends to hockey a crowd appeal unique among games. It may also detract from its appeal by making it the least strategic of the territorial games. Ross Atkin says that the major drawback of hockey may be its "disjointed" nature:

> *Even the polished Montreal Canadiens have a hard time controlling the puck for any length of time. With bodies zooming all over the ice, the puck is constantly being intercepted and deflected, leading*

> *to a great amount of offensive futility. In basketball, by contrast, a team can more easily control the ball and set up shots. The attacking team in hockey often resorts to dumping the puck over the blue [line], then chasing after it. This sort of catch-as-catch-can play results in a fast-paced yet chaotic game that is not always interesting to strategy-minded fans.*[43]

Another element making strategic control difficult may be the unique fact that, in hockey, substitutions are made while play is in progress.

The speed imparted by the ice increases the possibility of violence in hockey. The "bodies zooming all over the ice" bear lethal weapons in their hands and on their feet. The puck is also lethal because, being flat to slide on ice, it can gash as well as bruise. Violence ultimately converges on the goal. "A lone oncoming shooter against a goal tender is the true one-to-one relationship," says Gerald Eshkenazi, ". . . a pure confrontation."[44] A hockey slap shot does not travel much faster than a fast pitch in baseball, but the ball is round and **the batter is not standing on the plate**. The goalie is heavily padded, true. Until fairly recently, however, his face was not protected by a mask. He was wide open to the kind of thing that happened in 1928 when New York Ranger goalie Lorne Chabot stopped a Montreal shot just above his left eye. If his 44-year old coach had not skated out to take Chabot's place, the Stanley Cup finals would have been terminated by doctor's orders then and there.

Hockey players are tough. "They dress for a game without fanfare," says Eshkenazi. "First they take out their false teeth and drop them into paper cups. Then they put on the gear that protects their kidneys, shoulders, groin, kneecaps, and toes. They know they will be hurt, that sometime during the evening they will be bruised."[45] Dr. James Nicholas, the orthopedic surgeon who took care of Joe Namath's knees and has done research on the demands imposed by different sports, has said, "Their tolerance to pain is remarkable. Hockey players are the most uncomplaining athletes I've met."[46] Some young players are said to collect the stitches from their healed wounds, and to boast after a bloody game about the new trophies they have won. There is a hockey cliché, "If you can walk to the bench, you can play."

This toughness and willingness to play when injured are tied to an intense emphasis on winning, which is in turn tied to the fact that for many players hockey is the only way out of the life in which they grew up. All these factors explain why hockey, although it does not have the tactically controlled violence of football, at all times skirts much closer to the brink of uncontrolled violence. The temper tantrum is close to being an accepted part of the game. The practical question for officials is not whether players should fight, but how soon, and how the fights will be stopped. For example, although fighting is technically illegal **per se**, officials are not too concerned about two men fighting, but must intervene before a third man joins because that is likely to bring bench-sitters on the ice (which is illegal) or trigger crowd involvement.

Hockey, like basketball, is played in a confined area where the spectators are very close to the action. Although sport statistics generally show a higher percentage of games won by all teams at home, in hockey, as in basketball, the advantage is very great. For example, in 1971 the New York Rangers had a 19-16 record on the road, while at home they won 30 games and lost only 2.[47] Knowing the ricochets off one's home boards is an advantage, but probably the main reason why home teams win is that, although the officials are honest and the players physically tough, in a basketball-hockey type of crowd situation, both are psychologically intimidated by the home crowd.

A final point—hockey is still the only major sport to remain almost totally white (in the 1976-77 season there were two blacks in the National Hockey League). I have referred to the tendency of hockey to become the "white hope" for white spectators as basketball teams and crowds become more black. Why have blacks not moved into hockey as they have into baseball, football, and basketball? There is no reason to think that the same physical abilities that have brought success in these sports could not be transferred to ice. The answer probably takes us back to where we started this section—hockey is a game of sub-Arctic Canada. As long as there is a pool of young rural Canadians culturally attuned to the game and ready to use a stick and a puck to get up in the world, blacks from the ghetto, as well as whites from the mines and the mills, will probably seek their upward mobility in other sport channels.

The Democratization of Tennis

In November 1970, according to a Nielson survey, there were 10.6 million tennis players in the United States. In the same month of 1974, there were 33.9 million.[48] This is not the first time tennis has been a popular mass sport. In the early days of the modern era, two travel guides told their readers about tennis abroad. In his **Description of England and Scotland**, in 1558, the Frenchman Estienne Perlin reported, "Here you may commonly see artisans, such as hatters and joiners, playing tennis for a crown, which is not commonly seen elsewhere, particularly on a working day."[49] In 1598 Sir R. A. Dallington, in his **Method for Travell**, gave Englishmen this information about the French: "Ye cannot find that little. . . town in France that hath not one or more courts. . . Ye would thinke they were born with

Rackets in their hands. . . There is more tennis players in France than ale drinkers with us."[50]

Tennis has not always been for the masses. In fact, it seems to have begun in monasteries. The French game **jeu de paume**, so called because it was played with the palm of the hand instead of a racket, was **court** tennis (lawn tennis was invented in the late nineteenth century). "Court tennis is played on a court shaped like a stylized cloister. The ball must travel over the net, as in lawn tennis, but may also be bounced against the walls, or from the roof of a low gallery which extends along three sides of the court, much the same as the cloister in a cathedral."[51] **Jeu de paume** was played first at Easter. It seems to have been an adaptation to Christian architecture and tradition of the pagan spring fertility rites. "By the year 1287, at least within church walls, the rough and tumble ball games had become more refined, and. . . in certain churches. . . the game of tennis is officially recognized."[52]

The game was fun enough so that it ceased to be only an Easter ceremony, and became the favorite sport of young monks. An illustrated calendar of the early sixteenth century shows a game in which a priest has taken off his religious garb, and his undershirt is showing. The church took action against such "scandalous" performances, as it did also against priests who played with laymen on public courts.[53] By the sixteenth century the game had become a sport for the kings and nobility and then for the common people. The racket had been introduced; by the year 1400 the manufacture of rackets and balls in France was controlled by a Guild of Tennis Masters.

By the sixteenth century tennis was established in England as the game of the courtier and gentlemen. Charles II was an avid player, who once lost 4½ pounds of weight in a single match. Tennis was also the badge of an educated man. J. Early, a Fellow of Oxford, in 1628 described a "mere Young Gentleman of the University," saying that "the two marks of his Senioritie, is the Bare Velvet of his Gowne, and his proficiencie at Tennis, where, when he can once play a set, he is a Fresh-man no more."[54] Henderson points out that "by the time of Shakespeare tennis was the popular sport of the common people." However, because of its association with gambling and other vices, it had practically disappeared by the beginning of the nineteenth century. Lawn tennis was developed in 1873, but at the time Henderson wrote, in 1947, what he said was essentially true: "Today tennis is played in the private courts of a few wealthy men in England and America, and a few select sporting clubs in the United States, England, and France. It is a splendid game, ideal for exercise in the young and old, but unfortunately restricted in its use because of its excessive cost."[55]

The only exception is that it had developed also as a minor spectator sport, played by young men and women variously known as "tennis

Lawn Tennis as invented by Major Wingfield, 1873. Courtesy of Racquet & Tennis Club.

bums," "kept amateurs," "shamateurs," who received travel and expense money, and sometimes a little more under the table. The game was still on the face of it a gentlemen's (or lady's) sport, played for fun by people who had no monetary interest. The decorum was upper class; applause or booing was not permitted. Until a Mexican man named Gonzales and a black woman named Gibson shot to the top, the personnel was essentially WASP, the kind of people admissable to a place like the West Side Tennis Club.

The realities of tennis a quarter of a century ago are graphically demonstrated in an exchange between the English press and American tennis player Gardnar Mulloy over a 1953 incident in which Mulloy lost his temper at Wimbledon. Suggesting that Mulloy had violated the tennis code of the gentleman, columnist Jack Peart wrote in the Sunday Pictorial: "Don't run away with the idea that the pick of the world's semi-professional sun-chasers are out for the honor and glory that goes with a coveted Wimbledon title. Not on your life. Kudos mean cash to amateur tennis players—especially the men. No wonder they call it the tennis racquet."[56]

Mulloy's reply places the tennis "amateur" in social context. He describes a hypothetical young man who has been groomed for international tennis since the age of 13:

> *After seven years of training, practice, striving, playing, he goes on to the center court at Wimbledon. For a game of tennis? Baloney! There's only one thing in the whole wide world that kid wants—to win. What the hell else is he there for? What do the folks back home think he is doing there? Playing a game of tennis? Under these circumstances a player who loses his temper deserves to get his ear slapped back. But our boy is involved in an international contest. National honor and prestige are at stake. A chance of becoming a world Champion is within reach. He's got to win.*[57]

During the period of the "kept amateur," there were tennis pros. But their activity was essentially limited to exhibitions. The major tournaments and Davis Cup play were still open only to "amateurs." In this game of gentlemen, there were no open tournaments. In the 25 years since the incident related by Mulloy, tennis has become frankly professional. A top player in his or her twenties today can make as much money in a year as the best and most experienced "amateur" players were able to pick up in a lifetime of expense and under-the-table money. Tennis is broadcast to the nation as TV entertainment, and tailored to the needs of television.

As our beginning statistics indicated, the decline of "shamateur" tennis has had another outcome than money for TV networks and careers for rising young stars. It has changed tennis from a game played in stuffy hushed decorum by a minority for a minority, to a game for the expanding middle classes in an affluent society. It is, as the young monks found, an optimistic springtime and summertime game. Like baseball, tennis is non-contact, non-territorial, and non-time bound. Thus, it offers a respite from the clock and the rat race. Being a striking game, it provides movement against an object rather than against people. It is active enough to engage the cardiovascular and respiratory systems. For these reasons, played as singles into middle age and as doubles thereafter, tennis remains perhaps the best participatory sport for lifetime health and pleasure.

Ultimate Self-Confrontation: Golf

Golf, which like tennis has traditionally been an elite sport, likewise exemplifies clearly the transition from play to commercialism. Like tennis, golf involves no territorial imperative, is non-time bound, non-contact, and involves the striking of an object with a stick. For these reasons—with the shortcoming that it does not as actively engage heart and lungs—it also is an excellent lifetime participant sport. Golf is the ultimate solo sport. There is really nothing in golf to compare to doubles in the other "individual" sport of tennis. In his history of the pro golf tour, Al Barkow describes what he sees to be the essence of golf:

> *It can be said that there are only two things in life we do alone: die and play golf. . . Where a home run or a sixty-yard forward pass may have the captivating properties of a well-hit golf shot, . . . they depend on the machinations of others—a mispitch at the waist, a fleet, sure-handed receiver, or a lax defender. The golfer, though, stands alone. He starts and finishes the deed; every shot he plays is a one-on-one confrontation with his own nervous system, power of concentration, ego. He can blame no one for failure, can take full credit for success. It is just he and the golf course. . . . The golfer is Don Quixote attacking a windmill, a windmill that is literally . . . himself. Golf teases the existential soul with the loneliness of the long distance runner.*[58]

What about this solo act draws spectators? In 1900, the fine English golfer Harry Vardon toured the United States and had this to report: "The Americans were not sufficiently advanced to appreciate some of the finer points of the game. They did, however, appear to thoroughly appreciate the type of ball I drove."[59] Barkow describes the same thing in Space Age terms: "A golf spectator is satisfied when he gets to see. . . a ball struck with consummate power and amazing control; a ball sent soaring from a standing start, then floating to earth and stopping within a prescribed swatch of lawn. It is an awesome sensation, not unlike watching a rocket launch."[60]

The golfer has not always been alone. So far as we can trace its history, golf originated in a team game. In the French **jeu de mail**, as early as the 14th century, two teams would drive wooden balls about the size of tennis balls cross country with a mallet to a marker—a stone, a tree, or other vertical objects. The game was played along country roads with high ditches that furnished natural obstacles. In the 17th century **jeu de mail** became popular with the wealthy, and the "course" was reduced to a single set ground. The Dutch played a similar game, **kolven**, in the 16th century, both teams using the same ball, the distant goal still upright. It was in Scotland, out of a form of a shinty, that a game emerged that involved driving a ball into a series of holes, and thus the distinctive character of golf as a ball game developed. Henderson believes that golf can be traced back through shinty to the Egyptian fertility rites. "But," he says, "the development of the game itself is Scottish."[61]

Mary Stuart, Queen of Scots, was fond of golf. Here we see her playing at St. Andrews. Courtesy of The Bettman Archive.

Golf remained a predominantly British game until well into the twentieth century, with St. Andrews, in Scotland, its Mecca. The first United States Open was held in 1895, with ten players and a purse of $335. In the **Atlantic Monthly**, in June 1902, William Garrot Brown sized up the situation: "Empires, trusts, and golf were three topics of conversation in the land. The future historian. . . will not rate golf as the least of the three new things which came with the end of the century."[62] In 1914 a Harvard philosophy profesor saw a trend: "Where the English are content to muddle through, the Americans take a directly opposite, scientific approach. We are too bound to succeed to ignore the importance of method." They did succeed. In 1921 Jock Hutchinson (an American, not a Scotsman) won the British Open. In 1922 Walter Hagen won it. In 1930 Bobby Jones completed a "grand slam" of British Open, British Amateur, American Open, and American Amateur tournaments.

Jones was the last great amateur golfer in the best traditional sense of the word—a lover of the game and a Southern gentleman of culture and means. At the time of his grand slam, there were essentially three kinds of golfers in the United States, with status in this order: (1) amateurs, (2) club pros, and (3) touring pros. The amateur could afford to play without being seriously concerned about tournament purses. The club pro was primarily a golf teacher who occasionally played a tournament. The touring pro played the circuit for a living, traveling the country in Depression days in a beaten up car over beaten up roads for a hopeful cut in a meagre purse. The man most responsible for giving respectabiity to the touring pros was Hagen, the son of a German-born blacksmith, and a tremendous competitor; the most spectacular event was a severe trouncing of Jones in a special match-play engagement. Gene Sarazen, son of an Italian carpenter, was also influential in taking the game away from the "elite." An important part in professionalizing golf was played by George May, an ex-Bible salesman who, in the 1940s, promoted the Tam O'Shanter tournament in Chicago with bleachers around greens, name tags on players, and the first $100,000 purse. A pivotal point in the rise to recognition of pro golf took place in 1953 when Lew Worsham, before a national TV audience of two million, won the Tam O'Shanter by one stroke by holing out a wedge shot on the last hole for an eagle.

We have come a long way from **jeu de mail**, **kolven**, and St. Andrews. Post-war affluence and TV coverage have made the pro tour a major commercial event, organized of course more for the national television audience than for the spectators on the spot. As Robert Lipsyte points out in his history of sport in the 1970s, "Corporate America's television sponsorship made golf an enormously rich spectator sport—our latest livingroom heroes were men in picnic clothes who charted their comparative standings not by victories or even great performances but by the amounts of money they earned."[63] Lipsyte cites the case of Arnold Palmer who, even with fading skills, remained a culture hero jetting "from engagement to appearance to board meeting to match to the opening of a trade show."

The "old school" in golf is still represented by the Masters tournament, held since 1934 at the Augusta National golf club. By contrast with the Chicago gangsters who sometimes hung around Tam O'Shanter, at Augusta National "the membership list is composed of the quiet powers that are part of the industrial-military complex."[64]

Jones was prominent in initiating the Masters, and President Eisenhower was also president of Augusta National. At Augusta, says Barkow, golf is played in the Victorian manner, "and not without the attendant hypocrisy." It is said that at the Masters dogs do not bark and babies do not cry. To avoid a commercial image, attendance and the size of the purse are not publicized, but golf course architects and equipment and clothing manufacturers are on the scene making deals and taking orders. On one occassion a very pregnant young woman was refused use of the clubhouse restroom because she did not have proper credentials. The younger generation of pros are sometimes put off by the elitist atmosphere. Former National Open champion Lee Trevino has complained that at the Masters Mexican-Americans have less status than caddies. However, Barkow does believe that the Masters is one of the best-run tournaments.

Those who think golf is a pastoral escape from the rat race should consider the harassment of Jane Blalock, an ex-tomboy and college history major, who in her twenties became one of the most effective players on the women's tour. Blalock is, in the words of her coach and by her own agree ment, a very intense competitor. I have not seen a more concrete and insightful inside account than she gives of the physical and psychological stresses of athletic competition.[65] In 1972 the Ladies' Professional Golf Association suspended Blalock on the basis of unsubstantiated charges that she had repeatedly cheated in placing her ball in play. Under a temporary court injunction, she was able to continue tournament play with success despite ostracism by many of her fellow players. In 1974 federal judge Charles A. Moye finally sustained his earlier ruling that the suspension was in violation of the Sherman Anti-Trust Act because "imposed by competitors of plaintiff who stand to gain financially from plaintiff's exclusion from the market."[65] The court did not rule on the facts in the case, but only on the conspiratorial nature of the procedure.

In Chapter 10 we will strike a more positive note and consider the social psychology of how sport can teach people to get along with their fellow human beings.

FOOTNOTES

[1]George Grella, "Baseball and the American Dream," **Massachusetts Review**, 15, 1975, 562-573.

[2]**Ibid.**

[3]Leonard Koppett, **The Essence of the Game is Deception: Thinking About Basketball**, Boston, Little, Brown, 1973.

[4]Michael Novak, **The Joy of Sports: End Zones, Bases, Baskets, Balls, and the Consecration of the American Spirit**, New York, Basic, 1976, 58.

[5]John Updike, "Hub Fans Bid Kid Adieu," **New Yorker**, Oct. 22, 1960, 112.

[6]Grella, **op. cit.**, 557.

[7]David Q. Voigt, "Reflections on Diamonds: American Baseball and American Culture," **Journal of Sport History, 1**, Spring 1974, 3-25.

[8]David Halberstam, "Baseball and the American Mythology," **Harper's**, July, 1970, 22-25.

[9]Novak, **op. cit.**, 69.

[10]**Ibid.**, 64.

[11]William O. Johnson, **Super-Spectator and the Electric Lilliputians**, Boston, Little, Brown, 1973, 103.

[12]Novak, **op. cit.**, 64.

[13]Grella, **op. cit.**, 562.

[14]Novak, **op. cit.**, 57-58.

[15]Grella, **op. cit.**, 551.

[16]J. H. Duthie, "Athletics, the Ritual of a Technological Society?", **Play and Culture**, ed. Helen B. Schwartzman, 1978 Proceedings of the Association for the Anthropological Study of Play, West Point, N.Y., Leisure Press, 1980, 94-95.

[17]**Ibid.**, 97.

[18]Mark Melzer, unpublished manuscript, 1977.

[19]Wiliam Arens, "The Great American Football Ritual," **Natural History**, October 1975, 77.

[20]**Ibid.**

[21]Daphne Hurford, "I'll Do Anything I Can Get Away With," **Sports Illustrated**, July 25, 1977, 30.

[22]Patricia Edelman, unpublished manuscript, 1977.

[23]John Robinson, "Time Expenditure on Sports Across Ten Countries," **International Review of Sport Sociology, 3**, 1967, 79, n. This note is a summary of other research, not of Robinson's own study.

[24]Novak, **op. cit.**, 76.

[25]Harry Edwards, **Sociology of Sport**, Homewood, Ill., Dorsey, 1973, 270.

[26]Novak, **op. cit.**, 82.

[27]**Ibid.**, 98-101.

[28]Cited, **ibid.**, 104.

[29]**Ibid.**, 107.

[30]**Ibid.**

[31]**Ibid.**

[32]Edwards, **op. cit.**, 198.

[33]Edgar Z. Friedenberg in Howard S. Slusher, **Man Sport, and Existence**, Philadelphia, Lea and Febiger, 1967, ix.

[34]Grella, **op. cit.**, 555.

[35]Arens, **op. cit.**, 78-79.

[36]Chuck Cascio, **Soccer, U.S.A.**, Washington, Luce, 1975, 198.

[37]**Ibid.**, 169.

[38]**Ibid.**, 21.
[39]Novak, **op. cit.**, 96.
[40]Cascio, **op. cit.**, 201.
[41]**Ibid.**, 185.
[42]Novak, **op. cit.**, 96.
[43]Ross Atkin, **Christian Science Monitor**, May 12, 1977, 11.
[44]Gerald Eshkenazi, **A Thinking Man's Guide to Pro Hockey**, New York, Dutton, 1972, 21-22.
[45]Eshkenazi, **op cit.**, 13.
[46]**Ibid.**
[47]**Ibid.**, 14.
[48]**Christian Science Monitor**, April 2, 1976, 9.
[49]Robert W. Henderson, **Ball, Bat, and Bishop: The Origin of Ball Games**, New York, Rockport Press, 1947, 59.
[50]**Ibid.**, 64.
[51]**Ibid.**, 47-48.
[52]**Ibid.**, 50.
[53]L'Abbé Cochard, "Le Jeu de Paume á Orléans," **Mémoires**, Orléans, Société Archéologique et Historique de l'Orleanais, 1889, **22**, 297-340. Cited in **ibid.**, 54.
[54]J. Earle, **Micro-Cosmographie**, 1628, cited in **ibid.**, 66.
[55]**Ibid.**, 58.
[56]Gardnar Mulloy, **The Will to Win: An Inside View of the World of Tennis**, New York, Barnes, 1960, 160.
[57]**Ibid.**, 163.
[58]Al Barkow, **Golf's Golden Grind: The History of the Tour**, New York, Harcourt, Brace, Jovanovich, 1974, viii, 25-26.
[59]**Ibid.**, 42.
[60]**Ibid.**, 25.
[61]Henderson **op. cit.**, 120.
[62]Barkow, op. cit., 51.
[63]Robert Lipsyte, **Sports World: An American Dreamland**, New York, Quadrangle, 1975, excerpted in **Miami News**, July 3, 1976, lB.
[64]Barkow, **op. cit.**, 173.
[65]Jane Blalock, with Dwayne Netland, intro. by Billie Jean King, **The Guts to Win**, Norwalk, Conn., Golf Digest, 1977, especially Chapter 7, "Pressure Golf," pages 103-113.
[66]Cited in Blalock, **op. cit.**, 97.

PART THREE

THE SOCIAL PSYCHOLOGY OF SPORT

Christy Mathewson was, of course, a wonderful pitcher—no other man probably has ever brought a President of the United States half way across the continent to a seat at a crucial game; and certainly no other pitcher ever loomed so majestically in young minds, quite overshadowing George Washington and his cherry tree or even that transcendent idol of boyhood, Frank Merriwell. Such men have a real value above and beyond the achievements of brawn and sporting skill. They realize and typify in a fashion, the ideal of sport—clean power in the hands of a clean and vigorous personality, a courage that has been earned in combat, and a sense of honor that metes out justice to opponents and spurns those victories that have not been earned.

—**Commonweal** obituary to Hall of Famer Christy Mathewson, October 21, 1925.

CHAPTER 10 SOCIALIZATION: THE RULES OF THE GAME

There is a widespread belief that play, games, sport teach the rules of life. In this chapter we will examine this belief in the light of what we know about **socialization**, the process through which one becomes a participating member of society.

Let us look first at several representative statements of this belief.

H. G. Wells, the British author who wrote a comprehensive world history and was a forerunner of science fiction, also wrote in 1911 a little book on simple floor games for young children, in which he said, "Upon such a floor may be made an infinitude of imaginative games, not only keeping boys and girls happy for days together, but building a framework of spacious and inspiring ideas in them for later life. The British Empire will gain new strength from nursery floors."[1]

At about the same time the prominent American psychologist G. Stanley Hall wrote of the role of adolescent games in developing social qualities. In adolescence, Hall said, "a new spirit of organization arises which makes teams possible or more permanent. Football, baseball, cricket, etc., and even boating can become schools of mental and moral training. The rules of the game are intricate, and to master and observe them effectively is no mean training for the mind in controlling the body. . . . The reason for every detail of inner construction and conduct of the game requires experience and insight into human conduct. Then the subordination of each member to the whole and to a leader cultivates the social and cooperative instincts. . . . Group loyalty can be so utilized as to develop a spirit of service and devotion not only to town, country, and race, but to God and the Church."[2]

Otto Mallery, a contemporary of Wells and Hall, told political and social scientists about the socializing functions of organized play:

> *In the games of the street every boy is for himself. Victory belongs to the shrewd, the crafty, and the strong. Team games of the playground require the submission of the individual will to the welfare of the team. Rigid rules inculcate fair play. A boy has the option of obeying the rules or not playing at all. New standards are set up; standards of self-control, of helping the other fellow, of fighting shoulder to shoulder for the honor of the team, of defeat preferable to unfair victory. These standards when translated into the language of political life we call Self-government, Respect for the law, Social Service and Good Citizenship.*[3]

Somewhat later Stuart Sherman used tennis to illustrate dramatically the socializing effects of sport. In a game of tennis, he says, the server is **physically** free to do all kinds of things. He can walk up to the net and drop the ball over instead of serving, shoot it over the net with a gun, or hire a boy to carry it around the net. But he is not **mentally** or **morally** free to do any of these things. He realizes that the rules make the game, and he believes in the game. "The ethical implications of athletic games are immense. Democracy itself is a complex athletic game. Its existence depends, more than upon anything else, upon our hearty willingness, for the sake of the game, to refrain from doing what we are physically perfectly free and able to do."[4]

George Davis, the "soft-nosed" football coach best known because in the 1960s he compiled an unbeaten record while having his high school players vote on their starting line-ups, explains that team democracy in football is the best way he knows to help young men find themselves. A person's task in life, says Davis, is to find what he can do best and mesh it with what others can do best, so as to enrich the lives of all. "How do I know this is true?" he asks. "Football taught me. The better I blocked, the better my halfback ran. The better he ran, the better I blocked. Life is finding what is best in **you** and presenting it to society in performance. I don't mean giving society what it wants necessarily, but giving it what **you** have to give."[5]

The Process of Socialization

Now let us move from these preliminary impressions to analyze systematically the part played by play, games, and sport in the process of socialization. By way of definition, socialization is **the process by which we acquire personalities as functioning members of society**. The fact that we acquire them in a process of experience means that our social qualities are not as such inborn. Our basic physiological, psychological, and social drives—for food, sex, recognition, response, emotional support—are. Our capacity for adapting to new situations (intelligence) has an inborn neurological basis as well as a basis in experience. The same may be true of special mechanical, musical, and mathematical aptitudes. But we clearly develop social potentialities only through social interaction. In a sentence suggested by Lenin, socialization is the process of learning "the elementary rules of social life that have been known for centuries and repeated for thousands of years in all school books."[6] It was described by the sociologist Charles Horton Cooley when he said that "always and everywhere men seek honor and dread ridicule, defer to public opinion, cherish their goods and their children, and admire courage, generosity, and success."[7]

Where, now, do play, games, and sport fit into the process? Writing of play among the children of the Australian aborigines, R. M. Berndt says, "For the student of primitive life the chief interest in. . . imitative play lies in its educational value. The primitive child's school is its playground, and his playground is everywhere."[8] The best general statement I know as to how play is related to socialization also comes from "down under." In **The Games of New Zealand Children** Brian Sutton-Smith says:

> *Group life is very precarious among young children six to nine years of age; in their game organization these youngsters can rise above the limitations of their own relatively unorganized personalities; the structure of their games makes group activity possible amongst them when there might otherwise be none; their games provide the first behavior patterns that (as a group of children reaching toward* **social** *organization) they can readily comprehend, enjoy, and maintain.*[9]

The Rumanian sociologist George Ciuciu distinguishes two aspects of socialization—adaptation and innovation—and says that they correspond to two kinds of games—organized and extemporized. "With the help of the two kinds of games the child and the teenager get trained for two fundamental elements of the social life: the observation or integration into the social norms on the one hand, the change or modification of the social environment on the other."[10]

Earlier, Cooley had written of how our highest principles of social judgment grow out of concrete experience in the simplest group relationships like play:

> *Where do we get our notions of love, freedom, justice and the like which we are ever applying to social institutions? Not from abstract philosophy, surely, but from the actual life of simple and widespread forms of society, like the family* **or the play group** *[italics mine]. In these relations mankind realizes itself, gratifies its primary needs, . . . and from the experience derives standards of what it is to expect from more elaborate associations. Since groups of this kind are never obliterated from human experience, but flourish more or less under all kinds of institutions, they remain an enduring criterion by which the latter are ultimately judged.*[11]

Before we go into the socializing effects of sport as such, let me illustrate how socialization works concretely through a simple central person game that I played as a child in New York state in the 1920s and which a 1980 publication tells me is still played in southern California up to the age of 9.[12] Sutton-Smith does not list it among the games of the New Zealand children, but I imagine it is played there too, perhaps under a different name.

The game is Redlight. For those not familiar, it is played this way: Players (except one) line up at a starting line. The object is to reach a finish line. An It person, chosen by some chance procedure, turns his back to the starters, facing in the same direction, and shouts "Greenlight." Everyone tries to move toward the finish line. Periodically the It person shouts "Redlight" and turns and faces the other contestants. Everybody must stop. Anyone who doesn't will be sent back to the starting line. The game is won by the person who first reaches the finish line by advancing during the "greenlight" periods. The winner becomes It, and the previous It returns to the ranks. The process is repeated over and over.

We can call Redlight a metaphor of social authority—of leadership and followership, of superordination and subordination. The game is the authority system of home, school, work, and public life, and it is also **not** that system (see Chap. 3). Redlight raises and answers such questions as: How do leaders get where they are? (Possibilities in the game and in real life are chance, performance, deception, and cheating.) How much power should a leader have to judge and punish the actions of his followers, and what right do followers have to disagree and control him? (Suppose the It person says "You moved," and I say "I didn't" or "I didn't intend to" or "I didn't move enough to count" or "I moved but you didn't really see me." Or suppose the It person plays favorites. How are these situations to be resolved?)

The theme of Redlight, says Christine van Glascoe, is "the relationship between access to power and its exercise, and the social control of power in its abuse. . . In the game, one matures, as it were, from player to director in a period of about 10 minutes, and, furthermore, is allowed to practice the transition from player to director over and over again.''[13]

We will be able to examine just what sport does for our socialization by looking at it as **internalization of roles in a system of antagonistic cooperation**. Figure 10.1 portrays this visually.

Figure 10.1 The Game as a Social System

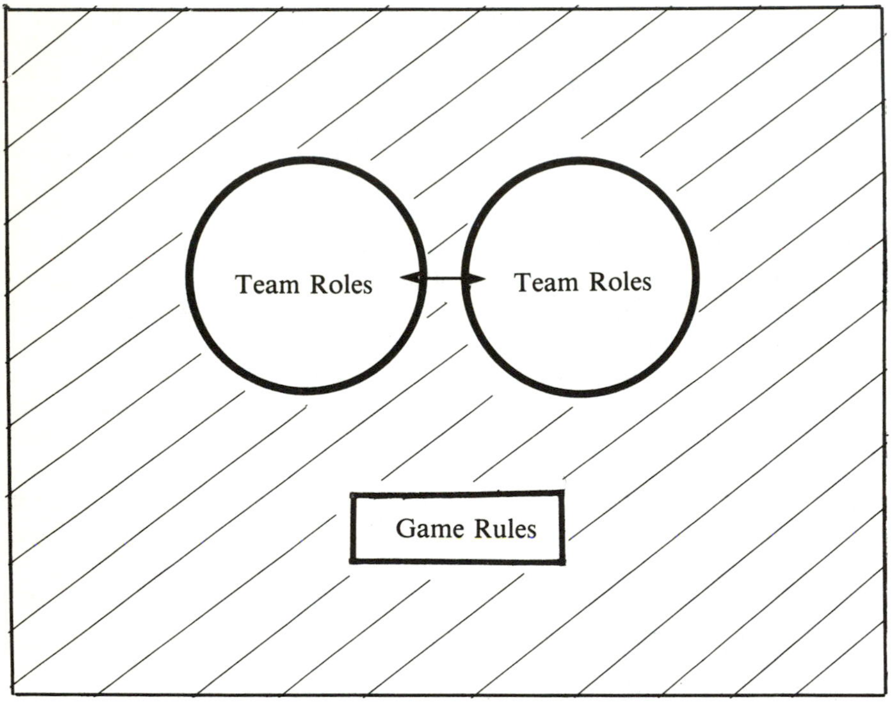

Antagonistic Cooperation

The term ''antagonistic cooperation'' comes from the book that also gave the words ''folkways'' and ''mores'' to our language.[14] William Graham Sumner used the term to describe a situation where two groups are in conflict within a wider system of cooperation. As an example he cited the kind of relationship by which predators refrain from killing their prey in order to avoid exterminating their source of food, thus benefiting both parties. He also saw industrial organization as an advanced form of antagonistic cooperation among groups struggling to wrest a living, and more, from nature and one another. Huizinga reminds us that the basis for preliterate tribal organization has typically been opposition of two "phratries" into which the tribe is divided. "The mutual relationship of the two tribal halves is one of contest and rivalry, but at the same time one of reciprocal help and the rendering of friendly service."[15]

A game is such a system of antagonistic cooperation. George Sauer, telling why he loved football even though he had to quit it, said, "At its highest level athletic competition is a cooperative venture much more than it is an antagonistic one."[16] Huizinga describes the potlatch (of which, we saw in Chapter 6, football may be a contemporary version) in terms of "two groups standing in competition but bound by a spirit of hostility and friendship combined."[17] Sutton-Smith observes that "it is clear that games can take place only between people who have confidence in each other, at least to some extent. Games and sports imply a higher level of agreement among the antagonists than exists between those who do not have games.[18] Writing of modern sport (especially football—soccer and rugby) Norbert Elias and Eric Dunning state clearly the nature of antagonistic cooperation:

> *In present-day industrial societies, a game is a group configuration of a very specific type. At its heart is the controlled tension between two sub-groups holding each other in balance. . . a "tension-balance." . . . Just as the mobility of a human limb is dependent on the contained tension between two antagonistic muscle-groups in balance, so the game depends on a tension between two and at the same time antagonistic and interdependent players keeping each other in fluctuating equilibrium.*[19]

Roles

Within this equilibrium of antagonistic cooperation, each person plays his role, as one does in life as a whole. The most famous statement about role is by Shakespeare: "All the world's a stage, and all the men and women merely players. They have their exits and their entrances, and each man in his time plays many parts." The classic scientific definition is by the anthropologist Ralph Linton:

> *A role represents the dynamic aspect of a status. The individual is socially assigned to a status and occupies it with relation to other statuses. When he puts the rights and duties which constitute*

the status into effect, he is performing a role. . . Each person has a series of roles deriving from the various patterns in which he participates and at the same time a role in general, which represents the sum total of these roles and determines what he does for the society and what he can expect from it.[20]

Linton's definition (as perhaps Shakespeare's) is a little too rigid: it sounds as though the roles we play in life (and also games) are the reading of a predetermined script. In real life, and real games, this is not the case. In life and games, we have two kinds of roles: (1) those in which we follow to the letter patterns assigned to us, and (2) those in which we exert initiative in meshing our behavior with that of other people whose precise response we can predict roughly but not exactly. The first are most likely to be stressed in Ciuciu's "organized" games, the second in "extemporized" ones. We can call these two kinds of roles **authoritarian** and **self-generated**. An illustration is the difference between the quarterback whose plays are called from the bench, and the quarterback who has a great deal of freedom to call the play as he "reads" the defensive alignment. The other players may also run the gamut, from carrying out assignments memorized from their playbooks to improvising their own tactics to conform to the quarterback's "audibles."

The two kinds of role-playing are likely to be promoted by two types of athletic leaders. Football coaches like Vince Lombardi and Paul Brown, or leaders in baseball like Little League manager Mike Maietta, are likely to demand rigid performance of predetermined roles or to call all plays from the bench. Ex-Green Bay Packer Bill Curry said of the Lombardi method: "What he seemed to do was to select a role for each player. He wrote the play, and he did the choreography, and if you didn't fit the role he would change your personality so you could play the part."[21] Martin Ralbovsky's **Destiny's Darlings** gives a similar profile of Maietta's authoritarian leadership as seen by his individual players and by himself in interviews twenty years later.[22] More humanistically oriented coaches like George Davis or Weeb Eubank of the spectacular 1969 New York Jets Super Bowl champions, or baseball managers like Red Schoendienst of the 1967 St. Louis Cardinals, are likely to encourage more flexible role performance. By contrast with the Lombardi image, Curt Flood describes Schoendienst as "a friendly, unobtrusive, considerate man who did not distract us from our jobs,"[23] Flood's picture of the Cardinals is one of genuine socialization:

Nobody on that team had occasion to utter the usual petty platitude, "I don't care if he's white, black, purple, or green, just so he does his job on the field." On that team we cared about each other and shared with each other and . . . inspired each other. As friends, we had become solicitous of each other's ailments and eccentricities, proud of each other's strengths. We had achieved a closeness impossible by other means. . .

There we were, Latins, blacks, liberal whites and redeemed peckerwoods, the best in the game and the most exultant. Victorious on the field and victorious off it, by God. A beautiful little foretaste of what life will be like when Americans finally unshackle themselves.[24]

Internalization

Roles, to be effective, have to be internalized, so that not only are they expected of us by others, but they are expected of us by ourselves. Freud once compared the upbringing of a child to the siege of a city. Having established its superiority, the attacking army (society), to avoid having to keep up the siege indefinitely, establishes a garrison within the city. We do not have to believe, as Freud seemed to, that the relationship between society and the unsocialized child is inevitably war. But his image of the "internal garrison" is valid to the extent that social controls over behavior are not effective until they are internalized.

The social psychologist George Mead's description of how internalization takes place is especially relevant for us because he specifically stresses the function played by games.[25] Role taking begins in the young child when he takes the role of **specific** others—plays Mommy, Daddy, cowboy, Indian, teacher, postman, policeman, and so on—and in these capacities carries on conversations with himself. In so doing he internalizes the character he plays. (Freud stressed the importance of internalizing the specific other of—identifying with—one's parent.) But in a game, says Mead, the process is carried farther. The child internalizes not an individual, but a group; not a specific other, but a **generalized other**. "If [a child] gets in a ball nine, he must have the responses of each position involved in his own position." To perform his role, he must be able to take in fantasy the role of everyone else on his team (and, we may add, the roles of the players on the other team). Mead, being a philosopher—no jock—is not as specific as he might be. We can take a specific illustration from baseball. Suppose there are runners on first and second. The batter drives a low liner to right field for a hit. Immediately we have ten players (the batter and the two runners on the team at bat, and the right fielder, the four infielders, and the pitcher and catcher on the fielding team) who are potentially involved in the play. Each, to play his role at this moment, must have inside him the roles of the other nine. The simplest outcome is a throw that goes directly to the plate, with the pitcher backing up the catcher. Another possibility is a cut-off throw and a play at third base. All the players have to have in them a range of possible actions by all ten men. With this illustration we can see what Mead means when he says: "The fundamental difference between the game and play is that. . . the child must have the attitude of all the others involved in the game. The attitudes of the other players, which the participant assumes, organize into a sort of unit, and it is that organization that controls the response of the individual."[26] The unit is the "generalized other."

In the game, the generalized other is the team, the little society that each player internalizes. Looking back at Figure 10.1, we could also say that the player internalizes the roles of **both** teams, who are involved together in the antagonistic cooperation of the game.

In the child's socialization, internalizing the generalized other in the game is a preparation for life in society. "What goes on in the game goes on in the life of the child all the time," ". . . He has to play the game." The sociologist Cooley found the basic sources of personality in the three main "primary groups"—family, neighborhood, and play group.[27] Mead says that games are such a powerful preparation for life because they may grip the child more intensely than either his family or the community to which he belongs. It is through internalization as generalized others that one's family, school, religious organization, clubs, country become a part of one's life—as also may the whole human race. "Ask not for whom the bell tolls," said John Donne. "It tolls for thee."[289]

Another perspective: the German sociologist Georg Simmel observed of the game that it is "not only that the game is played in a society (as its external medium) but that with its help people actually 'play' 'society'."[29] In his study of Little League baseball, Geoffrey Watson spells this out:

> *From the first step of the player's passage through the game—warming-up to bat—to the next step of the outcome of 'MAKING IT on base' or disconsolately returning to the dugout, to the final and ultimate stage of witnessing or making the third 'out,' parents are exposed to a symbolic 'departure' of their sons to the depths of game interaction where unpredictable and totally uncontrollable events flow with dramatic speed. The game adopts a position of central importance due to the public display of a son's ability: on center stage at bat, when base running, or when his skills are tested in decision-making fielding performances. Throughout the immediate concerns of the wider community are temporarily 'ruled out' as the late evening's action engrosses both parent and son in a family game which is as much a sport for mother and father as it is for an aspiring son. Families actually 'play' 'society' in what appears to be in every way an intensely competitive and achievement-oriented socialization laboratory. . .*[30]

Game Rules and Life History

The socializing function of play, games, and sport is a process that takes place within a person's life history. What is the chronology—what follows what? Ivor Kraft tells us what comes first: "Typically, the child first grasps the meaning of the abstraction, **rule**, in simple life situations which have nothing to do with games. He is punished, rewarded, deprived, or offered some pleasure in connection with what seem to be arbitrary aspects of life: He gets his bottle if he cries lustily; the cat scratches him if he pulls its tail. The child later applies this concept to games."[31] Mead sees a succession of play, with internalization of specific others, and games, in which a generalized other composed of one's peers is incorporated into one's personality. Several other students of play and games have stressed the transition that takes place as parents lose significance as the center of the child's life and are replaced by his peer group.

In a study published in the last years of the nineteenth century, Luther Gulick outlined five stages in psychological development in play, from babyhood to late adolescence. His conclusions were based on reminiscences of his own five children, and of children in Springfield, Massachusetts, and in English schools; on boys' books; and other studies.[32] Gulick found children before the age of 7 doing things like building with blocks, climbing, and investigating (even to the point of dissection of animals that he felt expressed not cruelty, but inquisitiveness). But "children before the age of seven rarely play **games** spontaneously." If they play them, it is generally on the initiative of adults or older children. Unless influenced by adults, play at this age is also "almost exclusively noncompetitive." There is typically little finely coordinated manual dexterity—hand-wrist movements.

Gulick found children between 7 and 12 playing games individualistically and competitively—making little streams and dams, paddle-wheels and boats, and simple machinery of all kinds. Typical games were blindman's bluff, prisoner's base, tiddly winks, marbles, somersaulting, and rolling over backwards. Boys were more competitive than girls.

Early adolescence (12-17) Gulick found marked by the beginning of team games. Young adolescents played baseball, football, hockey, and basketball, and formed gangs to play cowboys and Indians or cops and robbers. The key here was "co-operation among a number for a given end," with the individual subordinated to the group and to a peer leader.

In late adolescence, "the plays [games] are pushed to the limits of endurance and strength: they correspond more to organized savage warfare—for instance, college football. There is a depth and intensity about it that older people can hardly realize, unless they have themselves been through it. It seems to be a real thing and not merely a game."[33] We will remember that this was 1898.

In summary, "the plays of early childhood are individualistic, non-competitive, and for the accomplishment and observation of objective results. The plays of later childhood are individualistic, competitive, involve active muscular coordination and some judgments. The plays of adolescence are socialistic, demanding the heathen virtues of courage, endurance, self-control, bravery, loyalty, enthusiasm."[34]

The succession Gulick describes is from parent-centered (early childhood) to individualistic-competitive (later childhood) to team-competitive (adolescence). We well remember that, when Gulick wrote, there was no adult organization of Little League baseball or Pop Warner football for children.

Maximilian Stejskal's description of the traditional folk-athletic games of rural Finland (as contrasted with modern athletics) emphasizes the socializing role of games as **rites de passage** celebrating and legitimizing the transition from childhood to manhood.[35] Stejskal's conclusion that "under-eights rarely compete in their play consciously with one another" sounds like Gulick. From 12 to 15, Stejskal found, rural boys fight a lot, to test and demonstrate their strength and agility. But about 15, the age at which the church customarily confirms them adults, the matter gets serious. When boys can lift "confirmation stones" up to knee level "tradition occasionally defines that maturity or marriage ability is proven," although sometimes it may be necessary only to lift one end of the stone, not to raise it off the ground. But this weight-lifting may go so far as to resemble the severe puberty tests of some preliterate societies, or the competitive bench-pressing practiced by American athletes. With the help of a rope, these Finnish adolescents may lift up to 250 Kilos (550 pounds). Although Gulick had found them characteristic of the then-urbanized culture as early as the 1890s, team games, or "collective sport" in which "the individual subordinates himself to the team" are in Finland a part of the development of modern athletic games, which are much more structured and take place at sport grounds, rather than fields, backyards and country roads, the traditional scene of the rural folk-athletic games.

Constraint and Reciprocity

In the early twentieth century Jean Piaget studied children of both sexes in Geneva and Neuchatel, Switzerland to learn about the rules by which they played marbles.[36] Piaget found the same general progression from parent-governed to peer-governed games that Gulick did, and that Sutton-Smith found in New Zealand (see Chap. 6). Children under 10, if asked who

In Finland, the rural folk-athletic games of adolescence lead to organized sport. Statue of the great Finnish distance runner, Paavo Nurmi, in front of the Helsinki Olympic Stadium, site of the 1952 Games. Courtesy of Finnish National Travel Office.

had invented the game of marbles, would almost inevitably attribute it to their fathers or to the elders of the community. Asked whether one child or a group of children could change the rules if they wished, they typically answered "no," explaining that what has been handed down by the elders is right and should not be questioned. Strangely enough, although verbally the young children said the rules were unchangeable, in practice they did not observe them very well. To the question about who invented the game, the children over 10 were likely to answer something like "a bunch of kids." To the question whether the rules can be changed, their response was typically "Why not?" Unlike the younger children, who said the rules are sacred and unchangeable but broke them, the older children, while saying they are open to improvement, were more likely to observe them.

Piaget, like Mead, was studying games not for their own sake but for what they could teach about socialization—the development of social morality. He found a progression in marbles from a **morality of constraint**, which is **heteronomous** (other-directed) to a **morality of reciprocity**, which is **autonomous** (self-directed):

> *We have recognized the existence of two moralities in the child, that of constraint and that of cooperation. The morality of constraint is that of duty pure and simple. . . .The child accepts from the adult a certain number of commands to which it must submit whatever the circumstances may be. Right is what conforms to these commands; wrong is what fails to do so. . . .But first, parallel with this morality, and then in contrast to it, there is gradually developing a morality of cooperation, whose guiding principle is solidarity and which puts the primary emphasis upon autonomy of conscience.*[32]

A Harvard study by Michael Maccoby, also dealing with the game of marbles, supports the trend toward reciprocity found by Piaget. Maccoby asked boys: "When you are playing marbles with your father and you have each got ten marbles, how many are you prepared to lose to your father and how many are you prepared to win off him, and when you are playing with your best friend how many marbles will you lose and how many will you win?" The 5 year olds, when playing with their fathers, wanted to lose a lot; playing with their peers, to win a lot. The 11 year olds wanted to win a lot from their fathers but to break even with their best friend. Here we see a sharp change in attitude toward the authoritarian figure (from "let him have all" to "clean him out") and toward the peer (from "clean him out" to "share and share alike").[38]

Piaget's findings were stated as though they were true of all children, everywhere, at any time. But he did note that the children he studied were from the economically poorer areas. An Englishman, M. R. Harrower, compared responses to game rules and situations in two groups of British children: a group of lower income children comparable to those studied by Piaget, and a group from a "progressive middle class school.[39] Of the middle class school children, Harrower said, "There is certainly no evidence of Piaget's 100 percent in terms of appeal to authority at the age of 6-7 years in this group." It would seem (and this corresponds with other things we know) that respect for authority is much stronger in children of lower income families. Thus, Harrower found that "there is a much greater shift away from an arbitrary ethics of authority in the [lower class children]." Perhaps Piaget's results were biased by the socioeconomic group he studied.

Varieties of Group Success

The authoritarian and self-generated role behavior found by researchers can both produce effective teams. Here is a dramatic example of authoritarian role assignment, geographically and culturally very far from Vince Lombardi and Mike Maietta, taken from the textbook for Civics used in native schools in the Fiji islands in 1949:

Section 1 What does Government mean?

1. Here is a story:

Some boys wished to play [rugby] football. Sam had a ball, and Tom had one, too. But Sam hid his ball, so that they would use Tom's. Tom was angry.

When they played, they all wanted to play "forward." There were no "backs." Then they began to quarrel about it. Their game was stopped. They could not agree, so they could not play.

Inosa was the biggest boy. He said, "This is very foolish. We cannot play like this; I will be captain, and you must all do what I say. If you do not, then you shall not play."

They all said, "Yes." So he said, "We shall play with Sam's ball today. Tomorrow we shall play with Tom's ball." He then told each boy where to play. Now the game was good. They won the game.

When Inosa became captain, and made laws, that was GOVERNMENT. You cannot play games without laws, and you cannot play without a leader.[40]

A different answer to the question. "What does government mean?" and also to the question, "What does sport mean?" would be given by George Davis:

The biggest problem is motivating your athletes to perform. You know what he's going to have to do. Well, who will he do it better for? Will he do it better for an authority, or will he do it better for his peer group?

People associated with sociology know the answer. It's the peer group. Most of us all our lives have been cast in roles so tight that we don't dare escape them. I think many coaches feel if they take away the threat of not playing an athlete, the athlete won't obey them. That's not true. They'll be more closely disciplined by their peer group and what they think of them than they would possibly be by what their coaches think of them. Joe Namath is a good example. He's independent, a free soul, but his commitment to his teammates is complete. He would rather hurt himself than his teammates. I believe that. . . .

College and pro teams should vote on starting lineups. The coaches need not accept the players' veiw, but at least they will know what the athletes are thinking. Who knows? The vote might surprise them. It certainly will make for more cohesion and confidence between players and coaches. . . .

I. . .feel I know as much about democracy and its relationship to human beings as anybody. I know how it works—not by studying statistics or researching out somebody's opinions. . . .It's a great way to go. It's the only way.[41]

As I said, both constraint and autonomy can produce successful teams in many ways. Sutton-Smith points out the interesting fact that authoritarian role assignment can generate peer group solidarity. In the very young children in New Zealand playing games with a central figure ("It," for example, in tag), he shows how in play children can form a cohesive group through symbolically acting out their resentment against authority.

Although these players do not as yet have much experience in getting along with one another, they do not have in common their experience of the relationship between inferior and superior beings. Such common experiences, when represented in the form and fantasy content of these games, can bind the children into a group where other things might fail. . . .In the. . .games there is. . .identification with parent figures seen as arbitrary and fearsome. All children have had the experience of contending, in fact or fantasy, against such figures. In these games they can explore these feelings, but can do so without the dangers that would be involved in exploring such feelings in real life. The games invite exploration (screaming with fear, roaring with rage) but with their rules and the agreement that it is only 'play,' they safeguard the children from the anxiety which might otherwise result from unguarded exploration and expression of impulse.[42]

On the adult level, this kind of solidarity can be manipulated by intelligent authoritarians. Bill Curry relates how mutiny against Vince Lombardi erupted in the Green Bay locker room one day. One player, who had to be restrained from hitting the coach, told Lombardi off. Then Lombardi said, "All right. Now **that's** the kind of attitude I want to see. Who else feels that way?" One player said, "Yeah, me too!" Then all through the room rose cries, "Yeah, hell, me too!" "And suddenly," says Curry, "you had 40 guys that could kick the world." Then Lombardi went through the room and asked each man, nose to nose, "Do you want to win football games for me?" "And the answer was, 'Yes, sir,' 40 times, and we did not lose another game that year."[43]

Cheating, Winning, and Socialization

There are still further questions to be asked about socialization. In discussing how the child applies the concept of "rules" to games, Ivor Kraft comments, "The child. . .also quickly grasps the concept that sometimes one can get away with breaking the rules (cheating) in such a way as to enable the game to go on functioning. Cheating happens to be a widespread phenomenon wherever games are played."[44] Of the lessons taught by games, Sutton-Smith says, "In games children learn all those necessary arts of trickery, deception, harassment. . .and foul play that their teachers won't teach them, but that are most important in successful human relationships in marriage, business, and war."[45]

In **The Ultimate Athlete** George Leonard elaborates on this point. He says that we have come to take cheating for granted in the sports we watch on TV. In football, for example, along with the game between the two teams, there is a game between players and officials. Offensive holding is forbidden by the rules. But players, coaches, and officials all know that a certain amount takes place and is permitted. "The point, then, is not **whether** to hold, but **when** to do it and **how** to do it sneakily."[46] Leonard reminds us that fouling is accepted basketball strategy and an expected source of spectator enjoyment in hockey. This game of staying ahead of officials is not confined to sport, he reminds us. "We who cheat for a team are by no means individualistic tricksters. We are good corporation men. By playing sneaky games with officials, we prepare ourselves for success in the world outside of games. We learn to press for advantages in making out expense accounts and tax returns; we depend upon corporate and government officials to show us just how far we may go. We push to the limit traffic laws and antitrust laws and laws concerning political contributions."[47]

All this—which is **not** socialization in the sense of learning the basic rules necessary to get along with others—we will develop further in the next chapter.

Let us now look at Figure 10.1, which depicts a game as a system of antagonistic striving within rules, and ask two questions:

1) Is learning to win by violating the rules a socializing experience, even if it increases the solidarity of the "team"? (There is some ambiguity as to what "violating the rules" means, for a certain amount of technical rule violation falls within the "unwritten law" of accepted behavior—a hand at the base of the offensive center's spine in basketball, a certain amount of offensive holding in football and loose stick handling in hockey. Do we mean the written rule or the unwritten one?)

2) Is learning to win by observing the rules (even to the letter) always a socializing experience? Or can "fair" winning de-socialize a person?

Over the years one of my class assignments has been to ask students to write a critical review of the article in which George Sauer tells how the emphasis of winning and aggression forced him to leave football.[48] Every time a substantial number of students have replied like this: "George was a great football player and a beautiful humanist, but he's out of this world, a utopian dreamer. Doesn't he realize that what he found intolerable in football is a reflection of our culture? Football is no different from any other business, and to change it you will have to change the whole culture."

I believe the linking of football to our culture is accurate, and I also think George Sauer knows it is.

Is "winning" socializing? Many social scientists confuse people by using the word socialization loosely, to signify "learning the accepted culture pattern." I think we should limit the term, as I have tried to in this chapter, to learning of the elementary rules (and attitudes) necessary to human social life anywhere, anytime. It is quite possible for a culture to survive, temporarily, while violating "the elementary rules of social life." We don't know how long "temporary" is. Nazi Germany, which hoped to last a thousand years, is one example.

Fred Mahler, a Rumanian sport sociologist, made the point eloquently in telling the Fourth International Symposium on Sport Sociology at Bucharest in 1973 that play transmits the moral contradictions of a society and in calling for a "counterplay" to protect the players from the negative effects:

> *We certainly are in favor of competitive games but. . .one should awaken the consciousness of the participant. . .that affirmation*

of his personality integrated with the collective is the most precious result of play, success being nothing but a means and not an end in itself; that what is precious in a competition is the effort to surpass oneself, achieved not at the expense of the others, but together with them; that the true conquerer is the one who, thanks to a dignified behavior and observation of the rules, has unanimously been accepted, has obtained the affirmation of his human qualities, even if he is not the one who has personally conquered the laurels. This is how a 'pedagogy of play and counterplay,' without trying to construct a utopian 'play without competition,' should combat everything that transforms play into fight and should stimulate play where the winner is a collective of honest players who through competing respect and help one another.[49]

One can learn the rules of one's **cultural** game without learning the rules of the **human** game. So this chapter on socialization is followed by another on the relation of sport to **enculturation** in the "achieving society."

FOOTNOTES

[1]H. G. Wells, **Floor Games**, London, Frank Palmer, 1911, 9-10.

[2]G. Stanley Hall, **Adolescence**, New York, Appleton-Century-Crofts, 1937, Vol. 1, 221-222.

[3]Otto Mallery, "The Social Significance of Play," **Annals of the American Academy of Political and Social Science**, March 1910, 156.

[4]Stuart P. Sherman, "Towards an American Type," in **Points of View**, New York, Scribner's, 1924,21.

[5]Quoted in Neil Amdur, The Fifth Down: **American Democracy and the Football Revolution**, New York, Coward, McCann, and Geoghegan, 1971, 304.

[6]V. I. Lenin, **State and Revolution**, New York, International, 1932, 73-74.

[7]Charles Horton Cooley, **Social Organization**, New York, Shocken, 1962, 28.

[8]R. M. Berndt. "Some Aboriginal Children's Games," **Mankind** [Australia], **2**, Oct. 1940, 293.

[9]Brian Sutton-Smith, **The Games of New Zealand Children**, Berkeley, University of California Press, 1959. Reprinted in Sutton-Smith, **The Folkgames of Children**, Austin, University of Texas Press for the American Folklore Society, 1972, 44-45.

[10]George Ciuciu, "The Socialization Process of Children by Means of Extemporized and Organized Games." **International Review of Sport Sociology**, 9, 1, 1979, 9.

[11]Cooley, **op. cit.**, 32.

[12]Christine A. Van Glascoe, "The Work of Playing Redlight," in **Play and Culture**, ed. Helen B. Schwartzman, 1978 Proceedings of the Association for the Anthropological Study of Play, West Point, N.Y., Leisure Press, 1980, 228-231.

[13]**Ibid.**, 231, 230.

[14]William Graham Sumner, **Folkways: A Study of the Sociological Importance of Usages, Manners, Customs, Mores, and Morals**, Boston, Ginn, 1940, 18.

[15]John Huizinga, **Homo Ludens**, Boston, Beacon, 1955, 53.

[16]George Sauer and Jack Scott, "The Souring of George Sauer," **Intellectual Digest**, December 1971, 55.

[17]Huizinga, **op. cit.**, 59.

[18]Sutton-Smith, **The Folkgames of Children, op. cit.**, xv.

[19]Norbert Elias and Eric Dunning, "Dynamics of Group Sports With Special Reference to Football," **British Journal of Sociology**, **17**, 397.

[20]Ralph M. Linton, **The Study of Man**, New York, Appleton-Century-Crofts, 1936, 114-115.

[21]George Plimpton and Bill Curry, "The Green Bay Monster," **Quest/1977**, March-April 1977, 32.

[22]Martin Ralbovsky, **Destiny's Darlings: A World Championship Little League Team Twenty Years Later**, New York, Hawthorn, 1974.

[23]Curt Flood with Richard Carter, **The Way It Is**, New York, Trident, 1970, 87.

[24]**Ibid.**, 88, 90.

[25]George Herbert Mead, **Mind, Self and Society from the Standpoint of a Social Behaviorist,** Chicago, University of Chicago Press, 1967, especially "Play, the Game, and the Generalized Other," 152-164.

[26]**Ibid.**, 123-124.

[27]Cooley, **op. cit.**

[28]John Donne, "Devotions Upon Emergent Occasions," **Complete Poetry and Selected Prose**, London, Nonesuch, 1929, 538.

[29]Georg Simmel, **The Sociology of Georg Simmel**, trans. and ed. with intro. by Kurt H. Wolff, New York, Free Press, 1950, 50.

[30]Geoffrey G. Watson, "Games, Socialization and Parental Values: Social Class Differences in Parental Evaluation of Little Legue Baseball," **International Review of Sport Sociology**, 12, 1, 1977, 29.

[31]Ivor Kraft, "Pedagogical Futility in Fun and Games?" **NEA Journal**, January 1967, 71, 72.

[32]Luther Gulick, "Some Psychical Aspects of Muscular Exercise," **Popular Science Monthly**, **53**, October 1898, 793-805.

[33]**Ibid.**, 801-802.

[34]**Ibid.**, 802.

[35]Maximilian Stejskal, "Folk-Athlete Games," **International Review of Sport Sociology**, 5, 1970, 175-184.

[36]Jean Piaget, **The Moral Judgment of the Child**, New York, Free Press, 1948.

[37]**Ibid.**, 334, 335.

[38]Reported by Brian Sutton-Smith in discussion at symposium, "Aspects of Contemporary Sport Sociology," proceedings edited by Gerald S. Kenyon, Chicago, Athlete Institute, 1969, 185-186.

[39]M. R. Harrower, "Social Status and the Moral Development of the Child," **British Journal of Educational Psychology**, **4**, 1934, 75-95.

[40]Cited in Florence Stumpf [Frederickson] and Frederick W. Cozens, "Some Aspects of the Role of Games, Sports, and Recreational Activities in the Culture of Modern Primitive Peoples," **Research Quarterly**, **20** March 1949, 13.

[41]Cited in Amdur, **op. cit.**, 197, 307.

[42]Sutton-Smith, **The Folkgames of Children**, **op. cit.**, 213-214.

[43]Plimpton and Curry, **op. cit.**, 37-38.

[44]Kraft, **op. cit.**, 72.

[45]Sutton-Smith, **The Folkgames of Children**, **op. cit.**, 339.

[46]George Leonard, **The Ultimate Athlete**, New York, Viking, 1974, 17.

[47]**Ibid.**, 17-18.

[48]Sauer and Scott, **op. cit.**

[49]Fred Mahler, "Play and Counter-play: On the Educational Ambivalence of Play or its Utilization to Counter the Negative Effects of Play," **International Review of Sport Sociology**, 9, 1, 1975, 112-113.

CHAPTER 11 ENCULTURATION: SPORT AND THE ACHIEVING SOCIETY

I shall begin this chapter with a research project in which sociologist Harry Webb investigated the development in sport of attitudes central to the achievement culture. Introducing his study, Webb says:

> *In the transition from communal-agrarian to urban-industrialized society, 'achievement' criteria are presumed to replace 'ascription' ones as a basis for the allocation of positions and the distribution of rewards. The urban-industrialized society, based as it is on technological knowledge and a consequent division of labor, presumably requires a distribution of roles, at least in the economic and political institutions, based on qualifications of training and ability, and not necessarily on family background. 'To the swift goes the prize,' goes the saying indicating not only the constant connection between sport values and those of the economy, but the emphasis on individual differences in ability, training, and desire, and their consequences for influencing excellence presumably rewarded in a free competitive atmosphere.*[1]

Fairness, Skill, and Victory

In the ideology of the achievement culture, says Webb, there is a "trinity of values"—equity, skill, and victory ("fair play," "doing your best," and "winning"). Sport reflects, and reinforces, these general cultural values. The three are given different emphasis by different people in different situations. Webb's problem was: How, in attitudes toward sport, are these three values rated in importance at different stages of a person's growing-up "from jacks to linebacker"?

In 1967 Webb was able to ask 920 public school and 354 parochial school pupils in grades 3, 6, 8, 10, and 12 in Battle Creek, Michigan to rate the importance of these three values in sport. The question, as asked to grades 8, 10, and 12, was this:

> *What do you think is most important in playing a game?*
>
> *Number the items below from 1 to 3, starting with the one you think is MOST important (1) and finishing with the one you think is LEAST important (3)*
>
> _____________ *to play as well as you are able*
>
> _____________ *to beat your opponent*
>
> _____________ *to play it fairly*[2]

A simpler form was employed for grades 3 and 6.

There are six different ways in which the three values (hereafter abbreviated "play" [skillfully], "beat," and "fair") can be ranked. Webb scored the six combinations on a continuum from "play" to "professionalism." Figure 11.1 is an adaption of Webb's ranking. You can see that as we move from left to right, from 1 to 6, play orientation to professional orientation, "fair" (equity) becomes less important and "play" well (skill) and "beat" (winning) more important.

The results are shown in Figure 11.2. They are spelled out statistically in Table 11.1, which we will note is for males only (females we will discuss shortly). What we find, in general is that as children grow older, from grade 3 through high school, fairness loses in importance, and skill and winning take its place. The play orientation, with emphasis on fairness, is strongest in sixth grade (age 11), which is about where Piaget found the morality of reciprocity (cooperation) entering. But in Webb's study, it does not continue. From sixth to eighth grade (age 11-13) is the time at which professionalism enters in. Webb suggests that this is the time when the child moves from the elementary school, which is typically a neighborhood school, to the more impersonal junior high school; from a single classroom situation to a succession of rooms for different subjects. In the "child's play" and other life of the neighborhood, admission to participation was based upon such qualities as likeability, neighborhood residence, etc. In the more impersonal environment of the junior high school, one is rated less according to who she/he is as a whole individual person, and more according to observable achievement—ability to perform skillfully and compete successfully. At this point the child is moving out of the "ascriptive" communal situation in which he grew up and into the achievement society in which he will spend the rest of his life. Play and sport are a model of the outside rat-race, and are so presented by coaches and fans. Also, since age keeps the child or adolescent from winning his mark in the adult world, sport is the one area where his skill can be competitively rewarded. (Here I am expanding points that Webb touches on.)

Fig. 11.1 **Play-Professional Continuum**

	Rank Orders						
	1. Fair	1. Fair	1. Play	1. Play	1. Beat	1. Beat	
Play	2. Play	2. Beat	2. Fair	2. Beat	2. Fair	2. Play	Professional
Orientation	3. Beat	3. Play	3. Beat	3. Fair	3. Play	3. Fair	Orientation
	1	2	3	4	5	6	
	Degree of Professionalism						

Adapted from Harry Webb, "Professionalization of Attitudes Toward Play Among Adolescents," in **Aspects of Contemporary Sport Sociology**, Proceedings of C. I. C. Symposium on the Sociology of Sport, 1968, ed. Gerald S. Kenyon, Chicago, Athletic Institute, 1969, Table 1, p. 166.

Differences between girls and boys tell us more about sport in the achieving culture and about the roles of the sexes in that culture. As Figure 11.2 shows, from sixth to tenth grade both sexes become more professionally oriented (emphasis on playing skillfully, and winning). In the last two high school years, however, the girls move away from the skill-win orientation. The big factor in this seems to be the drop in the "beat" emphasis. Webb thinks the reason for this is that the adolescent girl's ambitions in the achievement culture (traditionally, to get a man) depend on qualities other than competitive skills, while the male's ambitions do require skill and winning. In this connection we can note that girls consistently rate fairness higher than do boys, and after sixth grade are consistently lower on winning at every point.

Figure 11.2 Play-Professionalism Continuum by Grade and Sex

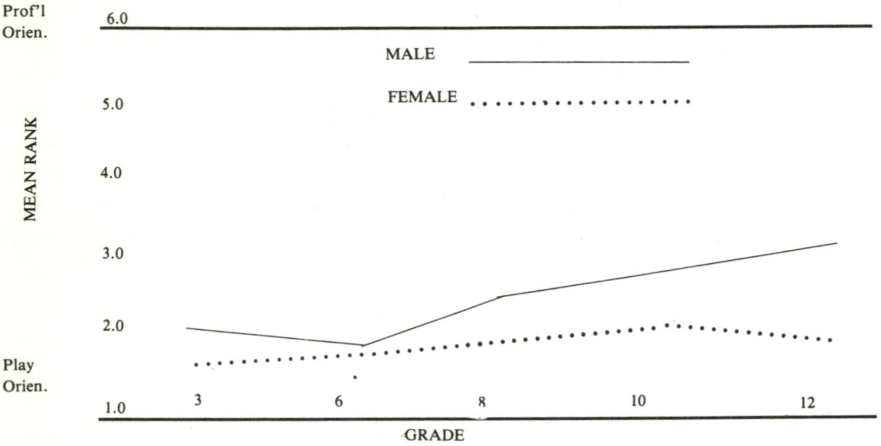

Source—Harry Webb, "Professionalization of Attitudes Toward Play Among Adolescents," in **Aspects of Contemporary Sport Sociology**, Proceedings of C. I. C. Symposium on the Sociology of Sport, 1968, ed. Gerald S. Kenyon, Chicago, Athletic Institute, 1969, Figure 4, p. 169.

Table 11.1 PROFESSIONALIZATION OF ATTITUDE BY GRADE IN PROPORTIONS: MALES

	Grade				
Scale Position	3(83)	6(94)	8(76)	10(131)	12(88)
1-2 (low)	78.2	72.4	31.6	28.2	19.3
3-4	12.1	20.2	52.6	48.1	58.0
5-6 (high)	9.7	7.4	15.8	23.7	22.7
	100.0	100.0	100.0	100.0	100.0

Source—Harry Webb, "Professionalization of Attitudes Toward Play Among Adolescents" in **Aspects of Contemporary Sport Sociology**, Proceedings of C. I. C. Symposium on the Sociology of Sport, 1968, ed. Gerald S. Kenyon, Chicago, Athletic Institute, 1969, Table 2, p. 170.

I will interject at this point two items that bear on the different sport enculturation of males and females in the achieving culture. In 1931, summarizing returns from women in the physical education profession in 98 leading colleges and universities, Mabel Lee said, "They prove how absolutely determined are the women of the physical education profession, and also how determined are the women college students of today, not to permit women's athletics to fall in the footsteps of men's athletics. They are determined to keep them free of all taints of professionalism and commercialization.[3] Forty-five years later Margaret Hennig, who organized a program at Simmons College to train women in management skills, spoke of the problem posed by the fact that girls do not usually have the long and intense team sport experience that boys have in working with others, taking risks, plotting strategy and experiencing victory and defeat. One of the first women admitted to the Harvard Business School, in 1963, Hennig reminisces, "My business policy professor began talking about goals, strategy, and objectives. I suddenly realized that I had no idea what 'strategy' meant. All the men just nodded their heads and the professor went on."[4] We may wonder how many women were disqualified (for better or worse) from managerial careers in the achieving society by the antiprofessional emphasis Lee reported.

Another difference that appears in Webb's research is between Protestants and Catholics. Until the eighth grade Protestants placed more emphasis on winning than do Catholics, but from then on Catholics rated it higher. By twelfth grade, Catholic boys **and girls** ranked fairness lower than did both Protestant groups. Historically, the achievement ethic was originally Protestant, as described in Max Weber's **The Protesant Ethic and the Spirit of Capitalism.**[5] David McClelland has impressibly demonstrated that Protestant countries are more economically advanced than Catholic countries.[6] Why, then, are the Catholic kids "more Protestant than the Protestants"? Webb thinks that it is because they are a minority. At about the eighth grade, when boys and girls settle down to what their respective roles are to be, there also comes the moment of truth at which Catholic youths realize that they are going to have to mobilize all their skills to survive or get ahead in a predominantly WASP culture.

In conclusion, Webb says, " Sport and economic structure are related not only on the basis of shared values, but sport experience additionally makes an important contribution. . . by providing a basis for attitudes and beliefs appropriate to adult participation in politics as well as the economy. . . This investigation demonstrates that participation in the play world is substantially influential in producing that final result, the urban-industrial man."[7]

Somewhat later, Brian Petrie used Webb's play-professionalism scale with 306 males and 318 females who constituted all American citizen undergraduates at Michigan State University.[8] Petrie found males, as we would expect, rating skill and competition as values of sport much higher than did females, who were more interested in social interaction, fun, and aesthetic pleasure. But he found neither college group showing results on the play-professionalism scale reported by Webb at the high school level. "It became apparent that both the male and female respondents were more strongly committed to the play, rather than the professional orientation, than had been the case among the children in the upper levels of high school studied by Webb.[9] Specifically, 87.8 percent of the Michigan State men and 98.4 percent of the women had the play orientation.

In a study of attitudes toward winning among young Canadian hockey players, Edward Vaz found results that were also different from Webb's. About his hypothesis and his findings Vaz says, "In an earlier paper we wrote, '. . . at the higher team levels the value of success, i.e., winning the game, rapidly takes precedence over other considerations among coaches and managers as well as players.' However our research findings do not substantiate this statement. . . In general, the importance of winning to the players decreases noticeably as one advances from the lowest (youngest) to the highest level teams."[10]

Strategic Competence and Achievement

Before going on to our next piece of research, I should introduce David McClelland's concept of need for achievement (abbreviated, **n** Achievement). A psychologist, McClelland became convinced that periods of economic advance are preceded by an increase in people's psychological need for achievement (so that the psychological change in a sense "causes" the economic advance). McClelland developed a modified form of the Thematic Apperception Test (TAT) to measure the individual's **n** Achievement. This is a "projective" test in which one is shown a series of unstructured pictures (for example, a child and adult) and is asked to tell a story about what is happening in the picture. Obviously what he "sees" tells more about the observer than about the objective picture. McClelland used other indicators, such as stories for children and artistic production, as clues to the level of **n** Achievement in cultures at other times and places. He reasoned that people with a high achievement need should be interested in competitive athletics as participants and spectators. He concluded on the basis of studies of games in 26 preliterate cultures that cultures with low **n** Achievement have noncompetitive games while those with a high Achievement have competitive games. He also tried to correlate scores of different

Fig. 11.3 Team-Sport and Individual Sport in Belgium

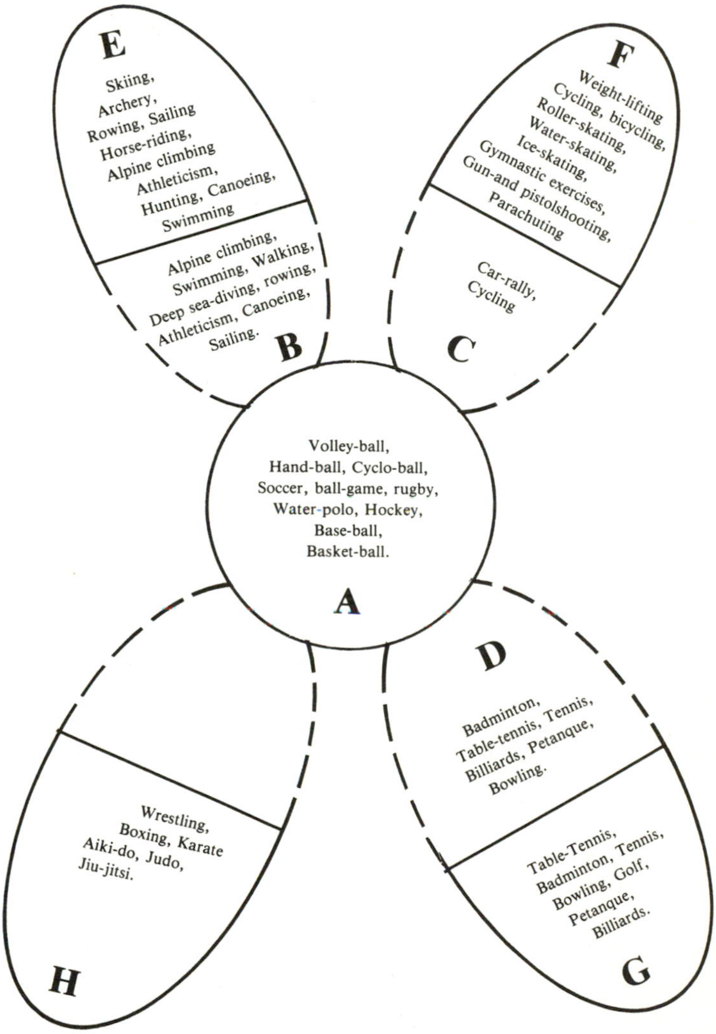

Source—A. Famaey-Lamon, M. Hebbelinck, and A. M. Cadron, "Team-Sport and Individual-Sport," **International Review of Sport Sociology**, 14, 2, 1979, 39.

economically advanced countries in **n** Achievement with the number of victories in Olympic years, but these results were inconclusive.[11]

How social background, individual achievement drive, and choice of sport activity can work together is indicated by Belgian research conducted by Famaey-Lamon, Hebbelinck, and Cadron, involving 5500 children of ages 6-12, and their parents.[12] The children, who were from 107 primary schools representing all parts of Belgium, should have been a pretty good sample from that country. The problem studied was choice of team sports as compared with individual sports. (Figure 11.3, taken from the Lamon-Hebbelinck-Cadron report, indicates the different kinds of sports included. Only the A-group are classified as individual sports; the rest are team sports.) How, the researchers asked, is this choice related to social position and educational attainment? They tabulated the choices of team versus individual sports for the parents of the 5500 children, and for the children themselves. The answer: For parents: "Team-sports are more practiced by manual workers. In the other professional groups, mainly individual sports are chosen, in a most pronounced way in the category of the self-employed and the intellectuals, that means the professions in which the sense of responsibility is most strongly developed."[13] The term "responsibility" seems here to refer to individualistic motivation and choice in a person's life. The children follow their parents: Team sport is practiced more by children whose parents left school after the primary grades, and individual sport by those whose parents went further in their schooling. It appears that those who "succeed" individualistically in the world outside-sport also choose those sports where they are most likely to star as individuals.

In an ingenious piece of literature related to **n** Achievement, Brian Sutton-Smith, John Roberts, and collaborators investigated what might seem a trivial subject for scientific study, the game of Tick Tack Toe.[14] This is not a sport, since sports are games combining strategy and physical skill. It is, however, a pure strategy game, with no elements of physical skill or chance. From it the researchers felt they might find out how people develop "strategic competence" in games and perhaps in society at large, and what kind of people develop it.

The research isolated people who play Tick Tack Toe so that they are likely to win from those who play so that a draw (tie) is likely. A "win" orientation is obviously more adventuresome, a "draw" orientation more conservative. The device that was used to measure performance was a set of six game situations, in each of which the subject was to indicate his next move (only one). The subjects were given these instructions:

These are six parts of six games of Tick Tack Toe. In each game your make only one move. You always use an X as your mark. Look at the first diagram. There is no mark on it. You make the first move. Put your X wherever you think it should go. Put it where you would put it if you were playing the game against someone else. Now look at the second diagram. The other person has already made one move. Now it is your turn to make a move. Put the X wherever you think it should go. (Repeat instructions for third diagram.) Now look at the fourth diagram. You both have had one move. Now it is your move again. (Repeat for fifth diagram.) In the last diagram, you have already each had two moves. Put your X wherever you think it should go.[10]

It is possible to calculate mathematically how many possible ways there are to win the game (outcome X) and how many possible ways to draw (outcome Y) after each possible move. Figure 11.4 shows in the left column the six problem situations and to the right, in each case, the number of possible ways of winning (X) and of drawing (Y) for each of the possible responses. (For example, in Problem 1, if the X is placed in any corner, there are 88 chances of winning (X) to 7 of drawing (Y) in every 100 games. If the X is placed in the center, there are 74 possible ways of winning to 14 ways of drawing. For any of the other possible placements the possibilities are X69 and Y18. So center and corner placements are more strategic.) This measure of strategic competence was developed by Robert Kozelka. The experimenters found that it is possible to predict whether a player will win or draw from his responses to the first four problems alone, and thus to classify him as an X (play to win) or Y (play to draw).

The problems were given at different times to 582 subjects from first grade to college sophomores in Bowling Green, Ohio; to 50 elementary school age children at the Fels Institute Summer Day Camp at Yellow Springs, Ohio; and to 40 elementary grade boys in Worcester, Massachusetts.

The results showed clearly that strategic competence (capacity for winning rather than drawing) is a quality that develops over time. In Bowling Green, **no** children from first to fourth scored the highest possibility of winning; 19 percent in 8th grade and 30 percent of college sophomores did. (Of course this means that 70 percent of the sophomores were not top winners at this "kids" game.") Responses in the center, which on problems 1, 2, 4, and 6 have a good chance of leading to a draw, predominated in the lower grades. Only in grades 5 and 6 did the likely-winning corner responses begin.

What kind of people win and which draw? Most of the evidence comes from the Fels camp at Yellow Springs, where Vaughn Crandall was the major collaborator. The children were given a measure of **n** Achievement responses to TAT-type pictures. They were rated by counselors on fine motor mastery, time spent alone on tasks, persistence in tasks, and independent achievement efforts. They were also rated on tendency to instigate physical aggression, and to instigate verbal aggression. They were rated on preference for types of play and games considered appropriate for their sex. These ratings, and the Bowling Green and Worcester studies, give us four profiles: the winning girl, the winning boy, the drawing girl, and the drawing boy.

The winning girl is of lower socioeconomic status than the drawing girl. She is likely to be more intelligent and achieving. In ratings by her peers on her group relations, she is significantly less likely to be seen as a failure. She is very much more likely to instigate physical aggression and to dominate other girls, and significantly less likely to withdraw in the face of aggressive attack. She engages in more muscular activity. In her choices of games she likes to play, she is likely to choose typically "masculine" games. She is likely to be independent of, and psychologically distant from, her mother. At the Fels camp X girls were found to have been punished significantly more by their mothers. "Winning scores (X) for girls give the picture of a girl who is hyperactive, domineering, and masculine."[16]

The winning boy is also seldom seen as a failure by his peers, and is more likely to be chosen as a leader. He is intelligent, and adept in arithmetic and language skills. He is strikingly persistent in carrying tasks to completion. He is likely to be heavier, and especially taller, than the drawing boy, and therefore beyond his peers in maturity. Like the winning girl, he is apt to be independent, especially of his mother.

The girl who plays to draw is of a higher socioeconomic class, unathletic, unaggressive, conventionally "feminine" in her game choice and her role playing. The drawing boy is also more "feminine" in his game choices.

The most surprising fact, which requires explanation, is that both the drawing girl and the drawing boy tend to rank **high** in **n** Achievement. If achievement is so important to them, why do they play to draw instead of to win?

Seemingly, they are afraid to take the chance that striving to win involves. The Y boys have been pushed by their mothers significantly more than have the X boys. This fits with the findings of Marian Winterbottom, who did pioneer work on how **n** Achievement develops.[17] So these boys are motivated to succeed on their own but, Sutton-Smith and Roberts suggest, only in an environment that is cut and dried for them by adults. At the Fels camp, drawing boys were observed to have a significantly higher need for adult approval. That is, their achievement is "other-directed" rather than "inner-directed." People with a high **n** Achievement, other research has found, don't like chance games, prefer to "play it safe." So they prefer to perform in an impersonal situation rather than in personal competition. A strategy game, in which the outcome depends on the uncertainties of another person's actions, as it does in Tick Tack Toe, is for each player actually a chance game. (Elsewhere Sutton-Smith and Roberts suggest that

Figure 11.4 Problems and Solutions with Probability-Derived Scores

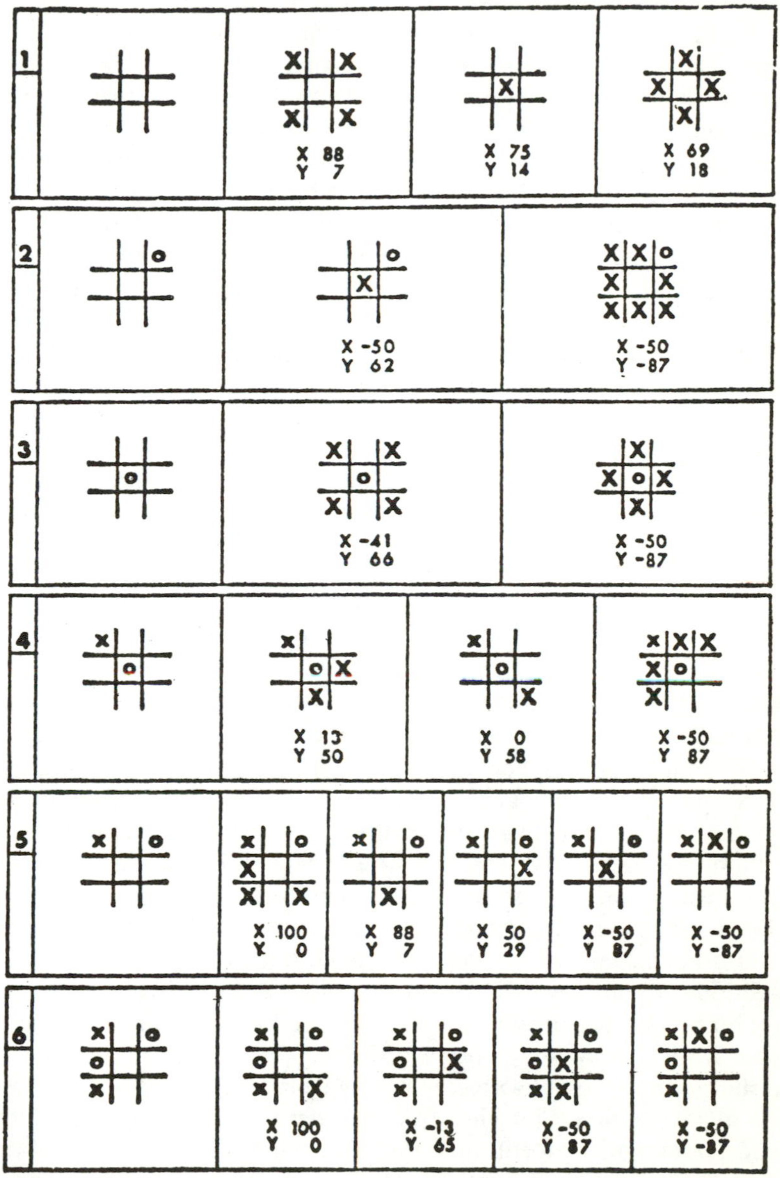

Source—Brian Sutton-Smith and John M. Roberts, **Genetic Psychology Monographs**, no. 75, 1967, Figure 1, p. 11.

pure physical skill games provoke less achievement anxiety than physical skill-strategy games. Probably the boys with **n** Achievement would have found a one-on-one basketball confrontation, even though personal, less chancy.) The person with high **n** Achievement eliminates both the chance of winning and the chance of losing by playing for a draw. Winterbottom found that boys with high **n** Achievement were highly concerned about success in their school work but were not usually as successful in fact. Likewise in the Tick Tack Toe study, the X boys who play to win are better in actual independent accomplishment, while the Y boys, pushed by their mothers but tied to their apron strings, dream better than they perform.

So the person with a strong achievement drive is essentially a passive, "feminine" individual (whether biologically female or male) who is driven to perform successfully when the job is mapped out in advance, but doesn't usually do well when on his/her own in an unpredictable situation. If, as Sutton-Smith and Roberts suggest, "strategic winning play at Tick Tack Toe models an underlying style of life in which strategic qualities find general manifestation."[18] This pure strategy game may also tell us about the general lifestyle of those who, in an other-directed society, dream grandly but actually play to draw.

Good and Poor Competitors

A somewhat earlier piece of research into the characteristics of winners was Francis J. Ryan's comparison of two kinds of people produced in our culture—college athletes who are good competitors and those who are poor competitors.[19] Ryan, a coach of field events and research assistant at the Yale Department of University Health, contributed his study in a symposium by members of the Yale Division of Mental Hygiene on problems of college men. His definition of "good" competitor is clear: a good competitor is one whose performance in competition exceeds his practice performance; a poor competitor is one who performs better in practice than in competition. In other words, Ryan was studying the difference between the man who rises to the occasion and the one who "chokes" under competitive stress. This is a commonly observed distinction in track and field events. Two shotputters who put 45 feet in practice may put 42 and 48 feet, respectively, in competition. Some high jumpers have frequently cleared 6 feet in practice, but not in competition; others have jumped 6 feet only in competition, never in practice. One athlete who barely made his college team had practice performances of Olympic calibre. Ryan felt that track and field performers would be a particularly good group to study because performance is measured simply and quantitatively. He granted that competitive performances, which are a matter of record, are easier to recall than practice performances, which are not systematically recorded. In fact, he said, to deliberately record practice performance for the purpose of such a study might really invalidate the results by making it, too, competitve. However, as a coach himself, Ryan was willing to trust the judgments of coaches who might have seen their athletes in more than 1000 trials over a period of four years.

He sent 65 coaches questionnaires on which each was asked to rate on 13 items the best competitor, past or present, he had ever coached, and the poorest. Although coaches were not asked to name the athletes they described, many did so, and Ryan says that "our good competitors include most American world record holders and Olympic champions."[20]

The questionnaires showed a substantial difference between good and poor competitors in general social qualities, practice habits, and attitudes toward performance. Socially, the good competitor was considered to be "very friendly," the poor one "a lone wolf." The good competitor was "usually in good spirits, with plenty of belly laughs;" the poor competitor smiled easily, but seldom laughed heartily. The good competitor's communication was good; the poor competitor was "about average," or "difficult to talk to." One coach worked four years with a man and never had a conversation with him. The good competitor was well liked by his teammates; the poor competitor was "about average" or "unpopular."

There was no significant difference in coming to practice early, on time, or late; both groups tended to arrive about the same time. When there, the good competitor was a hard worker; the poor competitor was about average or needed to be pushed. The good competitor usually followed coaching instructions without comment; the poor competitor would follow, but comment or make an argument for doing something different. After a poor performance, the good competitor was likely to blame himself, the poor competitor to blame conditions or officials. When he talked about future performances, the good competitor usually had in mind next week's performance; the poor competitor, some event in the indefinite future. This was related to the item that most sharply differentiated the groups: after a good performance, the good performer was **in all cases** likely to do well the next week; the poor performer would follow with an average performance or fall off badly.

As did our other researchers, Ryan felt that the sport behavior he studied reflected more general attitudes. "The poor competitor would appear to be unhappier, more constricted, and in general, more poorly adjusted. . . seems to have difficulty in expressing his aggression generally, and his inability to compete in athletics may be a specific instance of . . . an over-all difficulty."[21]

The last of Ryan's findings, that poor competitors tend to follow a good performance a week later with a mediocre or bad one, is the key to his explanation of the difference between good and poor competitors. "**Achievement** is the key word in the competitive situation, and . . . at least for the present the good and poor competitors are seen as separated by their differential ability to accept achievement."[22] A poor competitor is not a person who doesn't have the ability to do well, or who has a bad performance because of stress in a particular situation. The overstressed good performer may lose through a violent effort, faulted by gross errors. By contrast, the poor competitor's performance seems to be marked by "a feebleness of effort, almost a kind of paralysis."[23]

His problem is **fear of success**. This, says Ryan, is likely to affect his behavior in some other areas of life, though not all. Poor athletic competitors are sometimes, he points out, very successful in academic competition. This fact may indicate that the poor competitor is specifically afraid of performance that is culturally defined as "masculine." "He may be relatively free to express himself in a more neutral or possibly even traditionally feminine activity."[24] As for his future life as a whole, "the more patently masculine the vocation, the greater the disability."

Some aspects of Ryan's study raise questions about the whole "masculine" competitive syndrome as it appears in sport and in our culture as a whole. The good competitor, as defined by Ryan, is friendly and affable except in competition. Then he follows the model of the boxers who routinely touch gloves, then perform 45 minutes of mayhem upon one another, and at the end may fall into each other's arms like long-lost brothers. The good competitor, as discovered by Ryan, apparently lives in two worlds—the world of ordinary life, where people are fellow human beings, and the field of sport competition, where one's adversary is an enemy. By contrast, "the poor competitor prefers an atmosphere of friendliness."[25] He may even go so far as to offer encouragement or even coaching hints to an opponent. If the good competitor does anything like this, it is probably a con, "gamesmanship."

The good competitor may expect to have a number of "grudge matches," in some of which he doesn't even make a show of being friendly. Ryan says that some personality clashes are of course inevitable if one encounters many opponents, but that some good competitors seem psychologically to need these grudge matches. Contrariwise, "the poor competitor does not speak with anger or bitterness of his opposition; he does not have grudge matches." The good competitor Ryan finds hard to live with after a defeat: he may be bitter, morose, and even vicious. The poor competitor may on the other hand be relaxed, talkative, and in good spirits. One other contrast we will remember is that the good competitor accepts the coach's instructions without question, whereas the poor competitor is likely to make alternative suggestions.

At the time that he wrote, in 1958, it is clear that in Ryan's mind the poor competitor has a psychological problem, about which a conscientious coach may justifiably be concerned in terms of what it may mean for the athlete's whole future life. Twenty years later, after an athletic revolution, many would be inclined to feel that it is the good competitor, as described, who has a problem. This, I believe, would be the view of George Sauer, reflecting on football and the American ethos:

I think the values of football as it is now played reflect a segment of thought. . . that is prevalent in our society. The way to do anything in the world, the way to get ahead, is to compete against somebody, work your way up, and in so doing you have to judge yourself or be judged in relation to somebody else. . . As it is played now, football reinforces the social ethic that aggression and competition is a healthy thing—that that's the way to become a success. This kind of thought has a potential for tragedy and to the degree that it is exercised and carried out in football, it is tragic.[26]

Sex, Status, and Game Choice

Another contribution to our understanding of the role of sport in the achievement culture is research by psychologist Sutton-Smith, anthropologist Roberts, and mathematician Kozelka into what segments of the population are involved in different types of sport.[27] The researchers began with the **conflict-enculturation hypotheses** about sport on which we touched in Chapter 6: games must be understood as (1) providing a means for learning one's way into the "success systems" of one's culture while (2) "buffering" this learning by furnishing a sphere in which the child pressured by adult requirements or the adult pressured by the rat race can exercise mastery. In Chapter 6, I described cross-cultural research on the functions of physical skill, chance, and strategy games at different levels of social development. On the basis of this cross-cultural work, Sutton-Smith, Roberts, and Kozelka set up hypotheses about which game types will be preferred by different groups on modern society:

Because games of strategy are associated cross-culturally with severe . . . socialization, psychological discipline, high obedience training and complex cultures, they will be preferred in this culture by the persons who have had greater experience of such a child training pattern, that is, the higher status groups compared with the lower, and women as compared with men.

Because games of chance are associated cross-culturally with high responsibility training, punishment for the display of initiative, and a belief in the benevolence of the gods, they will be preferred in this culture by members of the lower status groups as compared with the higher and by women as compared with men.

Because games of physical skill are associated cross-culturally with high acheivement training, they will be preferred in this culture by the upper as compared with the lower status groups and by men as compared with women.[28]

At the two extremes, the groups who will be enculturated for achievement (males and upper socioeconomic groups) will participate in or watch games of physical skill; those who are enculturated for routine menial tasks (females and lower socioeconomic groups) will play games of chance. It will be helpful to review here the cross-cultural discussion of games in Chapter 6.

In an earlier report, the senior authors had analyzed game choices of 1900 third to sixth graders in 12 midwestern schools and had found the results abbreviated in Table 11.2.[29] These differences were all significant at the .05 level, that is, would have occurred by chance alone fewer than five times in 100 samples from such a population. It is interesting that the pure strategy games were predominantly female, and the physical skill-strategy games (sports) predominantly male.

The sources of information in the Sutton-Smith-Roberts-Kozelka study were (1) a 1940 Gallup poll asked 3242 subjects, "Which of the following games have you played in the last year?"; (2) a 1948 Minnesota poll that asked 598 respondents what sports they played and watched for recreation; and (3) a 1948 Roper-Fortune survey of the sport activities of 3008 people. In analyzing the Gallup poll results, the researchers selected golf and tennis as examples of physical skill games, bridge and checkers as strategy games, and dice, craps, and bingo as examples of chance games. For tennis and golf, a higher percentage of men than women played, and the most active occupational groups were professionals, proprietors, and clerks. Bridge and checkers were played significantly more by women, and the highest occupational groups were professionals and clerks. Dice, craps, and bingo were played significantly more by women, and were most popular occupationally with servants and semiskilled and unskilled workers.

The Minnesota poll showed males very significantly more active in playing and watching organized sports—fishing, hunting, bowling, football, baseball, golf, skating, and swimming. Educational level produced a similar significant difference, college, high school, and grade school graduates being involved in that order.

In the Roper-Fortune survey, men again predominated in performing and watching sports and listening to them on radio (this was 1948). In general, the higher the occupational status, the greater the interest in sports. However, **both** salaried executives and factory workers were more interested than professional people.

Sutton-Smith, Roberts, and Kozelka felt that their general hyposthesis held up: "In the present study, games of strategy have been shown to be associated with women and lower status, and games of physical skill with men and higher status."[30]

Sport and the Rise of Capitalism

In his study with which we began this chapter, Harry Webb said that the function of the "professionalization" of sport in the schools is to prepare people for their roles in a capitalist democracy. Although sport competiton and achievement are intensely important in the Communist world, historically the achievement ethic has been most prominent in the individualistic bourgeois society. Let us look at historic examples of how sport has been related to achievement.

Jean Jacques Rousseau, whose ideas were embodied in the French and other capitalist revolutions, gave sport an important place in preparing people to live in an achieving society:

Table 11.2 Game Choices of 1900 Boys and Girls, Grades 3 to 6

Game type	Girls	Boys
Strategy	5	0
Chance	7	1
Pure Physical Skill	4	9
Physical Skill and Strategy	1	11

Based on John M. Roberts and Brian Sutton-Smith, "Child Training and Game Involvement," **Ethnology, 1**, 1962, Table 7.

> *The children should not be permitted to play separately according to their fancy, but encouraged to play all together in public; and the games should be conducted in such a way that there is always some common end to which all aspire to accustom them to common action and stir up emulation . . . The most important thing is to get them accustomed from an early age to discipline, to equality and fraternity, to living under the eyes of their fellow citizens and seeking public approbation.*[31]

Writing of the drive to power of the business classes in nineteenth century England, Peter McIntosh says,

> *Team games encouraged just those qualities of cooperation and conformity to the needs of the herd which were so much prized by a middle class which was establishing its power and influence throughout the world . . . The great acceleration of athleticism and the growth of competitive games in the nineteenth century, with their supposed potential for training character, was an intrinsic part of the intensely competitive commercial development and imperial expansion of that era.*[32]

In Chapter 8, I referred to Allen Sack's study of the professionalization of American football in the late nineteenth century.[33] There I stressed the democratizing influence as Anglo-Saxon personnel gave way to immigrant ethnic groups. Sack points out that this was part of the revolution by which the manufacturing class come to power in the United States. The first ruling class was the seafaring New England commerical aristocracy. Harvard was their college. After independence from Britain, the urban industrial bourgeoisie gained power. From 1861 to 1865, in the Civil War, it broke the back of the planter aristocracy of the South. But the old aristocratic ideals of the merchant seamen lived on in New England, especially at Harvard, which was a symbol of contempt for the win-at-all-costs ethic in both athletics and business. Sack quotes a fictional Yale athletic hero, "Harvard is more status conscious; aristocracy is not important at Yale."[34] The 33 year string in which Yale beat Harvard 29 times represented in sport the rise to power of the business ethic and its Social Darwinist code of "survival of the fittest." Yale's coach, Walter Camp, the "father" of modern football, spoke the ideology of the successful business class. His biographer says of Camp, "He could not possibly have been described as a good loser. . . His spirit hated defeat, and he planned systematically with all his wits for victory." Camp himself said, "When you lose a match against a man in your own class, shake hands with him; do not excuse your defeat, do not forget it, and do not let it happen again if there is any way to prepare yourself for the next match."[35] Camp also said, "There were two things for which we were noted, our toughness and our tackling. No wonder we were tough, for [our practice] had been a general survival of the fittest."[36] It was no coincidence that Camp was the brother-in-law of the great Yale professor William Graham Sumner, author of **Folkways** and an outspoken and uncritical admirer of the successful business class:

> *The law of the survival of the fittest was not made by man and cannot be abrogated by man. We can only, by interfering with it, produce the survival of the unfittest.*[37] *. . . The strong and the weak are terms which admit of no definition unless they are made equivalent to the industrious and the ideal, the frugal and the unfrugal.*[38] *. . . All the achievements of the plutocrats which are denounced prove that they are men of transcendent ability, more powerful than thousands of other men put together simply by force of brains.*[39]

Achievement and the Sport Creed

Walter Camp shared the sentiments of a Boston surgeon of his time: "Football may twist a few joints, but it is building us a new race of men."[40] The theme of this chapter is the role of sport in enculturating for the achieving society. Part of this enculturation is a system of beliefs about sport. Some of these beliefs have a basis in fact, some are false, and some are unproved. This is typical of the belief-systems (ideologies) by which all social systems are supported. Sociologist Harry Edwards has systematically defined the ideology of the "dominant sports creed" and analyzed its validity point by point. Within his framework I shall add my own assessment on the basis of material in this and other chapters.

Edwards lists twelve things that sport is believed to do:[41]

1. Sports participation develops "good character."
2. It develops a value on loyalty.
3. It generates altruism.
4. It generates a value on social and/or self-control.
5. It develops fortitude.
6. It prepares the athlete for life.
7. It provides opportunities for individual advancement.
8. It generates physical fitness.
9. It generates mental alertness.

10. It is supportive of educational achievement.
11. It develops religiosity.
12. It develops patriotism.

Before we evaluate the creed, some things need to be clarified. First of all, the creed, in stating the qualities supposedly promoted by sport, usually implies that it develops them **better than do other activities**. Here there are three possibilities: (1) sport is the best way of developing these qualities, (2) sport develops them as do alternative activities, and (3) other activities develop them better. Take mental alertness, for example, of the kind needed to program a computer, teach an English class, fly a commercial airliner. You might hold that playing football or basketball would be the best kind of preparation for the physical-mental sharpness needed by a pilot. You might hold that it would contribute as much to staying on top of the English class as would a formal course in educational methods. You might say that a course in logic, or participation on the debate team would do more than basketball or football to develop the mental habits suited to computer programing. You might be right or wrong in these cases—they are simply illustrations.

Moreover, insofar as we find sport participation associated with positive values, we still have a question. Does sport participation **develop** the values, or does it **select** people who have them? We can take as an example No. 3 on Edwards' list. How do people in sport compare with people not in sport in their sensitivity to the feelings of others? There are four possibilities:

(1) sport experience in itself **develops** sensitivity to others.
(2) sport experience **selects** more sensitive people.
(3) sport experience selects **and** develops sensitivity to others.
(4) sport selects people who are more sensitive and **diminishes** their sensitivity, but not enough to cancel it out.

Now let's take the claims in the creed one by one.

(1) Sport promotes good character

There are two polar values in sport—sportsmanship and winning. I have asked my religious football players how they can show love to an opponent while they are "knocking the hell" out of him. Some are satisfied that they can. The studies of Webb show that the ethic of sportsmanship diminishes as one grows into organized sport. Ryan found admirable qualities of character in the "good" competitor—openness, sociability, humor, self-discipline. But he also found less admirable traits—hatred of opponents, a need for "grudge" matches, inability to accept defeat, and unquestioning acceptance of the coach's authority.

(2) Sport promotes loyalty

There is little doubt, I think, that sport in particular promotes strong group loyalties. What this means is best understood by applying to sport Sumner's treatment in **Folkways** of the characteristics of in-groups (which always have an enemy "out-group"). Strong feelings of hostility toward the opponent create intense feelings of loyalty within the team. The individual player identifies so strongly with his team that he will risk health or life for it. He has a double standard for judging the acts of his team and those of the adversary. What is "good clean aggressiveness" by his team is "dirty play" when the opponent does it. In-group loyalty may be less true of individual sports than of team sports. Even in team sports it has been weakened in the affluent society by the rise of the well-paid individual star for whom team victory may be less important than his personal record-making.

(3) Sport generates altruism

Altruism is, by definition, concern for the "other" (Latin, **alter**). Whether sport develops altruism depends on whether the other is a member of one's loyalty-group (team). Sumner reported that primitive (and not so primitive) cultures tend to define only members of their own group as "people." One does not feel toward members of the out-group, who are really non-persons, the obligation that he has to real people. There is much of this kind of thinking in sport, along with some real humanism. The Webb studies found altruism in sport declining with adolescence. Bruce Ogilvie and Thomas Tutko, summarizing intensive psychological research with athletes, reported a low need for giving support to others and receiving it from them.[42]

(4) Sport promotes social and self-control

An example of sport as social control is the way the athlete used to serve as a model, whom teachers and other adults could point out to youth, of the clean cut American boy (or girl) that they should be. Since the youth culture has rubbed off on jocks, this has changed a good deal. Another example is the possibility that sport may be an alternative to juvenile delinquency. Walter Schaefer, in a study of 585 midwestern senior high school boys, found that while 7 percent of the athletes had delinquent records, 17 percent of the nonathletes did. As suggested earlier, this could be because sport **selects** nondelinquents—boys who are likely to be delinquent are not likely to go out for sports, or to be accepted. (It may be that sport and delinquency are alternative ways of getting attention.) The difficulty of sorting out factors is illustrated by the fact that there was almost the same difference in delinquency rate between white collar and blue collar boys, and between high and low academic achievers, as between athletes and nonathletes. In fact, among white collar boys with low academic achievement, delinquency was **higher** among athletes than among non-atheltes. An interesting case of sport-related social and self-control is the outcome of three psychological tests of black and white athletes reported by Edwards.[44] Contrary to what coaches predicted, black athletes were more reserved, more orderly, more controlled, and more self-examining than white athletes. Blacks, for whom sport may be the only way out of the ghetto, are likely to work hard, follow instructions, and "keep their noses clean."

(5) **Sport develops fortitude**, "firm courage, patient endurance of misfortune and pain."

This claim is open to both of the questions I raised at the beginning of this section. There is no doubt that sport requires fortitude, but Edwards believes there is more evidence that sport selects people with fortitude than that it develops it significantly in athletes who lack it. Given this kind of strength to begin with, he says, sport experience may strengthen one's general confidence in his ability to endure. On the other hand, if sport serves as a crutch for a weak ego, failure may diminish one's strength and endurance. There is also the question, could other activities promote fortitude as well or better? If they are more like the situations one will meet in later life, they may. Fortitude in a prospective surgeon might be developed better by undergraduate in-service in an emergency ward than by playing on an intercollegiate team. Fortitude in a trial lawyer might be better fostered by similar in-service in a minimum security prison than by sport participation. The 1960s, with freedom rides, Peace Corps, VISTA, were rich in socially relevant and career-relevant opportunities to practice and develop fortitude, but it should not be too late to find other "moral equivalents of sport."

(6) **Sport participation prepares the athlete for life**

This is a general claim that rolls up all the previous ones—character, loyalty, altruism, self-control, fortitude—and more. Sport is believed to be a model of life, a period of play in which one enacts in miniature the basic experiences he will encounter in the rest of his stay on earth.

This idea of sport as rehearsal for life had some reality when school and college sport were still amateur. But now, as Edwards points out, on both the "amateur" and professional level, sport **is** life. For the fan, it may be peripheral, but for the athlete it is central. His sense of identity and self-worth are tied up with sport. Athletes don't spend their youth preparing for life because, in the achievement culture, **the successful athlete has no youth**.

What I mean is pointed up by a study of high-level sportsmen (and women) in Austria in the 1960s in which Hans Groll of the University of Vienna traced the typical pattern of sport development in the life cycle:

Footballers (soccer players) began around age 5, started to play competitively between 10 and 15, and reached top class between 18 and 25. Skiers had a similar pattern but began "as a rule" as early as age 3. Swimmers started from 8 to 13, were competitive about 13, and reached their top form about 16. Other athletes—cyclists, track and field performers, rowers, fencers, gymnasts, and basketball players—had a later start (typically about 11), but also became competitive by 15 and peaked before 25.[45]

What this precocious competitiveness can mean on a gut level is indicated by a study of the pulse rates of American Little Leagues at bat. At the plate they typically showed a rapid heartbeat that dropped when they finished batting. At the same time they denied **feeling** stressed.[46] Learning to endure extreme stress while suppressing awareness may enculturate the kid for life in the achieving society, but as a mental health practice it is very questionable.

In his non-youth, the athlete leads a very artificial existence that may handicap him in other lives of activity. President Eliot was speaking with the bias of a New England aristocrat who thought sport should be a gentleman's game, but what he said is still true: "The enfeebling theory that no team can do its best except in the presence of applauding friends is still another of the lesser evils of football. Worse preparation for the real interests and struggles of life can hardly be imagined. The orator, advocate, preacher, surgeon, engineer, banker, tradesman, craftsman, admiral, general, or statesman who cannot do his best except in the presence of a sympathetic crowd is distinctly a second-class man."[47]

Speaking to the 1968 International Congress of Sport Psychology, José Cagigal, Director of the Spanish Institute for Physical and Sport Education (Madrid) saw sport as disqualifying the athletic "prima donna" for the realities of life:

> *Generally speaking, to excel at any human activity calls for many years of sustained effort, making the individual spiritually mature enough to take his final triumph in stride. In sport, it is different; although effort and will-power are necessary to become an outstanding performer, public triumphs are obtained with relative ease in comparison with other walks of life . . . The caste of champions is in danger of becoming an outrageously spoiled social group, dragging its members down through successive stages of regressive immaturity to leave them finally with a wholly distorted sense of values incapable of taking their place in normal soicety. The champion who has belonged to the caste, when he leaves his hot-house world either on account of age or failure has the typical reactions of the unadapted psychopath.*[48]

Although his language was somewhat less strong, sociologist Walter Schaefer in the same year also told a Symposium on the Sociology of Sport that sport in our culture tends to create a severe conflict when the athlete confronts "real life":

> *Athletes whose sense of identity and self-worth is entirely linked to athletic achievement often experience an identity crisis when the athletic career has ended, and it becomes necessary to move on to something else. . . . successfully made the transitions, and as a result, linger on as marginal men in the world of athletics, have family or personal problems, or fail to adjust to a new work role.*[49]

So much for the successful athlete. Most athletes are not successful. Most are substitutes. Many parents of Little League youngsters have become acutely aware of what this fact implies. The sport experience does not really prepare the substitute for anything because he doesn't really share the experience. "Another prevailing myth in sports," says Tutko, "is that a hard-working substitute will come out of the experience with a stronger character. On the contrary, unless a child is extremely mature or unless he has a great deal of support from his parents, being a substitute will affect him adversely."[50] His being home on the bench labels him as inferior in the eyes of his peers. With no game experience, he generally gets worse instead of better. He may do poorly in school or shun friends to avoid ridicule. Dr. Jon Brewer, after studying boys of 8 to 14 in a California baseball program for nearly a year, said of poor players, "Like most young competitors, their athletic involvement constitutes a major part of their lives; they have fewer alternative activities than adults and thus if they are poor players, they define themselves as inferior human beings."[51]

A University of Miami football player whose rank was somewhat less than that of a substitute wrote bitterly of his experience:

> *Scout team players do not play or even travel. They just practice every day and watch with the rest of the spectators come game time. Playing, or rather not playing, is really not the major cause of my dissatisfaction and disenchantment with the game. Most of my grief is a result of the loss of respect. . . that is shown towards me. I, personally, feel I am treated very unfairly as a human being. Because I do not exhibit the talent that other players do, I am looked down upon by coaches and fellow players on and off the field.*
>
> *In high school I was one of the best players on the team. Because of this I was looked up to and respected by almost everyone in the school. Now all of a sudden I am a fourth team member and have lost all that respect. . . You are judged as a person on how well you perform on the field. Athletes should be treated as humans, not as machines.*

Why should someone be loved as a person because he plays good football, and someone else disliked because he does not play so well?

(7)Sport promotes individual advancement

The answer is always, for some it does, for most it doesn't. In Chapter 8 and elsewhere we saw how sport in this century has been an upward ladder for minorities—Irish, German, Polish, Jewish, Italian, Latin, black, and French Canadian. As a general formula, 5 percent of those who participate make it big, 95 percent either wind up where they started, or are actually held back by sport. Sport "tracks" some minority members up to a higher place in the world. On the other hand, it may track others down out of higher goals they might have reached had they not been atheltes. In this chapter, Ryan showed us that sport selects, develops, or reinforces qualities of leadership, aggressiveness, persistence, and accomplishemnt. Webb showed that as children are acculturated in our school system, they shed the attitudes of fairness that hold back competitive success, and take on those that encourage winning performance on and off the athletic field.

(8) Sport promotes physical fitness

This is true for active participants in the minor sports—tennis, golf, walking, swimming—who develop lifelong habits of exercise. We must distinguish these people from those who participate in the major, especially the bodily contact sports. Preparation for these involves physical drills that go far beyond health-promoting exercise. Edwards points out that both college and professional athletes are considered high insurance risks. This is related to the fact I pointed out earlier, that few "amateurs" or professionals in the major sports finish their careers without some permanent disability. This includes many participants in boys' baseball and football. Spectating, on the other hand, is not as passive as some imagine—the simplest observation of fans at a game shows them actively empathizing physically with the athletes they root for. But this grandstand recapitulation of competitive struggle hardly meets the body's exercise needs. Some, it is true, are also inspired to take up the sport they watch—this is clearly more likely in the minor sports. But in the last analysis, as I said in Chapter 1, even the overstressed and battered contact sport athlete will probably live longer and better than the person whose participation is limited to watching him.

(9) Sport participation promotes mental alertness

On this claim, in terms of research that will satisfy a hard-nosed sociologist, Edwards concludes that there is "no evidence pro or con." Clearly, organized sports, which are physical skill-strategy games, **require** mental alertness. Some of it is the kind of strategic alertness exemplified by Cleveland Browns' cornerback Bernie Parrish when he charted on blocked paper all the patterns run in past games on a key opposition pass play, and on the basis of this diagram was in a position to intercept two passes and knock down another. Some of it is the kind of psychomotor "feel" for fluid situations that Novak finds especially typical of basketball as played by blacks. Some of the required alertness is selected, some developed. The question is, how much is transferred to non-sport situations? Strangely, this claim is similar to the tone traditionally made for the mental sharpening effect of mathematics as a required school subject. In sport skills, as in math skills, "transfer of training" is likely to be greatest in areas similar to the original one, and less in more dissimilar areas. There is probably a considerable transfer of alertness habits from one sport to another. There is probably a lesser transfer to other physical skill activities such as piloting a plane. There may be some transfer to more removed activities like managing a corporation. As Edwards indicates, much research is needed here.

(10) **Sport promotes educational advancement**

Here we have quantitative data available (grade averages) but they are an invalid measure. The basic reason is that, in general, the grades of athletes are inflated. To keep their eligibility, athletes are often advised into "crap courses," in which a given grade represents less academic achievement than does the same grade in a more demanding course. In the courses they take, athletes may be graded by the same standards as other students. They may be graded down, because of prejudice or because they are stereotyped as "dumb jocks." But they are more likely to be graded up, because of overt athletic department pressure or because of the professor's school spirit ("we can't fail our ace quarterback"). Another basic fact is that athletes usually have to choose between their sport and their academic work—there are rarely time, energy, and attention enough for both. Sport does promote educational achievement in the sense that ahtletic "scholarships" enable poor youths to attend college who couldn't have afforded it otherwise. A few become professional athletes—whether this is an "educational" objective for an academic institution is open to question. But they do get off the track that dooms other poor youngsters to stay poor while their more affluent classmates get the prizes that go with a college degree. Some use an athletic scholarship to prepare themselves for a non-athletic vocation. But many others become so absorbed in sport that they are tracked out of such educational opportunities for advancement.

(11) **Sport participation develops religiosity**

Sport has traditionally been associated with the authoritarian syndrome, which enculturates people for conventional religiosity along with militarism, sexism, racism, and free enterprise capitalism. The ritual prayer before players go out to knock each other's heads off is as much a part of the syndrome as the Star Spangled Banner. The Fellowship of Christian Athletes links sport as properly expressing and promoting an orientation to "winning for Christ." Billy Graham enthusiastically proclaimed that "there are probably more really committed Christians in sports, both collegiate and professional, than in any other occupation in America."[52] The NCAA has allowed Graham's Crusade for Christ to put on halftime shows at authorized basketball games. The NFL sanctioned a special "Weekend of Champions" at the 1971 Miami Super Bowl, featuring Christian athletes from almost all major sports. However, the FCA and other religiously committed athletes are only a minority, and the ritual prayers, like the national anthem, are generally rather routine. Edwards is probably right in concluding that there is no hard evidence that sport either significantly promotes or detracts from formal religiosity.

(12) **Sport participation develops patriotism**

There are two aspects to the connection of sport with patriotism: (1) the role of patriotism in the militarist-sexist-racist-athletic syndrome and (2) the role of sport as an instrument of nationalistic policy. Two examples of the first: 1969 Berkeley football captain Jim Calkins' complaint that being filled with "super-patriotic stuff' had made white athletes subservient to authoritarian coaches; and General Douglas MacArthur's ode to sport:

> *Upon the fields of friendly strife*
> *are sown the seeds*
> *that upon other fields, on other days,*
> *will bear the fruits of victory.*[53]

In a 1971 article Sandy Padwe pointed to the linkage of the sport and political establishments: military jets flying over stadia in halftime shows; ABC refusing to televise a halftime program by the University of Buffalo band with an anti-war, anti-racist, and anti-pollution theme, but broadcasting an Army-Navy show honoring the Green Berets; the Rose Bowl committee refusing to allow the University of Michigan band to present a 4-minute "peace segment" in its halftime show, but authorizing the usual military floats and "red-white-and-blue pageantry"; a neon American flag over the Orange Bowl end zone and 50,000 spectators at the Memphis Liberty Bowl simultaneously waving little American flags provided by the management.[54]

The myth that international sport is good clean amateur fun has long been dead. The athlete who entered international competition on his own and paid his own way is also in the past. Of the competitions re-established in 1896 to further international friendship, Alex Natan says, "Olympic athletes have become soldiers of sport who are indoctrinated with grotesque notions of international prestige.[55] Nazi Germany was the first modern state to make sport a deliberate technique of military preparation. Since 1930 the Soviet Union has conceived of sport as a way to demonstrate superiority over the bourgeois world: "The triumph of our athletes . . . is proof of the superiority of the Soviet socialist culture over the rottenness of the culture of the capitalist countries."[56] China has likewise mobilized sport as a part of national policy. In both countries private sport is swallowed up in official state organization. Establishment of successful separate sport teams was one of the ways in which East Germany succeeded in getting recognition as a political entity separate from the German Federal Republic. Sport in the "free world" is still in the hands of private bodies, though not of individual athletes but President Ford's 1975 comittee expressed grave concern over the need for a centralized sport authority to produce medal-winning Olympic teams as an arm of national policy, and in 1980 President Carter assumed that the American Olympic Committee was subordinate to the government on the question of an Olympic boycott.

At this point I should note that Donald Ball, urging that we undertook to examine the idea that international sport is all politicized, especially the idea that the Cold War (East versus West) shapes the thoughts and actions of participants.[57] Ball did so by studying the scoring of figure-skating in international competiton. Scoring of figure-skating is subjective, depending upon assessments by judges who could easily reflect their political biases in their scoring. Most skaters are from either the Eastern or the Western bloc (there are few, for example, from Africa, Polynesia or Latin America). Ball studied judge's scoring for the World Figure Skating Championships from 1967 to 1971. If a Cold War bias were uppermost, the scoring of Eastern judges should have correlated with that of other Eastern judges, and that of Western judges with one another, to a significantly higher degree than all judges, East and West, agreed with each other, 974, scores of Western judges with one another, 961, and the correlation of scores of **all** judges with each other was 954. Since such high correlations could all have occurred by chance less than one time in a thousand, it appeared that judging was **not** dominated by the Cold War. Ball compared international judging for 1967 alone with judging in the Canadian and United States championships. The correlations of scores were, for world competion, 961; for the Canadian Championships, 832; and for the U.S. championships, 842. In the world events, he did find "home-towning": judges East, West, and neutral did rank their own nationals higher; but significant ideological differences he did not find. Contrary to the political bias theory he thought he had found a high degree of professional spirit in international judges: "the role definition of the skating judge emphasizes competence rather than (ideological) commitment; individual assessment as against international alliance; the good of the sport over the gain of the specific; fairness instead of favoritism; skating as contest instead of as cabal; and sportsmanship as versus partisanship.''[58]

In this and the previous chapter we have analyzed how sport is related to two lifelong aspects of the relationship between an individual and his society: the **socialization** through which one internalizes the patterns of give-and-take necessary to living with other people, and **enculturation**, the ''cultural brainwashing'' by which one internalizes the particular ways of behaving characteristic of one's culture. Although this is not necessarily the pure warfare that Freud thought it was, socialization and enculturation involve conflict and tend to produce, or release, hostile impulses. In Chapter 12 we shall deal with how sport is related to this hostility.

FOOTNOTES

[1]Harry Webb, ''Professionalization of Attitudes Toward Play Among Adolescents,'' in **Aspects of Contemporary Sport Sociology**, Proceedings of C. I. C. Symposium on the Sociology of Sport, 1968, ed. Gerald S. Kenyon, Chicago, The Athletic Institute, 1969, 161.

[2]**Ibid.**, 166.

[3]Mabel Lee, The Case For and Against Intercollegiate Athletics for Women, **Research Quarterly**, 2, May 1931, 127.

[4]**Christian Science Monitor**, April 1, 1976, 2.

[5]Max Weber, **The Protestant Ethic and the Spirit of Capitalism**, trans. Talcott Parsons, New York, Scribners, 1958.

[6]David C. McClelland, **The Achieving Society**, New York, Van Nostrand, 1961.

[7]Webb, **op. cit.**, 163, 177.

[8]Brian M. Petrie, ''Achievement Orientations in Adolescent Attitudes Toward Play,'' **International Review of Sport Sociology**, 6, 1977, 89-101.

[9]**Ibid.**, 96.

[10]Edward W. Vaz, ''What Price Victory? An Analysis of Minor Hockey League Players' Attitudes Towards Winning,'' **International Journal of Sport Sociology**, 9, 2, 1974, 40.

[11]McClelland, **op. cit.**, 322-324.

[12]A. Famaey-Lamon, M. Hebbelinck, and A. M. Cadron, ''Team-Sport and Individual-Sport,'' **International Review of Sport Sociology**, 14, 2, 1979, 37-50.

[13]**Ibid.**, 43.

[14]Brian Sutton-Smith and John M. Roberts, ''Studies of an Elementary Game of Strategy,'' **Genetic Psychology Monographs**, no. 75, 1967, 3-42.

[15]**Ibid.**, 10.

[16]**Ibid.**, 27.

[17]Marian Winterbottom, ''The Relation of Need for Achievement to Learning Experiences in Independence and Mastery,'' in J. W. Atkinson, ed., **Motives in Fantasy, Action, and Society**, New York, Van Nostrand, 1958, 453-478.

[18]Sutton-Smith and Roberts, **op. cit.**, 39.

[19]Francis J. Ryan, "An Investigation of Personality Differences Asociated with Competitive Ability," and "Further Observations on Competitive Ability in Athletics," in Bryant M. Wedge, ed., **Psychosocial Problems of College Men**, New Haven, Yale, 1958, 113-122, 123-139.

[20]**Ibid.**, 116.

[21]**Ibid.**, 119.

[22]**Ibid.**, 121.

[23]**Ibid.**, 125.

[24]**Ibid.**, 138.

[25]**Ibid.**, 127.

[26]Jack Scott, "The Souring of George Sauer," **Intellectual Digest**, December 1971, 53.

[27]Brian Sutton-Smith, John M. Roberts, and Robert Kozelka, "Game Involvement in Adults," **Journal of Social Psychology, 60**, 1963, 15-30.

[28]**Ibid.**, 16.

[29]John M. Roberts and Brian Sutton-Smith, "Child Training and Game Involvement," **Ethnology, 1**, 1962, 166-185.

[30]Sutton-Smith, Roberts, Kozelka, **op. cit.**

[31]Jean Jacques Rousseau, "Considerations on the Government of Poland," in **The Minor Educational Writings of Jean Jacques Rousseau**, selected and translated by William Boyd, reprint edition, New York, Teachers College, 1962, 99.

[32]Peter C. McIntosh, **Sport in Society**, London, Watts, 1963, 71-72, 106.

[33]Allen L. Sack, "Yale 29, Harvard 4: The Professionalization of American Football," **Quest**, Winter 1973.

[34]**Ibid.**, 20.

[35]Hanford Powel, Jr., **Walter Camp**, Boston, Little, Brown, 1926, 112-113.

[36]Sack, **op. cit.**, 30.

[37]William Graham Sumner, **Essays in Political and Social Science**, New York, 1885, 85.

[38]Albert Galloway Keller and Maurice R. Davie, eds., **Essays of William Graham Sumner**, New Haven, Yale, 1934, v. ii, 96.

[39]William Graham Sumner, "Bequests of the Nineteenth Century to the Twentieth," **Yale Review**, June 1933, 752.

[40]Powel, **op. cit.**, 99.

[41]Harry Edwards, **Sociology of Sport**, Homewood, Dorsey, 1973, 103-130, 318-330.

[42]Bruce Ogilvie and Thomas Tutko, "If You Want to Build Character, Try Something Else," **Psychology Today**, October 1971, 61-62.

[43]Walter E. Schaefer, "Some Social Sources and Consequences of the Interscholastic Athletics: The Case of Participation and Delinquency," in Kenyon, **Aspects of Contemporary Sports Sociology, op. cit.**, 29-55.

[44]Edwards, **op. cit.**, Table 7-4, p. 225.

[45]Hans Groll, "Participation in High-Level Sports of Young People Working in Industry and Trade," **International Review of Sport Sociology**, 6, 1971, 115-123.

[46]Dale L. Hanson, "Cardiac Response to Participation in Little League Baseball as Determined by Telemetry," **Research Quarterly, 38**, 3, October 1967.

[47]Charles William Eliot, "The Evils of College Football," **Woman's Home Companion**, November 1905, in William Allan Nielson, ed., **Charles William Eliot, The Man and His Beliefs**, New York, Harper and Row, 1926, v. 1, 116-117.

[48]José Cagigal, "Social Education Through Sport: A Trial," **Comtemporary Psychology of Sport**, Proceedings of the Second International Congress of Sport Psychology, ed. Gerald S. Kenyon, Chicago, Athletic Institute, 1970, 347.

[49]Schaefer, **op. cit.**, 35.

[50]Thomas Tutko and William Bruns, **Winning is Everything, and Other American Myths**, New York, Macmillan, 1976, 84.

[51]Cited, **ibid.**, 85.

[52]Quoted in "Are Sports Good for the Soul?," **Newsweek**, January 11, 1971, 51.

[53]Quoted in Philip Goodhart and Christopher Chataway, **War Without Weapons**, London, Allen, 1968, 63.

[54]Sandy Padwe, "Sports and Politics Must Be Separate—At Least Some Politics That Is," **Philadelphia Inquirer**, December 14, 1971, 35.

[55]Alex Natan, **Sport and Society**, London, Bowes and Bowes, 1958.

[56]**Physical Culture and Sport in the USSR**, Moscow, Fiskultura: Sport, 1954, 2.

[57]Donald W. Ball, "A Politicized Social Psychology of Sport: Some Assumptions and Evidence from International Figure Skating Competition," **International Review of Sport Sociology**, 8, 3-4, 1973, 63-71.

[58]**Ibid.**, 67.

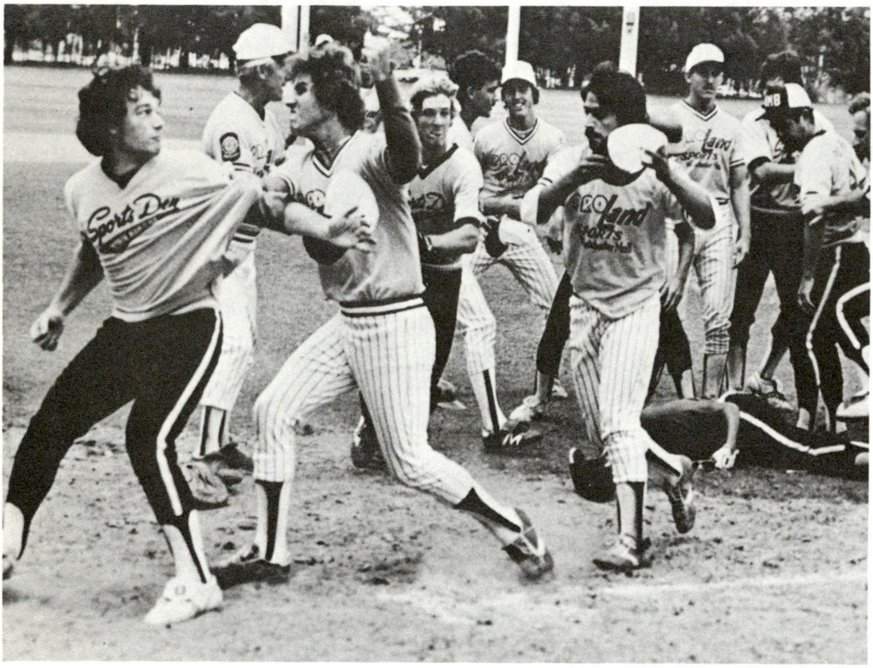

"Violence in Sport" Courtesy of **The Miami Herald.**

CHAPTER 12 VIOLENCE IN SPORT CATHARSIS OR REINFORCEMENT?

In this chapter we will explore one of the most important questions about sport, culture, and personality—the relationship between violence in sport and non-sport violence in society and in life in general.

Violence, Hostility, and Aggression

Violence we may define as **the use of destructive personal force against objects (including people) that are believed to stand in the way of one's goals**. Violence is related to **hostility**. Hostility embodies the wish to hurt another human being. It may or may not be acted out in the form of actual damage. There may be a hostile intent without a hostile act, or there may be a violent act without hostile intent. Dean Ryan suggests an important distinction between violence that is **hostile** and violence that is **instrumental.** Hostile violence is destructive behavior in which damage is intended. Instrumental violence may damage people in the course of achieving a goal (for example, incinerating a civilian population to win a war or disabling a key opponent to win a ball game), but the intention need not be hostile.[1]

Violence is also related to **aggression**. The term aggression, as used by some authors, is synonymous with hostility. Others use it to describe all outgoing manipulation of one's environment (by contrast with passivity, defense, and escaping behavior). A great deal of confusion is often created by loose use of the term aggression. In this chapter violence will mean destructive aggression, whether or not hostile in intent.

Does competitive sport increase or decrease violence and hostility in everyday life, for the participant and for the spectator?

It is argued by some that sport reduces violent and hostile tendencies in at least two important ways: (1) Vigorous and perhaps hostile physical activity has a **cathartic** effect through working off tensions, blowing off steam. (2) Since competitive sport is a form of **controlled** violence, in sport one learns how to be aggressive without letting one's hostility get out of hand. This control training, it is held, carries over into everyday life. Ryan suggests that "Bubba Smith could wipe out one entire end of town in an evening, if he chose. He doesn't, however. It may be that experience at controlling aggressive behavior gained through athletics keeps him from acting aggressively except in situations that he considers justifiable."[2] As for the spectator, there is a popular belief that by watching a prize fight, football game, or other violent event one is able to "get all one's aggressions out" and spare one's family, co-workers, and friends. The British psychiatrist Anthony Storr holds that competitive sport reduces the likelihood of war: "It is obvious that the encouragement of competition in all possible fields is likely to diminish the kind of hostility which leads to war rather than to increase it . . . rivalry between nations in sport can do nothing but good and it should be possible to encourage competition in other fields also."[3] In this connection, the historian Burckhardt once said that "a people knowing war has no need of tournaments."[4]

The opposite view about sport violence maintains that participating in or watching violent competition increases violence in both the athlete and the spectator. First, the athlete who is ordinarily afraid of giving expression to his hostile impulses may learn through athletic experience that he can do so and get away with it, without punishment. Having learned this on the playing field, he may also be less inhibited in daily life. Furthermore, in sport his violence is rewarded ("positively reinforced") and he also sees athletic heroes whom he admires being more richly rewarded. The spectator, according to this view, reacts in much the same way, except that the reinforcement of his violent impulses is vicarious rather than direct. Seeing athletes "getting away with murder" reduces the spectator's inhibitions against his own violent tendencies. He admires the same successful, "aggressive" heroes that the athlete does, sees them positively rewarded by their peers, and tends to imitate them as much as he can.

Violence in sport has many levels.

(1) The most extreme is the kind of violence that is outside the rules of even the bodily contact sports. (Although the sport Establishment tries to keep such things "in the family," such violence has recently been taken into the courts as also a violation of criminal law.) Among the violent operations that are almost standard operating procedure in the National Football League are sticking (ramming one's helmet into the base of an opponent's spine), stripping (pinching, biting, slugging, twisting arms and fingers to pry the ball loose from a ballcarrier), ringing the bell (slamming a fist into the earhole of a lineman's helmet), leg-whipping (kicking hard in the shins), and clotheslining (extending a forearm in front of a charging opponent's throat).[5]

(2) Extreme violence is also possible, indeed approved, **within** the rules of bodily contact sport. A University of Miami football player, describing a situation in which he whooped with glee over putting an opponent in the hospital, wrote, "There is a certain something that a football player has, and that is why he loves the game. He can go absolutely berserk and even hurt an individual without getting into any trouble." Frank Champi, before he quit as Harvard quarterback in 1969, described the "legitimate" violence of football: "You see people hit, getting hurt, it goes on and on. . . If somebody tries to break your leg, what can you expect? To play as hard as you can is to hit as hard as you can."[6] Boxing is the other major body contact sport. In it assault and battery are legitimized.

(3) All of the territorial games modeled on the spring festival contests described in chapter 7 (basketball, hockey, soccer, and lacrosse, as well as American football) easily cross the line into violence. Although Robert Ardrey has oversimplified and sensationalized the idea, possession and protection of a home and homeland have deep human roots. They can easily be associated with the defense of Good against Evil.The territorial games, like the original Osiris ritual at Papremis, involve a goal located in space that is attacked and defended. Intense emotions are easily mobilized. Although the rules of most territorial games theoretically minimize or outlaw bodily contact, in actual practice they are usually interpreted so as to maximize it.

(4) In the non-territorial and non-contact sports, power exerted against objects and people can play a large part. Most baseball fans prefer heavy hitting and scoring to close, low-scoring games featuring skill and finesse but little raw power. Force exerted on the inanimate baseball is not all that attracts fans. Baseball owner Branch Rickey, a devote Christian churchman, once said that his ideal ballplayer would break both legs of anyone who got between him and a base. Although the net makes bodily contact almost impossible in tennis, George Leonard gets the feel of contemporary tennis when he says of doubles that "net play more and more resembles World War II, with red-faced, tense-muscled middle-aged men crouching at the front lines every Sunday, itching to fire their nylon howitzers down their

opponent's throats."[7] In his history of pro golf, Al Barkow says the women's pro tour may never catch on as has the men's. Although golf essentially lacks the violence spectators seem to crave, men do provide some. But females, no matter how skillful, "just do not propel a golf ball with the same crack and rocketlike force as do the men."[8] Leonard, describing golf as a game of "contemplative strolls and shimmering distances," attributes much of the charisma of Arnold Palmer to the fact that even when past his prime, he could turn the game into a cavalry charge. (With respect to Barkow's comment, it is unlikely that a woman golfer could do that.)

(5) As Ryan suggests, "it is possible that competition, by its very nature, leads to aggression."[9] Muzafer Sherif and Carolyn Sherif describe how, in their famous Robber's Cave experiment with group behavior in adolescent boys, competitive athletic contests led to hostility so intense that the experiment had to be terminated. They state the principle that was illustrated: "When members of two groups come into contact with one another in a series of activities that embody goals which each urgently desires, but which can be attained by one group only at the expense of the other, competitive activity toward the goal changes, over time, into hostility between the groups and their members."[10] In short, a zerosum game (see Chapter 3) in which "winning is everything," is bound to become hostile. Therefore, from this viewpoint, the way we define competition in our athletic subculture makes it inevitable that it will teach us to be cut-throats. Dreams of "clean competition" are just that—dreams.

Evidence for Catharsis

Now, having posed the basic question, let's look at the social evidence for the theory of catharsis, and then at the evidence for reinforcement.

Our first case is the role of soccer among the urban Zulu of South Africa, as analyzed by the anthropologist N. A. Scotch.[11] Within a short time, these Zulu have moved from a preliterate tribal culture to an urban environment in Durban and other South African cities. The shift from rural to urban life is usually stressful for people anywhere. For the tribal Zulu, it meant moving to crowded housing and competition for scarce jobs. (Scotch does not mention that, as blacks, in the city the Zulu were brought into sharpest confrontation with **apartheid**—the South African separation of the races.) The whole result has been that in the city "interpersonal and intergroup hostility and aggression are much greater. . . than in the traditional rural Zulu community."[12]

Soccer football plays an important part in this rural-urban transition. Much of the limited leisure of male Zulu is spent playing, watching, and discussing soccer. "Organized football leagues, resembling in their hierarchies of skill our major and minor leagues in baseball, engage in complex rivalries no less extreme, bitter, and unremitting than in Chicago or Cleveland." Players, although "amateurs," are recruited, paid, and enticed away from one team to another. Star players have been known to pass from team to team looking for the "best deal."

The soccer syndrome transfers to football the emotions and rituals that in tribal life accompanied war. Players practice ritual sexual abstinence before a match as previously before battle. They smear on their jerseys and shoes the medicines traditionally put on weapons to give strength in battle. They purify themselves by an emetic the morning of the match as previously before combat. The teams approach the playing field in military formation. An educated Zulu describes the intensity of ritual preparation the night before a match, typically presided over by an **inyanga** (a tribal doctor):

> *All the football teams have their own* **inyanga** *who doctors them all for each match. The night before a match they must "camp" together around a fire. They all sleep there together, they must stay naked and are given . . . medicines by the* **inyanga**. *Incisions are made on their knees, elbows, and joints . . . Almost every team I know has an* **inyanga** *and does this—it is necessary to win. Even though players are Christians and have lived in towns for a long time they do it, and believe in it.*[13]

Scotch believes that this substitute warfare (whose tribal survivals clearly resemble some of our athletic rituals) play an important part in Zulu adjustment to the pressures of urban living: "Football . . . is one of the few opportunities open to the Zulu for release from the anxiety and tensions of . . . urban life; and more specifically, it allows the expression of the increased aggression and hostility that arises in the city between Africans, within the framework of a modern, acceptable form."

Scotch was mainly interested in the broad pattern through which tribal customs were translated to an urban setting. To give clear evidence on the cathartic effect of soccer, we would need to make two comparisons. We would need to know whether urban Zulu in highly frustrating situations were more involved in football than were people in less difficult situations. We would also have to compare the amount of intergroup and interpersonal hostility among Zulu involved in sport with the amount of Zulu not so involved. If we did this, we might have something of an anthropological equivalent of a psychological experiment conducted by Seymour Feshbach.[14]

Feshbach's research studied the effect of seeing a film of a violent athletic event. It involved the relationship among three factors: (1) treatment of a person by experimenters, (2) exposure to a violent film, and (3) testing of the level of aggressiveness after exposure.

One hundred and one male University of Pennsylvania students volunteered for the stated purpose of their judging the main character in two ten-minute films. One group was given fairly routine instructions. In the other group, instructions were given by Feshbach's assistant Abraham Wolf, in such a way as to arouse anger by questioning the student's intellectual and emotional maturity. These two groups were labeled Noninsult Group and Insult Group. (In a footnote Feshbach expresses his gratitude to Wolf for his competence **and courage** in doing the insulting.) Following this preliminary treatment, the students were then shown either a prize fight sequence from the movie **Body and Soul**, or a neutral film depicting the spread of rumors in a factory.

After this viewing, all were given two measures of aggressiveness. In a word association test they were asked to give ten written associations to each of five words (choke, massacre, murder, stab, and torture) shown them on 5 x 8 cards, mixed into a series of eleven cards, along with six neutral words (wash, travel, walk, relax, sleep, and listen). Each student was scored on the number of aggressive responses in his first ten associations to each of the five violent words (total possible score 50). In the second test of aggressiveness the original experimenter left the room and an associate entered and asked the students to fill out a multiple choice questionnaire evaluating the experimenter and the whole experiment. The questionnaire included six items, each with six possible responses, which were scored from 1 to 6 for aggressiveness (total possible score 36).

On aggressiveness toward the experimenter, among those who had previously been insulted, **those who had seen the fight film were significantly less aggressive than those who had watched the neutral film**. Table 12.1 shows the number of each group who fell above and below the average (in this case, median) aggressiveness score. A difference so large would have occurred by chance less than one time in a thousand ($p < .001$). The word association test also produced a significant difference in the same direction (students who had seen the fight film were less aggressive) but the level of significance was lower ($p < .05$—could have occurred by chance less than 5 times in 100, or less than 1 in 20).

Feshbach's conclusion was that vicarious exposure to violence has a cathartic effect when a person has been specifically angered, but not otherwise. He also hypothesized that under other conditions vicarious aggressive experience would have a stimulating effect, but the results for his Noninsult groups do not show this.

Table 12.1 Distribution of Aggression Questionnaire Scores Falling Above and Below the Median as a Function of Insult Fight Film and Insult Neutral Film Treatments.

Treatment	Below Median	Above Median
Insult Fight Film	20	6
Insult Neutral Film	7	22
		$p < .001$

Source—Seymour Feshbach, "The Stimulating Versus Cathartic Effects of a Vicarious Aggressive Activity," **Journal of Abnormal and Social Psychology, 53** (1961), Table 4, page 383. Copyright 1961 by the American Psychological Association. Reprinted by permission.

Evidence for Reinforcement

A study by Donald Hartmann several years later does show the stimulating effect that Feshbach did not find, and more.[15] Hartmann used as his subjects 72 male adolescent offenders under court commitment to the California Youth Authority for crimes ranging from minor offenses to strong-armed robbery. The young men were asked to take part in an investigation of teaching machines and audio-visual displays. As in Feshbach's experiment, the first step was arousal of anger by the experimenter's assistant in half of the subjects, through critical and unjustified statements about their intelligence and competence. The other half received neutral comments.

After the arousing or nonarousing instructions, the young men were each assigned at random to one of three two-minute films. The first minute of all three films was identical, showing two boys on a basketball court shooting baskets. The second minute of the first film showed the two boys in an active and cooperative basketball game. In the other two films the boys got into an argument that ended in a fist fight. These two films differed in that one showed one of the boys being hurt, while the other focused on his opponent's hostile behavior and attitudes. There were thus a neutral film, a "pain-cues" film, and an "instrumental aggression" film. "The pain-cues film focused almost entirely on the victim's verbal and gestural pain as he was ferociously pummeled and kicked by his opponent. The instrumental aggression film . . . focused on the aggressor's responses including foot thrusts, flying fists, aggressive verbalizations, and angry facial expressions."[16]

After he had seen one of the films, each young man was then told that he would eventually be questioned about its content. He was then invited to participate in an experiment on the effect of pain in learning. He was set in a room equipped with lights that were supposed to signal when a partner in another room had got a learning task right or had made an error. These lights were under the control of the experimenter; there was no actual learner. The young man also had at hand a panel of switches through which he was supposed to shock the learner when the light flashed that the learner had made a mistake. He was first invited to use each of the switches to shock himself, so as to know how strong a shock it delivered. Then the learner was supposedly put through a series of 25 tasks, for 10 of which the young man's light flashed an "error." Each time he was to pull a switch to shock the learner and thus help him learn. The duration and intensity of the shock were registered in an adjoining room and thus gave a measure of each young man's aggressiveness after seeing his film.

The results of the Hartmann experiment appear in Figure 12.1. Contrary to Feshbach's results, both violent films were followed by a **higher** level of aggression, as compared with the neutral film, regardless of whether the young man had been insulted or not. The difference shown would occur by chance less frequently than 1 time in 100: $p < 01$. The young men who had been insulted were more aggressive after seeing the film than those who had not been insulted. The opposite would have been expected from Feshbach's theory of catharsis. In addition, viewing a victim's pain stimulated more aggressive responses than did viewing of an aggressor's hostility. Also (not shown in Figure 12.1), young men with longer records of antisocial behavior, particularly when they were angered and saw pain, delivered more intense shocks than those with shorter records. Overall, Hartmann said, these results contradict the theory of catharsis as developed by Feshbach and others.

Hartmann's conclusions are supported by several earlier experimental studies by Leonard Berkowitz, also using an aggressive sport film and a neutral or less aggressive film. One violent film was the boxing picture, **Champion**, starring Kirk Douglas. Less aggressive control films showed a sailing race and the mile race between Roger Bannister and John Landy in which Bannister ran the first four-minute mile. Consistently, Berkowitz has found that his subjects behave more aggressively after seeing a violent film than after seeing a less aggressive one.

For example, in his experiment using the Douglas fight film, reported in 1965, Berkowitz used the same sequence of angering ⟶ exposure to film ⟶ opportunity to give shocks later employed by Hartmann, with the added twist that in some cases he identified his assistant, who was to receive the shocks, as a Boxer, and in others as a Speech Major. Angered subjects who saw the fight film gave the boxer an average of 5.35 shocks as compared with 4.95 for those who saw the neutral film. In average duration of shock, the figures were: fight film 16.56, neutral film, 11.47.[17] (Here, $p < .05$.)

Figure 12.1 Mean shock intensity for subjects viewing the control film, the instrumental aggression film, and the pain-cues film.

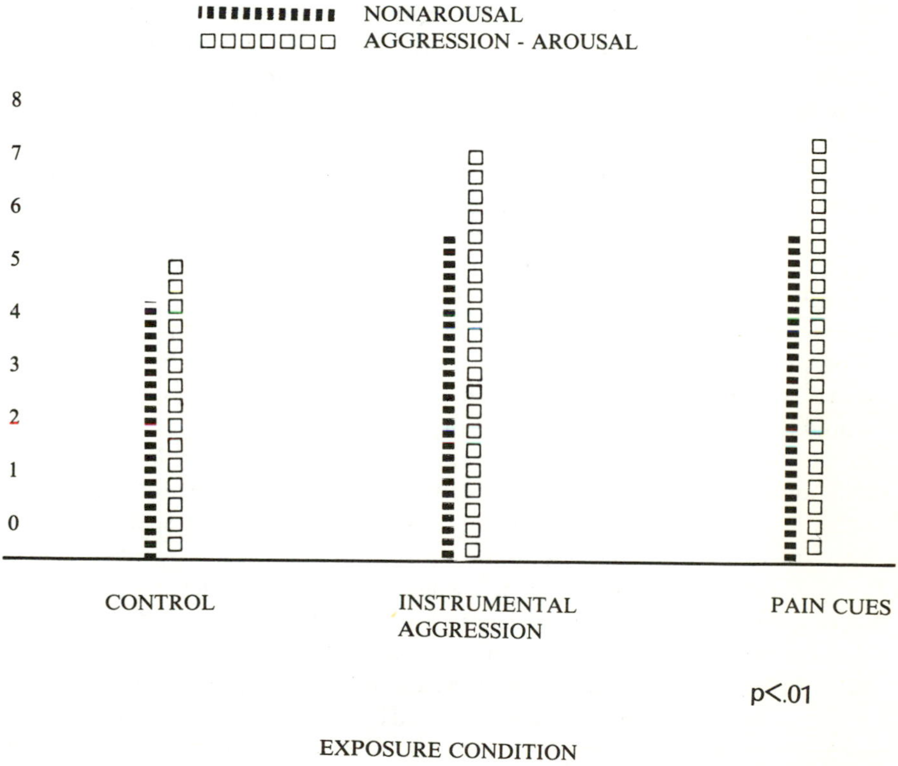

Source - Donald P. Hartmann, "Influence of Symbolically Modeled Instrumental Aggression and Pain Cues on Aggressive Behavior," **Journal of Personality and Social Psychology, 11,** 1969, Figure 1, page 283. Copyright 1969 by the American Psychological Association. Reprinted by permission.

Research dealing directly with the results of sport violence (of which there is not very much) is supplemented by a large body of experimentation on the general results of participating in or viewing violence. Richard Walters and E. L. Thomas compared a group that watched a fight scene from the James Dean-Sal Mineo movie **Rebel Without a Cause** with a group that watched a film showing adolescents doing art work. Afterwards, the fight scene group behaved more aggressively.[18] Albert Bandura has repeatedly found that children will repeat adult aggression seen live, on film, or on television.[19]

In 1969 Jeffrey H. Goldstein and Robert L. Arms took the catharsis-reinforcement question out into the "real world," comparing spectator attitudes before and after the Army-Navy football game in Philadelphia, and also before and after an Army-Temple gymnastics meet.[20] Student assistants from Temple University interviewed 97 fans coming into the stadium, asking them which team they favored. From a hostility scale constructed by Buss and Durkee[21] they asked the spectators 28 questions (9 scoring indirect hostility, 8 scoring resentment, and 11 scoring irritability), mixed with 8 "filler" questions about football. Having thus measured pregame hostility of a sample of fans by use of an accepted measure, the interviewers asked the same questions to another sample of 53 fans leaving the stadium after the game. The spectators leaving the stadium were significantly more hostile than those entering. This was true for both supporters of the losing team (Navy) and supporters of the winning team (Army). Table 12.2 shows the average before and after hostility scores. The range of possible scores was from 0 to 28 (the number of questions). A difference of this size would be expected by chance fewer than 25 times in 1000 ($p < .025$). "No support for a catharsis effect is obtained in the present study," said Goldstein and Arms, "contrary to the many popular notions that it would occur."[22] (The results would be more convincing if **the same** spectators had been interviewed before and after.)

At the Army-Temple gym meet, where the same interviewing techniques were used, there was no significant change in the level of hostility. Why? Although the gym meet was not a "neutral" non-competitive control situation, in terms of the scale presented earlier in this chapter, the level of violence was much lower. "One major difference between the nature of the two events is that a football game involves multiple players in direct physical contact, while a gym meet involves individual performance in which no contact can occur. It seems likely . . . that watching an aggressive sport leads to an increase in hostility among spectators."[23]

In another venture into the "real world," Edward Turner gave sentence-completion and thematic apperception tests to males at the University of Maryland after they had watched football and basketball games and wrestling matches involving tension and a doubtful outcome.[24] There was a significant increase in the number of aggressive words produced after these experiences as spectators.

Table 12.2 Mean Spectator Hostility Scores; 1969 Army-Navy Football Game

	Preferred			
	Army **(winning team)**	Navy **(losing team)**	No **preference**	**Total**
	n = 38	n = 47	n = 12	
Pre-game	10.42[a]	11.72	11.67	11.20
	n = 18	n = 30	n - 5	
Post-game	13.33	13.17	15.00	13.40

[a]The higher the score, the greater the hostility. $P < .025$

Source — J. H. Goldstein and R. L. Arms, "Effects of Observing Athletic Contests on Hostility," **Sociometry, 34**, 1971, Table 1, page 88.

A 1972 experiment by Dolf Zillman, Aaron Katcher, and Barry Milavsky applies not to the spectator but to the participant. It contradicted the catharsis theory in its simplest form, the belief that vigorous muscular activity reduces emotional tension. On the contrary, in this experiment, it raised it.[25]

Twenty-eight University of Pennsylvania students were recruited for research that was suposed to (1) test their ability to perceive while distracted, and (2) test the effect of electric shocks on learning. The procedure was this: The experimental group were first angered by giving them shocks for "wrong" answers to 12 questions. They were then put to work pedaling for 2½ minutes on a cycle machine (bicycle ergometer) and while pedaling shown a series of slides on which they were to report. (Control groups had no arousal of anger and performed a fairly simple manual task instead of pedaling.) Finally, all groups were invited to give shocks, from ten switches labeled "quite mild" to "rather painful," to help in a learning task. Throughout the experiment, the metabolic state of all groups was tested several times by taking a combination of pulse rate, systolic blood pressure, and skin temperature (the last as a measure of contraction or dilation of periphal blood vessels).

The arousal of anger through electric shock raised the level of metabolic excitation. The bicycle riding raised it very significantly ($p < .001$). Those who had been angered and had pedaled the bike (and thus were doubly aroused) gave significantly stronger shocks to the "learner" than the control groups ($p < .05$). Zillman, Katcher, and Milavsky said of their results: "The findings are clearly counter to the expectation that strenuous physical exercise, at least as long as elevated excitation lasts, and as long as the individual does not reach a state of acute exhaustion, can serve to drain aggressive tensions and thus induce catharsis.'[26]

In another kind of test of the catharsis hypotheses, anthropologist Richard H. Sipes studied the relationship between war and combative sport in 20 societies (all preliterate except for the Hutterites, a communal pacifist group in the United States and Canada).[27] Data on these societies were taken from J. P. Murdoch's **Ethnographic Index**, to which we were introduced in Chapter 6. Sipes selected what he thought were the 10 best examples of warlike societies and the 10 best examples of peaceful peoples. There are two main models, says Sipes, of the relationship betwen war and combative sport. According to the Drive Discharge model (which is the catharsis model), the members of every society have a certain amount of hostility that must be discharged somehow. War and violent sports are alternative ways. "Warlike sports serve to discharge accumulated aggressive tensions and therefore act as alternative channels to war, making it less likely."[28] According to the Cultural Patterning theory on the other hand, war and sport are both expressions of a common underlying pattern of cultural **mores**. "Behavior patterns and value systems relative to war and to warlike sports tend to overlap and support each other's presence."[29] If the Drive Discharge (catharsis) hypothesis is correct, in warlike societies we should expect to find few combative sports and in peaceful societies we should find many. If the Cultural Patterning hypothesis is correct, we should find that the more warlike societies have more violent games, and the peaceful societies have fewer. In a sentence, the catharsis hypostheses would predict an inverse (negative) correlation between frequency of warfare and number of combative games; the cultural patterning hypotheses would predict a direct (positive) correlation. Which hypothesis was supported by the data in the 20 societies? "The cross-cultural study shows that where we find warlike behavior we typically find warlike sports and where war is relatively rare combative sports tend to be absent."[30] There were dramatic exceptions. The Tikopians, a relatively peaceful people, have a combative sport consisting of a "mock fight with sticks in which, however, no one is hit. Each party moves forward with a rapid shuffling movement till they meet and clash their sticks together. [This] is played with the greatest zest and enjoyment." Sipes thinks this game may have survived from a less peaceful period. The Mundurucú, a people who are constantly attacking others, have no combative sports. Sipes feels that this is because internal relations in their society are so shaky that the Mundurucu cannot risk violent games. The overall results of Sipes' study are summarized in Table 12.3.

If a cross-cultural study of different societies shows a positive correlation between warlike patterns and combative sports, then within the same society participation in correlative sports, either as players or as spectators, should be higher in time of war than in periods of peace. Sipes did a study of the recent history of participant and spectator sports in the recent history of the United States. One of his findings was that football, a combative sport, boomed during World War II and the Korean war and baseball, a less competitive game, lagged. Before accepting this evidence against catharsis, we would need to examine other long-run trends in the two games.

Table 12.3 Relationships Between Warfare and Combative Sports in 20 Preliterate Societies

		Combative Sports: Yes	Combative Sports: No		
					$p < 0.003$
Warlike	Yes	9	1	10	
	No	2	8	10	
		11	9	20	

Source—Richard G. Sipes, "War, Sports, and Aggression: An Empirical Test of Two Rival Theories," **American Anthropologist, 75**, February 1973, Table II, page 71.

Sport anthropologist Kendall Blanchard agrees with Sipes' culture patterning view. He believes that **both** those who make general claims that combative sport reduces social aggression and those who claim that it generally increases it are wrong. Rather, "team sport behavior provides a specialized, artificial context for the expression of learned aggression needs through competitive forms of conflict."[31] It is a part of the culture, shaped by the culture. How combative sport in turn shapes the culture depends on the particular social situation. Sometimes sport competition may prevent unnecessary social violence. An example is the stickball games arranged by the traditional Mississippi Choctaw indians when two communities appeared headed for open hostility. "On the other hand, team sport contests can become the scene of violence. This is not to say that these competitive sports **cause** that violence."[32]

We may better understand what Blanchard means by considering three unrelated events that occurred in 1969. In Central America, Honduras and El Salvador went to war after a soccer game led to rioting. In Milwaukee,

Wisconsin, after losing a basketball game, black high school students threw a white college professor off a bus. In eastern Europe, a crisis between Czechoslovakia and the Soviet Union followed a Czech hockey victory which elated fans celebrated by tearing up the furniture in the Russian airlines depot. Did combative sport **cause** the war, the international crisis, the interracial violence? Could they have occurred without the sporting events? Were the clashes in the sport arena like the fuse that ignites the explosion of sticks of dynamite?

How does all the evidence on catharsis and reinforcement add up? Albert Bandura was probably carried away a little in an agonistic scientific dispute when he wrote:

> *It is highly improbable that even advocates of vicarious drive reduction would recommend community programs in which sexually aroused adolescents are shown libidinous movies at drive-ins as a means of reducing sexual behavior; famished persons are presented displays of gourmands dining . . . in order to alleviate hunger pangs; and assaultive gangs are regularly shown films of assailants flogging their antagonists in an attempt to diminish aggressive behavior.''*[33]

But it must be said for Bandura that his own very extensive researches, and most other research on the subject, support him in dismissing the theory of catharsis. As Ryan says, "while sport has many values, one of them does not appear to be the reduction of aggression."[34] Walters, summarizing research on the subject, was clearly correct in saying that the father who teaches his boy to hit a punching bag hard is increasing the chance that he will be aggressive toward other children.[35]

As far as the athlete himself/herself is concerned, the idea that combative sport teaches control of aggression is more plausible than the hypothesis of direct tension reduction with which Zillman and his colleagues dealt so thoroughly.There are such pieces of evidence as A. A. Stone's Harvard honors theses in which he found that football players at the end of a season were less aggressive generally and less personal in their aggression as measured by a Thematic Apperception Test (TAT) than were a control group of non-athletes.[36]

As for the spectator, in laboratory situations it seems that seeing the painful results of violence may alert people to the possible outcome of their own violence, and thus lead them to control it. In a series of experiments Richard Goranson showed two groups a fight film. One had a "positive outcome" showing the winner leaving the ring undamaged and going on to success. The other had a "negative outcome," stressing the loser's injuries, a cerebral hemorrhage, and agonizing death.[37] The subjects who had seen the negative outcome film afterwards gave fewer shocks to a "learner." Goranson had the subjects rate their mood before and after the film. Those who saw the negative outcome film felt significantly less happy after the film than before. If it had "drained off" tension cathartically, they should have felt better. So Goranson prefers the interpretation that "the horrible effects of the violence served to *sensitize* the subjects to the potential harm that they themselves might inflict [italics his]."

There is little or no direct evidence from sporting events to support the idea of catharsis. In laboratory experimentation, Feshbach's study with the fight film was an impressive piece of work, but does not stand up in the face of the later work of Berkowitz and Hartmann. Sipes' anthropological study was based on a very small sample, but I do not think that more extensive work is likely to come up with more cross-cultural support for catharsis.

The catharsis hypothesis is, I think, best seen as a cultural myth that supports behavior very central to our agonistic society, and also fits the interests of an entrenched sport Establishment. Cultural myths are not necessarily false, but are symbolically important beliefs that persist without the need for evidence. Usually there is **some** evidence supporting them and this is the case with the catharsis hypothesis, but its importance is blown far out of proportion. Conflicting evidence is ignored, sometimes actually censored.

A case of such censorship is very much to the point here, as illustrating the climate in which we study these matters. In the early 1970s the Surgeon General of the United States commissioned a panel of 40 psychologists, sociologists, and other social scientists who conducted 43 pieces of research involving 7500 young people from age 3 to 19, on the question, "Does violence on television cause children to be more violent?" These reports provided much evidence of children becoming more violent after watching TV. The Surgeon General then selected another panel to prepare a summary report of 260 pages, which was finally condensed down to 18 pages. The TV networks were allowed to veto members of this panel; seven were rejected because of opposition by NBC or ABC. By the time the research had been edited down to 18 pages by this loaded committee, any connection between TV programing and social violence had disappeared. The **New York Times** finally reported this abbreviated summary under a headline, "TV Violence Held Unharmful to Youth."

The objective evidence about sport violence tells us that the important question is not whether it reduces or teaches social violence, but **how and under what conditions it teaches it.**

First, what a participant or witness will do about violence in sport will depend upon how he/she sees it. In a study of Choctaw Indian youths and Anglo young people in Murfreesboro, Tennessee, Blanchard shows how the two groups, because of their cultural trianing, perceive the same sport activity in different ways.[38] Blanchard asked 13 Choctaw and 12 Anglo basketball players to pick out of a list of feelings the ones most important to doing well in the sport. Both groups named "aggressive," "tough," and "mean" as qualities of a good basketball player. But the Choctaws, unlike the Anglos, also picked feelings like "cheerful," "friendly," and "loving." When shown sketches depicting violent conflict in football games, the Choctaw high school students typically disapproved strongly, and the Anglos approved.

The Choctaws tended to see a game as a friendly contest, the Anglos to see it as a violent conflict. In the terms we used earlier (not Blanchard's) a basketball or football encounter seemed to be to the Anglos a zerosum game and to the Choctaws a non-zerosum game (see again Chap. 3).

The Choctaw fan may yell the violent words he has learned from the Anglo as part of the game—"tear off his head," "bust his ass," "kill him"—but since he also sees games as cheerful, friendly, and loving, the expressions are routine and don't convey the violence they do for the zerosum Anglo for whom "winning is the only thing." The same event in a game (for example, a legal football tackle) a Choctaw spectator is likely to see as less violent. This is because he does not see the person making the tackle as hostile, as the Anglo fan is likely to. In a basketball game, if a Choctaw is roughly guarded, he is less likely to see this as a hostile act and to react violently. "Violence is thus a more likely possibility in the Anglo situation."[39]

Perceived intent thus varies from situation to situation, person to person, culture to culture. When Berkowitz manipulated his scene from the movie **Champion** so as to make Kirk Douglas a "good guy," even subjects who had been angered didn't react aggressively, but when he was shown as a "bad guy," they did. Ryan summarizes the point: ". . . in sports if the opponent is perceived as a good guy, little aggression will result, but if the opponent is perceived as likely to act unfairly or aggressively, more aggression should be expected, both from the spectator and the participant."[40] Berkowitz says, "the scene really isn't an aggressive stimulus, unless the observer thinks of it as aggression, as the deliberate injury of others."[41]

In an experiment reported in 1967, Seymour Epstein and Stuart Taylor studied how willingness to inflict punishment in an aggressive competitive situation was affected by (1) whether one won or lost the competition, and (2) whether one saw the opponent as intending to inflict harm. On these two points, hostile response was significantly related to perceived hostile intent ($p < .001$) but not to winning or losing. "Instigation to aggression in a competitive aggressive interaction is determined largely by perception of the aggressive intent of the opponent, whether or not the attempt finds its mark."[42]

A. H. Hastorf and Hadley Cantril did an on-the-scene study of perceived intent in a real-life situation at the 1953 Princeton-Dartmouth football game.[43] Before the game, it was clear that Dartmouth needed to stop Princeton's All-American back, Dick Kazmeier. He was stopped early, leaving the game before the half with a concussion and a broken nose. How this was seen depended on who was seeing it. The Princeton student newspaper editorialized about this intentional unsportsmanlike crippling of a star. The Dartmouth paper pointed out that, as football injuries go, Kazmeier's were not really major and reminded Princetonians of previous games that season when **they** had won by ganging up on an outstanding opponent. On a questionnaire given to students of both schools, 39 percent of Dartmouth students saw the game as "rough and fair." Only 3 percent from Princeton saw it that way. Asked to check rule infractions by both teams while watching a game film, Dartmouth students checked an average of 4.3 by Dartmouth and Princeton students checked a mean of 9.8 infractions by Dartmouth ($p < .01$).

Another question is whether winners or losers respond more aggressively. Ryan reports that in a 1970 experiment in a competitive laboratory situation the aggression of losers was significantly increased while that of winners was reduced.[45] However, he thinks that his laboratory situation was somewhat artificial and might not be repeated in real life. Also in the laboratory, Epstein and Taylor found that winning or losing was not in itself significant, but that losing to someone whose intent was seen as hostile was.[46] In real life cases I mentioned earlier, in 1969 people became violent after **both** loss of a basketball game and victory in an important international hockey match. Goldstein and Arms found violent responses to be higher after the 1969 Army-Navy football game regardless of whether one's team had won or lost.[47]

I am going to lead from this chapter into the next by discussing Michael Novak's interpretation of the role of sport violence.[48] Novak sees its significance as culturally patterned and also existential in the sense that it makes us more aware of our place in the universe. To Novak the life of our culture and life in general are vicious and brutal. Violence in sport is a symbolic expression that enables us to experience directly or vicariously a dimension of existence that we often deny. Novak considers it healthy that males, unlike females, don't repress their anger but can feel it and act it out. He feels that sport, especially football, contributes to the richness of our life by providing a culturally approved area where those who are less repressed can help others to experience this aspect of existence. They are dramatic heroes who challenge others to be heroic. "Football externalizes the warfare in our hearts and offers us a means of knowing ourselves and wresting some grace from our true nature."[49] Thus, violent sport, particularly football, is essentially a religious drama. "If you think football is a violent liturgy reflect upon the Eucharist [the symbolic eating of the body and blood of Christ in the Mass]."

To think about what Novak says we have to distinguish the violence of **life** from the violence of **civilization** (defined in Chapter 8 as a game of strategy in which 5 percent of the population manipulate the other 95 percent within a system of rules). The world of nature does demand that we contest with the violence of fire, flood, earthquake, hurricane, microbic invasion, bodily decay. This calls for heroism. The world of civilization requires that we contend with the violence of man-made hunger, poverty, discrimination, and preparation for institutionalized mass extermination. This also calls for heroism. Organized sport, we have seen in this chapter, prepares people to participate in cultural violence. It is part of it, sharing the same values. It may help people to contend heroically with the ultimate violence of life. But it does not prepare them to contest the violence of civilization. It prepares exploited people, not to challenge the institutions that exploit them, but to act out their rage on one another, or catalyze a vicarious acting-out by spectators.

Muhammed Ali is probably the single best known person in the world. His survival of a brutal beating to conquer George Foreman in Zaire was heroic. But in the long view his heroism was **misplaced**. In a broad human perspective, one black man should not have been fighting another black man for the entertainment and profit of whites (or blacks). Ali's true heroism came when he used the qualities that conquered Foreman to take on Selective Service, the boxing Establishment, and the whole military-industrial complex. This is what the common (and uncommon) people of the world honor him for.

To say that for boxers, or football teams, to take out their anger and their fans' anger on one another is healthy is like saying that it was healthy for gladiators to kill each other in the Coliseum for the entertainment of the populace, when the long run interest of the human race called for "athletes" and spectators all to revolt against their masters.

In the movie version of Clifford Odets' **Golden Boy** Joe Bonaparte, an Italian violinist turned reluctant middleweight boxer, kills a black opponent in the ring with his fists. Afterwards he tells his gangster promoter, "I don't know why a poor kid like that had to die. If I had to kill anybody, it should have been a slob like you." A humanist like the dead fighter's father, who tried to console Joe, might have said nobody should die. But Golden Boy grasped the basic dynamics of his violence.

In Chapter 13 we will look at how sport can contribute positively to human freedom and self-realization.

FOOTNOTES

[1]E. Dean Ryan, "Sport and Aggression," in **The Winning Edge**, Walter C. Schwank, ed.,

Proceedings of the First National Sports Psychology Conference, Buffalo, 1973, Washington, American Alliance for Health, Physical Education, and Recreation, 1974, 24.

[2]**Ibid.**, 29.

[3]Anthony Storr, **Human Aggression**, New York, Atheneum, 1968.

[4]Jacob Burckhardt, **Griechische Kulturgeschichte**, iii, p. 69, cited in Johan Huizinga, **Homo Ludens**, Boston, Beacon, 1964, 72.

[5]Bill Surface, "Pro Football: Is It Getting Too Dirty?", **Reader's Digest**, November 1974, 151-154.

[6]Quoted in Neil Amdur, **The Fifth Down: American Democracy and the Football Revolution**, New York, Coward, McCann, and Geoghegan, 1971, 61.

[7]George Leonard, **The Ultimate Athlete**, New York, Viking, 1974, 111.

[8]Al Barkow, **Golf's Golden Grind: The History of the Tour**, New York, Harcourt, Brace, Jovanovich, 1974, 119.

[9]Ryan, **op. cit.**, 25.

[10]Muzafer Sherif and Carolyn W. Sherif, **Social Psychology**, revised edition, New York, Harper and Row, 1969, 239.

[11]N. A. Scotch, "Magic, Sorcery, and Football Among Urban Zulu: A Case of Reinterpretation Under Acculturation," **Journal of Conflict Resolution, 5**, 70-74.

[12]**Ibid.**, 71.

[13]**Ibid.**

[14]Seymour Feshbach, "The Stimulating Versus Cathartic Effects of a Vicarious Aggressive Activity," **Journal of Abnormal and Social Psychology, 53**, 1961, 381-385.

[15]Donald P. Hartmann, "Influence of Symbolically Modeled Instrumental Aggression and Pain Cues on Aggressive Behavior," **Journal of Personality and Social Psychology, 11**, 1969, 280-288.

[16]**Ibid.**, 282.

[17]Leonard Berkowitz, "The Concept of Aggressive Drive: Some Additional Considerations," in Berkowitz, ed., **Advances in Experimental Social Psychology**, New York, Academic, **2**, 1965, 315.

[18]R. H. Walters and E. L. Thomas, "Enhancement of Punitiveness by Visual and Audio Visual Displays," **Canadian Journal of Psychology, 17**, 1963, 244-255.

[19]Albert Bandura, **Aggression: A Social Learning Analysis**, Englewood Cliffs, N.J., Prentice-Hall, 1973.

[20]Jeffrey H. Goldstein and Robert L. Arms, "Effects of Observing Athletic Contests on Hostility," **Sociometry, 34**, 1971, 83-90.

[21]A. H. Buss and Ann Durkee, "An Inventory for Assessing Different Kinds of Hostility," **Journal of Consulting Psychology, 21**, 343-348.

[22]Goldstein and Arms, **op. cit.**, 89.

[23]**Ibid.**, 88.

[24]Edward T. Turner, "The Effects of Viewing College Football, Basketball and Wrestling on the Elicited Aggressive Responses of Male Spectators," cited by Thomas A. Tutko, "Conflict in Sports," in **The Winning Edge**, ed. Walter C. Schwank, Proceedings of the First National Sports Psychology Conference, 1973, Washington: American Alliance for Health, Physical Education, and Recreation, 1974, pp. 325-327.

[25]Dolf Zillman, Aaron Katcher, and Barry Milavsky, "Excitation Transfer from Physical Exercise to Subsequent Aggressive Behavior," **Journal of Experimental Social Psychology, 8**, 1972, 247-259.

[26]**Ibid.**, 258-259.

[27]Richard H. Sipes, "War, Sports, and Aggression: An Empirical Test of Two Rival Theories," **American Anthropologist, 75**, February 1973, 64-86.

[28]**Ibid.**, 64.

[29]**Ibid.**, 65.

[30]**Ibid.**, 71.

[31]Kendall Blanchard, "Team Sports and Violence: An Anthropological Perspective," in **The Anthropological Study of Play: Problems and Prospects**, ed. David F. Lancy and B. Allan Tindall, West Point, N.Y., Leisure Press, 1976, 97.

[32]**Ibid.**

[33]Albert Bandura, "Vicarious Processes: No-Trial Learning," in Leonard Berkowitz, **Advances in Experimental Social Psychology, op. cit., 2**, 1965, 15.

[34]Ryan, **op. cit.**, 27.

[35]Richard H. Walters, "Implications of Laboratory Studies of Aggression for the Control and Regulation of Violence," **Annals of the American Academy of Political and Social Science, 364**, 1966, 60-72.

[36]A. A. Stone, "The Effect of Sanctioned Overt Aggression on Total Instigation to Aggressive Responses," Harvard honors thesis, 1950, cited in E. Dean Ryan, "The Cathartic Effect of Vigorous Motor Activity on Aggressive Behavior," **Research Quarterly, 41**, 1970, 542.

[37]Richard E. Goranson, "Media Violence and Aggressive Behavior: A Review of Experimental Research," in Berkowitz, ed., **Advances in Experimental Social Psychology, 5**, 190, 21-22.

[38]Blanchard, **op. cit.**, 102.

[39]**Ibid.**, 106.

[40]Ryan, **op. cit.**, 26.

[41]Leonard Berkowitz, "Sports, Competition, and Aggression," paper read at the Canadian Sports Psychology Symposium, Waterloo, Ontario, 1972. Quoted in **ibid.**, 27.

[42]Seymour Epstein and Stuart P. Taylor, "Instigation to Aggression as a Function of Degree of Defeat and Perceived Aggressive Intent of the Opponent," **Journal of Personality, 35**, 288.

[43]A. H. Hastorf and Hadley Cantril, "They Saw a Game: A Case Study," **Journal of Abnormal and Social Psychology, 49** 1954, 129-134.

[44]**Ibid.**, 131.

[45]E. Dean Ryan, The Cathartic Effect of Vigorous Motor Activity on Aggressive Behavior," **op. cit.**

[46]Epstein and Taylor, **op. cit.**

[47]Goldstein and Arms, **op. cit.**

[48]Michael Novak, **The Joy of Sports**, New York, Basic, 1976, especially Chapter 5, pages 75-91, on football.

[49]**Ibid.**

CHAPTER 13
SELF-ACTUALIZATION: PLAY AS FREEDOM

Reflecting on a lifetime's experience as a physical educator, in a 1968 Temple university lecture, Eleanor Metheny said of why people play sports, "During the past ten years I have talked with countless people about the dimensions of their interest in the rule-governed competitions of sport. In those conversations I have heard the word 'freedom.' Freedom to go all out, holding nothing back—freedom to experience myself at my own utmost as a wholehearted, fully motivated, fully integrated, fully functioning human being."[1]

Let us make concrete what Metheny was talking about:

Pete Reiser, one of the all-time great outfielders in baseball history, looks back on his years in the game:

> *No, I don't have any regrets. Not about one damned thing. I've had a lot of good experiences in my life and they far outnumber the bad. Good memories are the greatest thing in the world, and I've got a lot of them. And one of the sweetest is of the kid standing out on the green grass in center field, With the winning runs on base, thinking, Hit it to me.* **Hit it to me.**[2]

Fleeting Moments

"I was in a (football) game last year that we lost by a very bad score but in the midst of it I was, seemed to be, having a fairly good day. And I just felt light-headed. . .—I played for the heck of it, for the fun of it, just because I wanted to. And . . . I'd be schmeared a couple of times—I'd get up and laugh my head off and I wouldn't know why I was laughing, and I certainly shouldn't have been laughing because I really got schmeared. And I'd go back to the middle and I'd be dying laughing and they'd think I was crazy, but I enjoyed it . . . After the game was over I felt terrible because we lost so bad. But during the game it was just this feeling of exuberance. I was having fun and nothing much could do anything about it, you know? And I was having fun because I was just—I was able to have fun. I was doing something that, at that time, I was doing reasonably well. And I just enjoyed it. During that game I was happy. But after the game I was not so happy, because we lost so badly. And that's the thing, I think that it's a temporary thing, when you're not realizing it, you're not really trying to think about it; you just know that you're enjoying what you're doing right now. . . . It's just **now**, *and you're hoping that two seconds from now it will be just like that. And that's the thing."*

—Fifteen year old high school athlete, to Edgar Z. Friedenberg, reported in Foreword to Howard S. Slusher, **Man, Sport, and Existence**, Philadelphia, Lea and Febiger, 1967, xi-xii.

John Brodie, San Francisco 49er quarterback, explains why he rejects both of the popular images of the football player as Beast or Computer:

Often, in the heat and excitement of a game, a player's perception and coordination will improve dramatically. At times . . . I experience a kind of clarity that I've never seen adequately described in a football story. Sometimes, for example, time seems to slow way down, in an uncanny way, as if everyone were moving in slow motion. It seems as if I have all the time in the world to watch the receivers run their patterns, and yet I know the defensive line is coming at me just as fast as ever. I know perfectly well how hard and fast those guys are coming and yet the whole thing seems like a movie or a dance in slow motion. It's beautiful.[3]

Another kind of football player, a 250 pound lineman, tells Metheny how it feels to smash another man as large as himself:

> *Have you ever hit anyone as hard as you can? . . . No, I suppose not . . . because you're not the type. But for me, when I really do get everything I have into it, there is such an explosion of joy in me that I can't possibly feel pain. . . . But when I goof off. . . if I hold back. . . . even when I do bring my man down, it hurts like hell.*[4]

A professional basketball player, Houston NBA guard Calvin Murphy, tells how it feels to sink a free throw before a hostile crowd: "The most beautiful sight in the world is that ball falling through the net, and then the sudden silence. It's like taking on 15,000 people at once and beating them all."[5]

Charlie Hodgson, who coached two University of Miami women's swimming teams to national championships, describes what keeps him going:

> *I don't have any super long-term goals, except that I like to be 100 percent successful in anything I do. I drive a '67 Volkswagen with the front end bashed in, I live at home and I can't afford much of anything . . . I figure I get paid about 15 cents an hour. But anything worthwhile is not easy. For something to be meaningful, you have to struggle and I'm willing to struggle—for a little while longer.*[6]

A rock-climber speaks of the self-actualization that draws him to this hazardous sport:

> *You see who the hell you really are. It's important to learn about yourself, to open doors into the self. The mountains are the greatest place in the twentieth century to get this knowledge. . . . Nobody hassles you to put your mind and body under tremendous stress to get to the top, there's nobody to . . . force you, judge you . . . Your comrades are there, but you all feel the same way anyway, you're all in it together. Who can you trust more in the twentieth century than these people? People after the same self-discipline as yourself, following the deeper commitment. The facades come rolling off. A bond like that with other people is in itself an ecstasy.*[7]

Now, having illustrated it, let us analyze in what ways play (or sport, so far as it **is** play) contributes to people's self-actualization and freedom. First, the play situation is an island in which the ordinary conditions and pressures of life are suspended and a new set of play rules set up. Sutton-Smith says, "For me play is what a person does when he can choose the constraints within which he will act or imagine. . . The player substitutes his own conventions and his own urgencies for those of society and nature." It is not a lone player, however, who ordinarily sets up the rules of play. In analyzing this, Metheny takes us back three thousand years, to the twelfth century B.C., to the legend of Patroclus as recorded in Homer's **Iliad**. The Greek nobleman Patroclus died a bloody hero in the Trojan war. To honor his brave life, his comrades at his funeral "threw javelins, hurled stones, drove horse drawn chariots at full speed, ran as fast as a man can run, and wrestled with each other in hand-to-hand combat." But they did not do these things just as Petroclus did them, for under the conditions of "real life" Petroclus could not perform his best. "On the battleground he had to throw on the run, and he had to throw at other men who were running toward him with their own spears at the ready; so he had to adjust his aim and force to the requirements of the movement, always keeping his own guard up to ward off the enemy spears and arrows. As he threw, other warriors often jostled him, or his feet slipped in the muck."[8]

So, at Petroclus' funeral, his companions tried to rule out all these hindrances and give everyone a free and equal chance to do his very best. They did this by establishing what Metheny calls "the paradoxical rules of sport competition", which imposed equal conditions on all competitors.

"Thus, each warrior . . . freed of all the hampering circumstances of war, . . . was free to go all out, holding nothing back; he was able to focus all the energies of his mortal being on one supreme attempt to hurl his own javelin at the nothingness of empty space . . . or he was free to run as fast as he could run, to hit as hard as he could hit, to leap, to jump as high, as far as he could leap or jump. He was free to bring all the forces of his own being to bear on the performance of one self-chosen human action."[9]

The **Iliad** is legend, based on fact, reconstructed later by a blind poet and not by the all-seeing eye of Wide World of Sports. But as a description of the paradox (seeming contradiction) by which rules bring freedom, the funeral of Patroclus, as analyzed by Metheny, comes very close to the core of what sport can be.

Aside from the mud and blood and other distractions of war, from what does play give relief? There are kinds of social freedom. In the play situation, people can overcome the group antagonisms that ordinarily separate them from one another. Stumpf and Cozens, who pioneered in introducing anthropological insights to physical educators, says, "it is above all in the leisure and play aspects of human culture that the hard crust of conservatism that divides one people from another is at its weakest."[10] I would suggest that in spite of the sometimes vicious competition in the stadium, life in the modern Olympic village does some of this for athletes from different nations.

Also, sport is freedom from work. The same authors quote the historian

Arnold Toynbee as saying that sport "is a conscious attempt to counterbalance the soul-destroying specialization which the division of labor under industrialism entails." This is no doubt true of many people's play, despite the fact that modern sport has in some cases embodied and raised to a peak this "soul-destroying specialization." Here is the truth in the image of football player as Computer to which Brodie referred. However I believe George Leonard in his book **The Ultimate Athlete** has best expressed what Toynbee was referring to. Leonard speaks of the running of O. J. Simpson "tuned into the rhythmic, pulsing, dancing nature of existence."

> *Out of a lifetime of sports spectating, the moments that live with us . . . are pure dance. We may forget league standings and final scores and even who won, but we can never forget certain dancelike moments: that supernatural Brodie to Washington pass in the 1971 playoff game with the Redskins, that classic, utterly pure blow with which Sugar Ray Robinson ended his 1957 bout with Gene Fullmer; that transcendent running catch by Willie Mays in the first game of the 1954 World Series in the Polo Grounds. Perhaps it is this desire for the transcendent rather than mere victory that keeps us locked to our television sets on those sunny afternoons when we ourselves might be out playing . . . Indeed, we can say that the whole complex structure of pro football was created so that O. J. (and others like him) can dance.*[11]

Another kind of self-actualization that sport gives is dramatic knowledge of self. Metheny describes the "moment of truth" in which the Greek Olympic athlete must stand, "naked of all pretense" and "stripped of all justifying excuses by the rules of sport":

> *In that self-revealing moment, no man can delude himself, for every competitor must experience himself as he is—in all the complexity and ambivalence of his own feelings about himself, his gods, and other men who claim the right to share the universe of his existence. If he is a proud man, he will experience his own pride. If he is a domineering man, he will experience his own need to dominate the lives of other men. So, too, a fearful man will know his own fears; a resentful man his resentments; and an anxious man his anxieties. An idealistic man must realize the reality of his own ideals—and the conflict he experiences as he tries to live up to them. A chauvinistic man must come to terms with his own chauvinism; a loving man must reveal the limits of his love; and a hating man will experience his own fearful hate.*[12]

Transcendence through dance and through self-insight are aspects of the "existential" experience of one's ultimate condition, a face-to-face encounter with how things really are that seems, for many people, to intensify their sense of aliveness. This encounter involves an intensified sense of being (life) and also a sharpened awareness of the possibility of non-being (death). Some find an ecstasy in their sport through this possibility of death. Let us begin with Janet Guthrie, in 1977 the first woman ever to drive in the Indianapolis 500:

> *Everything tastes better, smells better, looks better, feels better after a race. That's why I do it, I guess. It's the exhilaration, the worry of thinking you might not make it, the coming down afterward. I know of nothing else that is so life enhancing. . . . Every driver is immortal behind the wheel. The possibility of bodily injury does not occur out there. The cocktail party instinct, of course, is to say that race track drivers are suicidal. Well, I have a highly developed sense of self-preservation. Yet, the idea of putting yourself in a position where life is . . . forfeitable . . . I mean you tell all your friends and relatives that it's not really dangerous. But still . . ."*[13]

George Leonard is so impressed by the value of confronting death that he advocates protecting people's right to risk their lives through Right-to-Drown laws for those who do it in water and comparable legislation for those who find their confrontation on land or in the air. Leonard explains why:

> *We need no roundabout theories to explain the fascination of death and the solutary effects of calculated risk. We simply must remember that, from the vantage point of embodied consciousness, death provides us our clearest connection with the eternal. It can be said that in our present condition of flesh and blood, we are playing a game—I have called it the Game of Games—and somehow, at some level, are always aware of a boundary, a line we cannot cross and still return to this game. To cross that boundary we surrender the particular arrangement of molecules that we call the body. We surrender the particular arrangement of awareness that we call our ego. In surrendering, even in preparing to surrender, we begin to learn something about our present state. We learn something about the ever-shifting balance, the trade-off between the particular and the cosmic, about the necessary and unnecessary limitations imposed upon ourselves on this field of play. We gain hints of possibilities we had not dreamed of.*[14]

The Fascination of Risk

I am personally inclined to feel that one best intensifies life by focusing on life, but Bruce Ogilvie, a sport psychologist, has done some impressive empirical research that gives some support to Leonard's argument.[15] Ogilvie used questionnaires, standardized psychological tests, and depth interviews to study over 250 high-risk performers—professional and amateur football players, race drivers, sky divers, scuba divers, acrobatic airplane pilots. Why, Ogilvie asks, will a person fall free for 8000 feet while aiming at an eight-inch target on the ground; dangle at the end of a rope on a mountain 10,000 feet above the earth; strap himself into a high-powered midget plane for acrobatic competition; take the wheel of a racing car when Ogilvie's research showed that 67 percent of race drivers he studied were dead or disabled from competition within five years?

Ogilvie found some people explaining the risk-takers in terms of psychopathology—in brief, they are sick. His research shows us, Ogilvie believes, that the risk-takers are as psychologically healthy as the average person, perhaps healthier.

To get perspective, we may look at some of the negative interpretations of risk-taking, by psychologists and others.

(1) To some, sky-diving, mountain climbing, etc., are a form of what the psychoanalyst Alfred Adler called a "masculine protest"—an effort to overcome feelings of inferiority through being recognized as superior; to prove oneself omnipotent (we will remember Guthrie's statement that race drivers feel themselves immortal), to prove oneself sexually adequate and reassure oneself of one's masculinity.

(2) Some see the risk-taker as a psychopathic personality who has an immature, shallow contact with reality.

(3) Risk-taking has been described by some as a "counter phobic" reaction, through which one reduces anxiety by constantly and compulsively exposing oneself to the things of which one is physically and psychologically most afraid.

(4) Another view is that the risk-taker "displaces" fear from another situation in which the risk is greater. Thus, a woman who is afraid to stand up to her husband or a man afraid to confront his boss might overcome the sense of cowardice by conquering fear of falling off a mountain or jumping from a plane (my illustration, not Ogilvie's).

(5) Ogilvie says that the most frequent psychological explanation of habitual risk-taking behavior is an unconscious death wish. One flirts with death because one really wants to die. (Why one would want to die would need explanation, but there is plenty of clinical evidence of people who court death because somehow dying seems more attractive than living.)

There is, says Ogilvie, plenty of evidence that people take risks for all of these reasons. "Each has received support based upon clinical experience at every level from Pop Warner football through Olympic and professional sports over the past two decades."[16] But this is not the whole story. If it were, we should find two things: Risk-takers should score low on standard measures of mental and emotional health. Also, the different sports should vary in mental health according to the degree of risk, with the most emotionally stable athletes in the non-risk sports, and the most emotionally unstable in the risky sports. The tests and interviews do not show all this to be the case. Let us see what they do show.

Whatever risk takers may be, they are generally not stupid. Delk's study of skydivers found an average IQ in the superior range (122).[17] Another study of mountaineers gave a similar result. Ogilvie estimates that high risk-takers will score in the top 15 percent of the population in abstract reasoning ability. The Minnesota Multiphasic Personality Inventory and other personality tests show that risk-takers have a high energy level; are not anxious, depressive, or excessively dependent; and do not worry about their health. In ability to set goals, ambition, desire for success, and drive to be regarded as exceptional, Ogilvie says risk-takers will typically score in the top fifth or top quarter of the population. Some of the people he studied have been very successful in business and the professions.

Risk-takers are typically aggressive and take it for granted that they will dominate situations. They are independent. Unlike the traditional Establishment athlete, they are socially rebellious, reject traditional standards, and are impatient with routine.

It is in interpersonal warmth that the risk-takers come closest to being emotionally deprived. In keeping with their aggressiveness, they are forthright and have a strong interest in the opposite sex. but they have slight respect for the advice of others. Though their tough mindedness and unsentimentality may seem qualities of strength, and they appear extroverted, the risk-takers are "non-affiliative," that is, aren't joiners. Their typical emotional relationships, says Ogilvie, are "flat"—they are typically cool, reserved loners. In his study, the professional football players were an exception—"warmhearted and outgoing." (This may be partly because football is a team sport, while the other risk activities studied are individual.)

Ogilvie says that he found no significant differences between the female and male risk-takers, that they have an "almost identical personality structure." He thinks that for this reason we can dismiss the idea that risk-taking can be attributed to "some form of masculinity device." (This does not necessarily follow: in a male chauvinist culture, which the sport world generally is, the risk-taking women might well be trying to prove that **they** are men.)

The problem is to explain the paradoxical (seemingly contradictory) behavior of people who seem to relish life but habitually and deliberately risk ending it. These risk-takers, says Ogilvie, "are humans with a much greater need for stimulation and excitement who find that flirting with fate and living on the brink of their existence produce a special form of ecstasy that cannot be provided by any other form of behavior."[18] For them, risk-taking satisfies "a tremendous need to escape from the drabness of predictability," from the "bland tensionless states associated with everyday living." This, Ogilvie says, can be true of even a 747 pilot who controls his plane via an electronic master panel, or of the surgeon or the attorney for whom the youthful challenge of putting his skill on the line has waned. "I have found from my interviews with men and women who are the best in the world in their particular field of endeavor," says Ogilvie, "that they experience little joy in life when their true ability remains uncontested. They much prefer to place their considerable talent on the line and face the ultimate truth as to their ability.'[19]

Ogilvie's explanation receives some support from Bratton, Kinnear and Koroluk's study of 266 members of the Calgary Section of the Alpine Club of Canada.[20] There were two classes of members: hill walkers and rock climbers (the difference should be obvious). Both groups were asked to score on a 1 to 5 scale each of 22 reasons for climbing. The most prevalent reasons were enjoyment of fresh air, recreation and relaxation, enjoyment of scenery, exercise and physical fitness, and escape from routine. Except possibly for the last we have nothing very relevant to Ogilvie's explanation of high-risk athletes. But when the hill walkers and rock climbers were compared, the rock climbers scored much higher on reasons such as exhilaration, excitement, accomplishment and pride, challenge, self-expression, desire to test oneself, to conquer peaks, to do something that few others have done. Possibly contradicting Ogilvie's finding of no significant sex difference in the personalities of high risk athletes, on most of these reasons the male rock climbers scored higher than the women. "This," say the authors, "is in line with the culturally defined role of the male in Western society."

Even with the rock climbers, "to flirt with danger" scored only 0.93 out of a possible 5.00. "To flirt with danger was important for only three young male rock climbers thus supporting the view that most climbers play down the danger aspect of climbing." Before we accept the verbal response here as the complete "gut" reaction, let us remember how Guthrie minimized the risk in the Indy, but also stressed the thrill of mastering danger.

Autotelic Experience and Flow

Another very important piece of research on the self-actualizing aspects of play is the study of "autotelic" behavior in work and play by Mihaly Csikszentmihalyi.[21] As contrasted with extrinsic motivation, where the reasons for action lie outside the activity, autotelic behavior (Greek: **autos**, self; **telos**, goal) is valuable in itself. Examples of extrinsic motivation are playing for money, for fame, or to improve one's health. Autotelic motivations are pleasure in companionship, emotional release, enjoyment of the activity itself, the sense of "fun".

Csikszentmihalyi's study, which was not limited to sport in the sense of audience games, included 30 rock climbers, 30 male chess players, 23 female chess players, 22 composers of modern music, 28 female modern dancers, and 40 city high school championship basketball players.

Csikszentmihalyi asked the respondents to rank in order of importance eight motivations for their activity. For each motivation, the range of possible averages for the whole group would run from 8 (ranked highest by all respondents) to 1 (ranked last by all). Table 13.1 shows three highly autotelic motivations (enjoyment of the experience, the activity itself, and development of personal skills) ranked highest and the most extrinsic motivation (prestige, regard, glamor) ranked lowest.

Table 13.1 Rankings Given to Reasons for Enjoying Activity (rock climbers, composers, modern dancers, chess players, basketball players; N = 173)

Rank		**Mean**
1	Enjoyment of the experience and use of skills	5.99
2	The activity itself: the pattern, the action, the world it provides	5.78
3	Development of personal skills	5.37
4	Friendship, companionship	4.77
5	Competition, measuring self against others	4.22
6	Measuring self against own ideals	3.81
7	Emotional release	3.75
8	Prestige, regard, glamor	2.49

Source—Mihaly Csikszentmihalyi, **Beyond Boredom and Anxiety: The Experience of Play in Work and Games**, San Francisco, Jossey-Bass, 1975, Table 1, p. 15.

At this point Csikszentmihalyi studied the differences among his different groups. In "total autotelic rank," from most autotelic to most extrinsic, they ranked: 1. composers 2. dancers 3. rock climbers 4. male chess players 5. female chess players 6. basketball players.[22] The most autotelic item, "enjoyment of the experience and use of skills," was ranked very high by all the other groups but lower by basketball players. (The lower autotelic ranking of the basketball players may be due to the fact that basketball was the only competitive team game among the activities studied; or it may have to do with the fact that the basketball players were high school students and thus less mature.)

In another test, the 173 subjects were asked to rank a list of eighteen experiences from 1 to 18 in terms of how much they resembled their own activity. Unlike Table 13.1, here a **low** number is autotelic. On one of these items, "designing or discovering something new," the basketball players stood apart. Composers, dancers, and female chess players scored "designing or discovering something new" as the item most like their experience; basketball players scored it sixth, and gave "playing a competitive sport" first place. On another item, "running a race," basketball players ranked the item second in similarity to their activity; composers scored it 16.5, extremely dissimilar. On the item "making love," the answers were interesting and in line with the other results. Dancers ranked this 4.5 on a scale of 18 in similarity, rock climbers ranked it 6 and composers ranked it 6.5. Neither male nor female chess players nor basketball players could see a similarity between their activity and the experience of making love (ideally, perhaps, the most autotelic activity). The basketball players ranked love-making 14 on the 1 to 18 scale of similarity, male chess players ranked it 16.5, and for the female chess players making love, at 17.5 on a scale of 18, seemed to be the activity least resembling chess.[23] Here, again, both basketball and chess are intensely competitive, win-oriented games, as contrasted with the other activities.

On the basis of his studies, Csikszentmihalyi has developed the model of the "flow situation" to describe activity where extrinsic motivation is at a minimum and autotelic factors at a maximum. In the flow experience, action and awareness are merged—one does not stand apart at all and watch oneself playing, working, or whatever. Attention is intensely concentrated upon a very limited field. There is a loss of self-consciousness (not of consciousness as such). One's goals are very clear and one gets an intense and immediate feedback on how well one's action is approaching them. Abstractly, flow is described by Csikszentmihalyi in this way:

> *In the flow state, action follows upon action according to an internal logic that seems to need no conscious intervention by the actor. He experiences it as a uniform flowing from one moment to the next in which he is in control of his actions, and in which there is little distinction between self and environment, between stimulus and response, or between past, present, and future.*[24]

Elsewhere, he speaks of the "paradoxical feeling of simultaneously being in control and being merged within the environment." More specifically, the experience is expressed this way by a rock climber who is also a poet:

Climbing is recognizing that you are a flow. The purpose of the flow is to keep on flowing, not looking for a peak or utopia but staying in the flow. It is not a moving up but a continuous flowing; you move up only in order to keep the flow going. There is no possible reason for climbing except the climbing itself; it is a self-communication.[25]

Ten Seconds of Flow

"Your mouth goes as dry as cotton. Your palms are wet with perspiration. Your stomach is jumping. You feel as if your legs can't support your body. You feel all those things in a flash, an instant. . .

"Nine years of work and it's all over in 10 seconds. Your arms, your legs, your knee action. . . that's what you think of in those 10 seconds. You must keep them working together.

"You can't worry about the guy at your side or the guy behind you. You've got to get in front and they've got to catch you if they can. You've been trained for this. You can't let them catch you. They must not catch you.

"Then you hit the tape and all the joy flows. It comes through all at once. On that day, the dream is complete. A dream you've had for nine years. And when you step on the victory platform and watch your flag raised above the others and you hear the crescendo of your national anthem being played, you say to yourself, 'Today, I was the best.' "

—Jesse Owens on his gold medal 9.4 100 meters in the 1936 Berlin Olympics. **Miami Herald**, April 1, 1980, p. 2A.

Another rock-climber speaks of "one of those rare moments of almost orgiastic unity as I forget myself and become lost in action.[26]

Csikszentmihalyi cites George Steiner's description of what it is like to fall out of flow in a chess game and then get back in flow again as demonstrated in the Fischer-Spassky world championship match:

The bright arcs of relation that weld the pieces into a phalanx, that make one's defense a poison-typed porcupine shiver into vague filaments. The cords dissolve. The pawn in one's sweating hand withers to mere wood or plastic. A tunnel of inanity yawns, boring and bottomless. As from another world comes the appalling suggestion. . .

that this is, after all, "only a game." If one entertains that annihialating proposition even for an instant, one is done for. (It seemed to flash across Boris Spassky's drawn features for a fraction of a second before the sixty-ninth move of the thirteenth game.) Normally, the opponent makes his move and in that murderous movement addiction comes again. New lines of force light up in the clearing haze, the hunched intellect straightens up and takes in the sweep of the board, cacophony subsides, and the instruments mesh into union.[27]

In case rock-climbing and chess may seem a long way from the major spectator sports that are the main concern of this book, I should like to add at this point a description of a self-realizing flow situation in a football game:

> *. . . a man named Harlon Hill came sprinting down toward the dug-out end of the [Yankee Stadium] in the final seconds of a Chicago-New York football game, which the Giants were leading, seventeen to ten. A back named Jimmy Patton matched him stride for stride, and then Hill and Patton were leaping for the ball. I saw Hill go up twice on that single play, and I saw Patton go up twice with him. I saw Hill touch the ball three times before he pulled it in, held it, and stumbled across the goal to tie the game. I remember in that brief instant, Harlon Hill was the perfect receiver and Jimmy Patton was the perfect defensive back, and never have I seen anything that more personified the artistry and competitiveness and the poetry of what two professionals can achieve in a* **mano a mano** *confrontation.*[28]

Hill and Patton, as described by Izenberg, illustrate what Csikszentmihalyi feels to be the main condition for the existence of flow: a proper ratio between the abilities of the performer and the demands of the situation. Here we come to the title of Csikszentmihalyi's book, **Beyond Boredom and Anxiety**. If the demands upon one exceed one's aptitude and training, the result is likely to be anxiety. If aptitude and training are greater than situational demands, the performer is likely to be bored. Flow may occur when the balance is just right. Csikszentmihalyi illustrates this principle by rock-climbing, where both demand and aptitude are quantified (see Figure 13.1). Slopes are rated from F^{1} (a scramble) to F^{11} (the limits of human potential). Climbers are also rated from F^{1} to F^{11} in terms of the most difficult climb they have made. Faced with an F^{7} slope, an F^{4} climber (A) will feel worried, an F^{10} climber (C) will feel bored, and an F^{6} climber (B) will experience flow. On a very hard F^{10} slope, A (F^{4} skill) will feel anxious, B (F^{6} skill) will be worried, and C (F^{10} skill) will be in flow.

Figure 13.1 Example of Flow and Nonflow Situations in Rock Climbing

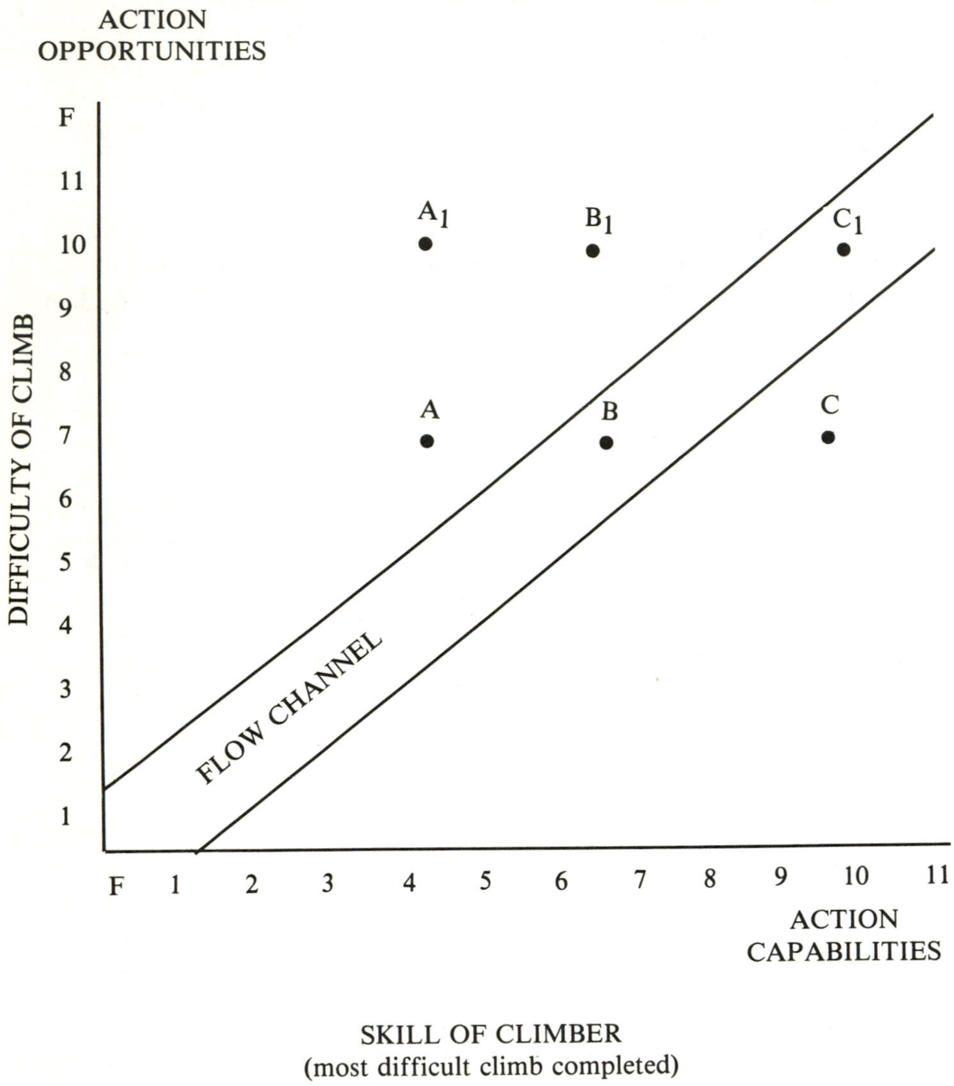

Source — Mihaly Czikszentmihalyi, **Beyond Boredom and Anxiety**, San Francisco, Jossey-Bass, 1975, Figure 2, p. 51.

However, Sutton-Smith thinks that the flow situation, where competence equals challenge, is more characteristic of work than it is of play. And the situation where abilities exceed challenge is not necessarily boredom. It can also be play: "In play our competence does exceed the challenge. Because of that it is a harbor to which we can retreat and envisage our possibliities rather than our real accomodations. When we rise out of play or in play tackle external objects in such a way as to be challenged excitingly (rather than to be overwhelmed or underwhelmed) then flow occurs. Flow is a state of integration with reality, play is not."[29]

Csikszentmihalyi studied flow in other activities, beyond his original 173 cases. In rock dancing, the dimming of lights and the overpowering loudness of the music so reduce distraction as to lead many dancers to report a "loss of self" and a "merging with the music." Because there are also other factors that impede "one-mindedness," Csikszentmihalyi rates rock dancing as a "shallow flow" activity as compared with the "deep flow" of chess and rock climbing. An example he cites of the distracting factors is the uncertainty that sometimes arises as to whether a partner's moves are part of the dance or a sexual advance.

Rock dancers were subjects for a further study of flow. On the basis of interview, Csikszentmihalyi selected dancers who he felt would be really "in flow" and others who he felt would not be. He asked the two groups to score themselves on a four-point scale (from "never" to "always") on their experience in rock dancing: sense of harmony with the environment, greater awareness of one's body, less awareness of distracting problems, less awareness of the passage of time, knowing what to do at all times, and getting immediate feedback from one's partner. The results showed that the "in flow" dancers were significantly closer to a 1-1 ratio between skill and challenge, in terms of the movements, the music, the partner, and the overall activity.[30]

Another group of subjects were 21 surgeons. Surgery is not usually considered a form of athletics, although one of the respondents did say, "Surgery is a body contact sport, not a spectator sport." Answering the question "Why do you do surgery?" only a third named a cure as the main reason. Another third spoke of the challenge. A final third described their work in such terms as "fun," "exciting," "feels great," "feels real good," "aesthetically pleasing," "dramatic and very satisfying," "like taking narcotics." They compared surgery to skiing, water skiing, mountain climbing, driving a fast car, competitive sailing, competitive softball, tennis. None of the 21 would exchange their specialty for another branch of medicine. Csikszentmihalyi sees surgery as possessing the main characteristics of flow activities: opportunities for action and enjoyment, limitation of stimulus field, clarity of goals and feedback, competence and control, transcendence of ego boundaries. All of these add up to the kind of fascination described by one surgeon: "It's incredible to put in a kidney [transplant] and have it start putting urine out even before you're closed."

Csikszentmihalyi's subtitle is "The Experience of Play in Work and Games." He believes that the autotelic satisfaction, flow, that he has studied, is possible in both. Surgery is a dramatic example. But flow can be part of the work life of the ordinary person. He cites the supermarket checker interviewed by Terkel who keeps in rhythm with the cash register ("It's like playing a piano"), learns to know each customer, and so as absorbed as the surgeon.[31]

The surgeon and the checker are two examples of how work in our society can have the autotelic quality of play. Three years after the publication of his book, Csikszentmihalyi reported interviewing a cross-section of working people in Chicago, reading them from the book descriptions of the flow experience, and asking them whether they had had work experiences of this sort. Twenty-six percent said Yes.[32]

In Chapter 5 we saw how the Puritan ethic rejected play as taking time from work. Perhaps it did this, Csikszentmihalyi suggests, because work was the Puritan's "game." Mex Weber said of the Protestant's money-making:

> *He [got] nothing out of the work for himself except the irrational sense of having done his job well. . . In the field of its highest development, in the Untied States, the pursuit of work, stripped of its religious and ethical meanings, tends to be associated with . . . passions which often actually give it the character of sport.*[33]

Some work is flow, but we know that most work, as yet, is not. What, then, is the role in society of the kind of activities that Csikszentmihalyi has studied? Using the language of the anthropologist Victor Turner, he suggests that flow activities are "antistructural" and also "protostructural."[34]

In everyday language, they **challenge** the accepted patterns of social life, and they also furnish a **model** of what it might become. He cites the study by Clifford Geertz of the addiction to cockfighting in Bali. The Balinese spend a great amount of time and resources training and wagering on roosters. Those who are successful gain temporary social status. "It is," says Geertz, "a Balinese reading of Balinese experience, a story they tell about themselves."[35] But, says Csikszentmihalyi, "The Balinese find true but unsettling what they see of themselves in the cockfight. The cockfight displays the social order in a new light."[36] A parallel example would be athletes like George Sauer, Dave Meggyesy, Chip Oliver, Bill Walton, and others who in the last fifteen years have come to see the structure of organized sport as an expression of a violent and competitive culture, and have rejected both.

The protostructural function of flow goes beyond criticism and rejection. The autotelic experience provides a model for change in the "normative order"—the system of cultural norms and institutions. "Deep play and other complex flow activities are like laboratories in which new patterns of experience are tested."[37]

In chess the structure involves the actor through intellectual competition, in climbing, danger draws the actor into physical and mental concentration. In each case, the person discovers a state of being which is rare in normative life. The comparison affords a relativizing perspective on the culture in which one is usually immersed.[38]

This confrontation is stated very strongly by a mountain climber:

Too many stimuli in the world, it's a smog, a quagmire. In civilization man doesn't really live reality. One never thinks about the universe and man's place in it . . . you think about cars, schools, parties . . . .

The mountains and nature bombard the mind with the question of what man is meant to be doing. The fact that man's mind freaks out in civilizations shows how abnormal and unhealthy they can be. We are the animals that have been the most fucked up in the last thousand years. Up there you know you're right, down here you think you're right.[39]

What do you know "up there"? Play or work for extrinsic motivations of status, money, and power are self-defeating. "Status differentials tend to follow a zero-sum pattern the psychic benefits for those who get recognized are paid for by the decreased self-respect of those who do not."[40] Play, says Csikszentimihalyi, should be the model for a "non-zero sum" society, where in work and play everybody wins, because all experience flows together.

What this might mean concretely is expressed by George Leonard in interpreting the views of a tennis instructor, Ms. Dyveke Spino:

She suggested the possibility of considering the person on the other side of the net not as your opponent but as your partner. In this context, a well-hit ball becomes a gift of energy, freely delivered. The gift may be returned, then exchanged again and again, linking the two players in a single energy field. The breathing of the two can be synchronized, with each player exhaling as the ball leaves [his] racket and inhaling upon its return.

Does this mean that you always hit the ball to the other player's strong side so that it is more likely to be returned? Far from it. In actual play you hit the ball to your partner's weakness, to the underdeveloped area of the energy field, and you expect the same. Thus both of you have the opportunity to achieve more of your potential and the total field between you is strengthened.

You might also be a "winner," which could be all to the good. But I can't help thinking that there are ways of keeping score that don't appear on the sports page.[41]

Two Human Beings

Jack Scott: Looking back on your years in sport, can you think of a particular occasion where sport existed as you believe it ought to exist, even if just for a fleeting moment?

George Sauer: I probably could think of more, but one of the outstanding ones in my mind is an incident that happened between Butch Byrd of Buffalo and myself in a game we played in Shea Stadium in 1969. The previous years, 1966, 1967, and 1968, I had pretty much what we call "owned" Butch. Even though he was always known as a hard-nosed player, I think he had a lot of respect for me. He was the kind of guy who wouldn't mind trying to intimidate you by occasionally giving you a cheap shot. Still, from mutual respect, we had built rapport, even an affection for each other that carried off the field as well as on. In 1969 he changed his style of playing me and shut me out in the first game of the 1969 season. In the second game he shut me out for the first half, but in the third quarter I caught a long pass over his head and he tackled me from behind. Given my speed, anybody could have. We rolled over, and as we started to get up, he looked at me and stuck out his hand. There is no way really to explain it. We just shook hands right there in the middle of the field. It was a very warm, human moment, and I think the story bears witness to the fact that opponents can get along as human beings, because once Butch got over the stage of trying to intimidate me and really concentrated on working on me, he was able to cover me more effectively. His excellence grew with his respect for my humanity. That one moment, which no one else probably understood, to me that was one of my most fulfilling experiences in football.

—Jack Scott and George Sauer, "The Souring of George Sauer, **Intellectual Digest**, Dec. 1971, p. 55.

Another example, which also uses the concept of teammates and opponents as partners in a field of flow, is John Brodie's description to Michael Murphy of his relationship to his receiver Gene Washington:

Brodie: *We room together, and we are good friends. We've worked out a series of signals that can change even after I've begun my snap count. But most of all, I guess, is that we read each other so well. He knows where I want him to be on a given pass play. Sometimes he will run a set pattern, but at other times he has to get to a place on the field any way he can.*

Murphy: *Could that place be marked by a set of coordinates, say at a particular yard line? Or is it better to say that you meet somewhere in the field of existence, in the field of your relationship, amidst all the flux on the playing field?*

Brodie: *I think the more poetic way says it better—it's a highly intuitive thing. Sometimes we call a pass for a particular spot on the field, maybe to get a first down. But at other times it's less defined than that and depends upon the communication we have. Sometimes I let the ball fly before Gene has made his final move,* **without** *a pass route being set exactly. That's where the intuition and the communication come in. But then we don't know what the other team, what those cornerbacks and safety men, might do next. That's part of the fun of the game, not knowing what they are going to do. The game* **never stops** . . . [40]

A novel and widely read treatment of sport as self-actualization is that of Timothy Gallwey, a tennis pro who applied eastern philosophy to the teaching of the game.[43] To Gallwey, a correct understanding of tennis (and of life) depends on distinguishing two selves: Self 1, which is the "teller," and Self 2, which is the "doer." The difference between the two selves Gallwey illustrates by the dance. With formal instruction as to which foot to put where, when, as a young man he took weeks to master the fox trot. Sometimes he would be so preoccupied with the next step that he would almost forget that he had a woman in his arms. At a disco today, a kid who may be failing both math and English can, by picking up the "body language" of his peers, learn the Monkey, Jerk, and Swim (all more difficult dances) in one night. The secret for tennis: The most important word in the language is "let." "You trust the competence of your body and its brain, and you **let** it swing the racket. Self 1 stays out of it."[44] Gallwey cites a personal case in which, just before a tennis match, an attractive girl phoned to break a dinner date for the third time. Neither he nor his opponent could understand the fantastic tennis Gallwey then played. It was not anger, mainly; he just played "out of his mind," letting go with a "what the hell" attitude that swept his opponent off the court.

What can Self 1 do, positively, in the game of tennis, and the game of life? It can help program Self 2, whose actions "are based on information it has stored in its memory of past actions of itself and the observed actions of others."[45] Self 1 can also establish goals for Self 2—for example, to break a service game by upsetting the opponent's net-rushing. Beyond this, Self 1 must trust Self 2 to react. Between points and games, Self 1 can plan. But in action Self 2 must execute. The reason, I would say: Self 1 can **talk** about Flow; Self 2 **is** flow.

FOOTNOTES

[1]Eleanor Metheny, "The Creative Process in Sport," in **Moving and Knowing: Sport, Dance, Physical Education**, Mountain View, Ca.: Peek, 1975, 140.

[2]Donald Honig, **Baseball: When the Grass Was Green**, New York, Coward, McCann, Geoghegan, 1975, 315.

[3]John Brodie, "I Experience a Kind of Clarity," Interview with Michael Murphy, **Intellectual Digest**, January 1973, 19-20.

[4]Metheny, **op. cit.**, 133.

[5]**Sports Illustrated**, Mar. 14, 1977, 10.

[6]University of Miami **Hurricane**, April 23, 1976.

[7]Mihaly Csikszentmihalyi, **Beyond Boredom and Anxiety: The Experience of Play in Work and Games**, San Francisco, Jossey-Bass, 1975, 94-5.

[8]Metheny, **op. cit.**, 136.

[9]**Ibid.**

[10]Florence Stumpf [Frederickson] and Frederick W. Cozens, "Some Aspects of the Role of Games, Sports, and Recreational Activities in the Culture of Modern Primitive Peoples," **Research Quarterly, 18**, October 1947, 215.

[11]George Leonard **The Ultimate Athlete**, New York, Viking, 1974, 230.

[12]Metheny, **op. cit.**, 137-138.

[13]Janet Guthrie, quoted in **Miami News**, May 29, 1977, 5B.

[14]Leonard, **op. cit.**, 224-225.

[15]Bruce C. Ogilvie, "The Stimulus-Addicts, a Psychosocial Paradox," in **The Winning Edge**, ed. Walter C. Schwank, Proceedings of the First National Sports Psychology Conference, Buffalo, 1973, Washington: American Alliance for Health, Physical Education, and Recreation, 1974, 43-50.

[16]Ogilvie, **op. cit.**, 45.

[17]"Why They Jump," **Parachutist**, May 1971, 12-15.

[18]Ogilvie, **op. cit.**, 50.

[19]**Ibid.**

[20]Robert D. Bratton, George Kinnear, and Gary Koroluk, "Why Man Climbs Mountains," **International Review of Sport Sociology**, 14, 2, 1979, 23-36.

[21]Csikszentmihalyi, **op. cit.**

[22]**Ibid.**, Table 2, p. 29.

[23]All these data on similarity are from **ibid.**, Table 3, p. 29.

[24]**Ibid.**, 36.

[25]**Ibid.**, 47.

[26]**Ibid.**, 86.

[27]George Steiner, "Fields of Force," **New Yorker**, Oct. 28, 1974, 94. Article reprinted as **Fields of Force: Fischer and Spassky at Reykjavik, New York, Viking, 1974.**

[28]Jerry Izenberg, **How Many Miles to Camelot: The All-American Sport Myth**, New York, Holt, Rinehart, and Winston, 1972, 221-222.

[29]Brian Sutton-Smith, **Newsletter of the Association for the Anthropological Study of Play**, 6, 1, Summer, 1979, 12.

[30]Csikszentmihalyi, **op. cit.**, Table 6, p. 113.

[31]Studs Terkel, **Working**, Pantheon, 1975.

[32]Letter to Phillips Stevens, Jr., reported in Stevens, "Play and Work: A False Dichotomy?", in **Play and Culture**, ed. Helen B. Schwartzman, 1978 Proceedings of the Association for the Anthropological Study of Play, West Point, N.Y., Leisure Press, 1980, 319.

[33]Max Weber, **The Protestant Ethic and the Spirit of Capitalism**, tr. Talcoff Parsons, New York, Scribner's, 1958, 71, 82.

[34]Victor Turner, **The Ritual Process**, Aldine, 1969.

[35]Clifford Geertz, **The Interpretation of Culture**, New York, Basic, 1973, 418.

[36]Csikszentmihalyi, **op. cit.**, 97.

[37]**Ibid.**, 93.

[38]**Ibid.**, 99-100.

[39]Cited, ibid., 95.

[40]**Ibid.**, 4.

[41]Leonard, **op. cit.**, 107.

[42]Brodie, **op. cit.**, 21-22.

[43]W. Timothy Gallwey, **The Inner Game of Tennis**, New York, Random House, 1974.

[44]**Ibid.**, 51.

[45]**Ibid.**, 53.

CHAPTER 14

PLAYER AND SPECTATOR

Agon, Self-Actualization, and Athlete

Many Americans worship at the church of sports. Services are held for each personal belief, whether it be football, racing, golf, or diving. One is thrilled by the splendor of the occasion and the beauty of the surroundings. On the walls hang the trappings and accounts praising past heroes. The offering freely asked is cheerfully given. The renditions of the colorfully clothed musicians stir one to action. Dramatically delivered is the powerful image of overcoming the adversary. Here each is brought to his own style of fulfillment. As one turns to leave, one muses, 'It is good to have been here, for I have felt the power.'

—From **In the Service of Sport**, unpublished free verse by Alyce Taylor Cheksa, sport sociologist.

The sense of self-realization in sport, as elsewhere, always involves a relationship to other people, to spectators present or absent. A sporting event is a dramatic ritual, an **agon**, of which the actions of the watchers are as much a part as are those of the performers. In a 1977 article on "the corruption of sport" Christopher Lasch critizes the view, seemingly held by some critics of modern sport, that "spectators are irrelevant to the success of the game."[1] "The attainment of certain skills," says Lasch, "unavoidably gives rise to an urge to show them off . . . the performer wishes . . . to ratify a supremely difficult accomplishment, to give pleasure, to forge a bond between himself and his audience, a shared appreciation of a ritual executed not only flawlessly, but with much feeling and with a sense of style and proportion.[2]

Social psychologists generally hold that our self-feeling depends on others who mirror us to ourselves. To William James, the self-sense was always social; we have as many selves as we have groups significant to us. In the absence of supporting social groups, a fantasied observer—God—may support our sense of fitness in our selves. Charles Horton Cooley used the simile of the "looking glass self"—what we feel ourselves to be is what we perceive others see us to be. George Herbert Mead said that to have a satisfying self is to receive a sense of satisfaction from significant other people who observe our activity. Later research in social psychology has verified and supported these early insights.

A sport event can be a tragic ritual **agon**, a dramatization of the struggle of human beings with nature or of the struggle of good people against antisocial people. By saying that sport can be a tragic drama I mean that it is a symbolic experience of the ultimate human condition. Alyce Cheska calls the "sport spectacular" a "ritual model of power," "a tenseness of victory and defeat communicated within the compressed arena of time and space."[3] In "The Athletic Contest as a Tragic Form of Art," Francis W. Keenan says, "The tragedy teaches us that for many men the ultimate achievement is defeat and that the highest level of performance, the most noble effort, may end in defeat."[4] The **agon** is "an example of man's plight in an uncertain world." I think Keenan understates the point: the world is uncertain, true, but one thing is certain—for **all** people (not "many") all effort **will** (not may) end in personal death. The tragic drama has a number of elements:

(1) the certainty that one performer, no matter how excellent, will lose.
(2) the "tragic flaw" that may undo even the most excellent player.
(3) the spectacular reversal of game momentum by which defeat may be snatched from the jaws of victory.
(4) the player's recognition, in action, of his identity, the revelation of his ultimate strengths and limitations as an athlete - and as a person.

(5) *the ability of the tragic loser to turn a natural defeat into a spiritual victory by contending to the end.*
(6) *the pity, fear, and empathic sharing in the transcendence of Fate through which the* **agon** may cleanse the spectator.

Because the **agon** is a microcosm of the spectator's life (all spectators' lives), it appeals to and enriches that life. It does this better than the stage play because "the stage must rely on imitation; athletics present life first hand and thereby increase the drama."[5]

A part of the tragic drama is heroic acts performed by athletes. The Polish sport sociologist Ryszard Swierczewski argues strongly that the typically American conception of the athlete as just a mass entertainer will not fit facts such as the letters written by fans about a dramatic Polish soccer victory over England. The admirers compared their feelings after the Wembley stadium game with their feelings at the end of World War II. Anyone who can produce that kind of reaction, he says, is no mere entertainer.[6] The athlete, says Swierczewski, is better described by Stefan Czarnowski's definition of a hero, "A hero is a man who within certain rites, due to services rendered during his life or by his death, possesses powers influencing a certain group or cause, of which he is a representative and the personification of its basic social value."[7] (This could also describe the 1980 U.S. hockey team).

The critics of whom Lasch speaks sometimes talk as though large sport audiences were something peculiar to the twentieth century. However, audiences much outnumbering the performers were part of the game scene at Papremus, at Olympia, at the Roman Coliseum, and at the medieval tournament. In these rituals, past and present, spectators have never been purely passive onlookers. As well as furnishing a mirror by which performers judge their own performance, crowd response stimulates and intimidates. If this were not true, it would not be a general principle in sport that home teams usually win. The agony and ecstasy of spectators shapes the outcome of the **agon** on the field, so that "bad guys" (visiting teams) generally lose.

What **is** different about contemporary sport we can visualize by thinking of a continuum of spectator participation. At one end is the informal gathering of people who may casually observe a pick-up game. The modern critics of sport, with whom Lasch disagrees, appear to idealize this kind of game situation, except that to some it would seem to be best if nobody were watching at all. In the middle of the continuum is the stadium crowd—Olympia, Coliseum, Yankee Stadium, Superdome. At the far end is something peculiar to the twentieth century—the radio or television audience of scattered observers. The difference between being part of a crowd of even 100,000, which is still an interacting group, and being part of an absent audience of 100 million separated viewers, is one of the most critical changes this century has brought to sport. Modern media of communication (telegraph in the late nineteenth century, radio and TV in the twentieth) have created audiences that are not only much vaster but are also absent and incapable of interacting immediately with the athlete on the field, or with one another.

In addition to the agonizing crowd, the athlete of today has a **public**. What difference does this make for his experience of self-actualization? The athlete does not hear the fan at home in front of the TV set when he blasts one out of the park, smashes a service ace, or makes an acrobatic catch of a forward pass. But he hears from him eventually, and Lasch believes that what he hears is reliable. Lasch argues that the modern sport audience, mainly composed of men who took part in sport as boys "and thus acquired a sense of the game and the capacity to make discriminating judgments," are a more trustworthy judge of quality than are the viewers of drama, dance, and painting, where skilled amateurs make up only a small part of the audience. Although he does not distinguish between the present crowd and the absent viewer, Lasch says that in sport, "the true connoisseur can easily distinguish between the performer who plays to the crowd and the superior artist who matches himself against the full rigor of his art itself." Furthermore, "constant experimentation in the arts . . . has created so much confusion about standards that the only surviving measure of excellence, for many, is novelty and shock-value, which in a jaded time often resides in a work's sheer ugliness or banality. In sport, on the other hand, novelty and rapid shifts of fashion play only a small part in its appeal to a discriminating audience." (Lasch's impressions are, incidentally, not supported by Harold Charnovsky's study of about 15 percent of all active major league baseball players, whom he found believing that "adult fans are 'squares,' people who lack understanding of baseball or the men who play it. They are seen as uninformed, naive, and volatile, as fickle as the weather, and to be trusted even less.")[8]

Agon, Self-Actualization, and Spectator

We have seen so far that an audience of some sort is indispensable for the athlete's self-realization as a player. What, in turn, does the athlete contribute to the self-actualization of the spectator? This can be boiled down to several basic questions: (1) Does sport make the spectator more passive or more active? (2) How does sport affect his health? (3) Does it make him more or less violent? (4) How does it affect his social power?

The answer in each case will be different according to the kind of spectator we are talking about. The biggest difference is between the participating spectator-at-the-event and the non-participating watcher-at-home (or elsewhere). Even at the event itself there are several kinds of spectators, as suggested by Leonard Koppett.[9] Koppet distinguishes the rooter, the bettor, the analyst, and the thrill-seeker.

The rooter is blindly loyal to "his" team. "Rooting is a form of patriotism attached to a smaller entity than native land, but rooted in the same complex of emotions." For the rooter, we may add, the game is significant because, as Sutton-Smith puts it, the game may invert the social experience of everyday life—those who are daily losers can be winners by identification with their heroes. A good example is the meaning for New Yorkers of the 1969 Jets and Mets. Another is Hans Hermann's study of east German soccer fans, whom he found participating as compensation for feelings of dissatisfaction and deprivation in their work or school life. "This is why there is such an excessive representation among the fans of those who have had bad experience at school."[10]

The bettor can be either a professional or a personal wagerer. Like the rooter, says Koppett, the bettor is interested primarily in who wins, rather than in how the game is played. He may love good playing, but is primarily a businessman. His difference from the rooter is that his loyalty is determined by the team he bets for, which may change from game to game.

The analyst is the spectator whose ego-trip involves knowledge of strategies, statistics, and esoteric information, all of which make him a more or less disinterested expert observer. "The armchair quarterback," Keenan reminds us, "plays a game of wits. He anticipates action and attempts strategic decision as if he were coaching or actually playing. He parades his expertise by announcing proper actions in advance of actual occurrence; when his pronouncements find concurrence with actual events, the spectator is fulfilled and delighted with the drama. The action becomes in a sense, imitative of his forecasts and representative of his will."[11]

The thrill-seeker is awaiting the "circus catch" (in baseball or football), the homer with the sacks loaded, the backboard-shattering slam dunk, the 60 foot three-point basket at the closing buzzer, the spectacular accident on the speedway, the 70 yard punt that bounces out of bounds on the one-yard line.

In terms of activity and passivity, we have seen that the spectator-at-the event tends to be emotionally and vocally involved in the **agon**. This will probably be truer for the rooter, the bettor, and the thrill-seeker than for the analyst. But the analyst too is a mirror for the participant's self-sense. He is adept at comparing today's performances with the great (or lousy) performances of the past. Particularly if he is a media writer or broadcaster, he is actively engaged. (No one is going to accuse Howard Cosell of being a passive bystander.) The spectator-at-home, of whatever type, is not active in the sense of giving immediate feedback to the players, or giving and receiving it in interaction with other fans. Being a viewer of TV may lead a person to become actively engaged in attending sports. But it may not. In 1954 the National Opinion Research Center found that over half the public (who had much less TV exposure then than now) had never attended an intercollegiate football game, that in any given season only one in seven attended, that only one in five was an active fan ("rooter").[12] We must remember that in Chapter 5 we saw that throughout this century the rise of commercial spectator sport has at times been paralleled by increase in mass sport participation (as the intensive commercialization of tennis on TV in the 70s was matched by a boom in sales of tennis equipment and a spread of tennis participation beyond the old "leisure classes"). So in many ways the late twentieth century spectator is not the passive dolt he has been caricatured as being.

The fact that the spectator is much less physically and emotionally inert than the stereotype says something about the effect of spectatoritis on health. Although some of the evidence cited in Chapter 12 may raise doubts, the athlete on the field is likely to work off the stress of **agon** physically and directly, while the equally stressed fan in the stands does not. Players rarely drop dead in a game; fans on occasion do. In Chapter 1, I suggested that although much has been made of the danger of "athlete's heart," it appears that over the long run the development of supplementary blood supply to the heart muscle is likely to make the athlete a lesser coronary risk than the fan. The same would be likely to be true for other diseases of stress.

In Chapter 12 we explored at length the experimental evidence on whether sport makes players and/or spectators more or less violent. The evidence did not seem to support the theory of catharsis, particularly for spectators. One of my football players commented that the average American's reason for coming to see football played "is really no different than the Romans watching the lions eat the Christians or the gladiators killing each other." Is this self-realization? Michael Novak would say, in a way, yes: football brings everybody face to face with his own usually hidden inner violence. It may be, however, that it obscures one's more loving potentialities.

Self-Realization Through Identification

In Chapter 8 we examined how sport is related to social power. Our emphasis was more on the athlete than on the spectator. We found that sport serves as a ladder of upward escalation for a few members of socially powerless groups, and that the upward mobility, as well as often increasing income and status, identifies the athlete with an athletic subculture that is exploitative, authoritarian, militarist, racist, and sexist.

Spectators share this upward mobility with athletes vicariously, that is, by identifying with their success. Do they thereby realize themselves more adequately? Some, like Novak, would say yes. He believes that it is healthy and positive for blacks, who are shut out of ordinary professional and business opportunities, to be able to identify with black basketball players who are running rings around their white opponents. Others would say that success by identification with successful black athletes, as with other successful black entertainers, makes it easier for blacks to accept their exclusion from other high-status careers. This, particularly, is the case for young blacks who could be successful physicians, lawyers, or architects but who are sidetracked into futile efforts to become Kareem Abdul-Jabbars, Reggie Jacksons, or Mean Joe Greenes.

Koppet compares the fan's loyalty to his local team to the patriot's unquestioning devotion to country. Through "his" team's success, the fan achieves a triumph that could never be his in "real life," outside sport. Consider the Detroit fan, as seen by Denny McLain, the major leagues' most recent 30-game winner:

> *Detroit's not a sophisticated city. It's a factory town. It's a blue collar place. The fans seem to have a closer identification with the player.*
>
> *They don't go away for weekends, they go to the ballyard. Their release is their favorite sports team, not a yacht or a trip to Acapulco. They live and die with their guys on the field, and they're a hardy group of sometimes rowdy, sometimes hard-drinking and leather-lunged people.*[13]

As McLain says, Detroit is a blue collar factory city. Specifically, it is an automobile city. A writer, Harvey Swados, worked on the assembly line in an auto plant to get background for his novel, **On the Line.**[14] If some day you buy a new car, says Swados, and along with the familiar new car smell there is a strange rotting odor, there may be no dark mystery. An assembly line worker, fed up with his job, may have had no better way to strike back than to leave his unfinished lunch in the body of a car as it went by him down the line. The same worker, on a weekend when his team was a contender, might be "rowdy" and "leather-lunged" at the ball park, and "live and die" with the team on the field.

Or take another worker with another job in another city, in a steel mill in Pittsburgh. As has been found of American workers in general, this "steeler" probably hates his job, and certainly finds in everyday life no triumph that can approach the four Superbowl victories of the Steelers football team.

Or, a touching little story, told by Woody Hayes, about a Filipino girl, married to a graduate student at Ohio State, who turns down her husband's suggestion that she sell their football tickets for $100:

> *Here's a little girl who wouldn't earn a hundred dollars in a week, and yet she's gonna work a week to see Ohio State play football because that was her only connection with Ohio State University. She was off campus all week. Her husband was on campus. But here was her connection—Ohio State football on Saturday, in there with 88,000 people. She's a little girl a half a world away, who comes to America, and the thing she likes best is football.*[15]

As good a profile of a fan as I have ever seen is James Michener's description of Herman Fly, a German-American locomotive plant worker. Herman's Odyssey, recounted in typical Michenerian style, embraces the fall of two great Connie Mack baseball teams in 1914 and 1931; the departure of the As to Kansas City and thence to Oakland (where Herman's allegiance still followed them); Fly's final switch to the basketball 76ers and at age 70 to the hockey Flyers. "Herman Fly never knew the joy of positive participation, but that he derived spiritual pleasure from being a mere spectator, there can be no doubt. In an age when big-league franchises were being callously shifted in order to pick up a few more dollars, he was unique in continuing to pay his devotion to a team which had abandoned him. . . For the small amount of money he spent each year on his admissions, Fly received a maximum return. For him, sports were a bargain."[126]

To what degree are all these experiences of spectators self-actualization? In the early days of European football, when local pick-up teams contested from one village green to another, a local citizen might have cheered them on with some meaningful sense that his neighbors' victory was his own. When my small college team won the state baseball championship over the state university in 1936, in the days I described in the opening pages of Chapter 4, all of the victors were "walk-ons" who shared my classes and dormitory and my identification with them was easy, reasonable, and gratifying. But when Detroit factory workers identify with baseball professionals who are Detroiters only temporarily, by contract; or Pittsburgh steel workers rise and fall with the fortunes of similarly hired diamond and gridiron aficiandos; or a Filipino girl finds the meaning of Ohio State University in a group of semi-professionals, most of whose only real tie to the institution is an athletic "scholarship," there is none of the same kind of organic connection, and it is hard to see how these people realize **themselves**.

Are Sport Spectacles Corrupt?

At the beginning of this chapter I referred to the idea that games would be better off without spectators. I said that this view runs counter to the basic principles of social psychology. However, it seems to be held by a number of concerned and competent people. What truth can we find, then, in the notion that in becoming spectacles, games have been corrupted?

Lasch agrees that there is some basic corruption in modern sport. Games are corrupted, he believes, when in order to appeal to a mass that doesn't really understand or care for the game, promoters introduce **irrelevancies**. Exploding baseball scoreboards are an example. The midget whom Bill Veeck sent up to bat for the White Sox would be another. So would cheerleaders without bras and bat girls in short shorts, who have nothing to do with the skillful playing of football or baseball. Encouragement of deliberate rough play and fighting draws to the hockey arena people who have no real appreciation of a well-played game. Lasch believes the game is corrupted whenever it is shaped to attract mass audiences rather than to promote the best play. Artificial tennis courts make possible profitable all-weather tournaments in unnatural surroundings, like Caesar's Palace, rather than promoting the fastest and most skillful play, as does grass. World Series night games geared to TV prime time and played in freezing weather change the whole nature of the "summer game" for both players and fans. The American League's designated hitter rule is aimed to promote high scoring that is supposed to be crowd-pleasing rather than demanding that a hurling ace be a completely rounded performer.

Sport is corrupted, says Lasch, when the **unpredictability** that is central to a good game is lost. This may happen, as in the fixed wrestling match, when the contest becomes pure show biz, a ritualized good guy-bad guy drama devoid of surprise. Sport may become routine when the dread of losing becomes so uppermost, as it understandably does with some coaches, that management "makes every effort to eliminate the risk and the uncertainty that contribute so centrally to the ritual and dramatic success of any contest." "When sports," says Lasch, "can no longer be played with appropriate abandon, they lose the capacity to raise the spirits of players and spectators, to transport them into a higher realm. Prudence and calculation, so prominent in everyday life but so inimical to the spirit of games, come to shape sports as they shape everything else."[17] Several dull "Stuporbowls" of the past are an example.

As far as it exists (and we have seen that it has been overestimated) sport is also corrupted by **spectator passivity**. Nineteenth century industrialism in the United States created an urban mass with no opportunity for the healthy play of town and country, who flocked to the stadium to get their exercise and experience their **agon** vicariously through the professionals on the fields. Although the same industrialism found that profit could also be made by selling baseball bats, footballs and basketballs, tennis rackets and golf clubs, bikinis and tanksuits, snow and water skiis, and jogging shoes, the fan who uses none of these himself, but only sits and roots, is still with us. To the extent that hired hands do people's playing and take their exercise for them, professionalism in sport is itself a corruption. Columnist Sydney Harris agress with Huizinga that play is a central and vital human activity, but feels that for grown men to play games for money before passive onlookers is a perversion.

> *"Professional sports" don't interest me, because I think that the phrase is a contradiction in terms . . . It is good and necessary that men should work for a living. It is a monstrous perversion that men should play for a living. . . .In true sports, the contestants are ranged against each other. In professional sports, they are ranged against the public. The ultimate object is to attract as many customers as possible. They are merchandisers and promoters and box-office accountants. . . .*
>
> *This is not to say that the players do not enjoy playing, or the spectators do not enjoy watching; but their enjoyment has lost the innocence it had for children—which means it has lost precisely the healing and redeeming quality that makes it good. . .*[18]

The nineteenth century industrial worker at the ballpark was less active physically than the farmer, or than the athlete on the field, but **he was still there**. In the late twentieth century McLain's leather-lunged blue collarites are still at Briggs Stadium and the Silverdome, but most of the audience (sometimes as much as 99.9 percent) is **not present**. (I take my figure from the 1980 Superbowl, where a little more than 100,000 fans watched in the Rose Bowl and about 100 million on the tube.) We do not have to have the view seemingly held by Jack Scott, Paul Hoch, Lewis Mumford, and Gregory Stone, that only spontaneous play for fun without an audience is healthy, to see this as unhealthy. James Michener argues that athletic stadia should be located downtown rather than in the suburbs because the ballpark crowd is about the only place where the isolated city dweller can get a concrete sense of community and civic pride![9] By contrast with watching a game from the stands, Michener would see watching it in front of TV as corruption.

Let's look at two examples of "medium events" as compared with "stadium events" (terms used by Brien R. Williams):

Baseball: "The fan does not see the half of what is going on to make baseball the pleasure it has become in 100 years. The televiewer lacks freedom; seeing baseball by television is too confining, for the novelty would not hold up for more than an hour, if it were not for the commentator. . . What would old timers think of such a turn of affairs—baseball from a sofa! Television is too safe. There is no ducking the foul balls."[20]

Football: "The networks with their zeppelins and zoom lenses, their dreamlike instant replays of color and violence have changed football from a remote college pastime to something like voyeurism.

"No matter how fine his TV reception, no beer and armchair quarterback can hope to see the true games. For all the paraphernalia, the tube rarely shows an overview; pass patterns and geometric variations are lost in a kaleidoscopic of close-ups and crunches."[21]

Do today's fans object? "Although it removes him from the true context of the sport situation," Susan Birrell and John Loy comment, "the American spectator seems more than happy to accept the television sport experience. . . . Television has trained America to focus on particular bits of action and ignore, or perhaps never come into meaningful contact with a live event experience. Perhaps this explains why many disgruntled fans leave a live game complaining that they could have seen it better on television."[22]

Even Lasch, who regards the spectator as an involved participant in an agonistic ritual, would have to consider watching on the tube a very diluted substitute for watching from grandstand or bleacher seat. He sees it as a positive source of corruption: "Television has enlarged the audience for sports while lowering the quality of that audience's understandings," and "As spectators become less knowledgeable about the games they watch, they become more sensation-minded and bloodthirsty." When this happens, "ritual, drama, and sports all degenerate into spectacle."

Sport is corrupted, Lasch also says, when it **ceases to be an end in itself**, enjoyed for itself and becomes a means to some external end—such as profit-making, patriotism, moral training, or the pursuit of health. We could add also, the prestige of the institution that sponsors sport. "When the game itself comes to be regarded as incidental to the benefits it supposedly confers on participants, spectators, or promoters, it loses its particular capacity to transport both participant and spectator beyond everyday experience—to provide a glimpse of perfect order uncontaminated by commonplace calculations of advantage. . .''[23] (Here we are back at Sutton-Smith's definition of play as an oasis of self-chosen rules in a world where one is ordinarily subjected to rules imposed from without.) When sport becomes instead the mirror image of a society compulsively fixated on money, status, power, and "entertainment," it is corrupt.

A football player turned philosophy professor, John McMurtry of the Canadian University of Guelph, charges that **competing for victory** also corrupts the search for excellence in sport.

"The pursuit of victory reduces the chance to work for excellence in the true performance by rendering it subservient to emerging victorious. I suspect that our conventional mistake of presuming the opposite—presuming that the contest for prize framework and excellence of performance are somehow related as a unique cause—and effect—may be the deepest lying prejudice of civilized thought. Keeping score in any game—especially team games—is a substantial indication that the activity in question is not interesting enough in itself to those who keep score."[24]

Of very different opinion is Andrzej Wohl, a sport sociologist from a communist country (Poland):

"The fundamental driving force of the development in sport technique is competition in sport. This is a characteristic feature of sport. In all spheres of human creativity, its development takes place through effort to obtain maximum results and through the accumulation on this basis of practical experience and rationalized knowledge. However, only in sport has an automatic mechanism been created, optimizing the aspirations to achieve maximum results in the form of an all-round, public system of sport competition, with precisely worked out rules and regulations and with such institutions as national and international championships and finally the Olympic Games."[25]

The corruption of sport is sweepingly summarized in the boxed position paper sent me by my sociologist father, Arthur Calhoun, in the 89th year of his life, when I taught my first class in Sport and Culture at the University of Miami. He uses the term "sport" in its original sense—disport (play). In the light of what I have said in this chapter I would seem to disagree with item 17. But not entirely. With all due respect for the important role of sport in dramatizing the agonistic human condition, I am inclined to feel that sport is properly **fun**, that *mass ritual drama is not fun*, but serious work, and that the agonistic spectacle, like money, status, power, and entertainment, is also a corruption of our profound need for release through play.

Assuming that the "sport spectacular" is a ritual morality play, I am inclined to apply James Dow's distinction between the psychology of ritual and the psychology of play.[26] "In the case of ritual, the effect is hypnotic

. . . Psychological effects of play are to provide the release of emotions in a benign setting, where these emotions and their accompanying actions can do no real harm. . . Ritual is staged so that it has real effects on things to which people are seriously attached. Play, on the other hand, is staged so that it will have no effects on things to which people are attached." To translate self-fulfillment or genuine catharsis into hypnotic possession is, I think, to corrupt it.

It's Not Sport

It's not sport, if it involves anything except fun; e.g.—

1. *If it is for health.*
2. *If it is for physical development.*
3. *If it is to reduce.*
4. *If it is a "pastime."*
5. *If it is a distraction, an escape.*
6. *If it is to impress someone.*
7. *If it is for social standing.*
8. *If it uses professional trainers or coaches.*
9. *If there is money involved (beyond "costs").*
10. *If competition is featured.*
11. *If a team uses players from elsewhere.*
12. *If it "represents" something.*
13. *If it has arbitrary rules.*
14. *If it keeps records.*
15. *If it appears on "Sports Pages."*
16. *If it deals in éclat.*
17. *If audiences are welcomed.*
18. *If it has "patrons."*
19. *If it is arbitrarily seasonal.*
20. *If it violates seasons (e.g., ice-skating in summer or swimming in winter).*

—Arthur W. Calhoun, personal communication, November 30, 1973.

The corruption of sport is sweepingly summarized in the boxed position paper sent me by my sociologist father, Arthur Calhoun, in the 89th year of his life, when I taught my first class in Sport and Culture at the University of Miami. He uses the term "sport" in its original sense—disport (play). In the light of what I have said in this chapter I would seem to disagree with item 17. But not entirely. With all due respect for the important role of sport in dramatizing the agonistic human condition, I am inclined to feel that sport is properly **fun,** that mass ritual drama is not fun, but serious work, and that the agonistic spectacle, like money, status, power, and entertainment, is also a corruption of our profound need for release through play.

FOOTNOTES

[1]Christopher Lasch, "The Corruption of Sports," **New York Review of Books**, April 28, 1977, 24.

[2]**Ibid.**, 24, 25.

[3]Alyce Taylor Cheksa, "Sport Spectacular: A Ritual Model of Power," **International Journal of Sport Sociology**, 14, 2, 1979, 51-72.

[4]Francis W. Keenan, "The Athletic Contest as a 'Tragic' Form of Art," **International Review of Sport Sociology**, 10, 1, 1975, 51.

[5]**Ibid.**, 45.

[6]Ryszard Swierczewski, "The Athlete—the Country's Representative as a Hero," **International Review of Sport Sociology**, 13, 3, 1978, 90.

[7]Stefan Czarnowski, **Works**, Warsaw, 1954, IV, 30.

[8]Harold Charnovsky, "The Major League Professional Baseball Player: Self-Conception Versus the Popular Image," **International Review of Sport Sociology**, 3, 1968, 52.

[9]Leonard Koppett, **The Essence of the Game is Deception: Thinking About Basketball,** Little, Brown, 1973.

[10]Hans Ulrich Hermann, **Soccer Fans**, Verlag Karl Hofmann, 1977, reviewed by Michael Klein, **International Review of Sport Sociology**, 13, 2, 1978, 112.

[11]Keenan, op. cit., 46.

[12]Cited in Leo Bogart, **The Age of Television**, 2nd ed., Ungar, 1958, Chapter 9, "Television's Effect on Spectator Sports."

[13]Denny McLain with David Niles, **Nobody's Perfect**, New York, Dell, 1975, 199-200.

[14]Harvey Swados, **On the Line**, Boston, Little, Brown, 1957.

[15]Woody Hayes, quoted in **Miami News**, September 9, 1977, p. C1.

[16]James A. Michener, **Sports in America**, New York, Fawcett Crest, 1977, 42-43.

[17]Lasch, **op. cit.**, 30.

[18]Sydney J. Harris, "Pro Sport is Mercenary Combat," **Chicago Daily News**, February 22, 1971. Reprinted by permission of Sydney J. Harris and Field Newspaper Syndicate. also in **The Best of Sydney J. Harris**, Boston, Houghton Mifflin, 1975, p. 140.

[19]Michener, **op. cit.**

[20]Orrin E. Dunlap, Jr., **New York Times**, May 21, 1939. Cited by Susan Birrell and John W. Loy, Jr., "Modern Sport: Hot and Cool," **International Review of Sport Sociology**, 14, 1, 1979, 12.

[21]Stephen Kanter, "Football: Show Business With a Kick," **Time**, October 8, 1973, 54-55. (Cited in Birrell and Loy, **ibid.**)

[22]Birrell and Loy, 13.

[23]Lasch, **op. cit.**, 26.

[24]John McMurtry in Thomas Tutko and Umberto Tosi, **Sports Psyching: Playing Your Best Game All of the Time**, Los Angeles, Tarcher, 1976, 201-202.

[25]Andrzej Wohl, "The Influence of the Scientific-Technical Revolution on the Shape of Sport and the Perspectives of its Development," **International Review of Sport Sociology**, 10, 1, 1975, 32.

[26]James Dow, "Ritual and Play," **Newsletter of the Association for the Anthropological Study of Play**, 67, 3, Winter 1980, 5, 6.

POSTSCRIPT

As Plato suggested, life is a game, to be played as a game, by agreed-upon rules, within limits of time and space. Because of its limits of time, it is a game we all must lose. But in another sense, it is a game we all must win—if we choose. For, to rephrase Grantland Rice's classic lines:

When the One Great Scorer comes
To write against your name
Whether you won or lost is
How you played the game.

So too it may be—also if we choose—in the games within the Game.

INDEX

PERSON INDEX

A

Adedeji, J.A. 36
Ager, Lynn 50, 51, 130
Ali, Muhammed 14, 276
Alvarez, Carlos 29, 31
Amdur, Neil 17, 64-65
Arens, William 171-172, 186
Aries, Philippe 132
Arms, Robert L. 268-269
Arond, Henry 162-163

B

Ball, Donald W. 254
Barkow, Al 200-201, 203
Barushimana, Antoine 36
Bateson, Gregory 48, 59
Bendict, Ruth 141
Betts, John Rickards 52, 95
Blalock, Jane 203
Blanchard, Kendall 271, 273-274
Bouton, Jim 22, 174
Brailsford, Dennis 89-90
Brodie, John 280, 297
Brown, Roscoe 104

C

Cadron, A.M. 233-234
Cagigal, Jose 249
Caillois, Roger 47-49
Calvin, John 83, 87, 88
Camp, Walter 244-245
Cantril, Hadley 274-275
Cascio, Chuck 191
Cheska, Alyce Taylor 300, 301
Cooley, Charles Horton 210, 211, 301
Cousy, Bob 163
Cozens, Frederick 113, 117, 282
Culin, Stewart 113
Csikszentmihalyi, Mihaly 288-295

D

Damon, Robert 19
Davis, George 209, 222
Dulles, Foster R. 89, 96, 101
Dunning, Eric 174-175, 213
Durant, Will 68, 69, 71, 74-76, 78, 80, 81
Duthie, J.H. 184-185

E

Edwards, Harry 11, 13, 40, 54, 103, 187
.... 190, 245-255
Elizas, Norbert 213
Eshkenazi, Gerald 195

F

Famaey-Lamon, A. 233-234
Farrar, Claire 115
Feshbach, Seymour 263-265
Flood, Curt 105, 214-215
Ford, Gerald 25
Frederickson, Florence S. 113, 117, 282
Friedenberg, Edgar Z. 190
Furst, R.T. 96, 97

G

Gallwey, Timothy 297, 298
Gardella, Daniel 105
Gardiner, E. Norman 10, 70-71
Gardiner, S.R. 88, 107
Gilbert, Bil 17, 105-106
Goellner, William A. 113
Goldstein, Jeffrey 268-269
Goodger, B.C. 65-66
Goodger, J.M. 65-66
Grella, George 179-184, 190
Grusky, Oscar 167
Gulick, Luther 217-218
Guthrie, Janet 284

H

Hall, G. Stanley 208-209
Hanford, George 24, 103
Hartmann, Donald 265-266
Hastorf, A.H. 274-275
Hayes, Woody 40-41, 138, 146
Hebbelinck, M. 233-234
Heffelfinger, Pudge 155
Henderson, Robert 144, 201
Hirschland, Ruth 26
Hoch, Paul 18, 102, 309
Huizinga, Johan 43,44, 45-46, 52-53, 54,
..67, 77, 138, 140, 143, 145, 146, 149, 150
.... 152, 213

I

Izenberg, Jerry 17, 78, 291

J

Jameson, Storm 86
Janowitz, Morris 31
Jones, Bobby 202, 203
Jurkiewicz, Bogdan 161

K

Kazmaier, Dick 275
Keenan, Francis W. 301-302
Koppett, Leonard 180, 189, 306
Kraus, Hans 19, 101-102
Krawczyk, Barbara 22-23, 55
Kuyper, Abraham 86

L

Lasch, Christopher 301-302, 308, 310-311
Leonard, George 223-224, 261-262,
.... 283, 284
Linton, Ralph 213-214
Lgsyte, Robert 17, 202
Lomax, Alan 125

Lombardi, Vincent 51, 214, 223
Lowie, Robert 112
Loy, John W., Jr. 158-160, 167-169, 310
Luschen, Gunther 92

M

Maas, Henry 133
Mahlen, Fred 224-225
Maksimento, A.M. 36
Malinowski, Bronislaw 139-140
Mathewson, Christy 207
Mayo, Elton 31
McClelland, David 86-87, 231, 232, 234
McElvogue, Joseph 167-169
McIntosh, Peter 53, 244
McLain, Denny 306
McMurtry, John 311
Mead, George H. 215-216, 301
Mead, Margaret 148
Medoff, Marshall 169-170
Meggyesy, Dave 21, 34, 165, 174
Meier, Heinz 54, 91-92
Metheny, Eleanor 279, 282, 283
Michener, James A. 10-11, 40, 158, 171
Miller, Stephen 46-47
Millett, Kate 148, 149
Morikawa, Sadao 102-103
Milloy, Gardnar 199
Mumford, Lewis 53, 77, 101, 180, 309

N

Niwi, Takaai 100
Novak, Michael ... 180-181, 183, 184, 186-188,
.... 189-190, 275, 305

O

Ogilvie, Bruce 11, 12, 285-287

P

Parrish, Bernie 34, 137, 252
Pearson, Kent 56-57
Petri, Brian 41, 231-232
Piaget, Jean 30-31, 33, 218-221
Polednak, Anthony C. 19

R

Ralbovsky, Martin 214
Rich, George 128-130
Riesman, David 131-132, 134,135
Roberts, John 50-51, 119-131, 232-238
Robinson, Jackie 156, 167
Rooney, John F. 158
Rosensteil, Annette 115, 130-131
Rostow, Walt W. 94-95
Roszak, Theodore 31
Rote, Kyle 119
Rote, Kyle, Jr. 191, 192
Rubin, Bob 16-17
Ryan, E. Dean 259-60, 272
Ryan, Francis, Jr. 238-241

S

Sack, Allen L. 54-55, 155, 244
Salter, Michael 55-56, 117-118
Sauer, George 27, 106-107, 165, 173, 213,
.... 224, 296
Savage, Howard 63-64, 82
Saxon, George 156
Schaefer, Walter 247-248, 250
Schwartzman, Helen 48, 59
Scotch, N.A. 262-263
Scott, Jack ... 27, 40, 109, 177, 225, 296, 309
Shaw, Gary 29, 31, 105, 165
Sheard, E.D. 174-175
Sherif, Carolyn 262
Sherif, Muzafer 262
Simmel, Georg 216
Sipes, Richard 270-271
Slater, Philip 31, 34-35
Smilansky, Sarah 133
Smith, Preserved 83, 86, 87, 95
Solberg, Winton 84, 89-91
Stejskal, Maximilian 218
Stone, Gregory 97-98, 100, 101, 102
Summer, William G. 212-213, 245, 247
Sutton-Smith, Brian .. 50-51, 119-131, 131-135,
..... 210, 213, 223, 232-238, 281-282, 311
Szot, Zbigniew 161

T

Tamasne, Foldesi 14
Tutko, Thomas 11, 12, 164, 150
Tylor, Edward 13, 113

V

Vaz, Edward 232
Veeck, Bill 106
von Glascoe, Christine 211-212

W

Watson, Geoffrey 134, 216
Webb, Harr 160-161, 227-232
Weber, Max 86, 87, 88, 294
Weinberg, S. Kirson 162-163
Wells, H.G. 208
Whyte, William F. 133
Williams, Ted 181
Wohl, Andrzej 14, 311

SUBJECT INDEX

A

abstinence, pre-game 34, 172-173, 263
achievement 125-135, 227-232, 232-238,
.... 241-243, 245-255
agon 47, 66-71, 87, 141, 144-152, 300-305
All-America football team 104, 155
amateurism 54-59, 61-66, 102-103
antagonistic cooperation 212-213

art as sport 149-152
athletic budgets 12-13, 64-65
athletic revolution 28-42, 43, 241
athletic "scholarships" 20-21, 106-107,
.... 155-164, 251
athletic subculture 165-275
Australian aborigines 116, 121
authoritarianism .. 11-12, 30-35, 166, 171, 214,
.... 218-221, 221,222

B

baseball 180-184
basketball 188-191
blacks 35, 166-171, 189-190
Book of Sports 88, 89, 93
buffered learning 116
buzkashi 53,144

C

catharsis 116, 259-276, 305
Camelot, myth of 78-82, 85
Carnegie Report 63-64
central person 50, 134
central position 168-170
children 50, 125-130, 210-212, 215-216,
.... 249, 250
civilization
  coldward course of 121
coaches 11-12, 166, 173-174, 214, 222-223
Colosseum 75-76
communication and sport 48, 98
conservatism
  and athletes 28
  and coahes 11-12
constraint 30-31, 218-220
counterculture 30-35

D

Dane's Head 53, 91
delinquency 247-248
depreciation of athletes 106
diffusion of sport 113
disability, physical 17-18
discrimination 166-171
drugs 18-19
drumming-match 145

E

economic life as sport 147-148
economic surplus 138-139
education as sport 148-149
educational testing 149
elderly persons 33
emulation, Trobriand 139-140
ethnic groups 32-33

F

femininity 172
fertility rites 142-144
feudalism 78-82
Fiji Islands 221
Finland 218
flow 288-298
  antistructural 294
  protostructural 295
football 184-188
fun 44, 280, 288, 311, 312

G

galumphing 46-47
games
  defined 50
  achievement 130-131, 134-135
  ascriptive 132-134
  central person 50, 134
  chance 122
  contact 180
  strategy 123-124
  striking 180
  territorial 143-144, 180, 261
  time-bound 180
  zero-sum 51, 295
game theory 51
gays 33, 173
generalized other 215-216
generation gap 148
Geography of American Sports, A 158
golf 200-203

H

health 17-20
high mass consumption 95
high-rish sports 285-287
hockey 194-196
homosexuality 33, 173

I

Iceland 129-130
identification 306-308
Indians, American 117-118
individualism 131-135
industrialism 94-107, 227-234, 238-241,
.... 243-245
internalization 215-216
invention, of sport 113

J

jeu de mail 201
jeu de paume 197

K

kayasa ceremony 140

L

latitude 120-121
Life Pass Holder (UCLA) 158-160
ludus 48-49

M

maintenance 119-125, 138-139
marbles 115, 218-220

Mayan civilization 113
Melanesia 116-117
Mescalero Apache 115
metaphor, play as 48, 211
mobility, upward 154-165
morality play, sport as 47, 311
Motu (New Guinea) 115, 130-131, 135
mu'agara 142

N

NCAA 10, 14, 23, 29
no-game cultures 122

O

obedience 125-126, 241-242
Olympics
  Greek 68-71
  Modern 25, 36-38, 184-185, 253-254
one-platoon football 62-63
Osiris 143-144

P

pachisi 113
paidia 48-49
pankration 69
Papremis 143-144, 179-180, 261
paro paro 115, 130-131, 135
pentathlon 69
philosophy, as sport 67, 150-151
play
  defined 43-46
  and work 54-59
poetry as sport 149-150
pok-ta-pok 113
polemics 150
political integration, and games 123-124
politics as sport 145-147
potlatch 140-142
professionalism 61-66, 96, 97
  .... 102-103, 228-232
Protestantism 85-87
Puritanism
  in Britain 86-92
  in U.S.A. 93-94
Puritan ethic 86-94, 95, 98

R

racism 32-33, 35-37, 166-171
reciprocity 31, 218-220
Redlight 211-212
reserve clause 30, 105
responsibility 126-127, 242
riddle-contest 67, 150-151
rising expectations 35
rites de passage 117, 218
ritual 47, 275, 301, 311-312
roles 213-215
  authoritarian 214
  self-generated 214-215
rugby 174-175, 178

S

Sabbatarianism 88, 89, 90, 91, 93-94
Samoa 116, 123
schools, musical 150, 151-152
seasons 142-143, 184
self-actualization 279-299, 306-308
sexism
  in Britain 174-175
  in Greece 70
  in Poland 22-23
  in U.S.A. 21-24, 32, 38-40
Sexual Politics 148, 149, 153
soccer 191-194
social class 133-134
social power 153-178, 306-308
social stratification 104-107, 154-165
socialization 208-226
South Africa 37, 262-263
specialization 53, 62-63
spectators 53, 101-102, 187, 300-312
sport
  defined 52-54
  American 95-99
  British 52-53
sport credd 245-255
spring festivals 142-144, 179, 261
stacking 167-170

T

Taiwan 37-38
take-off, economic 95
technical maturity 95
television 13-16, 302-303, 305, 310
tennis 196-200
terminal contest 56
Third World 36-38
tick-tack-toe 48, 234-238
Title IX 23, 39-40
tournament, medieval 81-82
tracking 106-107
transportation and sport 98

V

violence 259-278

W

WASPs 154
war, as sport 146-147
women 21-24, 32, 38-40, 171-175

Y

youth culture 40-41

Z

zero-sum games 51, 295

the Author

Photograph by Peggo Cromer

Donald W. Calhoun is Professor of Sociology at the University of Miami, where he has been a member of the faculty since 1962. He holds a Doctorate in Sociology from the University of Chicago, with previous pre-doctoral work at the University of North Carolina, Chapel Hill. He has taught at Kansas-Wesleyan University, Illinois Institute of Technology, the University of Minnesota, and Bethune-Coolsman College. He is author of **Social Science in an Age of Change** (1971, 1978) and **Persons-in-Groups: A Humanistic Social Psychology** (1976). Dr. Calhoun's non-academic experiences include two years as a field secretary with the American Friends Service Committee in Seattle, and two years growing and shipping "organic" citrus fruit from Fort Pierce, Florida. **Sport, Culture, and Personality** grew out of a class in Sport and Society that Dr. Calhoun has taught at the University of Miami since 1973.